British Prime Mir
Balfour to Brown

The origins of the post of Prime Minister can be traced back to the eighteenth century when Sir Robert Walpole became the monarch's principal minister. From the dawn of the twentieth century to the early years of the twenty-first, however, both the power and the significance of the role have been transformed.

British Prime Ministers from Balfour to Brown explores the personalities and achievements of those 20 individuals who have held the highest political office between 1902 and 2010. It includes studies of the dominant premiers who helped shape Britain in peace and war – Lloyd George, Churchill, Thatcher and Blair – as well as portraits of the less familiar, from Asquith and Baldwin to Wilson and Heath. Each chapter gives a concise account of its subject's rise to power, ideas and motivations, and governing style, as well as examining his or her contribution to policy-making and handling of the major issues of the time. Robert Pearce and Graham Goodlad explore each Prime Minister's interaction with colleagues and political parties, as well as with Cabinet, Parliament and other key institutions of government. Furthermore they assess the significance, and current reputation, of each of the premiers.

This book charts both the evolving importance of the office of Prime Minister and the continuing restraints on the exercise of power by Britain's leaders. These concise, accessible and stimulating biographies provide an essential resource for students of political history and general readers alike.

Robert Pearce, formerly Professor of Modern History at the University of Cumbria, is the author of many books on British and European history. The editor of *History Review* from 1998 to 2012, he is the General Editor of Routledge Historical Biographies.

Graham Goodlad is Director of Studies at St John's College, Southsea. He has written widely on nineteenth- and twentieth-century British political history, most recently an essay in the collection *Gladstone and Ireland* (2010), edited by D.G. Boyce and Alan O'Day.

British Prime Ministers from Balfour to Brown

Robert Pearce and Graham Goodlad

Routledge
Taylor & Francis Group

LONDON AND NEW YORK

First published 2013
by Routledge
2 Park Square, Milton Park, Abingdon, Oxon OX14 4RN

Simultaneously published in the USA and Canada
by Routledge
711 Third Avenue, New York, NY 10017

Routledge is an imprint of the Taylor & Francis Group, an informa business

British Library Cataloguing in Publication Data
A catalogue record for this book is available from the British Library

Library of Congress Cataloging in Publication Data
Pearce, R. D. (Robert D.)
British prime ministers from Balfour to Brown / Robert Pearce
and Graham Goodlad.
pages cm
Includes bibliographical references and index.
1. Prime ministers—Great Britain—Biography. 2. Prime
ministers—Great Britain—History—20th century—Biography.
3. Great Britain—Politics and government—20th
century—Biography. 4. Politicians—Great Britain—Biography. I.
Goodlad, Graham D. (Graham David), 1964– II. Title.
DA566.9.A1P436 2013
941082092'2–dc23   2012047792

ISBN: 978-0-415-66982-5 (hbk)
ISBN: 978-0-415-66983-2 (pbk)
ISBN: 978-0-203-59369-1 (ebk)

Typeset in Garamond
by Cenveo Publisher Services

Printed and bound in Great Britain by
TJ International Ltd, Padstow, Cornwall

Contents

Introduction

The Office of Prime Minister

'The office of Prime Minister is what its holder chooses and is able to make of it.'[1]

Herbert Henry Asquith (Prime Minister 1908–16), writing in 1926.

The British Prime Minister occupies one of the best known but also least well understood positions in public life. One of the difficulties is that the role has never had clear legal definition. The office is generally held to date back to Sir Robert Walpole (1721–42), who was recognized as the monarch's principal minister, responsible for managing both Parliament and the Cabinet, the group of senior ministers who collectively formed the supreme decision-making body in government. With a few exceptions, the Prime Minister – sometimes known as the premier – has simultaneously held the official title of First Lord of the Treasury. The term Prime Minister did not appear in a state document until the Treaty of Berlin in 1878 and the first office-holder to be granted a formal place in the order of precedence at the royal court was Sir Henry Campbell-Bannerman in December 1905. The first reference to the office in an Act of Parliament was in the 1917 Chequers Estate Act, which allocated Chequers, a country house in Buckinghamshire, to the Prime Minister as an official residence in addition to the better known address of Number 10, Downing Street.

If legal definition was slow to come, the political reality of the office was recognized much earlier. W.E. Gladstone, who served as Prime Minister four times in the Victorian era, wrote in 1878 that 'nowhere in the wide world does so great a substance cast so small a shadow; nowhere is there a man who has so much power, with so little to show for it in the way of formal title or prerogative'.[2] By the beginning of the twentieth century the main responsibilities of the office were well established: the management of the government as a whole, a task usually combined with the leadership of the largest party in Parliament; the power to determine the overall form and structure of the government, and to appoint its members; and a prominent role in the making of policy, especially in economic and foreign affairs. A responsibility which gained in importance as a result of the two world wars was the representation of the country in the international arena.

There is a great deal of truth in the quotation from H.H. Asquith with which this chapter begins. The nature of each premiership has been shaped to a great extent by the personality and aims of the individual office-holder; but all Prime Ministers also operate within a wider context which they themselves have not created. The flexibility of the role has sometimes been a source of strength, enabling successive office-holders to accrue new powers. Gladstone, for example, established in 1870 that only the Prime Minister had the right to call Cabinet meetings. In the special circumstances of December 1918, when Lloyd George sought King George V's permission for the first postwar general election, another important power passed from the Cabinet as a whole to the premier alone: the right to ask the monarch to dissolve Parliament. Other powers, for example the Prime Minister's right to dismiss ministers, were clarified over time. Late nineteenth-century premiers generally believed that if a minister had proved politically or personally unacceptable, they should wait until the next general election, and then refuse to reappoint the individual in question. This was the fate of two ministers in Lord Salisbury's government, for example, Sir Matthew White Ridley and Henry Chaplin, after the autumn 1900 'khaki election'. An important step forward was taken in September 1903 when Arthur Balfour removed three Cabinet opponents of changes to the free trade system. Even then, however, the actual method employed was to provoke their resignations rather than to dismiss them outright. It seems that it was the demands of running governments in wartime after 1914 that enabled premiers simply to sack a colleague outright.

In the course of the twentieth century a range of processes combined to enhance the power and significance of the premiership. The evolution of an increasingly rigid party system, both at Westminster and in the country, combined with the extension of the right to vote to increasing numbers of men, and eventually to women, made it increasingly important for governments to command the loyalty of their supporters. The fruits of this included the tightening of party discipline, increased government control over the parliamentary timetable and – as a consequence of the 1911 Parliament Act, which curbed the powers of the House of Lords – the establishment of the Commons as the pre-eminent legislative body. These developments gave the premier increased power, as the head of a government committed to driving a policy programme through Parliament. At the same time the rise of a new kind of career politician, more intent than their predecessors on securing government office, increased the patronage powers of the Prime Minister. These developments coincided with the rise of the mass media, with radio supplementing the press as a platform for political leaders from the 1920s, and television emerging as an even more powerful means of communication after the Second World War. The establishment of the Downing Street Press Office in 1931 marked the beginning of a process whereby prime ministerial aides sought to manage the projection of the government's message to the electorate. The media's growing focus on individual leaders was encouraged by the introduction of a regular slot for Prime Minister's Questions in the Commons in 1961 and by the televising of party conferences and general election campaigns.

Another factor in the development of prime ministerial power was the widening reach of government from the late nineteenth century; a process which received added impetus from the two world wars. Visible signs included the creation of Whitehall ministries concerned with education, agriculture, transport, health and housing and numerous other areas. As the volume and complexity of government business increased, it became customary for important decisions to be taken in Cabinet committees. The Committee of Imperial Defence, established by the Balfour government in 1902 to give advice on military matters, was the first real example, although it lacked executive capacity. The use of committees became routine from the end of the First World War. The role of the full Cabinet was increasingly confined to confirming decisions that had already been taken by a committee, or to resolving inter-departmental disputes. The Prime Minister's power was enhanced by possessing the right to decide the chairmanship and composition of these committees. For example, in January 1947 Clement Attlee ensured approval for the decision to build a British atomic bomb by setting up a committee from which potential opponents were excluded, and whose membership included the supportive figure of Ernest Bevin, the Foreign Secretary. This had the added advantage of maintaining secrecy around a highly sensitive policy area.

The twentieth century witnessed the emergence of an increasingly professional and bureaucratic approach to government. The pressures of running the First World War ended the more informal character typical of Victorian and Edwardian Cabinets, in which discussion proceeded without a formal agenda, and the only record of their conclusions was a weekly letter from the Prime Minister to the sovereign. Lloyd George's appointment as Prime Minister in December 1916 led to the creation of a body which later evolved into the Cabinet Office, whose officials took formal minutes of meetings and communicated Cabinet decisions to the relevant government departments. This organization, headed by the Cabinet Secretary, officially served the Cabinet as a whole but in practice provided crucial support for the Prime Minister as its chairman. The power to set the agenda – to bring certain items forward or to defer discussion on others – was an important source of prime ministerial influence. Thus on taking office in October 1964, Harold Wilson was able to prevent consideration of devaluation of the pound as an alternative economic strategy, until compelled to do so in July 1966 by the pressure of external events. The Cabinet Office was supplemented by the Private Office, staffed by permanent officials whose function was to manage the premier's daily schedule and correspondence. From the 1960s premiers were supported by the Political Office, which managed links with their party and constituency base. They also made increasing use of 'special advisers', who came and went with each change of government. Their advice supplied a party political dimension which neutral civil servants were professionally unable to provide. In 1974 Wilson instituted the Policy Unit, which was retained by his successors, whose task was to support the Prime Minister in driving forward initiatives across different Whitehall departments. By the late twentieth century Prime Ministers had a significantly expanded staff at their disposal. Tony Blair's restructuring of Number 10 in 2001 combined the functions of the Private Office and Policy Unit in a new directorate, whose purpose was to advise the Prime Minister and to co-ordinate the implementation of government policy across different departments. The Press Office became part of a new and more powerful unit dedicated to government strategy and communication. To some commentators these developments amounted to the creation of a 'Prime Minister's department' in all but name.

It is not surprising that many writers have argued that the power of the premier was growing inexorably over the course of the century, and that the office was assuming an increasingly 'presidential' character. As coalition premier in 1918–22, Lloyd George was criticized for his use of the so-called 'Garden Suburb', a collection of private advisers housed in temporary accommodation behind Number 10. He was also accused of unduly neglecting Parliament and indulging in too many conferences with other heads of government, a practice which was later dubbed 'summit diplomacy'. After the Second World War claims that Cabinet government was being replaced with 'prime ministerial government' were aired with renewed intensity. A landmark was the publication in 1963 of Labour MP and writer Richard Crossman's new introduction to a classic Victorian text, Walter Bagehot's *The English Constitution*. Crossman argued that the powers of the Prime Minister, already considerable a century earlier, had been immeasurably increased by 'the centralisation of the party machine under his personal rule' and 'the growth of a centralised bureaucracy, so vast that it could no longer be managed by a Cabinet behaving like the board of directors of an old-fashioned company'.[3]

It is, however, important to be aware of the extent to which the personality, aims and circumstances of individual premiers have influenced the development of the office. Lacking specific departmental responsibilities, Prime Ministers have had considerable freedom, unless a major crisis arises, to intervene in areas of their own choice. In the words of James Callaghan, 'it is the Prime Minister himself who takes the initiatives, who pokes about where he chooses and creates his own waves'.[4] The period witnessed a range of governing styles: from the detached chairmanship of Asquith or Attlee to the more active, interventionist approach of, for example, Neville Chamberlain or Margaret Thatcher. In a number of cases incoming premiers consciously sought to differentiate themselves from the governing style of their predecessors, largely in order to establish their own authority. Thus on his appointment in October 1922, Bonar Law explicitly distanced himself from the personal dominance exercised by Lloyd George as premier: 'my idea is that of a man at the head of a big business who allows the work to be done by others and gives his general supervision'.[5] In the 1990s Tony Blair defined himself in contrast to what he depicted as John Major's weak management style, evidently modelling himself on Thatcher in his desire to run a highly centralized operation. He outlined the dilemma facing Prime Ministers in a television interview in January 2000: 'if you have a strong idea of what you want to do and believe in pushing it through, then you're, in inverted commas, a "dictator". And if you're not, then you're "weak". And, you know, you pays your money and you takes your choice on that one.'[6]

Yet, as the experience of a number of premiers, including Blair, demonstrated, the power of an individual office-holder has been strongly influenced by external circumstances. The state of the economy is an ever-present limitation: one thinks of the contrasting experiences of Tony Blair, governing during the boom years at the turn of the century, and Gordon Brown, grappling with the onset of financial crisis after 2007. The sheer workload of a Prime Minister, and the routines imposed by the structures of government, is another important factor. Marcia Williams, who served as Harold Wilson's Political Secretary, later warned that 'the civil service runs No 10 and Whitehall. Eighty per cent of a Prime Minister's time is spent on government, only at most twenty per cent on his political role as leader of his party.'[7] The ability to command a parliamentary majority is a vital element in prime ministerial success or failure. James Callaghan's ability to deliver his government's social programme was compromised by the disappearance of his majority after April 1976, and his defeat in a vote of no confidence three years later paved the way for 18 years of Conservative rule. The power of a premier is also bounded by the need to conciliate powerful members of the governing party, and to strike a balance between different factions and interests in the composition of a Cabinet. Thatcher's inability to find common ground with key individuals on the issue of closer European integration led to the resignation of her longest serving colleague, Deputy Prime Minister Sir Geoffrey Howe, in November 1990, triggering a successful challenge to her leadership from within the Conservative Party shortly afterwards. Luck is a very important, yet often underestimated factor in the making and unmaking of Prime Ministers. It is interesting to speculate what Neville Chamberlain – a Prime Minister with a solid record in domestic policy, prior to his arrival in Number 10 in May 1937 – might have achieved, had his premiership not been dominated by the issue of how to deal with Nazi Germany. Conversely Winston Churchill, an outsider to government throughout the 1930s, owed his conquest of power to his predecessor's failure to rise to the challenge of the Second World War. Harold Macmillan, who owed his appointment as a junior minister to the elevation of his patron, Churchill, in May 1940, recalled this turn of fate many years later: 'I reminded Winston again that it took Hitler to make him P.M. and me an under-secretary. The Tory Party w[oul]d do neither.'[8]

Our book highlights the influence of these factors as it explores the work and legacy of the 20 figures who occupied the premiership between the retirement of Lord Salisbury in July 1902 and the arrival of David Cameron in May 2010. Each chapter provides essential background by giving a concise account of its subject's rise to the highest office, and the shaping of his (or in one case her) ideas and values. The focus, however, is on the individual's impact on government structures and events whilst in Number 10. We examine the different Prime Ministers' governing styles, their contributions to policy-making and the ways in which they handled the major domestic and international issues of their time. Their relationships with key colleagues and with their political parties, and the ways in which they related to Cabinet, Parliament and other institutions, are discussed. We aim to give enough explanation of the key issues of modern British politics – from tariff reform in the Edwardian era to the banking crisis of 2007–8 – so that the context for a study of each premier's term of office is made clear. In each case we assess the significance of the Prime Minister in question and the current state of the individual's reputation. Each chapter concludes with a short list of suggestions for further reading, to guide those who wish to extend their knowledge. We hope that our readers will gain an enhanced understanding, not only of the individual post-holders but also of the way in which the office of Prime Minister has evolved since the beginning of the twentieth century.

History, of course, does not constitute a scientific laboratory: there can be no controlled experiments, and no judgements which will command universal agreement. But in the chapters which follow we see individuals in different ways scaling what the Victorian premier Benjamin Disraeli called 'the greasy pole', and premiers grappling with issues great and small. We examine prime ministerial successes and failures, and many attempts which fall somewhere between these categories. We see premiers who undoubtedly made a difference and others who did not. There were consensus premiers, who went with the grain of their times, and conviction premiers, who sought to break the mould in pursuit of their own agendas. Here are 20 individuals who were unique but who also represented parties, movements and interest groups and also ideas and ideals. They form a vital part of the fabric and texture of modern British history.

Notes

1 The Earl of Oxford and Asquith, *Fifty Years of Parliament*, London: Cassell, 1926, p. 185.

2 W.E. Gladstone, quoted in Andrew Blick and George Jones, *Premiership: The Development, Nature and Power of the Office of the British Prime Minister*, London: Imprint Academic, 2010, p. 71.

3 R.H.S. Crossman, 'Introduction' to Walter Bagehot, *The English Constitution*, London: Fontana, 1963, pp. 51–2.

4 James Callaghan, *Time and Chance*, London: Collins, 1987, p. 403.

5 Bonar Law to the Conservative Women's Organisation, reported in *The Times*, 2 November 1922, quoted in R.J.Q. Adams, *Bonar Law*, London: John Murray, 1999, p. 333.

6 Tony Blair, interviewed by Michael Cockerell on *Blair's Thousand Days: What Makes Tony Tick?*, BBC2, 30 January 2000.

7 Quoted in *the Sunday Times*, 4 May 1997.

8 Peter Catterall (ed.), *The Macmillan Diaries: The Cabinet Years, 1950–1957*, London: Macmillan, 2003, p. 361, entry for 13 October 1954.

1 Arthur Balfour (1848–1930)

Prime Minister: July 1902–December 1905

> 'Arthur could never bring himself to dip his hands into dirty or troubled waters.'
>
> One of Arthur Balfour's Cabinet colleagues, quoted by his niece and biographer, Blanche Dugdale, 1939.[1]

Arthur Balfour has frequently been dismissed as a dilettante who was ill-equipped for the pressures of an increasingly democratic and professional political environment. In the cutting words of David Lloyd George, 'he will be just like the scent on a pocket handkerchief'.[2] Posterity has not been kind to a premier who was believed to have owed his elevation to aristocratic family connections rather than to personal merit. The once popular phrase, 'Bob's your uncle', refers to the fact that Balfour served his political apprenticeship under his uncle, Robert, Marquess of Salisbury, whom he succeeded without challenge as the tenant of Number 10 in July 1902. His premiership was one of the shortest and least successful of the twentieth century. His resignation, after just three and a half years in office, paved the way for a general election in which his government's record was comprehensively rejected and in which he suffered the humiliation of losing his own parliamentary seat.

Balfour's premiership was an unhappy interlude in the career of a man whose total of 27 years in office made him the longest serving Cabinet minister in British political history. Uniquely, he served in the Cabinets of three later premiers – Asquith, Lloyd George and Baldwin – and was arguably more effective and at ease in a subordinate role. As Foreign Secretary during the First

World War he issued the 1917 Balfour Declaration, offering the Jewish people a 'national home' in Palestine and indirectly laying the foundations for the future state of Israel. Our concern here, however, is with Balfour's period as Prime Minister. First, however, it is necessary to give some account of his personality and ascent to the highest office.

The rise to the premiership

The product of a wealthy Scottish landowning family, Balfour was sophisticated, charming and well-read. He never married and was happiest in a small circle of like-minded friends and family members. He had a wide range of interests, writing several volumes of philosophy and in 1882 co-founding the Society for Psychical Research, whilst remaining a committed member of the Church of England. He was fascinated by technology, becoming the first Prime Minister to own a motor car. Erudite conversation, tennis, golf and country house parties occupied a great deal of his time. All of this tended to create an impression not only that he was to some extent bored with politics but also that he lacked steel and determination. Yet as Chief Secretary for Ireland in 1887–91, he responded to Irish nationalist agitation with a combination of stern police measures and constructive reform designed to win support for the Union with Great Britain. With the Prime Minister, Lord Salisbury, in the upper house, Balfour was the indispensable manager of government business in the Commons in 1891–92 and again in 1895–1902. He was an excellent debater who impressed both his supporters and his adversaries in the parliamentary arena.

Nonetheless there were real grounds for doubt about Balfour's fitness for the highest office. Although he sat for a 'popular' constituency, East Manchester, he was never comfortable with the rough and tumble of mass electoral politics. A leading Conservative newspaper, the *Morning Post*, hinted at his aloofness, noting that the party's commercial interests admired him as an individual but 'from the business point of view they are not absolute devotees of his'.[3] Balfour retained a lofty detachment from average party opinion and press comment. At the time of his appointment as premier he told Winston Churchill, then a backbench Conservative MP, that 'I have never put myself to the trouble of rummaging an immense rubbish-heap on the problematical chance of discovering a cigar-end'.[4]

Balfour was fortunate not to face an acceptable alternative candidate for the premiership in 1902. Salisbury had presided over a coalition of Conservatives and Liberal Unionists, which had come together after 1886 in opposition to the Liberal Party's plans for Irish Home Rule. Although popularly known by the end of the nineteenth century as the 'Unionist Party', the two sections did not formally come together as one organization until 1912. The outstanding personality was the radical Liberal Unionist, Joseph Chamberlain, who had served as Colonial Secretary since the formation of Salisbury's last administration in June 1895. Although the Conservatives admired his dynamism and wished to harness his presentational skills, they were not prepared to elevate a member of the Unionist alliance's junior wing to the highest position. At a time when the party did not formally elect its leader, Balfour's undisputed succession was assured when the ageing Salisbury retired.

Governing style

Like Anthony Eden in 1955, another premier who succeeded a dominant and long-serving leader, Balfour made very few alterations to his ministerial team. The only really significant move was the appointment of the Home Secretary, C.T. Ritchie, as Chancellor of the Exchequer. This change occurred only because the previous incumbent, Sir Michael Hicks Beach, insisted on retiring. Like his uncle, Balfour showed a preference for surrounding himself with family connections in government, including his brother Gerald as President of the Board of Trade and his brother-in-law, Lord Selborne, as First Lord of the Admiralty. This perpetuated the image of the government as a cosy aristocratic club, the 'Hotel Cecil', a tag which recalled the outgoing Prime Minister's family name.

Although Balfour was capable of ruthlessness – Churchill memorably wrote that 'had his life been cast amid the labyrinthine intrigues of the Italian Renaissance, he would not have required to study the works of Machiavelli'[5] – he did not find it easy to dismiss close colleagues. Balfour did not want to remove

George Wyndham, a friend who served as Chief Secretary for Ireland, when it became clear in March 1905 that he had caused political embarrassment by allowing a senior civil servant with nationalist sympathies to formulate a scheme for devolution. He also allowed a dispute between the Viceroy of India, George Curzon – another personal connection – and the commander-in-chief, Lord Kitchener, over civil-military control of the Indian army, to drag on. Cabinet colleagues noted the greater informality of meetings. The premier's intimates were addressed by their Christian names rather than, as had been the custom under earlier premiers, the titles of their government posts. After the fall of the government the Unionist MP, William Bridgeman, recalled a gathering of ex-ministers at Balfour's house, in a room dominated by the painter Burne Jones' ethereal female figures, 'whose anaemic and unmanly forms seemed to give the meeting a nerveless and flabby character, and were to me painfully symbolic of their owner'.[6]

The key relationship in the government was between Balfour and Chamberlain, who continued as Colonial Secretary. The latter accepted that his radical, nonconformist past disqualified him from the leadership of an alliance which was still dominated by landowning, Anglican Conservatives. Nonetheless Chamberlain remained in politics in order to rally Unionist forces around what he deemed a worthwhile cause. As Prime Minister, Balfour would unavoidably be overshadowed by his energetic colleague, whose background and political creed were so different from his own. Lord George Hamilton, the Conservative India Secretary, later reflected that in spite of the two men's undoubted strengths as individuals, in association their clashing personalities were a recipe for disunity. 'Balfour's philosophical temperament and indifference to attack', he wrote, 'made him a master of original and tenacious defence.' Meanwhile Chamberlain's 'impulsive and imperious temperament' inclined him to an aggressive approach to political issues, so that 'coupled together as the leaders of a single party they were a hopeless combination'.[7]

The record in government

The tension at the heart of the Unionist leadership was to be demonstrated after May 1903, when Chamberlain decided to initiate a campaign for tariff reform or imperial preference – a proposal to reverse Britain's relative economic decline by turning the empire into a united trading bloc through a system of selective taxes on imports. The policy was controversial because it represented a breach with the tradition of free trade, which had been established as economic orthodoxy since the 1840s. Chamberlain's scheme would require Britain to impose taxes on foreign goods, including foodstuffs, in order to give preferential treatment to empire produce. Support for these proposals extended beyond traditional advocates of agricultural and industrial protection, who faced growing foreign competition. Chamberlainite 'whole-hoggers' viewed tariff reform as a means of consolidating the ties between Britain and the empire countries, whilst funding old age pensions, which were moving up the political agenda by the turn of the century. The policy met strong opposition from the Liberals and from a section of the Unionist Party, who viewed free trade as the foundation of Britain's prosperity. They regarded tariff reform as economically unsound and likely to lose the party support from an electorate which would react adversely to the threat of higher food prices.

Intellectually Balfour had long been sceptical of pure free trade orthodoxy. As party leader he was concerned to find a position around which he could unite the bulk of his followers. Near the end of his life Balfour told his biographer that he had been determined not to repeat the example of Sir Robert Peel, the nineteenth-century Conservative leader who had twice split his party by executing U-turns on the issues of Catholic emancipation and the repeal of the Corn Laws: 'he smashed his party, and no man has a right to destroy the property of which he is a trustee'.[8] In pursuit of a viable middle way Balfour entered into a devious series of manoeuvres. In November 1902 Chamberlain had secured Cabinet agreement to use a one shilling duty on imported corn, which had originally been imposed for revenue-raising purposes during the Boer War, as the basis for a tentative move in the direction of imperial preference. The duty was to be remitted in the case of Canada, to reward the latter for cutting tariffs on British goods. In the Colonial Secretary's absence on a visit to South Africa, Balfour and his colleagues gave way to pressure from the pro-free trade Chancellor, Ritchie, to abandon this initiative.

With hindsight this was probably a tactical error since it removed the opportunity to test the impact of preferential taxes.

By September 1903 the division between the Unionist free traders and those who supported tariff reform was widening. In order to keep control of his Cabinet Balfour effectively dismissed Ritchie and two other committed ministerial supporters of free trade. In a highly devious manoeuvre, he provoked them into resigning whilst concealing the fact that Chamberlain had secretly undertaken to leave the government in order to initiate a public debate on his proposals. Only the slightly delayed resignation of the widely respected Duke of Devonshire, a moderate free trader, spoiled the plan. Balfour had hoped to retain him as a reassuring symbol of stability. At the same time the premier sought to paper over the cracks by articulating a more limited plan, entailing the use of retaliatory tariffs as a bargaining tool in international trade, a position which he elaborated in speeches at Sheffield in October 1903 and Manchester in January 1904.

Balfour's machinations gave him the option of leading the government in the direction of full-blooded tariff reform if Chamberlain's campaign won wider support, without committing him in advance to a potentially risky new departure. He was, however, unable to reconcile two deeply held, conflicting positions. Failing to appreciate the depth of feeling aroused by tariff reform, he alienated free traders without winning the confidence of Chamberlain's hard-core supporters. 'Retaliation' was too complex and subtle a concept to appeal to the wider electorate. Much more powerful was the argument, put by Liberal Party spokesmen, that tariffs would unavoidably raise the cost of daily necessities. They portrayed Balfour's stance as an unworkable, incoherent position, which failed to offer clear leadership. One memorable image, by the Liberal cartoonist, F. Carruthers Gould, depicted him as a storm-tossed sea captain on the flooded deck of a ship, with the caption: 'Please do not speak to the man at the wheel. He has no settled convictions. An inquiry is being held as to the right course.'[9] The spectacle of division presented by the Unionist Party contributed to their reduction to a mere 157 seats, out of 670, in the January 1906 general election.

Nonetheless it would be unfair to see Balfour's administration exclusively through the prism of tariff reform. He became Prime

Minister at a time of rising concern, across the political spectrum, with Britain's capacity to remain a pre-eminent imperial power. The fact that it had taken three years to achieve victory in the Boer War, a localized colonial conflict, had encouraged a vigorous debate on the theme of 'national efficiency'. Attention focused on the backwardness of provision in a number of fields, including military planning, education and social welfare. Although he did not possess an overarching reform programme, Balfour was in sympathy with some aspects of the contemporary desire for modernization. He had been involved in educational reform before his appointment as Prime Minister. Balfour described current provision as 'chaotic' and 'utterly behind the age'.[10] Although primary education was a responsibility of the state from 1870, its provision was complicated by conflict on religious lines. At local level education was provided by voluntary schools, most of which were controlled by the Anglican Church, and by state schools run by locally elected boards, which were more popular with the nonconformist community. In 1901 the landmark Cockerton judgment ruled that it was not legal for the board schools to provide education beyond the age of twelve. The 1902 Education Act, which Balfour piloted through Parliament, abolished the school boards and placed responsibility for primary, secondary and technical education in the hands of local education committees of the county and borough councils. It also allowed Anglican schools, which were closely associated with Conservative interests, to receive support from local taxation. The move infuriated nonconformist activists and helped to galvanize support for a reviving Liberal Party. Viewed from a broader perspective, however, it was a much needed measure of administrative rationalization, which cemented local accountability and created a structure which endured for the greater part of the twentieth century.

An area of greater personal interest for Balfour was the reform of defence policy, which assumed considerable urgency in the light of Britain's poor performance in southern Africa. The Committee of Imperial Defence, created in December 1902, was his response to the need for a body capable of assessing the overall strategic needs of Britain and its empire. Unlike a weaker forerunner established under the last Salisbury government, the committee's membership included the professional army and navy chiefs as well as the responsible ministers. Initially chaired by the Duke of Devonshire, from October 1903 his place was taken by the Prime Minister, who thereby set a precedent for most of his successors. Of even greater importance was the reorientation of British foreign policy. This had begun with the negotiation of an Anglo-Japanese alliance in the closing stages of Salisbury's government, an important step towards closer co-operation with other powers where specific national interests – in this case the threat from Russian ambitions in the Far East – were involved. In 1904 Balfour's Foreign Secretary, Lord Lansdowne, concluded the *entente cordiale* (friendly understanding) with France. The primary purpose of this agreement was to resolve outstanding differences over colonial policy in North Africa, which had marred relations between the two countries in the late nineteenth century. It did not amount to a formal alliance, and Balfour and Lansdowne did not envisage it becoming a basis for closer collaboration between Britain and France on matters of European strategy. Nonetheless, in face of Kaiser Wilhelm II's increasingly erratic diplomacy, this was how the *entente* evolved, and in 1914 it was to be the foundation for a joint military response to German aggression.

It was Balfour's tragedy that initiatives in foreign and defence policy, however important in the long run, made little or no impression on the electorate. The same could be said of the government's 1903 Irish Land Purchase Act, the most ambitious manifestation of a Unionist strategy designed to counter the appeal of nationalism in rural Ireland. It sought to create a class of Irish peasant-proprietors by using government funds to transfer the estates of landlords to their tenants. The Act did not, however, prevent a revival of the demand for Home Rule in the following decade. At home, the 1905 Unemployed Workmen's Act allowed local authorities to provide work for those who lost their jobs through the vicissitudes of the trade cycle. Less enlightened was the 1905 Aliens Act, a response to public concern over an influx of poor European Jewish immigrants. The government failed, however, to address the broader question of the legal rights of trade unions. Their status had been called in question by the 1901 Taff Vale judgment, which resulted in a rail union being fined for loss of profits incurred during a strike. Balfour's unwillingness to offer substantial benefits to the organized working class encouraged the conclusion in 1903 of an electoral pact between the Liberals and the Labour Representation Committee, the forerunner of the Labour Party.

Balfour lacked the sureness of touch which is the mark of a successful leader. His decision to resign in December 1905 was prompted partly by exhaustion caused by the struggle over tariff reform, and partly by a mistaken belief that Liberal differences on the Irish Home Rule issue would make it impossible for them to form a stable minority government. In fact Balfour had catastrophically underestimated the Liberals' desire to regain office after a decade in the wilderness. By surrendering power he allowed the incoming premier, Sir Henry Campbell-Bannerman, to consolidate his position by dissolving Parliament at a time of his choosing. The result conclusively demonstrated Balfour's unsuitability for the task of leadership in an increasingly democratic society. Few would have believed, as he left Number 10 at the age of 57, that the best years of the ex-premier were still ahead of him.

Notes

1 Blanche E. C. Dugdale, *Arthur James Balfour, First Earl of Balfour, Years 1848–1906*, London: Hutchinson, 1939, p. 295.

2 Thomas Jones, *Whitehall Diary Volume I, 1916–1925*, London: Oxford University Press, 1969, p. 201, entry for 9 June 1922.

3 The *Morning Post*, 14 July 1902, quoted in John Ramsden, *The Age of Balfour and Baldwin 1902–1940*, London: Longman, 1978, p. 3.

4 Winston Churchill, *Great Contemporaries*, London: Macmillan, 1937, p. 213.

5 Churchill, *Great Contemporaries*, p. 204.

6 Philip Williamson (ed.), *The Modernisation of Conservative Politics: The Diaries and Letters of William Bridgeman, 1904–1935*, London: The Historians' Press, 1988, p. 28, entry for 23 May 1906.

7 Lord George Hamilton, *Parliamentary Reminiscences and Reflections, 1886–1906*, London: John Murray, 1922, p. 322.

8 Dugdale, *Arthur James Balfour 1848–1906*, p. 259.

9 'Wheel and woe: Balfour attempts to steer a middle course,' reproduced in Denis Judd, *Balfour and the British Empire*, London: Macmillan, 1968, p. 112.

10 *The Times,* 15 October 1902, quoted in Ruddock F. Mackay, *Balfour: Intellectual Statesman*, Oxford: Oxford University Press, 1985, pp. 108–9.

Further reading

R.J.Q. Adams, *Balfour: The Last Grandee*, London: John Murray, 2007
Max Egremont, *Balfour*, London, Collins, 1980
E.H.H. Green, *Balfour*, London: Haus, 2006
Ruddock F. Mackay, *Balfour: Intellectual Statesman*, Oxford: Oxford University Press, 1985

2 Henry Campbell-Bannerman (1836–1908)

Prime Minister: December 1905– April 1908

'If people should say of me that I tried always to go straight there is perhaps no credit to me in that. It may have been mere indolence. The straight road always seemed to me the easiest.'

Campbell-Bannerman to a friend, shortly before his death, April 1908.[1]

Although brief, Sir Henry Campbell-Bannerman's two and a half year premiership was significant in several respects. Aged 69 in December 1905, he was the oldest Prime Minister, at the time of his appointment, in the twentieth century.[2] His arrival in Number 10 also represented a minor constitutional landmark, in that he was the first individual formally to be designated as 'Prime Minister' rather than to be known by the older official title of 'First Lord of the Treasury'. He was also the last premier to lead the Liberal Party to win an independent parliamentary majority. On a more sombre note, a fortnight after his resignation in April 1908, he became the only holder of the post to die in Number 10, the address he called 'his rotten old barrack of a house'.[3] Yet Campbell-Bannerman remains one of Britain's least remembered Prime Ministers. Outside his native Scotland, where the centenary of his death occasioned modest commemorative activities, his name has little resonance, except amongst those with a specialist interest in the history of the Liberal Party.

The rise to the premiership

There was little in Campbell-Bannerman's earlier career to indicate that he would rise to the highest office. From a well-to-do mercantile background in Glasgow, he moved away from his family's Conservative beliefs as a young man, towards the Liberal Party of W.E. Gladstone. His views were broadly those of the party's centre-left: a belief in individual freedom, a desire to help the disadvantaged, an aversion to imperialism and support for Irish self-government. Known originally as Henry Campbell, he took the additional name 'Bannerman' as a condition of an inheritance, though he was usually referred to as 'CB' for short. After entering Parliament in 1868 as Member for Stirling Burghs, he held junior office in Gladstone's first two governments. His first Cabinet appointment was as Chief Secretary for Ireland in 1884–85, followed by two stints as War Secretary in 1886 and 1892–95. It was on an issue relating to Campbell-Bannerman's department, his alleged failure to procure adequate supplies of cordite explosive, that the Conservatives engineered a vote in the Commons which led to the resignation of Lord Rosebery's ill-starred Liberal government in June 1895.

In spite of this setback, by now Campbell-Bannerman had gained a reputation as an affable, dependable individual, an unexciting speaker and a quietly competent administrator. His only real defect was a tendency towards laziness. His political commitments were never allowed to interfere with the routine which he and his wife had established, with large parts of the year spent in Scotland, Paris and the Bohemian spa town of Marienbad. His willingness at one point to consider running for the Speakership of the House of Commons demonstrated that the struggle for power was not the driving force of his life.

What propelled Campbell-Bannerman to the top was the ineffectiveness of Gladstone's two successors, Lord Rosebery and Sir William Harcourt, as Liberal leaders during the party's long spell in opposition after 1895. On Harcourt's resignation in December 1898 the party's most outstanding parliamentarian, H.H. Asquith, who had served as Home Secretary in 1892–95, was widely tipped to take over but for personal reasons he declined the opportunity. With the more obvious candidates eliminated, Campbell-Bannerman was chosen as the person most likely to provide a degree of unity. His position was, however, far from secure. Following the convention of the time, only a former premier had an automatic claim to be recognized as leader of the party *as a whole* in opposition, so that Campbell-Bannerman was leader only of the Liberals in the Commons. Aged 62 in February 1899, when he assumed the leadership, he was widely expected to be no more than a 'caretaker' figure.

Within months of his elevation, Campbell-Bannerman faced the challenge of holding the party together amid the divisions occasioned by the outbreak of the Boer War. The conflict was politically difficult because it highlighted the tension within Liberalism over imperial policy. On the one hand were the so-called 'little England' radicals, including John Morley and David Lloyd George, who abhorred imperial expansion and sympathized with the Boers' struggle for independence. They were opposed by the 'Liberal imperialists', who took a more positive view of Britain's overseas responsibilities and favoured consensus with the Unionists in external policy. This group, whose most senior members were Asquith, Richard Burdon Haldane and Sir Edward Grey, represented a challenge to Campbell-Bannerman's leadership since they clearly wanted to see the return of Rosebery to front-line politics.

Campbell-Bannerman slowly earned respect for the way in which he prevented the internal conflict from inflicting worse damage on the party. To have reduced the Unionist majority from 152 to 134 seats at the October 1900 election, when the war appeared to be going Britain's way, was a significant achievement. Although personally sympathetic to the anti-war position, he avoided unnecessarily antagonizing the imperialists by concentrating on the way in which the Unionist administration conducted the conflict, rather than on the issue of Britain's involvement. His approach was exemplified by his well-known June 1901 condemnation of the use of farm burning and the confinement of Boer civilians in concentration camps as 'methods of barbarism'. Campbell-Bannerman was helped by the fact that, although Rosebery continued to make hostile interventions in the party's affairs, he lacked the determination to mount a serious bid to recover the leadership – a characteristic which deterred his disillusioned admirers from giving him their unequivocal loyalty.

A number of developments helped Campbell-Bannerman to focus Liberal energies on the goal of returning to power. The party was able to unite in opposition to the 1902 Education Act, which offended nonconformists, a key Liberal interest group, by granting local taxation support to Anglican schools. The scandal of 'Chinese slavery', which centred on the British authorities' employment of indentured Chinese labour in the South African gold mines, further damaged the Unionist administration's public image. Most damaging of all for the beleaguered Balfour government was the launching of Joseph Chamberlain's tariff reform campaign in May 1903, which raised the threat of higher food prices. Liberals of all kinds united in defence of the traditional policy of free trade, whilst the Unionists presented an electorally unappealing appearance of internal disunity.

Campbell-Bannerman showed his real political skill and inner toughness when the opportunity of taking office materialized at the end of 1905. Following a speech at Stirling in November, in which Campbell-Bannerman announced his support for a 'step by step' progression towards Home Rule for Ireland, Rosebery publicly dissociated himself from the party leadership. Mistakenly believing that this indicated a fatal division in the Liberal ranks, Balfour resigned the premiership, anticipating that his opponents would not be capable of forming a minority government. Instead Campbell-Bannerman seized the chance to establish himself in office and then to call a general election, which would focus attention on the unpopular outgoing Unionist administration. He then faced down the so-called 'Relugas compact', a prior agreement by Asquith, Haldane and Grey – named after the latter's Scottish fishing lodge, where it was concluded – to refuse to serve unless Campbell-Bannerman became a purely nominal premier in the House of Lords. Their intention had been to make Asquith the real power in the government, as Chancellor of the Exchequer and leader of the party in the Commons, and thus to avert the Liberal imperialists' nightmare of a 'little England' government in which their influence would be marginal. Campbell-Bannerman, however, reacted decisively by securing Asquith's unconditional acceptance of the Exchequer. He exploited the latter's unwillingness to stand by an informal agreement if it meant jeopardizing the prospect of a viable Liberal government after a decade in the wilderness. Once Asquith, the only indispensable member of the trio, had accepted a position as the new premier's chief lieutenant, the plot rapidly crumbled.

Campbell-Bannerman was then able to bring Grey and Haldane on board as Foreign Secretary and War Secretary respectively.

Perhaps Campbell-Bannerman made too many concessions to his strongest critics, especially to Haldane, whom he privately viewed with a mixture of contempt and mistrust: 'Haldane always prefers the backstairs to the front, but no matter for the clatter can be heard all over the house.'[4] With an election in prospect, however, it was important to present a united front to the country, reflecting the main strands of party opinion. The leading Liberal imperialists were balanced in the new Cabinet by the appointment of Morley at the India Office, Lloyd George at the Board of Trade, the centrist Herbert Gladstone at the Home Office and former labour activist John Burns as President of the Local Government Board. W.T. Stead, a well-known journalist, testified to Campbell-Bannerman's skill in holding his team together: 'he is the hub because he is the solidest, most seasoned, best balanced of all Liberals'.[5]

The record in government

In the January 1906 general election the Liberals secured a majority of 130 seats over the other parties, although in practice they possessed a staggering majority of 356 when combined with their Irish Nationalist and Labour allies, who were unlikely to vote with the severely depleted Unionist contingent. A contributory factor was the 1903 electoral pact with the newly formed Labour Representation Committee, negotiated by Herbert Gladstone as Chief Whip, which saved Liberal candidates from three-cornered contests. Although Liberal plans for social reform featured in the election, the campaign focused primarily on the negative record of the Unionist government. Campbell-Bannerman himself did not offer a specific programme of reforms in launching the party's campaign at the Albert Hall. He stressed the importance of popular control in licensing, education and Irish policy, and promised action 'to make the land less of a pleasure-ground for the rich and more of a treasure-house for the nation',[6] to modernize the Poor Law and tackle issues of urban overcrowding and unemployment. He struck a classically Gladstonian Liberal note in his opposition to the growth of armaments and extravagance in public spending, and in his robust defence of free trade. In drawing attention to the iniquity of Unionist plans for the taxation of food he set the tone for the subsequent campaign: no fewer than 98 per cent of Liberal candidates mentioned the issue in their election addresses. The new premier also attacked the Unionists for running away from their responsibilities, and for putting political tactics ahead of coherent policy-making. He took up this theme again when Parliament reconvened and Balfour tried to take up the time of the new House of Commons with a series of verbal pyrotechnics. Campbell-Bannerman contemptuously dismissed his opponent's mannered subtlety as 'utterly futile, nonsensical and misleading ... I say, enough of this foolery'.[7]

In office Campbell-Bannerman offered not the unrelenting dynamism of the radical reformer but, in the words of the junior Home Office minister, Herbert Samuel, 'common sense enthroned'.[8] His advanced age and poor health perhaps limited his horizons. Another factor was his wife's prolonged illness and death in August 1906, which drained his energies and undermined his morale. He was also conscious that an extension of the state's role, in a bid to tackle poverty and inequality, would be controversial in a party which remained an ideological broad church. Its ranks included traditional advocates of non-interventionist *laissez-faire*, such as Morley, as well as ambitious protagonists of government action, headed by Lloyd George and the young Winston Churchill. Campbell-Bannerman was also anxious to avoid giving grounds for the allegation that the Liberals were excessively deferential to their working-class supporters. As he wrote to Asquith when framing the 1906 King's Speech, 'if we have two sops for Labour, we ought to have some other Bills of general interest to balance them. Otherwise ... colour will be given to the assertion which seems to be [the Unionists'] main weapon just now that we are in the hands of Labour.'[9]

Campbell-Bannerman was capable of using the Prime Minister's authority to take decisive action when he considered the case to be justified. A good example was in March 1906, when the Cabinet considered its response to the 1901 Taff Vale case, a legal ruling which had made trade unions liable for damages incurred by strike action. This was a major grievance for the government's

Labour allies and remedial action of some kind was necessary. A majority of ministers, headed by Asquith, favoured a bill which would have given trade unions only limited rights. On the floor of the Commons, however, Campbell-Bannerman abandoned the agreed line and supported a more wide-ranging bill introduced by a Labour member, which gave the unions total immunity from civil actions. In December 1906 he again signalled his sympathy for the Labour movement by deciding, on the basis of listening to the debate in the Commons, to support the inclusion of domestic servants in the provisions of a Workmen's Compensation Bill, which extended workers' rights to make claims for industrial accidents and diseases. Imperial policy furnishes another example of Campbell-Bannerman's willingness to take an independent line in defiance of his more cautious colleagues. His was the decisive voice in determining that the two defeated Boer states, the Transvaal and the Orange Free State, should be granted self-government, a step which paved the way for the creation of the Union of South Africa in 1910. The premier's insistence on adopting the most generous available option ran counter to the advice of the Colonial Office and of a Cabinet committee, which had recommended a more limited solution based on proposals made by the previous government.

No less important for the future was Campbell-Bannerman's response to the action of the House of Lords in obstructing and mutilating his ministry's legislation. The upper chamber's use of its power to veto measures of which the dominant Unionist element disapproved was a major obstacle to any Liberal government. In 1906–7 it disposed of an education bill designed to strengthen public control over church schools receiving rate aid, and an attempt to abolish plural voting, a practice which favoured the Unionists by giving greater weight to property-owners. On Campbell-Bannerman's initiative the Cabinet adopted the idea of a suspensory veto in June 1907. This sought to give the elected chamber the authority to force legislation through as a last resort, within the lifetime of a Parliament, in the event of conflict between the two houses. In the ensuing debate Campbell-Bannerman tellingly characterized the Lords as 'a mere annexe of the Unionist party'.[10] Although the motion in favour of the suspensory veto was carried in the Commons, there was as yet no appetite for a showdown with the Lords. Campbell-Bannerman had pointed the way towards the settlement of this crucial constitutional issue, which would occur under his successor with the passage of the 1911 Parliament Act.

None of this, however, amounted to a consistent effort to drive through a coherent set of government policies. Some issues were ducked because they were simply too divisive. For example, Campbell-Bannerman personally sympathized with the growing demand for female suffrage. He encouraged a delegation to continue lobbying in May 1906 and ten months later spoke and voted for a women's enfranchisement bill. He was not prepared, however, to run political risks in support of a cause to which many of his colleagues were strongly opposed. The issue was simply too sensitive, with traditional chauvinism reinforced for some Liberals by the fear that the enfranchisement of property-owning women might favour the Conservative Party.

To a large extent this was a government of departments, in which individual ministers were allowed an unusual degree of autonomy. The Prime Minister acted as a facilitator, who enabled rather than initiated. The most independent minister was Sir Edward Grey at the Foreign Office, who supported the idea of Anglo-French 'military conversations'. These were secret discussions between the two countries' general staffs, first held in the winter of 1905–6, which assumed that Britain would be prepared to provide military support in the event of a Franco-German conflict. The premier was clearly uneasy, telling his French counterpart, Clemenceau, in April 1907 that public opinion would not 'allow of British troops being employed on the Continent of Europe'.[11] Nonetheless he chose not to reveal the growing links with France to the full Cabinet, where it would have encountered strong opposition from the 'little Englanders'. Perhaps persuading himself that the talks did not represent a definite commitment, he made no attempt to take foreign policy in a different direction from that charted by his Foreign Secretary.

Campbell-Bannerman earned the respect of his colleagues for his low-key style of management. Morley, a veteran of the Gladstone and Rosebery administrations, described the Cabinet in December 1906 as 'the most harmonious that ever was'.[12] As Campbell-Bannerman's health broke down in the spring of 1908, and his colleagues prepared for Asquith's succession, the previously critical Haldane privately doubted the latter's capacity to keep the party and Cabinet united: 'C.B. is the only person who can hold this motley crew together.'[13] By now, however, the prospects for the Liberal government were darkening. The onset of an economic recession in late 1907 boosted the Unionist claim that only tariff reform could guarantee prosperity. The Liberals' strong initial position was weakened by three by-election losses in 1907 − one to Labour, one to the Unionists and a third to an independent socialist candidate − followed by three more defeats at the hands of the Unionists in the first three months of the following year. The problems of the House of Lords, women's suffrage, Ireland and relations with the labour movement were soon to become acute. In each case Campbell-Bannerman had outlined an authentically radical Liberal response, but his departure meant that it would be left to others to decide how to proceed.

Notes

1 J.A. Spender, *The Life of the Rt. Hon. Sir Henry Campbell-Bannerman, G.C.B.*, Volume II, London: Hodder and Stoughton, 1923, p. 407.

2 This excludes Sir Winston Churchill, who was 76 when his *second* term as Prime Minister began in October 1951.

3 Anthony Seldon, *10 Downing Street: The Illustrated History*, London: HarperCollins, 1999, p. 120.

4 F.W. Hirst, *In the Golden Days*, London: Frederick Muller, 1947, p. 264.

5 *Review of Reviews*, January 1906, quoted in John Wilson, *CB: A Life of Sir Henry Campbell-Bannerman*, London: Constable, p. 466.

6 Spender, *Life of Campbell-Bannerman*, Volume II, p. 209.

7 Wilson, *CB*, p. 497.

8 Viscount Samuel, *Memoirs*, London: Cresset Press, 1945, p. 56.

9 Campbell-Bannerman to Asquith, 17 January 1906, quoted in A.K. Russell, *Liberal Landslide: The General Election of 1906*, Newton Abbot and Hamden, CT: David and Charles/Archon, 1973, p. 210.

10 Wilson, *CB*, p. 563.

11 George Monger, *The End of Isolation: British Foreign Policy 1900–1907*, London: Thomas Nelson, 1963, p. 325.

12 John Viscount Morley, *Recollections*, Volume II, London: Macmillan, 1918, p. 197.

13 Haldane to his sister, 1 February 1908, quoted in Stephen Koss, *Haldane: Scapegoat for Liberalism*, New York and London: Columbia University Press, 1969, p. 55.

Further reading

Jose F. Harris and Cameron Hazlehurst, 'Campbell-Bannerman as Prime Minister', *History*, 55 (185), October 1970: 360–83

Iain Sharpe, 'Campbell-Bannerman and Asquith: an uneasy political partnership', *Journal of Liberal History*, 61, Winter 2008–9: 12–19

John Wilson, *CB: A Life of Sir Henry-Campbell-Bannerman*, London: Constable, 1973

3 Herbert Henry Asquith (1852–1928)

Prime Minister: April 1908– December 1916

'He is like a great counsel in whom solicitors and clients have faith ... He has splendid judgment and, as a rule, deals with great subjects, in council and in the H[ouse] of C[ommons], in the same imperturbable manner as small ones. It, however, remains to be seen how he will conduct himself if he has to fight a failing cause.'
David Lloyd George on Asquith, 28 April 1912.[1]

Lloyd George's observation encapsulates a widely accepted interpretation of his predecessor as Prime Minister. H.H. Asquith presided over one of the most remarkable peacetime administrations of modern times, forging a highly creative partnership with Lloyd George as Chancellor of the Exchequer. His government laid the foundations of the welfare state and weathered a prolonged conflict with the Unionist-dominated House of Lords. Following two general election victories in 1910 it passed the 1911 Parliament Act, which decisively curbed the powers of the unelected upper chamber. Asquith attracted the loyalty and admiration of a generation of Liberals. Typical was the tribute paid by Sir John Simon, who served in his governments for six years. In his memoirs, written almost a quarter of a century after Asquith's death, Simon described his former leader's statue in the House of Commons as 'an admirable representation of the man as he was – compact with intellectual power, fearless and confident in the course he ought to take'.[2]

By contrast, the two years of war in which Asquith remained at the helm form a largely disappointing sequel. After grappling unsuccessfully with the challenges of a new kind of conflict, he

was replaced as premier by Lloyd George, whose dynamic leadership is popularly regarded as having turned near-disaster into
ultimate victory. Symptomatic of the rapid decline of Asquith's
reputation was the derogatory connotation applied to one of
his best-known phrases, 'Wait and see'. When first uttered in
response to his opponents in March 1910, at the height of his
government's confrontation with the Lords, it indicated a refusal
to be pushed into prematurely declaring his hand. Amid the
demands of total war, however, it was flung back at him as an
indication of dilatoriness. Asquith has also taken a share of the
blame for the decline of the Liberal Party, which emerged from
the war years severely weakened and soon to be replaced by
Labour as the strongest force on the centre-left of British politics.
Although he inherited a united parliamentary following, with a
sizeable independent majority, by the time he left office his party
was seriously divided. In the December 1918 general election the
Liberals effectively disappeared as a viable party of government.
Asquith lost his own parliamentary seat, which he had held for
22 years, to an unknown challenger whose posters declared,
'Asquith nearly lost you the War. Are you going to let him
spoil the Peace?'[3] Although he returned to the Commons at a by-
election, and remained Liberal leader until October 1926, he
never held office again.

The rise to the premiership

Asquith's story began in unremarkable circumstances in September 1852, the child of a small employer in the West Yorkshire
woollen trade. After his father's early death Asquith steadily
moved away from his northern provincial roots, attending school
in London before embarking on an academically distinguished
career at Balliol College, Oxford. Here he came into contact with
the teachings of T.H. Green, a leading moral philosopher. Green's
concept of an enlarged role for the state was a key influence on the
'New Liberalism' of social reform, which was to be put into practice in Asquith's peacetime premiership. Yet abstract thought
of this kind never enthralled him. Whilst struggling to establish
himself as a barrister Asquith wrote political articles for *The
Spectator*. In his writings he demonstrated a commitment to a

practical Liberalism, wary of the wilder shores of radicalism but definitely anti-Conservative. By giving legal advice to senior members of the party, and cultivating a friendship with another rising Liberal star, the highly intellectual and earnestly progressive Richard Burdon Haldane, he secured nomination for the Scottish constituency of East Fife in 1886. With Haldane, who held a neighbouring seat, he was to form a crucial political relationship. A second significant association was with another newly elected MP, Sir Edward Grey, a Northumberland landowner on the right of the party. In spite of important temperamental differences between the three, they drew support from each other in the following decades.

It was a measure of Asquith's rapidly acquired parliamentary standing that he was appointed Home Secretary in Gladstone's final government, formed in August 1892, without serving an apprenticeship in junior office. By the time Gladstone's successor, Lord Rosebery, left office in June 1895, Asquith had established himself as a politician with leadership potential. In opposition, however, he initially assumed a relatively low political profile. This was partly because, following the premature death of his first wife, he had married the eccentric London society figure Margot Tennant, whose extravagant lifestyle compelled him to return to legal practice in order to earn money. As a result he declined to stand for the Liberal leadership when a vacancy arose in December 1898 – a decision which opened the way for the unexpected succession of Sir Henry Campbell-Bannerman.

As the Liberal Party became divided over its response to the Anglo-Boer War of 1899–1902, Asquith identified himself with the Liberal imperialist wing which supported British military action. Yet he was never as committed as Grey and Haldane to this protest movement within the party, always keeping open his links to mainstream Liberalism. He emphasized his orthodoxy by taking the lead in countering Joseph Chamberlain's campaign on behalf of tariff reform in 1903. He joined Grey and Haldane in the 'Relugas compact' of September 1905, an agreement to make the 'little Englander' Campbell-Bannerman Prime Minister in name only, with a seat in the Lords, when the Liberals returned to power. Yet he was also the first of the trio of plotters to abandon the attempt, accepting without hesitation when Campbell-Bannerman offered him the post of Chancellor of the Exchequer following the fall of the Unionist government in December. In the end the lure of senior office reinforced the unwillingness of the party loyalist to abort the first opportunity in a decade to form a viable Liberal administration.

Asquith's term as Chancellor consolidated his credentials as the elderly Campbell-Bannerman's heir. In office the differences between the premier and his Liberal imperialist colleagues were less important. Asquith's three budgets were mildly progressive and in his last one, introduced just after he had become Prime Minister, he signalled a move towards the 'New Liberalism' of social reform by announcing plans for a non-contributory, tax-funded old age pension. In the Commons Asquith's capacity for clear exposition and forcefulness in debate made him an effective defender of government policies; 'send for the sledge-hammer'[4] was Campbell-Bannerman's response to difficulties. As the latter's health failed, Asquith deputized for him, unchallenged in both Parliament and Cabinet. He was the logical choice as premier when Campbell-Bannerman finally resigned in April 1908.

Governing style

As manager of his ministerial colleagues Asquith acted more as a co-ordinator and a mediator than as a dynamic innovator. Provided that policy broadly evolved along the lines of which he approved, he was content to let others take responsibility for new initiatives. This was particularly true of the ministry's principal social reformers, Lloyd George, who succeeded Asquith as Chancellor, and Winston Churchill, who entered the Cabinet for the first time as President of the Board of Trade. The latter described Asquith in November 1913 as 'supreme in the Cabinet but very self-contained, reserved and slow to speak. He holds the casting vote and thinks it unfair to use it till all have spoken'.[5] Those who worked with him frequently compared him to a judge, exercising authority in a spirit of calm reserve. The Chief Whip, Jack Pease, described him as 'always decided and approachable … ready to listen to anything that is said before giving a decision'.[6] The Prime Minister's temperament was ideal for holding together a diverse and talented team. In February

1909, for example, he resolved a potentially damaging clash between Reginald McKenna, the First Lord of the Admiralty, and a group of 'economists', headed by Lloyd George and Churchill, who objected to the proposed acceleration of naval building. The Admiralty insisted on a programme of six ships for the coming financial year, whilst their opponents maintained that they had exaggerated the threat from Germany and that four would suffice. It was Asquith who brokered a compromise, whereby four ships were to be laid down immediately and a further four, if and when the necessity was demonstrated.

Asquith exuded a cool detachment in his relationships with his colleagues. Margot Asquith's startling description of her husband in April 1908 as 'a cold hard unsympathetic man loved by none, admired by a few'[7] contained an element of truth. There was no permanent inner Cabinet although certain ministers had easier access than others to the Prime Minister. Pre-eminent among these was Sir Edward Grey as Foreign Secretary, who was allowed a considerable degree of autonomy in running his department. Asquith also confided in the Earl of Crewe, who occupied a series of middle-ranking posts. In the later stages of his premiership he became close to Reginald McKenna, who moved from the Admiralty to the Home Office in October 1911 and to the Exchequer in May 1915. Asquith worked closely with Lloyd George on account of the latter's seniority, though even he was not privy to all areas of government policy. When Lloyd George complained that he was kept in the dark about foreign policy, Asquith conciliated him by admitting him to a Cabinet committee in December 1910 but this was allowed to wither away after seven months.

Yet if he was self-contained and capable of devious manoeuvre, Asquith rarely exhibited outright ruthlessness. He was usually forgiving of his colleagues' failings. The only major casualty of his appointment as Prime Minister was the Earl of Elgin, by common consent a poor performer, who was removed from the Colonial Office. Lord Tweedmouth, whose growing mental instability was well known in high political circles – Asquith himself referred to him privately as a 'raving lunatic'[8] in May 1908 – was relieved of the Admiralty but retained as Lord President of the Council until October. The striking exception to the indulgence with which Asquith habitually treated his colleagues was his abrupt dismissal of Haldane as Lord Chancellor, as the price of sharing power with the Unionists in May 1915. Asquith jettisoned his oldest political friend, whom a section of Unionist opinion unfairly regarded as a pro-German sympathizer, without a word of commiseration. He was not willing to lose the chance of an accommodation which would guarantee his own political survival.

A certain remoteness also typified Asquith's relationship with his own parliamentary party. Although effective at the dispatch box, he made little effort to keep in touch with the Liberal backbenchers, delegating day-to-day management of the Commons to a succession of capable Chief Whips. Unlike Lloyd George, he did not seek to enthuse mass gatherings of the party faithful or to cultivate the press. In a tentative populist gesture in the autumn of 1909, he had a speech on the House of Lords' opposition to the budget relayed to a wider audience by means of gramophone recordings. He was the last Prime Minister to run a Cabinet without the apparatus of a formal agenda or minutes – a deficiency which was later addressed by Lloyd George in response to wartime pressures.

Although efficient in the discharge of business, Asquith rarely allowed public life to divert him from the pursuit of his many personal interests. With the possible exceptions of Clement Attlee and Harold Macmillan he was the best read Prime Minister of the century. He enjoyed golf, bridge, motoring and the society of attractive, intelligent women. The intense emotional attachment which he formed with Venetia Stanley, a woman 35 years his junior, is recorded in an amazingly detailed correspondence which ended only with her sudden engagement to one of his ministerial colleagues, Edwin Montagu, in May 1915. Asquith's liking for alcohol, which had been known in high political circles before 1914, became a matter of satirical public comment in wartime. The music hall comedian George Robey entertained audiences with the refrain, 'Mr Asquith says in a manner sweet and calm/Another little drink won't do us any harm'.[9] By this stage his physical deterioration was becoming evident, the writer Lytton Strachey describing the effects of high living on the premier in May 1916: 'a fleshy, sanguine, wine-bibbing medieval-Abbot of a personage – a gluttonous, lecherous, cynical old fellow'.[10]

It would, however, be a mistake to underestimate Asquith's capacity to react to events. He was unusual among Prime Ministers in taking on additional Cabinet posts for short periods when crises occurred. Thus in the Curragh incident of March 1914, he took over the War Office after its ministerial head, J.E.B. Seely, resigned following the revelation that he had turned a blind eye to pro-Unionist army officers, who had signalled their unwillingness to support the government's policy of implementing Irish Home Rule. He acted as War Secretary until the outbreak of war in August 1914. Asquith resorted to the same tactic when the Easter Rising threw the British administration of Ireland into confusion, holding the post of Chief Secretary for three months from May 1916 until the situation had stabilized. Some colleagues, however, were sceptical about his brand of crisis management. Lord Morley, for example, noted the premier's confidence 'in his ability to furnish at least some provisional solution when the situation created by neglect threatens to get out of hand'.[11] Almost to the end of his premiership Asquith's public image remained one of stoic indifference in the face of adversity, summed up in Max Beerbohm's 1913 cartoon, which showed him seated on a stone, unconcerned by the threats of opponents including a member of the House of Lords, a militant trade unionist and a campaigner for female suffrage. 'Come one, come all, this rock shall fly/from its firm base as soon as I', read the caption.[12] There was a fine line, however, between imperturbability and a lack of drive and direction, which was to be crossed amid the more urgent challenges of world war.

The record in government

Domestic policy

Asquith's disinclination to provide bold, flamboyant leadership has led some commentators to underestimate his personal commitment to the Liberal government's social reforms. In fact without his support, the reforms which are usually associated with Lloyd George and Churchill, notably old age pensions, labour exchanges and National Insurance, would not have come to fruition. Although essentially a safety net for the poorest and most vulnerable, rather than an all-embracing welfare programme for the whole of society, these reforms marked a decisive breach with the Victorian choice between self-help, private charity and the stigma of the Poor Law. The Asquith ministry established a precedent for state intervention on behalf of the elderly, the sick and the unemployed, upon which subsequent governments would build. Politically the reforms enabled the Liberals to hold off the emerging challenge of the Labour Party as a rival for working-class votes.

The Prime Minister's most important contribution to the success of the reforms was the way in which he rallied the Cabinet behind Lloyd George's controversial 1909 'People's Budget', which sought to raise money for increased social expenditure as well as meeting the rising costs of naval defence. The budget targeted the wealthy to an unprecedented degree, with proposals for increases in income tax and death duties, and for a super-tax on incomes above £5,000 per year. By seeking to do so without abandoning the Liberal principle of free trade, it provoked the determined opposition of Unionist tariff reformers, who maintained that social reform should be funded by the revenue generated by import duties. Unionist domination of the House of Lords led to the budget's rejection by the upper house in November 1909, in defiance of convention and of the Liberals' 350-strong Commons majority. This, the latest in a series of rejections of Liberal government measures, was a major challenge for Asquith. If the unelected, hereditary peers were to be allowed to use their power of veto in this way, it would be impossible for a radical, reforming government to function effectively. Although he avoided the overtly demagogic, class war language of Lloyd George, Asquith was clear that this action could not be tolerated. Faced with King Edward VII's refusal to create sufficient Liberal peers to override the Unionist majority in the Lords, he fought a general election in January 1910, which left the Liberals in power but without an independent majority. With 275 seats against the Unionists' total of 273, they were now dependent on the support of the 82 Irish Nationalists and 40 Labour MPs. Although the resulting 'progressive alliance' was able to unite in a campaign against the Lords, it was still a disappointing outcome.

Asquith's colleagues were divided: some wanted to reduce the Lords' powers at once whilst others viewed reform of the composition of the upper house as a more pressing priority. His Chief Whip, the Master of Elibank, privately described the Cabinet in February 1910 as 'absolutely discredited' by internal disagreement, whilst 'the Prime Minister ... had lost his nerve, he had no grip of the situation'.[13] Asquith soon recovered his poise and united the Cabinet behind a series of resolutions, later embodied in the Parliament Bill, which sought to end the Lords' veto power. The solution in essence was a revival of the concept of a 'suspensory veto', outlined by Campbell-Bannerman in 1907. All money bills were to be passed automatically, and the Lords would be allowed to delay other legislation for no more than two parliamentary sessions. Following the death of Edward VII in May, Asquith attempted to reach an agreed solution using the device of a constitutional conference. After this broke down in November, as a result of Unionist intransigence, he led his party into a second general election, whose outcome almost replicated that of the earlier contest. This time he had obtained the reluctant private consent of the new sovereign, George V, to the creation of peers in the event of a second Liberal victory. Asquith stood his ground in the face of furious Unionist opposition when the terms of the deal became known. His strategy was vindicated when a divided upper house finally allowed the Parliament Bill through in August 1911. Through his persistence he had obtained a constitutional settlement which left the Lords still with a significant capacity for obstruction, but with the primacy of the elected chamber now unambiguously asserted. A solution had been found to a problem which had dogged Liberal governments since the time of Gladstone.

In other areas of domestic policy the Asquith government proved less productive. He conciliated the government's Labour Party allies by introducing salaries for MPs in 1911 and by reversing the effects of the 1909 Osborne judgment, a legal ruling which had barred trade unions from using their funds for political purposes. The government averted a national coal strike in March 1912 by conceding a minimum wage for miners, whilst making clear that intervention of this kind would not be extended to other industries. To the demand for female suffrage, which reached a peak in 1910–14, Asquith gave a negative response. In refusing to entertain the notion of political equality between the sexes he was out of step with the trend of Liberal opinion and with a number of his own Cabinet colleagues. It is possible that his hostility inflamed the violence of the campaign waged by Emmeline Pankhurst's Women's Social and Political Union, some of whose members personally attacked the Prime Minister. He offered a half-hearted concession to the suffrage movement in July 1912, when the government introduced a general reform bill, with provision for a free vote on an amendment to give women the same voting rights as men. When the Speaker of the Commons declared in January 1913 that such an amendment would compel the withdrawal and recasting of the bill, Asquith abandoned it with relief.

It was Ireland, however, which absorbed most of Asquith's energies in the two years prior to the First World War. The introduction of a Home Rule Bill in April 1912 was the price that Asquith paid for the Irish Nationalist Party's support in the Commons. It was also a belated attempt to honour an historic Liberal commitment. Now, however, the passage of the Parliament Act meant that the government could eventually overrule the Unionist majority in the Lords, which had blocked Gladstone's last attempt to establish a Dublin parliament in 1893. The Liberals faced a serious obstacle in the form of the Protestant community in Ulster, who could count on the support of the Unionist Party in resisting any attempt to place them under the authority of an Irish legislative body. One solution was to grant special treatment to the Protestant parts of the north for a specified period. This would not, however, appease the Unionists, whose objective was not merely to exempt Ulster but to destroy the Home Rule Bill. Nor was it acceptable to the Nationalists, led by John Redmond, who viewed Ireland as a single unit and who feared that a self-governing entity deprived of the industrial resources of the north would not be economically viable.

Asquith was probably mistaken in deciding to postpone making concessions to Ulster until 1914, in the belief that the Unionists would abandon their opposition as the passing of the legislation became imminent. He approached the question with a cool detachment which took little account of the deep feelings of the opposing factions. He recorded his exasperation with the refusal of Home Rulers and Unionists to accept a pragmatic division of the partly Catholic, partly Protestant county of Tyrone in a private letter: 'I have rarely felt more hopeless in any practical affair: an impasse, with unspeakable consequences, upon a matter which to English eyes seems inconceivably small, & to Irish eyes immeasurably big.'[14] The reflection indicates Asquith's inadequate grasp of a situation which seemed to be descending into civil war. The Irish Unionists, headed by the uncompromising figure of Sir Edward Carson, were preparing to defy London by creating a provisional government defended by a well-drilled armed force. They had reason to believe that Asquith could not count on the co-operation of the army in an attempt to impose Home Rule on the north, and every expectation that they could secure Ulster's permanent exclusion from a self-governing Ireland. After a cross-party conference at Buckingham Palace in July 1914 failed to produce an acceptable settlement, the prospects looked bleak. Asquith was fortunate that the outbreak of European conflict shortly afterwards diverted attention from the growing crisis in Ireland, bringing the rival factions together in support for the British war effort. Under the terms of the Parliament Act the Home Rule Bill was placed on the statute book in September 1914, but with its provisions suspended for the duration of the war. In this way Asquith ensured his own political survival, but at a price of the increased contempt of the Unionists. One of his most outspoken critics, Leo Amery, attacked his avoidance of decision-making in a *Quarterly Review* article written in July 1914: 'he has held a season ticket on the line of least resistance and has gone wherever the train of events has carried him, lucidly justifying his position at whatever point he has happened to find himself'.[15] It was a charge to which his opponents would return in wartime.

Foreign policy, defence and war

An important constraint on Asquith's conduct as Prime Minister was his position as the leader of a very diverse party, whose many strands of opinion were reflected in the composition of the Cabinet. Nowhere was this more evident than in foreign and defence policy, where the spectrum of views ranged from advocates of closer military ties with France to opponents of increased defence spending who would not contemplate British intervention in a continental conflict. Germany's aggressive conduct in the summer of 1914 provided a severe test of Asquith's managerial skills. Characteristically, he did not set out a clear policy in advance but moved in response to events. He was aware that a premature decision, whether to intervene or to declare British neutrality, would have broken up the government. Only a small number of ministers – Grey, Haldane and Churchill – were unequivocally in favour of the former course of action. A larger number were prepared to resign if Britain gave France military support without a clear justification. Germany's invasion of Belgium in early August 1914, in pursuit of its attack on France, helped Asquith to unite the doubters behind a moral case for intervention. It was a measure of his skill that he took Britain into the conflict with only two relatively minor Cabinet ministers, Lord Morley (Lord President of the Council) and John Burns (President of the Board of Trade) choosing to resign. Crucially, Asquith was assisted by the decision of Lloyd George, the only credible leader of an anti-war radical movement, to stay. Asquith acted in step with the movement of public opinion, which was markedly anti-German and supportive of 'gallant little Belgium'. He consolidated his government's unity by appointing the non-party Field Marshal Lord Kitchener, Britain's most popular military figure, as War Secretary. The latter's prestige helped to offset criticism of the government as it became apparent that it did not possess ready answers to the growing military stalemate in the trenches of northern France and Belgium.

By May 1915, however, it was becoming clear that a wider reconstruction of the government was necessary. Two issues brought matters to a head. The First Sea Lord, Admiral Fisher, resigned his post as the professional head of the Navy in a dispute over the handling of the Dardanelles expedition, an ill-conceived attempt to drive Turkey out of the war. At the same time allegations of a shell shortage on the Western Front cast severe doubt on the competence of War Office administration and made it hard for the Unionist leader, Bonar Law, to restrain his parliamentary supporters from an all-out attack on the government. To the surprise of his followers, Asquith agreed to form a coalition. Controversy continues to surround his precise motives but it seems likely that both he and Bonar Law separately wanted to avoid fighting a general election at an unfavourable time. Asquith kept the Treasury and Foreign Office in Liberal hands, appointed Lloyd George to run a new ministry responsible for the production of munitions, and fobbed Bonar Law off with the relatively junior post of Colonial Secretary. In the longer term, however, the decision to share power with the hereditary enemy weakened Asquith's standing, with one disillusioned Liberal minister, Augustine Birrell, lamenting the creation of the 'twopenny halfpenny coalition' which left the premier with 'a Cabinet composed of warring, uncongenial, and it may be traitorous elements'.[16]

Most serious was Asquith's failure to create a body with executive power to take responsibility for overall war planning. The full Cabinet was too large to assume a strategic decision-making role yet it retained formal authority over all areas of policy. None of the smaller committees created by Asquith – the war council which met from November 1914 to June 1915 and its successors, the Dardanelles committee and the war committee – had clearly defined powers. Sir Edward Carson, who served as a member of the coalition ministry from May to October 1915, harshly but not entirely inaccurately described Cabinet government in this period as '22 gabblers round a table with an old procrastinator in the chair'.[17] His impatience with Asquith's indecisiveness reflected a widening gulf between those who believed that the war could be fought with minimal disturbance of peacetime methods, and those who wanted a more active role for government.

The division was highlighted by the growing pressure from the majority of Unionists, and a small but influential number of Liberals headed by Lloyd George, for the adoption of conscription. In his handling of the issue Asquith sought as far as possible to maintain unity. By the autumn of 1915 he had reached the conclusion that compulsion would be necessary in order to meet the army's needs. At the same time he was conscious of the attachment of traditional Liberal individualists to the principle of voluntary recruiting. He also feared the implications of any move towards the compulsory direction of manpower for the government's delicate working relationship with organized labour. His priorities were clear in a letter to one of his female confidantes: 'I am bridge-building, a difficult kind of architecture. But it has to be done – or at any rate attempted.'[18]Accordingly Asquith allowed the argument for conscription to evolve, first seeking a compromise in the form of the so-called Derby scheme, named after the director-general of recruiting, whereby men were invited to attest their willingness to serve, should this prove necessary. Only after this had been tried did he push for the outright conscription of unmarried men, which was carried in January 1916 with the loss of only one Cabinet minister, the Home Secretary, Sir John Simon. The conscription of married men followed four months later.

Asquith's capacity for artful compromise is understandable in terms of the need to hold the coalition together. It did him no good, however, with principled Liberal opponents of the growth of state power, and still less with those at the other end of the spectrum, who were impatient for a more ruthless prosecution of the war. His position was further undermined by a series of blows. Although he acted to restore order in Ireland after militant republicans tried to seize control of Dublin in the Easter Rising, the government was blamed for its failure to anticipate the rebellion. Asquith's Liberal credentials were damaged by the brutality with which the military authorities carried out the executions of captured rebels, whilst Unionist opposition at home destroyed the last chance of a constitutional settlement. On the Western Front British forces failed to make headway in the Battle of the Somme, which cost 415,000 casualties between July and November. Among the dead was Asquith's son, Raymond, whose loss further impaired his effectiveness at a time when his own health was deteriorating.

Criticism of the premier's conduct of the war found a focus in Lloyd George, who had moved from the Ministry of Munitions to the War Office following the death of Kitchener at sea in June 1916. By November Lloyd George had become convinced that the creation of a small war committee, independent of the Cabinet and with full decision-making powers, was essential. The sticking point was his insistence, supported by Bonar Law and Carson, on the exclusion of the Prime Minister from the committee. The War Secretary's impatience with his chief had been growing for some time. In early December he confided in the editor of the *Manchester Guardian*, C.P. Scott, his exasperation with a Prime Minister who saw himself solely as a chairman of a committee: 'He came to Cabinet meetings with no policy which he had decided to recommend, listened to what others said, summed it up ably and then as often as not postponed the decision. It was a futile method of carrying on a war.'[19] To Asquith, however, Lloyd George's desire for stronger direction of the war was little more than a mask for personal ambition. After initially accepting the proposal in outline, he changed his mind after the appearance of a highly critical article in *The Times*, now known to have been inspired by Carson, but in which Asquith detected the hand of Lloyd George. This prompted Asquith to resign the premiership, possibly in a vain bid to demonstrate his own indispensability, but more likely in despair at the way in which real authority had ebbed away from him. With not only Lloyd George but also key Unionist ministers ready to resign, his position at the head of the coalition had become unsustainable.

Asquith was far from a complete failure as war leader. Like all the participant nations, Britain was unprepared for a worldwide conflict which required the large-scale mobilization of manpower and material resources. Asquith's government expanded government control of vital war industries and worked out arrangements with the trade unions to facilitate increased production. It survived significant military reverses and managed the transition from voluntary to compulsory service. It established a framework on which the Lloyd George government was able to build in the final two years of the war. Asquith was, however, too much absorbed by the tasks of deflecting criticism and maintaining consensus. He lacked his successor's capacity for inspirational leadership and his willingness to subordinate everything to the goal of victory. In part this was a matter of temperament. Both in his personal routine and in his attitude to policy-making, Asquith sought to salvage as much as possible of the calmer, more orderly pre-war way of working. He failed to heed Bonar Law's advice, that 'in war it is necessary not only to be active but to seem active'.[20] Yet he clung to the premiership for as long as possible. That was why, in December 1916, he rejected Lloyd George's attempt to impose a command structure which would have left him with the shadow but not the substance of power. Lloyd George later recalled an indignant Asquith asking: 'What is the proposal? That I who have held first place for eight years should be asked to take a secondary position.'[21] His refusal to serve in a subordinate capacity, in the interests of party unity and the national interest, inevitably prompts an unfavourable comparison with Neville Chamberlain's willingness to take office under Winston Churchill in May 1940.

Asquith's fall was to a large extent a natural consequence of his own limitations. The tribute paid to him by some of his admirers, 'the last of the Romans', hints at his weaknesses as well as his strengths. His judicious approach to problems, his respect for established methods and institutions and his dignified aversion to the vulgar arts of self-dramatization understandably aroused respect. Yet in an unprecedented national crisis his cautious, conservative nature became a positive handicap. The political crisis of December 1916 saw the replacement of Britain's last truly Victorian premier by an individual better attuned to the challenges of the twentieth century.

Notes

1 J.M. McEwen, *The Riddell Diaries 1908–1923*, London and Atlantic Highlands: Athlone Press, 1986, p. 42.

2 Viscount Simon, *Retrospect*, London: Hutchinson, 1952, pp. 140–1.

3 Earl of Oxford and Asquith, *Memories and Reflections 1852–1927*, Volume 2, London: Cassell, 1928, pp. 171–2.

4 Roy Jenkins, *Asquith*, London: Collins, 1964, p. 193.

5 Austen Chamberlain, *Politics from Inside: An Epistolary Chronicle 1906–1914*, London: Cassell, 1936, p.576.

6 Cameron Hazlehurst and Christine Woodland (eds), *A Liberal Chronicle: Journals and Papers of J.A. Pease, 1st Lord Gainford, 1908–1910*, London: The Historians' Press, 1994, p. 58, entry for 23 July 1908.

7 Stephen Koss, *Asquith*, London: Allen Lane, 1976, p. 90.

8 Hazlehurst and Woodland, *A Liberal Chronicle*, p. 25, entry for 25 May 1908.

9 A.J.P. Taylor, *English History 1914–1945*, London: Pelican, 1970, p. 41.

10 Koss, *Asquith*, p. 209.

11 Sir Almeric Fitzroy, *Memoirs*, Volume 2, London: Hutchinson, 1923, p. 475, quoting his diary for 17 January 1912.

12 Reprinted in Stephen Koss, *Asquith*, and also in Michael and Eleanor Brock (eds), *H.H. Asquith: Letters to Venetia Stanley*, Oxford: Oxford University Press, 1982, illustration 12.

13 A.C. Murray, *Master and Brother*, London: Murray, 1945, p. 40.

14 Michael and Eleanor Brock (eds), *H.H. Asquith: Letters to Venetia Stanley*, Oxford: Oxford University Press, 1982, p. 109, letter dated 22 July 1914.

15 Cameron Hazlehurst, *Politicians at War, July 1914 to May 1915: A Prologue to the Triumph of Lloyd George*, London: Jonathan Cape, 1971, p. 21.

16 Stephen Koss, *Haldane: Scapegoat for Liberalism*, New York and London: Columbia University Press, 1969, pp. 209–10.

17 David French, *British Strategy and War Aims, 1914–16*, London: HarperCollins, 1986, p. 102.

18 Asquith to Pamela McKenna, 13 October 1915, quoted in Martin Farr, 'Winter and Discontent: The December Crises of the Asquith Coalition, 1915–1916', *Britain and the World*, Volume 4(1), 2011, p. 118.

19 Trevor Wilson (ed.), *The Political Diaries of C.P. Scott 1911–1928*, London: Collins, 1970, p. 243, entry for 3 December 1916.

20 Robert Blake, *The Unknown Prime Minister: The Life and Times of Andrew Bonar Law 1858–1923*, London: Eyre and Spottiswoode, 1955, p. 290.

21 Jenkins, *Asquith*, p. 515.

Further reading

Michael and Eleanor Brock (eds), *H.H. Asquith: Letters to Venetia Stanley*, Oxford: Oxford University Press, 1982

George H. Cassar, *Asquith as War Leader*, London: Hambledon Press, 1994

Roy Jenkins, *Asquith*, London: Collins, 1964

Stephen Koss, *Asquith*, London: Allen Lane, 1976

4   David Lloyd George (1863–1945)

Prime Minister: December 1916– October 1922

'This siren, this goat-footed bard, this half-human visitor to our age from the hag-ridden, magic and enchanted woods of Celtic antiquity.'

Maynard Keynes, *The Economic Consequences of the Peace*[1]

Though he was born in 1863, so that his formative years were Victorian, and though for a time he seemed identified with narrow causes like temperance and Welsh disestablishment, David Lloyd George now seems a surprisingly modern political figure, in a way that his contemporaries do not. Partly this is due to the series of sexual and financial scandals that beset him, and which have so many recent counterparts that they seem somehow contemporary; partly, also, to his determination to alleviate poverty, an issue almost as important now – the poor, like the rich, being always with us – as in the first quarter of the twentieth century. Similarly, his political style seems distinctly modern. Here was no *primus inter pares* but a presidential leader, complete with a bevy of personal advisers: a man who liked to cut a dash on the national and international stages, always conscious of the need to influence the media. Belying his years, he was a person of great flexibility of mind. He adapted more successfully than any other British politician to the transition from peace to war in 1914, just as he was, in the 1920s, the first politician to espouse Keynesian economic policies. Though the office of premier had an aura of solemnity about it, Lloyd George often seemed a fresh and even playful figure, a rebel within the establishment. Even his irreverent jokes are still funny.[2]

Yet if few doubt that Lloyd George was a man of enormous ability and energy, and could charm the birds from the trees, that is where consensus ends. To contemporaries he was a remarkably controversial figure, and he remains so to historians. What part did principle play in his career, what part opportunism? More specific questions must also be asked. Why did he become Prime Minister in December 1916? Was he motivated by patriotism, in that the war desperately needed a new energetic impulse, or did he indulge in unscrupulous intrigue against the honourable H.H. Asquith out of ambition? We also have to ask whether he was really, as his supporters insisted, 'the man who won the war', and what he achieved by carrying on a coalition into the equally momentous and challenging years of peace.

The rise to the premiership

Though born in Manchester, David Lloyd George was brought up in North Wales by his uncle Richard Lloyd, a self-educated shoemaker and Baptist preacher who was devoted to his nephew and did all he could, emotionally and financially, to further his career. Leaving school at 15, Lloyd George became articled to a solicitor in Portmadoc and, having passed the law examinations in 1884, set up his own firm in Criccieth. Here his younger brother did most of the work, while he concentrated on entering Parliament, winning Caernarvon Boroughs for the Liberal Party in 1890 by a mere 18 votes. He was to represent the constituency for the next 55 years.

At first he was very much the radical, and some thought the irresponsible, critic. The House of Commons, he decided, was 'the House of Snobs'[3] controlled by wealthy landowners – whichever party was in power. His opposition to the Boer War – and his escapade in having to dress as a policeman to escape angry crowds in Birmingham in December 1901 – brought him notoriety, while his spirited opposition to Balfour's Education Bill in 1902 impressed his party. It was no shock when, in 1905, at the age of 43, he was made President of the Board of Trade, with a seat in the Cabinet. He was to be continuously in office for the next 17 years. Nor had he long to wait for promotion. In April

1908, when Herbert Asquith moved to 10 Downing Street, Lloyd George replaced him as Chancellor of the Exchequer.

Lloyd George was one of the thrusting 'New Liberals'. The worst kind of Tory, he averred, was the nominal Liberal, whereas he himself judged that 'for Liberalism stagnation is death'.[4] The Liberals had to seize the initiative, introduce bold reforms, tackle the poverty to which social scientists had recently drawn attention, and show there was no need for a specifically Labour Party. Otherwise, as the franchise inevitably widened, there would be no future for the Liberals. That such views, though often presented in stirring speeches, were not merely rhetoric is shown by his record in office. As Chancellor, he was lucky in bringing to fruition, in 1908, measures that Asquith had masterminded, including graduated income tax and old age pensions for those over 70 who were in poverty. But the 'People's Budget' of 1909 ('a war budget ... raising money to wage implacable warfare against poverty and squalidness')[5] was very much his own work. It raised income tax and inheritance tax, introduced a 'super-tax' on the highest incomes and began, in a modest way, the taxation of land. When the Lords unexpectedly rejected the measure, he took the initiative in rousing opinion against the peers, his outspoken language shocking Edward VII, and he worked closely with Asquith to produce the Parliament Act of 1911. No longer could the Lords veto money bills, and they could only delay other measures for a maximum of two years. Also in 1911 Lloyd George introduced National Insurance against ill health, so that all manual workers would receive treatment from a general practitioner, as well as some unemployment insurance.

Lloyd George told friends that the driving force in his career was a determination to better the lives of the poor, and his record before 1914 goes a long way to bear this out. He had also ensured for himself a momentous political future. In a Cabinet that is sometimes described as the most able of the twentieth century, he was undoubtedly the star. Yet there was no real rivalry or rancour between the Prime Minister and his hyperactive, talented Chancellor. Indeed many rate their partnership as more harmonious and constructive than that between any other two holders of their offices. 'Asquith', Lloyd George remarked, was 'a big man': though he 'never initiates anything' himself, he was a 'great judge' in Cabinet.[6] Asquith was 62 in 1916, Lloyd George 51, and some believed the premiership was sure to pass to the younger man, but only in the fullness of time and when the older man decided to retire. Yet, as Asquith once quipped, in politics the inevitable rarely happens.

Lloyd George supported Britain's declaration of war against Germany on 4 August 1914. Despite his previous opposition to the Boer War, he had never been a pacifist, and Germany's violation of Belgian neutrality brought him down in favour of intervention. Yet he was immensely depressed at the cataclysm of war: he would bear his share of the ghastly burden, he said, 'though it scorches my flesh to do so'.[7]

Unlike his colleague Winston Churchill, roused to fever pitch by physical conflict, Lloyd George had little stomach for warfare. The sound of bombs always sent him scurrying for shelter and the sight of suffering made him physically ill. After visiting a hospital in France in February 1916, he was visibly unnerved: 'I was not made to deal with things of war. I am too sensitive to pain & suffering.'[8] Even so, he told Churchill that the 'only thing I care about is that we win the war'.[9] Earlier he had judged that stagnation could be the death of Liberalism; now he realized that for Britain itself stagnation could be death in a war whose scale diminished that of any previous conflict.

Continuing as Chancellor, Lloyd George calmed fears of financial panic. He doubled income tax, very nearly quadrupled beer duty, and began to borrow on the scale needed to finance the conflict. He also made rousing patriotic speeches that identified him in the public mind with the wholehearted prosecution of the war. Even more important, it was he who negotiated the 'Treasury Agreement'. Already the trade unions had agreed to an industrial truce, so that the number of strikes declined dramatically. Now, in March 1915, Lloyd George hammered out a 'no strike' agreement for key groups of workers, with compulsory arbitration, and secured an acceptance that 'restrictive practices' would end. The way was open for 'dilution', so that skilled jobs could be undertaken by a larger number of unskilled men – or, increasingly, by women. The Agreement, together with a new Defence of the Realm Act, which gave the government unparalleled power to direct industry, signalled that the state was being mobilized to win the war. It was soon clear, however, that even more had to be done.

'One Big Push' from the West, it had been said, combined with the advance of the 'Russian Steam-roller' in the East, and the war would be 'all over by Christmas'. Yet such facile optimism proved unfounded. Early in 1915, with around half a million men in the British army and with troops digging themselves in on the Western Front, constructing 500 miles of fortifications from the Channel coast to Switzerland, it became clear that the conflict would be a long war of attrition. Each side's defensive weapons negated the artillery bombardment and infantry assaults of the enemy, inflicting enormous casualties.

In the spring of 1915, shell shortages and the failure of the Gallipoli campaign in the Dardanelles produced a demand for political change at the top. In May 1915 Asquith bent before the storm and accepted Conservative demands for a coalition. It was in fact a very imperfect political union. Asquith gave the Conservatives only 8 out of 21 Cabinet posts and none of the great offices of state. Their leader, Andrew Bonar Law, was fobbed off with the position of Secretary of State for the Colonies. The one success of this period was Lloyd George. He was working harder than ever before in his life, setting up and running a new Ministry of Munitions.

Asquith had entrusted Lloyd George with a crucial task, as the war had created a seemingly endless demand for weapons, shells and other *matériel* of war. The keynotes of his work were improvization (he even had to find his own office space and requisition hotels for his staff) and unorthodoxy (businessmen were brought into Whitehall for the first time). He was not the most orderly of administrators, John Grigg tells us, but he had a genius for 'animating ... an organisation' and he gave the Ministry of Munitions 'the breath of life'.[10] He successfully cut through red tape, insisted that more firms switch to war production, brought armaments works under his control and even set up his own new munitions factories. War was too vital a business to leave to the operation of free market forces. As revisionists have pointed out, there was much inefficiency, but what is remarkable is the degree to which Lloyd George succeeded. By the time he left the Ministry, in June 1916, it had 12,000 staff at headquarters, while shell production had been revolutionized, with a fivefold increase within a year.

In July 1916, Asquith again turned to Lloyd George, appointing him Secretary of State for War on the death of Lord Kitchener. It seemed a sensible measure, for the versatile Welshman was the one undoubted political success of the war. But, no longer overworked at Munitions, he was able to consider the overall war effort, including military strategy. As casualties mounted on the Western Front, he was determined that fundamental change must come about. The root of the problem, he decided, lay with Asquith's leadership.

Asquith had been a formidable politician in his early days and, since becoming premier in 1908, had established a reputation as a brilliant chairman of Cabinet. Now, in quite different conditions, he wanted 'Business As Usual'. His lifestyle changed very little. He still drank too much and enjoyed the theatre, bridge and several lengthy correspondences, as well as weekends away. He was also the same expert chairman of Cabinet: patient, restrained, courteous, scholarly and impartial. He did his best to ensure balance and unity among a group of men who were, in fact, hotly divided. There were two broad factions – those who clung to *laissez-faire* and those who saw the need to intervene more and more in the life of the nation. Each approach was, in theory, a perfectly reasonable response to warfare in general, but not to the 'total war' in which Britain was now embroiled.

The non-interventionists wished, in particular, to maintain civil liberties, and were adamant that conscription – and other forms of 'Prussianism' – should be avoided. If the Prime Minister was not actually of this group, which included friends like Reginald McKenna, then he was determined to work with them and keep them in the Cabinet – much to the frustration of the interventionists in general and of Lloyd George in particular. At one point, he judged irritably that 'if he [Asquith] were in the pay of the Germans he could not be of more complete use to them'.[11] Admittedly Asquith bowed before the pressure, accepting the conscription of single men in January and of married men in June 1916, but these concessions were made with such reluctance that they brought him little political reward.

Asquith had no intention of surrendering the premiership. Indeed he did not take his opponents quite seriously. He believed that Balliol men, like himself, had 'effortless superiority', whereas in fact what he possessed was effortless complacency, and snobbery too. He decided that Lloyd George was 'not quite *au fond* a gentleman', while Bonar Law, another individual without a university education, 'had not the brains of a Glasgow baillie'.[12] Such men were irritants motivated by nothing more substantial than personal ambition.

It was the civil servant Maurice Hankey who first put forward the idea of setting up a small War Committee to run the war: Asquith would be excluded but would remain Prime Minister. Bonar Law put the scheme to him, but he turned it down. He won't fight the Germans, Lloyd George decided, 'but he will fight for Office'.[13] In the end Asquith resigned, half expecting that no one else would be able to form a government and that he would soon resume his rightful position. It was a fatal error, however, for Lloyd George, with the backing of the Conservatives, successfully formed a government.

There was certainly an element of intrigue about it all – inevitably so, as there was no other way of removing the premier – but it was hardly a Lloyd George plot. Admittedly he was personally ambitious, but in December 1916 his primary motivation was patriotism. He genuinely believed, and for good reasons, that there had to be a change at the top and that he was the best man to provide it. Bonar Law and other Conservatives agreed. Balfour insisted that he had no prejudice in favour of Lloyd George, his old political enemy, but that 'he is the only man who can, at this moment, break down the barriers of red tape and see that the brains of the country are made use of'.[14]

Asquith might have retained the premiership, but he was too clouded with his own conceit to realize the need to stand aside from the central direction of the war. Even after resigning as premier he could have stayed in the government – an idea that earned his scorn. 'What is the proposal? That I who have held first place for eight years should be asked to take a secondary position?'[15] Not merely pride but pomposity came before his fall.

Lloyd George must be acquitted of putting personal ambition before national need. Some at the time, and numberless historians since, have accused him of splitting the Liberal party, and certainly the party was torn asunder. Only around half of the 129 Liberal MPs supported him, and initially none of the Liberal ministers. But he knew that there were far bigger issues than party unity. In the critical national situation at the end of 1916, which is sometimes described as being as dangerous as that of June 1940, it is to Lloyd George's credit that party unity did not weigh in the balance. 'Unity without action is nothing but futile carnage', he insisted; 'And I cannot be responsible for that. Vigour and vision are the supreme need at this hour.'[16]

Wartime premiership

Lloyd George became Prime Minister on 6 December 1916. Labour's National Executive Committee voted narrowly to support his government, and so the new coalition had support from all three parties, though Lloyd George himself was at first the only leading Liberal member of the new government.

A small War Cabinet was appointed, initially comprising Lloyd George (who dominated proceedings), Bonar Law, Labour's Arthur Henderson, and two Conservative peers, both former proconsuls, Lords Curzon and Milner. Later others became members, including the South African leader, Jan Christian Smuts, though he was a member of neither the Commons nor the Lords. In addition, a Cabinet secretariat was formed, under Maurice Hankey and later with Thomas Jones as his assistant, so that for the first time there was an agenda for each meeting and proper minutes were taken of proceedings. Earlier Asquith, wedded to the old amateurism, had believed it impossible even to have an agenda.

Lloyd George also created completely new ministries, to meet wartime needs. These included Labour, Pensions, National Service, Food Control, and Shipping. Although many of the men chosen as ministers were the obvious choices, several were highly unorthodox. For instance, he chose the Oxford historian H.A.L. Fisher to head the Board of Education. Even more remarkably he appointed Sir Joseph Maclay, a Glaswegian shipping magnate, to lead the new Ministry of Shipping. No matter that Maclay refused to become a Member of Parliament or accept a peerage. In wartime Lloyd George could get away with breaking the rules.

He himself expanded his own secretariat of personal advisers, so that a 'Garden Suburb', headed by the Gladstone Professor of Government at Oxford, W.G.S Adams. appeared in huts at the back of 10 Downing Street. Critics complained that the normal procedures of the civil service were being undermined, a judgement with which the new Prime Minister must have concurred. He wanted new thinking, not the mandarins' time-honoured procedures. Similarly he broke precedent by detaching the Leadership of the House of Commons from the premiership. Unlike previous premiers, he had no time to spend sitting through debates. A more presidential figure than any of his predecessors, he embraced reform and unorthodoxy so that Britain might survive and win the war.

The Prime Minister undoubtedly symbolized new vigour, and it seems that the British public approved of the political events of December 1916. There was a new mood of confidence and hope, so that morale was undoubtedly raised. But what tangible difference did Lloyd George make?

Perhaps the most constructive act of statesmanship would have been to try to end the war. Certainly a compromise peace was being talked about. President Woodrow Wilson hoped the warring nations would see sense, and end the slaughter, and in November 1916 a former Foreign Secretary, Lord Lansdowne, mooted the idea in Cabinet and resigned the following year to raise it in the press. An opportunity seemed to arise almost as soon as Lloyd George entered 10 Downing Street, as the German Chancellor, Bethmann-Hollweg, put out peace feelers on 12 December. Yet the Prime Minister and his Cabinet decided that to negotiate at that time would be tantamount to surrender: the Germans, in a position of strength, would not consider withdrawing from Belgium or Serbia, and had other territorial demands too. The Russians rejected Bethmann's note on 15 December, and Britain and France followed suit at the end of the month. Thereafter the faint possibility of a compromise peace faded still further, as in 1917 the German War Lords, Hindenburg and Ludendorff, engineered the resignation of the civilian Chancellor and exercised virtually dictatorial control in Germany. They were determined to fight on, and met similar mettle from the British. Lloyd George, like H.G. Wells'

Mr Britling in a best-selling novel of 1917, was determined to 'see it through'.

The key issue in 1917 was not victory but survival. Already German submarines in the Atlantic were sinking merchant ships, so that there were serious food shortages. Now, at the start of 1917, the War Lords began a campaign of unrestricted submarine warfare. This was a high-risk strategy, as sinking US vessels might well bring the Americans into the war, as indeed it did in April; but the Germans were gambling on early victory, by starving Britain into submission. They were very nearly successful, as in one month alone 371 vessels bringing food into Britain were sunk, and only a small proportion could be replaced by newly built ships. There was simply no solution, according to commander of the Grand Fleet, Admiral Jellicoe, and he was backed by the First Lord of the Admiralty, Edward Carson.

That merchant vessels should travel in convoy, with an armed guard, was a proposal favoured by many. It was not Lloyd George's brainchild, and yet without his powerful support it might well not have been adopted from May 1917, first on a small scale and then, after its utility had been proven, on a larger scale, so that by the end of the war 80 per cent of shipping to British ports came by this means. By the middle of 1918 shipping construction was greater than shipping losses. Jellicoe and Carson were both replaced. Lloyd George had undoubtedly made a vital contribution to winning the war.

The German U-boat menace was neutralized, but even so there were few causes for celebration on the home front, which in 1917 seemed close to collapse. Food production at home had decreased as farm workers – and farm horses – had gone to the front, and though improvements were made, with guaranteed corn prices to farmers and the utilization of disabled soldiers, prisoners of war and the small women's land army, food shortages remained and prices were too high for many to afford. There was real hunger and malnutrition, and babies died as a result in the mining villages of Durham and elsewhere. There were also signs of civil disobedience, as shops were looted and strikes, though technically illegal, became more common. The number of working days lost in unofficial stoppages in 1917 reached 5.6 million, more than twice the previous two years combined. Some ministers wanted to declare martial law and conscript the strikers, but Lloyd George believed that grievances were 'genuine and legitimate'[17] and instead arranged for pay rises. Nevertheless it was only in 1918 that food rationing was finally introduced and prices controlled, after Lloyd George's first appointment as Food Controller, the grocer Lord Devonport, had been replaced by a prominent Welsh businessman, D.A. Thomas. Now, for the first time, every British family was guaranteed basic rations.

Britain's survival on the home front was a close run thing. All too often crisis management, rather than the orderly implementation of effective plans, had characterized Lloyd George's government, as it had Asquith's. Yet at least the British home front fared better than Germany's, where there was mass starvation and real dislocation by 1918, and where strikers were often conscripted or put on trial.

The home front was the Prime Minister's obvious area of responsibility, but Lloyd George believed, controversially, that politicians should also have overall control of military affairs. He had long been against the basic strategy of the generals. The British High Command, he had decided, was fighting the last war, the military mind making up 'in retentiveness what it lacks in agility'.[18] He abhorred the mass slaughter on the Western Front, and hence had supported the Dardanelles campaign, though never as wholeheartedly as Churchill. In particular, he developed a contempt for Douglas Haig, since December 1915 Commander-in-Chief of the British Expeditionary Force and the author of the costly Somme offensive of 1916. He believed him not only unintelligent but callous: Haig squandered men's lives because he thought of the soldiers as his 'property', whereas Lloyd George said he was their 'trustee'.[19]

Ideally, Lloyd George would have liked to sack Haig, but he was too uncertain of his ground. The upper-class Scot had the backing of the royal family and of many Conservatives. Had Lloyd George dismissed him, he would almost certainly have had to resign himself, with the uncertain expectation of being reappointed. Instead he rejected Haig's offensive plans early in 1917 and favoured instead those of the French General Robert Nivelle. Not only did Nivelle inspire more confidence than Haig, but Lloyd George wanted to secure greater co-operation and co-ordination between the British and the French allies. In addition, if the offensive failed, most of the casualties would be French. And fail it did. By the end of April, after little more than two weeks of fighting, the French had suffered a quarter of a million casualties and gained 500 yards of territory.

Afterwards there was great pressure on the Prime Minister to accept Haig's plan for a third battle of Ypres. It was strongly backed by the Conservatives, and Lloyd George later insisted that the government would have fallen had he continued to resist. Whether he could have done more is open to debate. What is certain, however, is that Passchendaele was another bloodbath. Time and again Haig professed to see the enemy tottering on the verge of collapse, but time and again he was wrong. From July to November 1917, Britain lost 300,000 killed and wounded in the Passchendaele quagmire, the Germans far fewer. Lloyd George might have used his authority to call off the continuing slaughter; that he took no action is perhaps his greatest failing of the war. Clearly the new premiership had not signalled a new phase in warfare. Its basic pattern was set rigid.

Yet Passchendaele at least allowed Lloyd George to push ahead with Anglo-French co-ordination. A Supreme War Council was set up in November 1917. This comprised the allied Prime Ministers and their military advisers, and Lloyd George made sure that Haig was not one of them. When the Chief of the General Staff, Sir William Robertson, refused to co-operate with the Council, he was replaced in February 1918. Lloyd George took heart that ultimately victory was assured. The USA had joined the war the previous April and it seemed just a matter of time before their troops arrived in sufficient numbers to make a crucial difference. In the meantime he favoured a defensive posture that would minimize casualties There is some truth in the allegation that, as a result of this strategy, Lloyd George denied Haig enough troops for yet another 'big push' in the spring. It was soon apparent, however, that it was the enemy who were on the verge of victory.

The Ludendorff offensive began on 21 March 1918. Firing one million shells in five hours, German forces broke through British lines, capturing 21,000 troops in a day and achieving the biggest breakthrough for three years. Paris itself was actually shelled, and

Allied forces were falling back in disarray. Rising to the occasion, Lloyd George acted swiftly and confidently. He took over the War Office and arranged for the return to France of thousands of troops on leave, also diverting men from Palestine and Italy. In addition, without consulting his Foreign Secretary, he successfully appealed to President Wilson for the immediate use of American troops on the battlefield. The scope of conscription was also extended, to include men up to the age of 50, up from 42. Lloyd George also arranged that a leading French general, Ferdinand Foch, should become General-in-Chief of the Allied forces in April. That the German offensive failed, however, was really due to Ludendorff's tactics. Obsessed with the amount of territory his troops could take, regardless of the larger strategic picture, his men penetrated too deeply, outstripping their supply lines. The last attack began on 15 July, and proved a clear failure. A million German soldiers had died.

At this stage the Allied forces were able to counter-attack, and Haig had a largely free hand. The British had learned lessons from painful past experiences, especially that soldiers should advance under cover of a 'creeping barrage' of heavy gunfire, rather than moving forward after a bombardment. In addition new technology, like tanks and planes and innovative percussion fuses, were used effectively. Haig's summer offensive of a hundred days broke through the Hindenburg line. Some military historians judge his ensuing victories to be among the most impressive in British military history. In November the Germans sued for an armistice. His reputation restored, Haig was soon able to imply that the war had been won in spite of Lloyd George and his 'conceit and swagger'.[20]

For most Britons, however, amidst the celebrations, Lloyd George was 'the man who won the war'. Does the claim carry any credence today? A case for it was argued by Maurice Hankey. He pointed to key factors: Lloyd George created the Ministry of Munitions; he streamlined the Cabinet; he introduced the convoy system; and then he secured acceptance of the Supreme War Council 'which prepares the way for the unified command within six months and victory within a year'.[21] Hankey was right in that, in assessing Lloyd George's contribution to victory, we cannot confine ourselves to his premiership, but he surely exaggerated the significance of his co-ordination of Anglo-French strategy. It was the Germans who took the initiative, Ludendorff losing the war by his last-ditch attempt to deliver a knock-out blow as much as the Allies winning it, though Haig and Foch deserve a share of the credit. Even on the home front, it can be argued that in many ways Lloyd George's government was little better than Asquith's. Certainly several of the new ministers did little better than their earlier counterparts.

Nevertheless, there is no reason to suppose that Asquith's government would have fared any better in 1917–18, and many reasons to suppose it would have been more timid in its work. Many contemporaries agreed with C.P. Scott in May 1918 that, 'whatever his faults George is at least an incomparably better war minister than Asquith'.[22] Certainly Admiral David Beatty, Commander-in-Chief of the Fleet from April 1917, believed that Lloyd George was 'the one man in the whole rotten crew who had his heart set on winning'.[23] Lloyd George worked tirelessly for victory. He was not '*the man* who won the war', for no one man could possibly have done so, but he contributed much more than any other single politician, and it is all too easy to believe that without him Britain would have lost.

Postwar premiership

At the end of the war, Lloyd George again broke ranks with his prime ministerial predecessors. Hitherto the Cabinet as a whole had decided on the date of a general election; but now, with patriotic feelings running high, he alone took the initiative and called a snap general election, for 14 December 1918. Labour went into opposition, but he had no trouble persuading the Conservatives to continue their coalition into peacetime. They hoped to profit from their association with the charismatic premier. It was he – and his promises to 'make Germany pay' and to create a land fit for heroes, complete with homes fit for heroes to live in – who dominated the hustings. According to Bonar Law, Lloyd George 'commands as great an influence in every constituency as has ever been exercised by a Prime Minister in political history'.[24] When he saw the results, with the coalition securing a massive 478 seats, compared to Labour's 62 and the

Asquithian Liberals on 28, he decided euphorically that the 55-year-old Lloyd George could be Prime Minister for life. His position seemed impregnable.

There has probably never been a more popular Prime Minister than Lloyd George at the end of 1918. His political future looked assured, and it seemed that Britain would begin a golden age of prosperity and reform under his leadership. Yet he was to have less than four years in office and his peacetime premiership seemed to contemporaries, as to most historians, to be an abject failure. The seeds of his downfall were in fact already present at the moment of his greatest success. His seemingly unassailable political position was, in reality, highly insecure. Furthermore, people's expectations were grossly inflated: too much was expected too soon, so that even substantial achievements might be perceived as failures. Finally, although Britons rejoiced that they had won the war, it was in many ways a Pyrrhic victory. Old problems had been exacerbated and new ones created. Any government was likely to fail in the period after 1918.

That the Prime Minister was actually in a vulnerable position was soon apparent. Lacking the support from his own majority party that a premier can usually depend on, Lloyd George was dangerously dependent on the support of the Conservatives, who by themselves constituted a secure majority in the parliament. They would continue to support him only so long as he was a vote-winner, and this meant that he had to be seen to be dominant and successful. This suited his temperament, but it was a dangerous strategy nevertheless. The corollary was that he would be responsible for failures, as well as successes. Furthermore his policies, having to receive the assent of the Conservative backbenchers, had of necessity to follow their basic wishes. The alternative, the creation of a new party from the fusion of Lloyd George's Liberals with all but the extreme Conservative Diehards, soon foundered, revealing the all too obvious differences in policy and temperament that separated the two groups. Hence the Prime Minister had little choice but to walk a political tightrope. At first he received invaluable support in this balancing act from Andrew Bonar Law, the experienced and popular leader of the Conservatives, an effective mediator between the two wings of the coalition. His resignation due to ill health in

March 1921 was a real blow to Lloyd George, especially since his successor, the aloof Austen Chamberlain, seemed out of touch with backbench opinion and too much controlled by the Prime Minister. Conservative discontents multiplied over the next year, exploding at the Carlton Club in October 1922.

Lloyd George had the bad luck to be in office when the continent of Europe was impoverished and overseas markets had been lost. In Britain a brief postwar boom gave way to a severe depression. The war had led to tremendous expansion in the steel, coal and textile industries, and when it was clear that their products were no longer needed in such vast quantities, unemployment mounted. At the beginning of December 1920 it stood at only 300,000, but six months later it passed the two million mark. The Conservatives called for government retrenchment. This was not necessarily Lloyd George's favoured solution. As his Chancellor in 1921 he chose Sir Robert Horne because he was 'the least orthodox of all the possibles, and the most indifferent to financial and economic orthodoxy';[25] but he had little choice but to acquiesce in their wishes. In 1921 there were cuts of £75 million, followed by a further £64 million; and the following year there was a further 12 per cent reduction. Similarly, Lloyd George was unable to accept the recommendation of the Sankey Commission – admittedly by the narrowest of margins, the casting vote of the chairman – in favour of the nationalization of the coal mines. Such a policy would have been anathema to the Conservatives. The results were inevitably harmful for Lloyd George: a rash of strikes (totalling 86 million working days in 1921) and the ending of the high hopes of social reconstruction.

There is much to be said in mitigation. There were, for instance, far more bitter and violent strikes on the continent, and Lloyd George did at least manage to avert a potential general strike in April 1921, so that the seemingly mighty 'Triple Alliance' of miners, railwaymen and transport workers became to satirists the 'Cripple Alliance'. Furthermore, the number of days lost due to industrial conflict fell significantly in 1922, to 20 million. Similarly, important social reforms were implemented. Although a planned further extension of the school leaving age was abandoned in 1921, Fisher's Education Act of 1918 had improved vastly upon previous educational provision, making attendance compulsory until the age of 14. Free milk was also supplied to children in need for the first time in 1921. Critics complained that, as central grants were discontinued, the vaunted 'homes fit for heroes to live in' had become, by 1922, homes only heroes would be willing to live in. Even so, around 170,000 new subsidized houses had been built. There were also very important extensions to the national insurance scheme that Lloyd George had originated in 1911. The Unemployment Insurance Act of 1920 extended the existing scheme to far more workers, so that a total of 12 million were covered, and the following year another Act provided 'uncovenanted benefit' (or 'the dole') for those whose unemployment benefit had expired, and in addition there were extra benefits for the wife and children of an unemployed worker. Much was in fact achieved, and the years 1918–22 compare favourably in terms of social welfare provision with any other four-year period between the wars. Yet it was less than the people wanted, and less than they had been led to expect.

Even so, perhaps Lloyd George might have achieved more, even in the inauspicious postwar conditions, had he not been overwhelmingly busy, as problems overlapped and impacted upon each other. There was little let-up in the Prime Minister's schedule, as domestic and foreign issues called for his personal intervention.

From January to June 1919 he was in attendance at the Paris Peace Conference. It was the largest international conference ever, as 32 nations sent delegations to decide the future of large parts of the world. At first it was assumed that peace treaties would somehow emerge from plenary sessions, but in time the key decisions were made by the 'Big Three' of Lloyd George, America's President Wilson, and chairman of the Conference Georges Clemenceau, the Prime Minister of France. Their work has been variously estimated, the critics judging that their short-sighted failures led directly to a second world war 20 years later. But this is an unbalanced judgement, giving far too little weight to the period after 1919, and in particular to the deterioration of international affairs that followed the onset of the Great Depression from 1929.

The peacemakers had a whole series of daunting tasks. They had to attempt to bring about national self-determination in parts of

Europe where ethnic groups did not occupy discrete land areas, and at the same time construct states large enough to be viable and thus likely to survive. Yet self-determination had to be denied to the Germans, as the aggressors had to be made weaker not stronger. Also, they had to disarm the defeated powers, dispose of their colonies and arrange for the payment of reparations. Furthermore, a new international peacekeeping body had to be set up. They had somehow to satisfy states as diverse as France, which had suffered more than any other during the war and was consequently bent on revenge, and the United States, which had suffered minimal damage and so could adopt a more disinterested approach.

That agreements were reached, and treaties written, was undoubtedly impressive, and for this Lloyd George must take some of the credit. Several times he acted as a broker between Clemenceau and Wilson. He did much to ensure that the Rhineland remained under German sovereignty, that plebiscites were held in Upper Silesia, and that the controversial issue of a final reparations bill was to be decided later, by a commission, once Germany's capacity to pay had been assessed. The economist Maynard Keynes was highly critical of Lloyd George: here was a man of enormous ability, indeed with six or seven extra senses not available to ordinary mortals, able to sense with 'telepathic instinct' what everyone else was thinking and was going to say next; yet he was concerned solely to do a deal that would 'pass muster for a week'.[26] Lloyd George was indeed concerned to do deals that would pass muster. What was the alternative? – not a perfect treaty, for there could be no immaculately conceived treaties, not in these circumstances. The alternative was deadlock. Lloyd George certainly hoped the arrangements were workable and would last a reasonable amount of time, but he knew that no settlement could be final.

The Prime Minister was criticized by Liberals because the treaty of Versailles, with Germany, was too harsh, and by Conservatives because it was not harsh enough. But the problems did not end there, for Lloyd George attended a further 23 full-scale international conferences, as he and other leaders grappled with the problems of postwar Europe. A crisis arose in August–September 1922 when the Turks refused to accept the harsh Treaty of Sèvres and, for a time, as British and Turkish troops confronted each other at Chanak, it seemed that another war might be imminent. Perhaps, his growing number of critics suspected, he was engineering a war-scare as a pretext for calling another khaki election.

By this time the coalition was under heavy pressure and seemed unlikely to survive much longer. One major issue centred on the agreement that the Prime Minister had recently engineered for Ireland. This had been preceded by violence, from January 1919 to July 1921, in which around a thousand people had been killed. Irish Republicans had unilaterally declared independence after the war, and the British had responded by sending in troops, including the notorious 'Black and Tans', meeting terror with terror and shocking liberal opinion not just in Britain but overseas as well. Lloyd George had then negotiated personally with the leaders of Sinn Fein and the Irish Republican Army. They had wanted a united Ireland and a republic, but Lloyd George – employing the full gamut of his skills, including charm, sober reason, deceit and finally the threat of renewed violence – had managed to persuade them to accept the partition of Ireland and Dominion Status. He had been remarkably successful, securing a deal that the republican team accepted and which the Conservatives in the House of Commons endorsed by their votes. In fact, however, the Conservatives would have much preferred a united Ireland under British rule, and when a faction of the IRA refused to accept the Anglo-Irish Treaty, so that virtual civil war waged in Ireland for much of 1922, they were aggrieved with the Prime Minister and began to regret accepting the treaty.

Added to the battalion of Lloyd George's woes was financial scandal. Sleaze had long dogged him. He had been involved with shady financial deals earlier in his career; and though extra-marital affairs had been kept out of the divorce courts, many knew that his secretary, Frances Stevenson, was also his mistress. Now he was accused of selling honours: £10,000 for a knighthood and £50,000 for a peerage – and Lloyd George had created 1,500 of the former and 90 of the latter. When, in July 1922, particularly disreputable characters were given honours, the storm broke.

It is not surprising that at the Carlton Club, on 19 October, the Conservatives voted, probably by 187 votes to 86, to leave the coalition. Lloyd George was no longer acceptable as Prime Minister. Yet it is worth remembering that Chanak did not result in war, that the situation in Ireland was soon calmed and became generally accepted, and that Lloyd George survived a Commons debate on the honours scandal. We can now see that – despite his failings and in the teeth of huge problems – Lloyd George's peacetime administration has substantial achievements to its credit.

Conclusion

Lloyd George did not regret leaving office in 1922. Indeed he seems to have had a 'genuine sense of relief'.[27] After 17 continuous years in office he needed a break, and time to devise new radical policies. Many have said that he was a demagogue corrupted by power, and there were certainly times when he seemed almost dictatorial in his manner. Yet he did not feel himself to be one of the great men of history: he was not 'among the Caesars and the Cromwells', being too aware of the importance of circumstances in his own fortunes. Had Balfour been Tory leader in December 1916, he mused, there would probably have been a Conservative government not a coalition.[28] This was a becoming modesty, but a faulty one nevertheless, as all 'great men' require good fortune. A better judgement was provided by Bonar Law, after he had himself become Prime Minister. He decided that Lloyd George was 'the most outstanding figure in our politics, the best fighting man'.[29] Small wonder that almost everyone expected that he would return to power at some point.

Lloyd George's career would have been remarkable even had he not attained the premiership. As a social reformer and as Minister of Munitions, he had achieved more than any contemporary. As Prime Minister, in six long and momentous years, he helped Britain survive one of the supreme tests in its history and provided important benefits afterwards. The words 'charisma', 'genius' and 'orator' are over-used, but one cannot avoid them when discussing Lloyd George.

His faults were obvious. Frances Stevenson certainly recognized them. He was 'a past master in craft': if ever he put his cards on the table, she insisted, he would be sure to keep one or two up his sleeve.[30] He could be devious, he lied, and he used corrupt means. Fortunately he used such tactics to get things done. His virtues were on the same scale as his vices: indeed they were often inseparably intertwined. No wonder he remains a fascinating and controversial figure.

Notes

1 Margaret MacMillan, *Peacemakers*, London: John Murray, 2001, p. 46.
2 For example: 'When they circumcised Herbert Samuel, they threw away the wrong bit.'
3 Roy Hattersley, *David Lloyd George*, London: Little, Brown, p. 52.
4 Trevor Wilson (ed.), *The Political Diaries of C.P. Scott*, London: Collins, 1970, p. 70, entry for 16 January 1913.
5 R. Pearce and R. Stearn, *Government and Reform 1815–1918*, London: Hodder & Stoughton, 1994, p. 130.
6 John Campbell, *Pistols at Dawn*, London: Cape, 2009, p. 153.
7 Hattersley, *David Lloyd George*, p. 155.
8 A.J.P. Taylor (ed.), *Lloyd George: A Diary by Frances Stevenson*, London: Hutchinson, pp. 92–3, entry for 1 February 1916.
9 Ibid., p. 52, entry for 19 May 1915.
10 John Grigg, *Lloyd George: Peace to War*, London: Methuen, 1985, pp. 274–5.
11 *Lloyd George: Diary by Frances Stevenson*, p. 68, entry for 12 October 1915.
12 M. and E. Brock (eds), *H.H. Asquith Letters to Venetia Stanley*, London: Oxford University Press, 1982, p. 544, entry for 16 April 1915; *Diary by Frances Stevenson*, p. 129, entry for 27 November 1917. A baillie was a Scots magistrate and town councillor.
13 *Lloyd George: Diary by Frances Stevenson*, p. 133, entry for 5 December 1916.
14 Hattersley, *David Lloyd George*, p. 418
15 Campbell, *Pistols at Dawn*, p. 172.
16 Ibid., p. 171.
17 Robert Pearce, *Britain: Society, Economy and Industrial Relations 1900–39*, London: Hodder & Stoughton, 2002, p. 45.
18 Hattersley, *David Lloyd George*, p. 363.
19 *Lloyd George: Diary by Frances Stevenson*, p. 139, entry for 12 January 1917.
20 Hattersley, *David Lloyd George*, p. 475.
21 David Thomson, *England in the Twentieth Century*, Harmondsworth: Penguin, 1991, p. 268.

22 *Political Diaries of C.P. Scott*, 10 May 1918, p. 344.
23 Hattersley, *David Lloyd George*, p. 421.
24 Ibid., p. 486.
25 Michael Kinnear, *The Fall of Lloyd George*, London: Macmillan, 1973, p. 7.
26 Robert Pearce, *Britain: Domestic Politics 1918–39*, London: Hodder & Stoughton, 2nd edition, 2000, p. 35.
27 *Political Diaries of C.P. Scott*, p. 429, entry for 23 October 1922.
28 Ibid., p. 383, entry for 16–17 March 1920.
29 Ibid., p. 431, entry for 6 December 1922.
30 *Lloyd George: Diary by Frances Stevenson*, p. 143, entry for 14 February 1917.

Further reading

John Grigg, *Lloyd George: War Leader, 1916–1918*, London: Penguin Books, 2003
Roy Hattersley, *David Lloyd George: The Great Outsider*, London: Little, Brown, 2010
Hugh Purcell, *Lloyd George*, London: Haus, 2006
Alan Sharp, *David Lloyd George: Great Britain*, London: Haus, 2008

5 Andrew Bonar Law (1858–1923)

Prime Minister: October 1922–May 1923

> 'I have known one honest politician: Bonar Law. He was without guile.'
>
> Lord Beaverbrook[1]

At the funeral of Andrew Bonar Law, in Westminster Abbey on 5 November 1923, Herbert Asquith sneered that 'the unknown Prime Minster' was being buried by the side of the Unknown Soldier. The phrase has served as epitaph to the man who was Prime Minister for only 211 days, the shortest tenure in the twentieth century. Yet this dismissive remark – by a Liberal of the Conservative leader who had effectively ended his career – must not obscure the political importance of Bonar Law. King-breaker and king-maker, and a formidable politician, he was not the 'political pygmy'[2] of all too persistent legend.

The rise to the premiership

It was a long and circuitous road from New Brunswick, where Bonar Law was born in September 1858, to 10 Downing Street. He spent the first 12 years of his life in Canada, and never fully lost his Canadian accent. His mother, originally from Scotland, died when he was two, but the influence of his father, a Presbyterian minister from Ulster, was far more persistent. Certainly he was later identified with Irish Unionism and struck acquaintances as dour and Calvinist in temperament. He was brought to Scotland by an aunt in 1870, when his father remarried, but did not, belatedly, receive the public school and Oxbridge education that has so often equipped men to become Conservative leaders. He left school at 16, worked in a local bank and then bought a partnership in a firm of iron merchants. As the business expanded under his hard-working stewardship, he married, fathered six children and seemed set for a future of commercial prosperity that was essentially non-political.

The turning point in his life came in 1900 when, aged 42, he won a hitherto safe Liberal seat in Glasgow in the 'khaki' election at the height of the Boer War. Soon he was Parliamentary Secretary at the Board of Trade and one of the key figures on the Conservative front bench. Though never openly critical of Arthur Balfour's leadership, Law became committed to Joseph Chamberlain's ideas on tariff reform; and on Balfour's resignation, in November 1911, he was elected party leader. Significantly, the aristocratic Balfour had been replaced by a member of the middle classes – a man, noted a Tory grandee distastefully, who would not even recognize a pheasant, let alone know how to shoot one. An outsider had taken centre stage. Now the Liberal government would surely be faced by the smack of firm opposition.

Yet, while the government focused on popular social reforms, the Conservative Party was still divided over tariffs. In addition, Bonar Law's policies on Ireland struck many as unconstitutional. Law believed that the Liberals were cynically favouring Home Rule because they were dependent on Irish Nationalist votes at Westminster, with results that would be disastrous for the Protestants of Ulster; and therefore he was prepared, as a last resort, to endorse force to resist such a catastrophe. Perhaps this hardline stance was designed to elicit compromise from Asquith's government. Nevertheless, by 1914, he had contributed to the very real possibility of civil war in Ireland.

Law's Conservatives stiffened the resolve of Asquith and the Liberals to fight at the outbreak of war in August 1914. Thereafter it was 'Business as Usual' – until, that is, shell shortages, and Britain's poor performance in the Dardanelles campaign, led to a chorus of Tory criticisms. Bonar Law's pressure then secured a coalition in May 1915, though it was certainly not a coalition of equals: the Conservatives did poorly from the distribution of offices, with Law himself becoming merely Colonial Secretary. But he was an influential figure whose growing disillusionment with

Asquith led him to work closely with the Liberal David Lloyd George and, eventually, to insist on new executive control. The result was Asquith's resignation in December 1916. The King then called on Bonar Law, the leader of the largest party in the Commons, to form a government; but he, wisely, preferred to serve as Chancellor of the Exchequer under Lloyd George.

This was a time of personal tragedy for Bonar Law. His wife had died in 1909, and during the war two sons also perished within six months of each other. No wonder almost everyone sensed an aura of melancholy about him. Almost certainly on the verge of a nervous breakdown, he found an antidote in work. An observer judged that he had 'the tireless energy of a man who never wasted a moment by performing an unnecessary act or saying an unnecessary word, and therefore did three ordinary men's work quite smoothly'.[3] He was certainly a success as Chancellor. In 1917 he raised the enormous sum of £600 million via a War Loan campaign, and at a lower rate of interest than either his officials or the Governor of the Bank of England thought possible, and in total he raised 26 per cent of wartime expenditure from taxation, more than in any other belligerent country. He also formed a remarkably constructive partnership with Lloyd George. Normally they would meet for two hours every morning, the Prime Minister allowing the Chancellor to subject his ideas to detailed scrutiny. If they survived, he knew they would pass through both the Cabinet and the Commons. Having made Lloyd George Prime Minister, Bonar Law kept him there. Indeed it was he who enabled Lloyd George to maintain the life of the coalition beyond Germany's defeat in November 1918.

That the postwar phase of the coalition lasted as long as it did owed much to Bonar Law. As Lord Privy Seal, but still occupying 11 Downing Street, Law mediated effectively between the two wings of the coalition. As long as he was their leader, Conservatives were confident that their views were being treated with respect. His resignation on 17 March 1921, due to dangerously high blood pressure, was therefore a body-blow to Lloyd George. Moreover, after six months recuperating in the South of France, Bonar Law returned to Britain critical that Lloyd George's Irish settlement, though safeguarding six counties of Ulster for the United Kingdom, was breaking down. He also complained that the Prime Minister was provocatively risking war with Turkey at Chanak. 'We cannot alone act as the policemen of the world.'[4] It was far from surprising that, at the Carlton Club on 19 October 1922, the Conservative backbenchers voted, by a majority of 100, to end the coalition and be free of Lloyd George. The finest speech of the day was delivered by Stanley Baldwin, President of the Board of Trade, but it was Bonar Law's rather hesitant words that had more effect. Here was the alternative Prime Minister without whom the Tory rebellion might have fizzled out. Bonar Law had given the premiership to Lloyd George; now he took it from him.

The record in government

Key Conservative figures, like Austen Chamberlain and Lord Balfour, remained loyal to Lloyd George. Therefore, after Law had first been elected party leader, the 64-year-old Prime Minister had to patch together what critics called 'a government of the second eleven' prior to calling a general election. In the campaign he gave a simple message, that Britain's 'first need, in every walk of life, is to get on with its own work, with the minimum of interference at home and disturbance abroad'.[5] It was not the most inspiring of messages, and Lloyd George considered it more a yawn than a policy, but after the upheavals of the previous years – with their high hopes and bitter disappointments – it appealed to enough electors for the Conservatives to be returned with an overall majority of 77 seats. It was the first solely Conservative victory since 1900 and it ensured that the party survived.

No one can argue that Bonar Law was a great success as Prime Minister. His tenure was too short and his successes too few. He accepted some of the substance of Lloyd George's work, so that for instance the Irish Treaty was ratified; but he had no wish to replicate Lloyd George's 'presidential' style as premier. Hence, though sensibly retaining the Cabinet Secretariat, he scrapped Lloyd George's 'Garden Suburb' of personal advisers. He also, in sharp contract to his predecessor, refused to intervene in industrial disputes, arguing that market forces should be allowed to operate undisturbed. Nor would he see a delegation of the unemployed, directing them instead to the appropriate minister. A Prime Minister, he believed, should be analogous to 'a man at the head of a big business who allows the work to be done by others and gives his general supervision'.[6] Hence it was Foreign Secretary Lord Curzon who negotiated the replacement of the Treaty of Sèvres, which had been imposed on Turkey in 1920, with the more moderate Treaty of Lausanne; and Neville Chamberlain was given a free hand with his Housing Act, the most beneficial piece of domestic legislation from this period. But there were two major problems with which Bonar Law had of necessity to become involved.

The first was the French occupation of the Ruhr, after Germany defaulted on its reparations payment. The British Prime Minister had disapproved of the proposed French action, arguing that the French were 'trying to cut beef steaks from the cow which they would like also to milk'; and at one stage he had even told Poincaré to 'go to hell'.[7] But it was in vain. The action soon resulted in ten million unemployed in Germany and a savage deterioration in Anglo-French relations. But no blame could attach to the Prime Minister, for Britain was little more than an impotent spectator of events.

The second issue concerned British war debts to the United States, and here Bonar Law was more closely involved. Sensibly, he wanted a general settlement – and if possible a cancellation – of inter-allied war debts, but the Americans were insisting on a unilateral settlement with Britain, and nothing Chancellor Stanley Baldwin could say or do would divert them from this course. Nevertheless the Prime Minister was appalled with the terms his Chancellor had negotiated, and then accidentally revealed to the British press, which involved repayments over 63 years at an average annual interest rate of around 3 per cent. The Prime Minister expostulated, 'I would be the most cursed Prime Minister that ever held office in England if I accepted those terms'[8] and threatened to resign. Yet though he huffed and puffed, the over-whelming majority of the Cabinet supported Baldwin, and Bonar Law contented himself writing an anonymous letter to *The Times* deploring the terms.

Law resigned in May 1923, having been diagnosed with incurable cancer of the throat, and was dead six months later.

Preferring not to nominate his successor, he allowed George V to take soundings and then to choose the new Prime Minister.

Conclusion

Bonar Law was the first, and so far only, Prime Minister to be born abroad, as well as the first businessman and the first Presbyterian to become premier. Yet he is remembered, above all, for having the shortest premiership of modern times. Not only was his party divided, but there was too little time for an ill man to make much impact.

Could he, in other circumstances, have become a great Prime Minister? Certainly it might seem that, as understudy to Lloyd George in 1916–21, he had undergone the perfect apprenticeship. He was also a good debater – with 'a neatly balanced armoury of hard-hitting phrases, coupled with acid politeness, to direct against his opponents'[9] – and was able to attract devoted admirers. Baldwin remarked privately that 'I loved the man'[10] and fellow Canadian Lord Beaverbrook admired him tremendously. To be called honest and without guile is no mean accolade, though it is far from certain that these qualities constitute unalloyed advantages in a politician. Certainly Lloyd George judged Bonar Law 'honest to the verge of simplicity'.[11] A.J.P. Taylor judged that he was 'a backbencher in spirit',[12] and though an ideal Number Two Law lacked the hard cutting edge of impervious self-confidence that leadership often demands.

Every new incumbent at 10 Downing Street is inclined to believe that he or she is inaugurating a new era in political history. This was not so with Bonar Law. Yet, though his premiership was a disappointment, it was certainly not a dead end. His victory in 1922 not only began a period of Tory dominance, but he adumbrated the theme of 'tranquillity and stability both at home and abroad'[13] that constituted the broad ideal of his party for the remainder of the interwar period.

Notes

1 A.J.P. Taylor, *Beaverbrook*, Harmondsworth: Penguin, 1970, p. 281.
2 Anthony Howard in the *Sunday Times*, 11 April 1999.

3 R.R. James (ed.), *Memoirs of a Conservative*, London: Weidenfeld and Nicholson, 1969, p. 50.

4 Ibid., p. 118.

5 Andrew Taylor, *Bonar Law*, London: Haus, 2006, p. 111.

6 R.J.Q. Adams, *Bonar Law*, London: John Murray, p. 333.

7 James (ed.), *Memoirs*, pp. 145, 143.

8 Robert Blake, *The Unknown Prime Minister*, London: Eyre & Spottiswoode, 1955, p. 494.

9 Lord Winterton, *Orders of the Day*, London: Cassell, 1953, p. 59

10 Ibid., p. 120.

11 John Ramsden, *An Appetite for Power*, London: HarperCollins, 1998, p. 248.

12 A.J.P. Taylor, *Essays in English History*, Harmondsworth: Penguin, 1979, p. 272.

13 Blake, *Unknown Prime Minister,* p. 466.

Further reading

R.J.Q. Adams, *Bonar Law*, London: John Murray, 1999

Robert Blake, *The Unknown Prime Minister: The Life and Times of Andrew Bonar Law,* London: Eyre & Spottiswoode, 1955

E.H.H. Green, 'Andrew Bonar Law (1858–1923)', *Oxford Dictionary of National Biography*

6 Stanley Baldwin (1867–1947)

Prime Minister: May 1923–January 1924; November 1924–June 1929; June 1935–May 1937

'Baldwin was one-half contemplative and non-political. He was more preacher than statesman. He had no profound faith in political action as a cure for man's miseries.'

Thomas Jones, civil servant[1]

Conservative leader for 14 years, Stanley Baldwin was Prime Minister on three separate occasions and for a total of seven years. Yet not even these figures do justice to his political success. His election victories in October 1924 and November 1935 constitute two of the largest of the twentieth century, with overall majorities of 210 and 159 respectively, and he also led the Conservative Party to the greatest victory of modern times in October 1931: the Tories won an overall majority of 325 seats, or 492 with their coalition allies. Though not Prime Minister in 1931–35, Baldwin wielded more power than the nominal premier, Ramsay MacDonald. Even when Baldwin lost elections he also won them: in December 1923 he gained significantly more votes and seats than the party that went on to form an administration, and in May 1929, though Labour totalled 28 more seats, Baldwin's Conservatives polled over a quarter of a million more votes. No wonder that the interwar period is sometimes dubbed the Age of Baldwin, or that Winston Churchill called him 'the most formidable politician I have ever known'.[2] To many ordinary English people he was not only the dominant political figure of the age but also a profoundly reassuring one, a man whose honesty and breadth of vision elevated him above the political fray. Englishness personified, he seemed to embody the deep stability and harmony of Britain between the wars. Kings might come and go – and in 1936 there were three of them – but Stanley Baldwin, 'the man you can trust', seemed to go on for ever.

Yet the above gives a totally misleading impression of perhaps the least dynamic but the most fascinating political figure of his times.

The rise to the premiership

That Stanley Baldwin should have become a Member of Parliament was entirely predictable. After Harrow and Trinity College, Cambridge, and a decision not to enter the Church, he helped run the family's successful ironworks in Worcestershire. He was following in his father's footsteps, and on Alfred Baldwin's death the son inherited not only the firm but also his father's seat in the Commons. He was elected unopposed at the by-election in West Worcestershire in March 1908 caused by his father's demise. That such a man as Stanley Baldwin should have become Prime Minister, however, was truly astounding.

At school a master commented that he was 'a nice enough boy, but without the brains to do anything big';[3] and most MPs would have endorsed the verdict. He called his maiden speech in June 1908 'a deadly experience',[4] and from then till the outbreak of war he spoke on only four other occasions. He was one of that large number of MPs described, unkindly but not altogether inaccurately, as lobby fodder. He had married Lucy Ridsdale in 1892, after watching her score a half-century in a ladies' cricket match, and their family eventually included five children. Baldwin moved three times a year from Astley Hall, with its large complement of servants and gardeners, for the parliamentary sessions in London, while also maintaining the vice-chairmanship of Baldwins Ltd and holding several other directorships. It seemed a wealthy, civilized and successful existence – but only until August 1914.

The outbreak of war was a turning point in his life. At 47, he was too old to enlist, but the massive suffering Britons endured, with an eventual total of around 750,000 killed, mobilized his energies as never before. That so many younger MPs did fight meant there were vacancies in government, and at the end of

1916, on the formation of the Lloyd George coalition, Baldwin became Parliamentary Private Secretary to Conservative leader Andrew Bonar Law. Six months later he was promoted to Joint Financial Secretary to the Treasury, in which position he gave around one fifth of his wealth, £120,000, in order to help pay Britain's war debts, hoping that others would follow suit. Then, in 1921 he entered the Cabinet as President of the Board of Trade; and a year later, appalled by what he saw as Lloyd George's immorality, he spoke out at the Carlton Club in favour of ending the coalition. With an eloquence of which few thought him capable, he castigated the Welshman as 'a dynamic force ... a very terrible thing; it may crush you but it is not necessarily right'.[5] Against his expectations, Baldwin and his fellow rebels won the vote. Lloyd George found himself in the political wilderness and Baldwin found himself at the Exchequer in a Bonar Law Conservative government deprived of the party's big figures – including Austen Chamberlain, Balfour and Birkenhead – who might otherwise have occupied the highest offices. Furthermore, six months later, when ill health forced Law's resignation, they had still not rejoined the fold. Baldwin had not proved a particularly successful Chancellor, and indeed Law had disapproved of the deal he struck with the Americans for the repayment of British war loans, but the only other possible premier, Lord Curzon, was disliked for his aristocratic hauteur and had the disadvantage of being in the House of Lords. Against all the odds, Stanley Baldwin – 'a man of the utmost insignificance' according to Curzon[6] – entered 10 Downing Street.

Baldwin had not plotted or schemed for office. That he should have reached such a pinnacle was due to what he once called a 'succession of curious chances'.[7] Yet he believed that something profound lay behind mere chance and coincidence. Schooled from early days in the Church of England, and kneeling at prayer every morning with his wife, he could not help seeing the finger of the divine. During the war he had felt he was being called upon to work for his country, and now it became clear that this work included the premiership. 'I could see the hand of God in it ... *I knew* that I had been chosen as God's instrument for the work of healing the nation.'[8]

Baldwin felt no special pride, since all service – 'whether a man is driving a tram-car or sweeping streets or being Prime Minister' – ranks the same with God.[9] But he did feel confident that he would not be called upon to do anything beyond his strength. He simply had to build upon his past experience. As an employer at Baldwins he had treated his men well, and there had never been a strike: now, on a larger scale, he would exercise similar qualities of decency and human sympathy. He would give his whole strength to 'the binding together of all classes of our people'.[10] This was especially necessary after the upheavals of war and after the coming to power in Russia of the Bolsheviks, with their doctrines of class hatred. Similar tensions had to be avoided in Britain, while the Labour Party, with its provocative commitment, in clause four of its 1918 constitution, to bring about the common ownership of the means of production, had to be encouraged to channel its energies into peaceful and parliamentary directions. Baldwin also recognized that democracy itself could not be taken for granted. The vote had been extended at a gallop, with the enfranchisement of all men over 21 and women over 30 in 1918, and there was no guarantee it would flourish. Voters had to learn to trust their politicians, and that meant that politicians had to behave responsibly and not make promises they could not keep. The alternative was demagoguery and eventual dictatorship. Musing on demagogues, Baldwin decided that his time in what he called the 'thieves' kitchen'[11] that was Lloyd George's Cabinet had not been wasted: he must be a Prime Minister as unlike Lloyd George as possible.

Governing style

Baldwin was not a typical premier. There were no particular changes or reforms he burned to effect. He was not a modernizer, and disliked many aspects of the modern world, including the telephone, fast cars and aeroplanes. (Hell, he decided, would be full of 'electric trams tearing about and getting nowhere'.)[12] Nor did he wish to pose as a larger-than-life 'great man'. Indeed he disbelieved in the whole concept. Winston Churchill had many of the attributes of greatness, including imagination, eloquence, industry and ability, but such qualities counted for little without 'judgment and wisdom'.[13]

Baldwin was content to seem ordinary. He certainly looked it. His trousers were generally baggy, his jacket pockets bulged, and his tie was often awry. The *Tailor and Cutter* unkindly devoted a special article to his 'suburban' appearance.[14] Baldwin was even at pains to deny that he was clever, and certainly never thought of himself as a member of the intelligentsia ('a very ugly word for a very ugly thing').[15] He was 'just a wheel-greaser' and 'a lazy devil by nature',[16] and would even admit to mistakes. He was not bothered about fame, keeping no diary and writing no memoirs. 'Here was a politician,' one biographer has written, 'who was scarcely a politician at all.'[17]

This image was partly natural but also partly constructed. Baldwin consciously exaggerated his ordinary qualities. He was not an energetic figure, but he was certainly not as lazy as he liked people to believe. Admittedly he did not work as hard at his desk as Ramsay MacDonald or, from a later generation, Margaret Thatcher. But he was not that kind of politician: arduous, excessive hours would simply lead to nervous collapse. He did, however, put in long hours in the House of Commons, and even when engaged in such seemingly apolitical pursuits as walking in the countryside, reading or playing patience, his mind was often mulling over important political or moral issues. He was making a virtue of what he lacked in order to project himself as the archetypal modest, ordinary Briton; and the quality he wished to project above all was an honesty that made him trustworthy. His appeal for trust was the leitmotive of his career. When, at the 1935 general election, he insisted 'I think you can trust me by now',[18] that was the culmination of a whole series of similar claims which, repeated often enough, were accepted as true by many people. Clearly Baldwin was a successful image-maker: by stressing his ordinary human qualities he had transformed himself into a decidedly extraordinary politician.

In most respects Baldwin was an unexceptional premier. He was certainly no more than a decent chairman of Cabinet and manager of a government. Having learnt from Lloyd George how not to do it, he chaired his Cabinets in a relaxed style and sought consensus.

The main criticism made of him was that, in his unwillingness to appear to dictate to colleagues, meetings could sometimes last 'an unconscionable time'.[19] He disliked having reshuffles and tended to choose ministers and then let them get on with their work. After all, he said: 'Ministers are not servants of the Prime Minister, they are responsible Cabinet Ministers.'[20]

Baldwin was assiduous in attending the House of Commons, but made no attempt to outshine possible rivals. He did not want to slay the opposition front bench, as Lloyd George was said to do, so that each sat squirming in his seat. Instead, Baldwin was reasonable and courteous. No one ever saw him lose his temper. He was very concerned to encourage the Labour Party to tread the constitutional path, and so avoided jibes and did his best to be on friendly terms with their MPs. Left-winger Manny Shinwell found him 'friendly and approachable'.[21] Clement Attlee believed Baldwin liked Labour MPs better than Conservative ones; Arthur Henderson admired him more than any other Liberal or Conservative figure; and Beatrice Webb found him 'an engaging personality with no side or solemnity ... He glories in having no expertise in political and economic questions and no cut-and-tried theories. He is a big man and an ugly-featured man, but he has a most attractive voice and the pleasantest of smiles'.[22] Surely no Prime Minister made fewer political enemies than Stanley Baldwin.

He was not a natural orator, and indeed he once spoke in favour of a motion at the Cambridge Union that 'Rhetoric is the Harlot of the Arts'. His son revealed that before a major speech 'the colour would leave his face, the sweat would sometimes roll off his brow and he has confessed time and time again he felt he might be sick'.[23] Nevertheless, many found Baldwin's speeches unforgettable, and it was his feel for words, and also his uncanny ability to sense the mood of the audience, that made him something of an artist in politics. He had shocked people with his verbal skill at the Carlton Club, deep feeling lending eloquence to his words, and it was a similar depth of emotional sincerity that coloured the speeches he really cared about. He was impressive in the Commons in November 1922 when he insisted that the world would never be cured by repeating the French penta-syllablic word *proletariat*:

The English language is the richest language in the world in monosyllables. Four words of one syllable each are words which contain salvation for this country and for the whole world. They are, 'Faith, Hope, Love and Work'. No Government in this country today which has not faith in the people, hope in the future, love for its fellow men, and which will not work and work and work will ever bring this country through into better days and better times.[24]

A homily was hardly the usual parliamentary fare, but it was Baldwin's stock-in-trade. His earnest plea was to re-echo the prayer 'Give us peace in our time, O Lord'.[25]

In numerous speeches all over the country, Baldwin lifted his eyes from current political problems to address what he saw as far bigger issues – especially what bound people together, making them into a nation able to overcome their differences. Typical titles were 'Christian Ideals', 'Democracy and the Spirit of Service', 'This Torch of Freedom', 'Unto Whomsoever Much Is Given', 'The English Heritage' and 'On England'. Baldwin gave enormous thought to such speeches. Similarly he made a series of addresses on the radio, showing himself an adroit political broadcaster. Instead of trying to orate into the microphone, he spoke naturally, as though he were in the room with his listeners. In his first election broadcast, in 1924, he even broke off in mid-sentence to light his pipe, the sound of the striking match being clearly audible. Over a decade later, in 1935, he was still the master. It was said that he had 'his feet on our fenders'.[26] He was also adept at utilizing cinema newsreels.

The record in government

First premiership

Words not actions were king with Baldwin. Hence those who expected a politician to be concerned, above all, with acts of parliament and reforms could not understand him. To George Orwell he was 'simply a hole in the air'.[27] Yet, at first, it seemed he might be a bold executive. Neville Chamberlain's Housing Act was proving successful in Baldwin's first administration, and more was expected, given that the government had a substantial majority and several more years left to run. Yet Baldwin decided that he needed to introduce tariffs in order to reduce unemployment in Britain. Since Bonar Law had promised that protection would not be introduced without consulting the electorate, Baldwin – insisting that he knew 'nothing of political tactics' but that he was 'not a man to play with a pledge'[28] – called an election for December 1923. When the Conservatives lost seats, leading to the formation of the first Labour government, it was clear that Baldwin had made the biggest mistake of his career. His first, brief government might well have been his last. He was saved partly because of the lack of any obvious successor, the leading Tories still not having returned to the party, partly because Labour might collapse at any time and it seemed unwise for the Conservatives to change horses in mid-stream.

Second premiership

The general election of October 1924 resulted in a resounding victory for Baldwin, with 48 per cent of the vote and an overall majority of over 200. The size of the victory was due to large elements of luck, in that the Liberals put forward so few candidates and the 'Red Scare' led Liberal voters to turn to the right.

This was the first postwar government to run its full course and there were undoubted successes to Baldwin's credit. He managed to bring the dissidents back into the party, so that the Conservatives were now at full strength, and in addition welcomed back the biggest dissident of them all, Winston Churchill, who had left the Tories back in 1904 and had been a Liberal until early in 1924. Many were astounded that he became Chancellor of the Exchequer. Baldwin must also take a share of the credit for the work of his ministers. At the Foreign Office, Austen Chamberlain was undoubtedly a success. In 1925 he helped negotiate the Locarno treaties, whereby France, Belgium and Germany accepted their common frontiers, and the following year Germany entered the League of Nations. Later such developments would be written off as dangerous illusions, but at the time *détente* seemed real enough. Neville Chamberlain, as Minister of Health, was the constructive force on the home front, aided by Churchill. His 1925 pensions reforms were important. Henceforth pensions would be given at 65 to insured workers and their wives, and also to widows, with allowances for dependent children and orphans. The 1929 Local Government Act gave local councils greater power than anywhere else in Europe, and reorganized finance to pay for them. The Equal Franchise Act saw women receive the franchise on the same terms as men, so that all those aged 21 and over could vote. In truth, however, the Prime Minister could not claim much credit for this enfranchisement. To his way of thinking, it would have been more sensible to disenfranchise some men, so that all could vote on reaching the age of 25.

Yet what stands out most about Baldwin's second government was not reform but industrial confrontation, and this was an area in which the Prime Minister took a real personal interest. He genuinely wanted to 'heal' Britain, and he condemned the purveyors of class hatred on the left and right. He found communism anathema, but he also castigated the 'hard-faced men ... who look as if they had done very well out of the war',[29] believing that those who indulged in 'vulgar luxury' were 'the best propagandists of revolutionary doctrine'.[30] It is supremely ironic, therefore, that Baldwin faced Britain's first, and so far only, general strike.

The origins of the strike can be traced back decades, into the chronic inefficiency and poor industrial relations of the coal industry. But Britain's return to the gold standard in April 1925, at the pre-war value of the pound, made a bad situation worse in that, at a stroke, exports became more expensive. Churchill felt in his bones that the move was unwise but acquiesced in the almost unanimous opinion of the financial establishment; Baldwin, a former Chancellor who knew even less about finance than Churchill, was content that the experts understood the situation, or thought they did. The result was that, in July 1925, colliery owners announced wage reductions and a longer working day, and when the Trades Union Congress supported the miners, a general strike looked imminent.

At this crisis point, Baldwin showed a courageous willingness to defy his own right wing. On 31 July, dubbed 'Red Friday' by the left, he gave a subsidy of £23 million, to maintain wages at their existing levels while Sir Herbert Samuel, a former Liberal minister, headed a Royal Commission into the mining industry. In fact, a strike was merely postponed rather than averted, but there is no doubt either that Baldwin wanted a settlement or that the Samuel Report might have provided the basis for one, had the colliery owners and the miners been prepared to compromise. Could Baldwin have done more to avert a strike? Possibly. Certainly a more adroit negotiator, a Lloyd George for instance, might have been able to drive a wedge between the miners' leaders, who wanted a strike, and the TUC leaders, who merely wished to threaten one. But Baldwin resolutely refused to take the initiative. Perhaps he shared too much of the employers' outlook to be an impartial arbiter. Certainly he and his ministers were immediately at ease with the owners, but not with the TUC delegates. In the end, exhausted and depressed, Baldwin called off negotiations, and went to bed, even though the union leaders wanted talks to continue. The general strike began at 11.59 p.m. on Tuesday 3 May 1926.

Once the strike was under way, the government's contingency plans worked well, while the TUC had to improvise arrangements at the very last minute. Although the strike, involving 80 trade unions and three million people, was solid, it showed little sign of paralysing the country. The government fostered the opinion that the strike was illegal, and consequently that union funds might be seized, while Baldwin broadcast effectively on the radio on 8 May saying that he was 'longing and working and praying for peace' and asking to be trusted to 'secure even justice between man and man'.[31] Many historians have praised him for his statesmanlike stance, and yet it was Samuel's intervention as unofficial mediator that gave the TUC a chance to back down, calling off the strike at 12.20 p.m. on Wednesday 12 May, after only nine days. Had they not done so, the hawks in the government would have introduced legislation making the strike illegal and prohibiting picketing. Baldwin had been lucky in that the TUC were not, as the government's newspaper, the *British Gazette,* provocatively insisted, challenging the constitution.

Trade union leaders hoped that Baldwin would use his influence, as he seemed to promise, to prevent the victimization of returning workers and then to broker a decent deal for the miners, who stayed out on strike until the end of the year. In fact he did neither. On the verge of a nervous breakdown, he was ordered by his doctor to take an immediate holiday. Labour's young left-wing firebrand Jennie Lee was not the only one to decide that Baldwin was guilty of a 'piece of deliberate deception',[32] and for a time many miners would gladly have murdered not only Winston Churchill but Stanley Baldwin.

Such successes as the Conservatives enjoyed did not result in their re-election in 1929. The government seemed to many to be running out of steam. In fact, Baldwin deliberately played down positive proposals in the election campaign and put forward the slogan 'Safety First' in order to face down Liberal Party leader Lloyd George and his, to Baldwin's mind, wild and irresponsible plans to cure unemployment. Baldwin did indeed see off the Liberals, but the Labour Party won the highest number of seats and formed another minority government.

The years in opposition were difficult ones for Baldwin. He did not relish adversarial politics. Furthermore, he came under sustained attack from two political enemies, the press barons Lords Beaverbrook and Rothermere. Critics insisted that Baldwin should adopt the protective tariffs he had abandoned after the fiasco of the 1923 general election. As a result, he came very close to resigning before by-election victories were won in 1931 and the campaign against him petered out. A Conservative victory under Baldwin seemed likely at the next general election – until, that is, the events of August 1931 resulted in a National Government.

Third premiership

Baldwin was not one of the instigators of the coalition formed in August 1931, but he acquiesced willingly enough. After the general election of October that year, MacDonald, with 13 supporters in the Commons, was at Number 10, while Baldwin, as Lord President of the Council, occupied Number 11 and had 473 MPs behind him. It was not a case, as in 1918–22, of a dynamic Prime Minister without a party holding the Conservatives in thrall; nor was there any Machiavellian plot whereby Baldwin was able to pull MacDonald's strings. The fact is that Baldwin simply enjoyed being number two in the government. As Tom Jones wrote: 'This being second and not first suits him perfectly and frees him from final decisions and from worry.'[33] The charge against him is that he allowed 'Ramshackle Mac'[34] to stay on, during 1933–35, when he was plainly not up to the job.

Baldwin's own health was poor around this time. He was growing increasingly deaf and occasionally had trouble walking. He complained in September 1933 that 'the world is stark mad' and that he was 'sick to death of being an asylum attendant'.[35] He intended to bow out of politics by the time of the next election, in the meantime using his influence to keep the Conservatives united and also to help Sir Samuel Hoare with his mammoth task of producing a new constitution for India. Yet MacDonald's belated resignation, in June 1935, gave Baldwin, now aged almost 68, a third premiership; and when Labour's leader, George Lansbury, resigned in October, the Prime Minister decided to cash in by calling an immediate general election, instead of waiting till the following spring, as Central Office had advised.

The election was fought amidst controversy over foreign policy. How far should Britain rearm to combat the growth of Nazi Germany's armed forces, and what should be done about the invasion of Abyssinia (present-day Ethiopia) by the Italian dictator Benito Mussolini? Almost everyone agreed that Baldwin handled the issues well. He promised to repair the gaps in British rearmament without beginning a new arms race, and he backed the stance of his new Foreign Secretary, Sir Samuel Hoare, in pledging full support for the League of Nations against Italian aggression. Baldwin also made superb use of radio broadcasts. 'What I likes about Baldwin', commented one working man, was that "e don't sling no mud.'[36] He was widely trusted, as against the unknown quantity of Labour's caretaker leader Clement Attlee. The result was that the government won an overall majority of 242 seats.

Baldwin's government passed the Public Order Act at the end of 1936, banning the wearing of political uniforms. It was a blow to Oswald Mosley's British Union of Fascists. Yet it owed little to the ageing Prime Minister, who had commented on 12 June 1934, just five days after Blackshirt violence at Olympia, that 'we need not bother' about Mosley.[37] Far more troublesome were continental Fascists. Having won the November 1935 general election on a pro-League of Nations policy, Baldwin and his

Cabinet authorized Hoare to do a deal with his opposite number in France, Pierre Laval, outside the League: they would buy off Mussolini by giving him two-thirds of Abyssinia. When the deal was leaked to the press, egg could be discerned all over Baldwin's face. He survived only narrowly by accepting Hoare's resignation and at the same time making a 'take-you-into-my confidence' speech of brilliant obfuscation in the Commons, successfully confusing the issues 'with platitude after platitude'.[38] He also successfully squared Tory elder statesman Austen Chamberlain: he appealed for Chamberlain's support by implying that he would soon be asking him to take over at the Foreign Office. Afterwards, however, he gave the post to Anthony Eden.

It looked as though Baldwin would bow out of politics under a cloud. He was certainly not the man to concert British policy towards the dictators. He was finding it difficult to get to grips with Adolf Hitler. He saw the need to rearm, and did so, yet he could scarcely credit that another major war might have to be fought so soon after the horrors of 1914–18 – and next time casualties would be even higher for, as he told the Commons in November 1932, 'the bomber will always get through'.[39] Baldwin believed that God had made him Prime Minister to bind the British people in brotherhood, not to spearhead a response to Nazism. Hence he was not inclined to believe some of the worst stories about Hitler. 'Most governments seem not better or worse than the people they govern,' he insisted; 'Nor am I on the whole disposed to conclude that the people are such a helpless ineffective flock of sheep as those who claim to speak in their name often imply. They have a way of making their opinions known and heard when they feel deeply.'[40] As a result, he focused not on rearming at the optimum speed to counter the Nazi menace, but upon securing agreement from the British people – and that meant rearming at a pace they would accept. He was highly conscious of the limits of his power. Yet when he spoke plaintively of how little governments could do, he really meant that he would not attempt much. He was elevating a personal weakness into a universal fact.

It was time for political change at the top, but one issue kept Baldwin in office: his worry about the new king, Edward VIII, who acceded to the throne on 20 January 1936. Baldwin had been feeling run-down, and his doctor had prescribed phosphorus pills, but now he perked up. Perhaps 'Providence has kept me here' to deal with the new monarch.[41] Many found the unstuffy Edward an attractive figure, but Baldwin and others, including the Archbishop of Canterbury, Cosmo Gordon Lang, were convinced that Edward was not a man of regal timbre. Baldwin believed him to be 'an abnormal being, half-child, half-genius'.[42] After a string of affairs, he now wanted to marry someone totally unsuitable, Wallis Simpson: an American, a commoner, and a divorcee. Furthermore the Prince meddled too much in politics and seemed far too sympathetic to the unemployed and perhaps even to the Nazis. Lang insisted that Edward must go, to be succeeded by his younger brother. Baldwin would have been content if Edward had kept Mrs Simpson as 'a respectable whore ... kept out of the public view'.[43] The idea, put forward by Winston Churchill, of a morganatic marriage, met with Baldwin's disapproval. He told Edward that the people in Britain and also in the Commonwealth would not countenance any such thing: Edward had either to put aside all thoughts of marriage or he had to abdicate. Baldwin always rather preened himself on understanding the British people, and at one stage Edward felt he was being talked to by a Gallup Poll. But in fact Baldwin was being disingenuous: not only was British public opinion hotly divided but so too were Commonwealth leaders. The Prime Minister of New Zealand was in favour of a morganatic marriage, while the leaders of Canada and Ireland sat firmly on the fence. Nevertheless, Baldwin got his way, and in December 1936 Edward VIII abdicated.

Baldwin was able to retire to an 'immense Hallelujah Chorus of gratitude and admiration': Neville Chamberlain, for one, judged that he had reached the 'highest pinnacle of his career'.[44] Yet it must be said that he was fortunate. Had Edward VIII refused to take his Prime Minister's advice, there would have been a full-scale constitutional crisis. 'Royalists' like Churchill and Beaverbrook felt let down, for, as the latter complained, 'Our cock won't fight'.[45] As with the TUC in May 1926, Baldwin was lucky in his enemies.

He stayed on for the coronation of George VI, retiring in May 1937 and consoling himself for the loss of office with the comforting thought that he would no longer have to 'answer fatuous questions' in the House of Commons.[46] On retiring, he became a Knight of the Garter and was created Earl of Bewdley.

Conclusion

The *real* Stanley Baldwin is elusive. Certainly Winston Churchill could not make up his mind. At one time he praised the political success of a man who, time and again, had got the better of him. Yet he also judged, at one point, that it would have been better if Baldwin the passive appeaser had never been born. He was also in the habit, when playing chess, of referring to his pawns as 'Baldwins'. His son Randolph went even further: though he was in favour of the castration of 'political ineffectives', this would not be necessary in the case of Stanley Baldwin, who was already an old woman.

A bevy of biographers have reached different verdicts too. His official biographer, G.M. Young, soon became disenchanted with his subject. He even made the bizarre comment of the newly married, but indolent, Stanley Baldwin and his wife that: 'There was not much passion in their mating.'[47] Most biographers have been sympathetic, but some of their praise has been equally unbalanced. Philip Williamson goes so far as to say that the poem 'If', by his cousin Rudyard Kipling, could have been written about Baldwin.[48] Admittedly Baldwin could walk with kings and not lose the common touch, but he certainly could not always meet with Triumph and Disaster and treat those two impostors just the same. His self-righteous reaction after the 1923 general election testified to that: 'Everyone who tries in politics to do the thing he believes in simply and honestly is sure to come a smeller [i.e. "a cropper"]. The martyrs did. Christ did.'[49] Above all, Baldwin did not dynamically fill the unforgiving minute with sixty seconds' worth of distance run. He did not deserve the nickname Dormouse, after Lewis Carroll's narcoleptic rodent, but it is not altogether surprising that the soubriquet was applied to him.[50]

Baldwin was a man of genuine goodwill: he surely exuded more human sympathy than any other premier. Yet if he meant well, sometimes – as Theodore Roosevelt said of his successor as US

President, William Howard Taft – he meant well feebly. Nor was he always the man who could be trusted. He was not above political chicanery. Certainly Austen Chamberlain said he would call a chapter on Baldwin 'Sly, Sir, Devilish Sly!'[51] Tom Jones was right, in that Baldwin was indeed 'one-half contemplative and non-political', but he cultivated that image as a most effective political weapon.

Clearly the traditional image of Baldwin is inadequate. He remained at the top in politics for a long time, but he only seems a dominant and stable figure in retrospect. From 1923 to 1937 he lurched from one crisis to another, and survived partly by luck. Furthermore, though his wife called him Tiger, he was essentially a ruminant. No clear-cut reforms stand to his credit, and it is difficult therefore to assess his achievements.

Baldwin undoubtedly had a major impact on the Conservative Party. It was he who reunited it, after the adventure of the Lloyd George coalition. He led from the centre, or perhaps from left of centre, and prevented the party lurching to the right. Under Baldwin the Tories were prepared to intervene rather more than in the past, and social reforms became an integral part of the party's appeal, as Baldwin not only chose reforming ministers but gave them consistent support. It is not true, however, that he personally produced victory after victory. Although he attracted working-class votes, there are more than enough *structural* explanations of Conservative dominance between the wars. Rather than Conservatives owing their power to him, it is truer to say that his political longevity was due to their acceptance of his leadership. Similarly, there are good reasons why democracy was preserved in Britain, while it was collapsing elsewhere in Europe at the same time, and why class tensions on the whole decreased. Baldwin played a part in these developments, but his role was not crucial.

Baldwin did not embody Britain between the wars. Nor did he understand the British people to the extent that he claimed. Yet he was a remarkable man nevertheless. Not only was he an unmistakable figure, he was one of the characteristic figures of his age, helping to infuse it with elements of goodwill, compromise and moderation, but also with inefficiency, feebleness and muddle-headedness. Remove him and the history of the period would have been different. On that we can surely all agree. As to whether it would have been better or worse, essentially whether God got it right in 1923 – that will provoke endless debate.

Notes

1 Thomas Jones, *A Diary with Letters 1931–1950*, London: OUP, 1954, xxxii.
2 H. Montgomery Hyde, *Baldwin*, London: Hart-Davis, MacGibbon, 1973, p. 564.
3 Francis Williams, *A Pattern of Rulers*, London: Longmans, 1965, p. 7.
4 A.W. Baldwin, *My Father: The True Story*, London: Allen & Unwin, 1956, p. 74.
5 Keith Middlemas and John Barnes, *Baldwin: A Biography*, London: Weidenfeld and Nicolson, 1969, p. 123.
6 A.J.P. Taylor, *English History 1914–1945*, London: OUP, 1965, p. 205.
7 Kenneth Young, *Stanley Baldwin*, London: Weidenfeld and Nicholson, 1976, p. 45.
8 Williams, *Pattern of Rulers*, pp. 29–30.
9 Arthur Bryant, *Stanley Baldwin*, London: Hamish Hamilton, 1937, p. 99.
10 Baldwin, *My Father*, p. 127.
11 Thomas Jones, *Whitehall Diary*, vol. II, 1926–30, London: OUP, 1969, p. 23, entry for 26 April 1926.
12 Kenneth Young, *Stanley Baldwin*, London: Weidenfeld and Nicolson, 1976, p. 13.
13 Jones, *Diary with Letters*, p. 204.
14 Bryant, *Baldwin*, p. 101.
15 Young, *Baldwin*, p. 39.
16 Philip Williamson, *Stanley Baldwin: Conservative leadership and national values*, Cambridge: CUP, 1999, p. 62.
17 Bryant, *Baldwin*, p. 100.
18 Williamson, *Stanley Baldwin*, p. 86.
19 *The Modernisation of Conservative Politics: the Diaries and Letters of William Bridgeman*, 1904–35, London: The Historians' Press, 1988, p. 226.
20 Young, *Stanley Baldwin*, p. 29.
21 Manny Shinwell, *Lead With The Left*, London: Cassell, 1981, p. 116.
22 N. and J. MacKenzie, *The Diary of Beatrice Webb*, vol. 4, London: Virago, 1985, p. 207, entry for 5 Feb. 1930.
23 Williams, *Pattern of Rulers*, p. 33.
24 Robert Rhodes James, *Memoirs of a Conservative: J.C.C. Davidson's Memoirs and Papers*, London: Weidenfeld and Nicolson, 1969, p. 140.

25 Young, *Baldwin*, p. 66.
26 C.T. Stannage, *Baldwin Thwarts the Opposition*, London: Croom Helm, 1980, p. 179.
27 George Orwell, *The Lion and the Unicorn*, Harmondsworth: Penguin, 1982, p. 56.
28 Montgomery Hyde, *Baldwin*, p. 177.
29 J.M. Keynes, *The Economic Consequences of the Peace*, London: Macmillan, 1919, p. 133.
30 Baldwin, *My Father*, p. 139.
31 Montgomery Hyde, *Baldwin*, pp. 271–2.
32 Jennie Lee, *My Life with Nye*, Harmondsworth: Penguin, 1981, p. 58.
33 Jones, *Diary with Letters*, p. 93, entry for 19 Feb. 1933.
34 Young, *Baldwin*, p. 112.
35 Jones, *Diary with Letters*, p. 115.
36 Stannage, *Baldwin Thwarts the Opposition*, p. 177.
37 Jones, *Diary with Letters*, p. 130.
38 Harold Nicolson, *Diaries & Letters 1930–39*, London: Fontana, 1969, p. 226, entry for 19 Dec. 1935.
39 Williams, *Pattern of Rulers*, p. 44.
40 Williams, *Pattern of Rulers*, p. 45.
41 Jones, *Diary with Letters*, p. 164, entry for 24 Jan. 1936.
42 Anna Sebba, *That Woman*, London: Weidenfeld & Nicolson, 2011, p. 122.
43 Sebba, *That Woman*, p. 149.
44 Montgomery Hyde, *Baldwin*, p. 513.
45 A.J.P. Taylor, *Beaverbrook*, Harmondsworth: Penguin, 1974, p. 481.
46 Jones, *Diary with Letters*, p. 314, entry for 15 Feb. 1937.
47 G.M. Young, *Stanley Baldwin*, 1952, p. 23.
48 Williamson, *Stanley Baldwin*, p. 112.
49 Thomas Jones, *Whitehall Diary*, Volume I: 1916–1925, London: Oxford University Press, 1969, p. 259, entry for 7 Dec. 1923.
50 *Chips: The Diaries of Sir Henry Channon*, ed R.R. James, Penguin, 1970, p. 47, entry for 29 May 1935.
51 Montgomery Hyde, *Baldwin*, p. 412.

Further reading

Jeremy Dobson, *Why Do the People Hate Me So?* London: Matador, 2010
Anne Perkins, *Baldwin*, London: Haus, 2006
Philip Williamson, *Stanley Baldwin: Conservative leadership and national values*, Cambridge: Cambridge University Press, 1999

7 James Ramsay MacDonald (1866–1937)

Prime Minister: January–November 1924; June 1929–August 1931; August 1931–June 1935

> 'I … asked him [Ramsay MacDonald] to form a Government, which he accepted to do. I had an hour's talk with him, he impressed me very much; he wishes to do the right thing.'
>
> George V in his diary, 22 January 1924[1]

For most of his career, James Ramsay MacDonald was acknowledged as one of the great figures in the Labour Party, serving as Secretary from its inception in 1900 and becoming the first ever Labour Prime Minister in 1924, with a second period in office from 1929 to 1931. He was, to quote the title of a 1929 biography, *Labour's Man of Destiny*. Yet when he agreed to serve as the Prime Minister of a predominantly Conservative National Government in August 1931, he was expelled from the party and instantly demonized. 'We'll hang Ramsay Mac on a sour apple tree,' sang the chorus of execration from the left; 'For that's the place where traitors ought to be.'[2] When he stood down as Prime Minister in June 1935, he was a forlorn figure on the margins of politics. Consequently there is no Prime Minister more difficult to evaluate fairly or to pigeon-hole with standard terms such as effective or ineffective, success or failure. Where stands Ramsay MacDonald today in the panoply of modern premiers?

The rise to the premiership

There is perhaps no such thing as a 'self-made man', for everyone is indebted to the help of countless individuals. Yet James Ramsay MacDonald had none of the traditional privileges that usually accompany, and facilitate, a political career. On the contrary, born in October 1866 in the small Scottish fishing village of Lossiemouth, 40 miles east of Inverness, the illegitimate son of a seamstress and a ploughman, he knew poverty and privation in his youth. He was brought up in a two-room thatched dwelling, sometimes described as a cottage, sometimes as a hovel. A turning point came when the teacher at his local Free Kirk school drowned, and he had to tramp across the fields for four miles to the parish school at Drainie. Here the single qualified teacher, charged with the education of 70 pupils, spotted his intelligence and gave him the encouragement he needed to work, read and aspire. Instead of becoming a fisherman or farm labourer, MacDonald was taken on as a pupil-teacher. He might have become a fully-fledged teacher himself, but at the age of 18 he opted to move to England, first to Bristol and then to London, where he subsisted at times on a diet of bread and water before taking a variety of low-paid clerical posts. But what mattered to him was not employment but politics.

At one time a member of the revolutionary Social Democratic Federation, MacDonald turned to the more moderate Independent Labour Party and, from 1886, to the gradualist Fabian society. An assured 'networker', with countless contacts but few intimate friends, he was also a member of the philosophically radical Rainbow Circle, composed mainly of collectivist Liberals.

His career was enhanced when in November 1896 he married the wealthy Margaret Gladstone, with whom he had six children. It was at their house that the Labour Representation Committee began meeting after its formation in 1900. Six years later it changed its name to the Labour Party. MacDonald served as Secretary and then Chairman of the Labour Party until 1914. He was important in negotiating the famous Lib-Lab Pact of 1903. Each party would allow the other a free run against the Conservatives in 30 constituencies, with the result that, in 1906, MacDonald himself became MP for Leicester, and Labour representation increased from 4 to 30. From 1911 to 1914 he led the Parliamentary Party. He co-operated wholeheartedly with the Liberals, endorsing all the legislation they put forward, including pro-trade union measures and the payment to MPs of a salary of £400 a year, a sum of enormous benefit to Labour. Sensitive to left-wing criticisms that he was too moderate, MacDonald nevertheless maintained that his ideals were socialist.

He was, in fact, making a name for himself as political theorist, writing *Socialism and Society* (1905), *Socialism* (1907), *Socialism and Government* (1909) and *The Socialist Movement* (1911). A cynic might argue that, had he been clear about the meaning of socialism and the methods of reaching it, one book would have sufficed. Certainly these writings were discursive, rhetorical and in parts plain impenetrable, but they marked out their author as the most intellectual of Labour's MPs. His basic theme was that as capitalism became more and more powerful, the state would have to intervene in the interests of social justice. There would be no class warfare or violent revolution: in essence, socialism would slowly evolve out of a successful capitalism. MacDonald was also a fine speaker. Tall and handsome, with a deep voice and an emotional and romantic style, he was a master of parliamentary ritual. 'The authoritative grasping of the lapel, paper in hand; the stressed syllable of earnest conviction; the slow, quiet statement; the outstretched arms; the waving fist; the precise, indicative finger – he employed them all with theatrical skill.'[3] He also tried to redress the concentration of his fellow Labourites on industrial matters. If they were parochial, he would raise his eyes to the wider world. He was a key critic of British foreign policy and also interested himself in India, producing *The Awakening of India* in 1910, the first of two books supporting the moderate and gradualist wing of the Indian nationalist movement.

One forms an impression of MacDonald as a man overwhelmingly busy, perhaps as a compensation for personal tragedy. His wife died in 1911, shortly after the death of his mother and eldest son, and the blow was a heavy one. 'My fireside is desolate,' he wrote in a rare revelatory moment; 'I have no close friend in the world to share either the satisfaction of success or the disturbance of defeat. So I get driven in upon myself more and more.' He added, with typical self-dramatization, that he felt the 'mind of the solitary stag' growing upon him.[4] Relief from depression came not from close friends, for there were none, but from that universal antidote, work and more work. His huge industry helps account for his political success, though his loneliness and isolation go a long way to explaining his later failure.

MacDonald opposed Britain's intervention in war in 1914. He was not a pacifist, but believed that the war had been caused by Grey's foreign policy and by 'secret diplomacy'. He resigned the leadership of the Parliamentary Labour Party in August 1914. It was a principled stand, but it led to venomous attacks in the press, and particularly from Horatio Bottomley, who published his birth certificate in *John Bull*, a popular right-wing nationalist publication, to show that he was illegitimate and also accused him of being a traitor to his country. In the general election of 1918, which saw a widened franchise working to Labour's advantage, MacDonald lost his seat. He used his time outside Parliament to produce two more books (*Parliament and Revolution* and also *Parliament and Democracy*) arguing, at a time when 'direct action' was in the air, the case in favour of evolutionary parliamentary socialism. The vote could give Labour all the power Lenin had won by violent revolution.

He returned as MP for Aberavon in 1922, along with 141 other Labour MPs, and soon became leader of the Parliamentary Labour Party, beating the duller figure of J.R. Clynes by 61 votes to 56. In the general election of 1923 Stanley Baldwin's Conservative Party won the largest number of seats, 258 compared with 191 for Labour and 159 for the Liberals, but it was a hung parliament. Quite unexpectedly, MacDonald found himself invited to form the first ever Labour government.

There were some on the left who were against taking office without the power that only a majority in Parliament could confer. Others, however, more naively, rejoiced that Labour could take the reins of government and put forward fundamental changes. Bishops, financiers and lawyers – and similar spongers on the working class – were warned that a Labour government would be, for them, the beginning of the end. Yet what were inspiring hopes to some were diabolical fears for others. It was said that a Labour administration would confiscate people's post office savings, disband the armed forces, abolish the monarchy, liquidate the British Empire, outlaw Christianity, and institute sexual promiscuity so that women would be 'held in common' in a socialist dystopia. Winston Churchill insisted that Labour was simply 'not fit to govern'.

MacDonald decided that, by leading a minority government, he would be ideally placed to tame the left and give the lie to right-wing scaremongers. By orderly, moderate, competent administration, he could show Labour was fit to govern, so that in future more votes would be gained, and from a whole cross-section of the nation, so that eventually the party would achieve an overall majority and could then introduce socialist reforms. He even managed, at the Albert Hall, to make these aims emotionally attractive. Labour, he insisted, dreamed of a society more perfect than mankind had ever known, but they could not reach it in one almighty bound. 'We are going to walk there. We are upon a pilgrimage. We are on a journey. One step is enough for me. One step. Yes, on one condition – that it leads to a next step. If we shirked our responsibilities now we ... would be inflicting upon ourselves the defeat that our enemies could not inflict upon us.'[5] The danger, however, was that in trying to work the system, perhaps being just a little more progressive than the Conservatives, Labour might lose its soul. The austere Beatrice Webb was worried that, instead of the philistine citizen being permeated by the socialist creed, the socialist creed might well be permeated by the philosophy of the philistine citizen.

First premiership

MacDonald kissed hands with the king, and became Prime Minister, on 22 January 1924. He was the first person of working-class origins to become Prime Minister, and it showed. Though his ministerial salary was now £5,000, or £3,500 after taxes, he could not afford the rich furniture, furnishings and retinue of personal servants that a premier traditionally paid for himself. He was also the first Prime Minister without any prior ministerial experience. Similarly, this was the most working-class Cabinet in British history, though with a smattering of middle-class intellectuals like Sidney Webb. For the House of Lords, MacDonald arranged that hereditary peerages should be given to several childless Labour men, but also relied on non-partisan figures like Lord Haldane, who became Lord Chancellor, and former Viceroy Lord Chelmsford, who became First Lord of the Admiralty. Philip Snowden, Labour's acknowledged financial expert, seemed the obvious choice as Chancellor of the Exchequer, while Arthur Henderson, who had sat in Lloyd George's War Cabinet, became

Home Secretary. The astute and affable ex-railwayman J.H. Thomas was given the Colonies. The only daring appointment was that of the left-wing John Wheatley as Minister of Health.

Lloyd George urged Labour to nationalize electricity and the railways and believed that, with Liberal support, they could be in office for five years, but MacDonald would have none of it. He did not trust the Welshman and believed that, though the Tories were gentlemen, 'the Liberals were cads'.[6] The Prime Minister simply wanted his ministers to gain experience and operate the system, without proving incompetent or rocking the boat. And this is largely what happened, perhaps inevitably so, as it was bound to take time for new men to master their briefs. MacDonald himself noted, after a month in office, that 'officials dominate Ministers. Details are overwhelming & Ministers have no time to work out policy with officials as servants; they are immersed in pressing business with officials as masters.'[7]

MacDonald could take heart that Snowden, concerned above all to balance the budget, was proving as orthodox a Chancellor as his predecessors. He ruled out expensive reforms, though there were some progressive changes nevertheless. Public works measures, which included the construction of 40 new secondary schools, were undertaken, and there was also reform of the unemployment benefit system, so that there would henceforth be no gap between the two periods of 16 weeks in any one year in which benefits could be claimed. State scholarships to the universities were also revived. Most important of all, John Wheatley, a largely self-educated ex-miner who had devised slum clearance schemes in Glasgow, was a success. Building upon earlier legislation, his Housing Act gave government subsidies to house-builders. The novelty was that his Act supported municipal builders, providing houses to be rented not bought, and that it gave the subsidy over a long, 40-year period. Since initial outlay would be limited, it received Snowden's support.

The success of the government would depend to a large extent on MacDonald himself, for he doubled up as Prime Minister and Foreign Secretary. In the latter role he enjoyed undoubted success. Franco-German enmity had resulted in the French occupation of the Ruhr in 1923, but both sides had lost from the confrontation and were willing to compromise. Hence they accepted an invitation to London in August, out of which emerged the Dawes Plan. This scaled down German reparations, instituted a new German currency that cured inflation, and provided for the withdrawal of French troops from the Ruhr. A new era of *détente* seemed to be under way in Europe.

The Prime Minister also helped to invigorate the League of Nations. He and his opposite number in France, the socialist Edouard Herriot, were the first two national leaders to appear at Geneva, in September 1924. MacDonald called not only for the admission of Germany and the USSR to the League but for a system of compulsory arbitration of international disputes, a proposal soon embodied in the Geneva Protocol. Under its terms, those states that did not accept arbitration would be branded aggressors and subject to a variety of sanctions. In fact the next British government refused to accept the Protocol, but MacDonald had certainly made a name for himself. Newspaper editor C.P. Scott described the speech at Geneva as 'wise, far-seeing and courageous'.[8]

Yet foreign policy seemed likely to lead to the downfall of the government. Labour accorded diplomatic recognition to the Soviet Union in February 1924, and two treaties were agreed and signed in August. This was dangerous ground, as critics were all too willing to tar Labour with the communist brush, and when it emerged that there was going to be a loan to Russia, it looked as though the Liberals would withdraw their support. Before this could happen, however, MacDonald decided to go out of office on the more minor issue of the Campbell case. In September Labour's Attorney-General decided to withdraw a prosecution against J.R. Campbell, editor of the *Workers' Weekly*, for urging troops not to fire on fellow workers. The case was unlikely to succeed anyway, but the Conservatives complained of government interference with the course of justice, and MacDonald decided that a vote in favour of a Liberal call for a committee of enquiry was a matter of confidence.

After ten months in office, MacDonald called a general election. Many thought that he was worn out by the strains of office. He was indeed a compulsive worker whose minimum working day stretched from 7 a.m. to 1.a.m. He was notoriously bad at delegating, and the strains seemed to be telling. Critics called the

Prime Minister 'over-sensitive' at best, 'womanish' or 'childish' or worst. He never really liked the atmosphere of the Commons and did not understand the place, taking it as a personal affront that, instead of listening reverentially when he rose to speak, some would 'lie back with eyes closed'.[9] It was a crass error to accept a Daimler car and a package of shares from the head of McVitie and Price, the biscuit manufacturers, and then to recommend him for a baronetcy. No matter that the man's charitable donations made him a worthy recipient. MacDonald himself admitted privately that, by the time of the election, 'his nerves had gone all to pieces'.[10]

Nevertheless, MacDonald believed that his government had been a substantial success. He told the king that Labour had shown 'that they have the capacity to govern in an equal degree with the other parties ... that patriotism is not a monopoly of any single class or party ... that they have left the international situation in a more favourable position than that which they inherited'. He added that Labour had 'done much to dispel the fantastic and extravagant belief ... that they were nothing but a band of irresponsible revolutionaries intent on wreckage and destruction'.[11] In short, he had achieved his aims. Sidney Webb, who had served as President of the Board of Trade, was less solemn. He thought that, on the whole, the episode of a Labour government had been good for the education of the party: it was a good joke, though not one that should be repeated.

These opinions were voiced before the Red Scare of the election campaign. The so-called Zinoviev letter, which was almost certainly a forgery, seemed to associate Labour with the Soviet Union's attempts to foment revolution. The owner of the *Daily Mail*, which printed the letter, judged that it probably won 100 seats for the Conservatives. Certainly they gained an overall majority of over 200. The old slur that associated Labour with communism had not been destroyed. Yet though Labour's tally of seats fell by 50, their vote had increased by over one million.

MacDonald could hope to form a second administration in due course. In the meantime, as well as popping out another book (*Wanderings and Excursions* in 1925), he continued to pursue his course of moderation. There was a new mood of confrontation on the left but, after the fiasco of the General Strike of May 1926, union leaders decided to rally behind him. Prime Minister Stanley Baldwin called for 'safety first' at the 1929 general election, hoping the electorate would look to him as a symbol of stability; but Ramsay Macdonald was no less a reliable figure. A moderate manifesto was presented to the electorate, and only 6 per cent of Labour candidates' election addresses mentioned 'socialism' at all. As a result, Labour won 288 seats, the Conservatives 260, and the Liberals 59. There was no overall majority, but Labour was now the largest single party. MacDonald's strategy seemed vindicated. At 62, he became Prime Minister for a second time.

Second premiership

MacDonald was more optimistic than for several years. Privately he remarked that whereas in 1924 he had been 'a squatter, in constant danger of eviction', now he was 'a tenant with a lease'.[12] He told Parliament that he intended to continue in office for at least two years and that he would seek consensus in the Commons to achieve this, urging MPs to look upon themselves 'more as a Council of State and less as arrayed regiments facing each other in battle'.[13] Unemployment totals had just dipped, and MacDonald himself was a little less lonely, having recently established friendships with several society ladies.

MacDonald's recipe was a repeat of 1924. There would be further competent administration, so that residual fears would be calmed and more votes, and possibly even a majority, won next time. Once again Lloyd George urged bold action, but the cost of Liberal support, which included some form of proportional representation, did not attract MacDonald. Hence it was another moderate government, symbolized by the return of Snowden to the Exchequer, the only novelty being the appointment of Britain's first woman Cabinet Minister, Margaret Bondfield, at the Ministry of Labour.

The government did enjoy some successes, both at home and abroad. MacDonald found it impossible to deny the Foreign Office to the experienced and highly respected Arthur Henderson, and he helped to negotiate the Young Plan, which further scaled down German reparations, and to secure the withdrawal of the last foreign troops from the Rhineland in 1930, five years ahead of schedule. MacDonald himself took charge of Anglo-American relations, visiting President Hoover in Washington and holding a conference in London in 1930 that laid down limitations in the respective sizes of the navies of Britain, the United States and Japan. Domestically, the 1930 Coal Mines Act reduced the standard 8-hour shift by 30 minutes and the Unemployment Insurance Act removed the onus on applicants to show that they were 'genuinely seeking work'. More reforms were due to follow, including the raising of the school leaving age to 15. But in fact reforms were soon off the agenda. Britain's economic survival was all that mattered.

Five months after Labour came to power the stock market crashed on Wall Street in the USA. Soon its catastrophic effects were being felt worldwide. In Britain unemployment rose every month from November 1929 onwards. In July 1930 it exceeded 2 million, and by the end of the year it reached 2.5 million. British exports fell in value by 50 per cent between 1929 and 1931. This was no mere recession, this was the Great Depression. Commentators came to believe that the whole capitalist system might well be breaking down.

What could Labour do in this economic blizzard? The orthodox response was to deflate. This meant that, at a time when tax receipts and hence government revenue were falling, the budget had to be cut. There was tremendous pressure on the Chancellor to slash spending, and the main item of escalating expenditure was unemployment benefit, which rose from £12 million in 1928 to £125 million in 1931. The alternative was reflation, to borrow money and use this to employ people, in the hope that eventually enough prosperity would be generated to repay the loans. Lloyd George had suggested a massive public works scheme in the 1929 general election campaign, and Labour's young Chancellor of the Duchy of Lancaster, Oswald Mosley, put forward similar ideas in a memorandum in May 1930. Snowden and the Cabinet rejected it, however, and at the annual conference later that year MacDonald rallied the party faithful with a powerfully emotional speech in which he appealed to them to 'go back to your socialist faith. Do not mix that up with pettifogging patching – either of a Poor Law kind or of Relief Work kind'.[14]

At this stage MacDonald himself took personal charge of unemployment policy, but was totally out of his depth. He set up committees and commissions to investigate possible solutions, but the situation worsened in 1931. Crisis was reached in August 1931, after a 'run on the pound'. The Cabinet was in almost constant session from 19–24 August. Snowden insisted that, in order to negotiate a foreign loan, he must make expenditure cuts of £78 million, including a cut of 10 per cent in unemployment benefit. A bare majority of the Cabinet, including MacDonald, supported him. The whole Cabinet could only agree on cutbacks totalling £56 million. There was deadlock, Arthur Henderson rallying nine members of the 20-strong Cabinet in implacable opposition to making the poor even poorer. MacDonald felt he had no choice: he went to Buckingham Palace to tender his resignation and bring the second Labour government to an end. When he returned, however, he announced that he was Prime Minister of a National Government.

How can we explain the most controversial event in twentieth-century political history? There was certainly no conspiracy on MacDonald's part. He had not plotted to bring about these events. On the contrary, his health was poor (so that he was sleeping only a couple of hours a night and often felt that 'my brain is going' and that he could not carry on);[15] and he was all but overwhelmed by events. He had fully expected to resign until George V, perhaps exceeding his constitutional duty, pressed him to stay. Acting Liberal leader Herbert Samuel and Neville Chamberlain for the Conservatives added to the pressure, and MacDonald acquiesced. Consciously, he was putting country before party. Cuts were needed, Labour would not make them, and therefore a National grouping, in which Labour would be represented primarily by himself, Snowden and Thomas, would have to deal with the emergency. 'I have changed none of my ideals,' he broadcast to the nation, but 'I have a national duty.'[16] Afterwards there would be a return to normal party politics.

The real charges against MacDonald are twofold. The first is that, as Labour Prime Minister, he refused to take positive actions to combat the Depression. There was certainly no lack of advice coming his way, in favour of protective tariffs, withdrawing from the gold standard, and public works. Instead he took refuge in a beatific, utopian and irrelevant vision of the socialist future. The second is that he became a coalition Prime Minister before getting the permission of his party or even explaining his intentions. But then MacDonald had always been an aloof and enigmatic leader, unable to communicate to his Cabinet. As a friend, Molly Hamilton, wrote of him: 'MacDonald, on the platform, can stir the whole gamut of feelings: meet him and he is as secret as an oyster.'[17] Beatrice Webb called him 'a magnificent substitute for a leader', for he was 'the only artist, the only aristocrat by temperament and talent, in a party of plebeians and plain men'.[18]

National Prime Minister

On the formation of the National Government on 24 August 1931, MacDonald was perceived by many as a national saviour. 'Thank God for Him' wrote J.L. Garvin in the *Observer*.[19] His National Government had the job of making cuts and balancing the budget, in order to solve the national emergency, and then of disbanding. At least that was the theory. The practice was very different. Cuts were indeed made, including a 10 per cent reduction in unemployment benefit, and loans negotiated; but in fact Britain was forced off the gold standard on 21 September. The effects of this, and of the significant devaluation of the pound that it entailed, were undoubtedly beneficial; but to many it seemed to presage further financial and economic upheaval, and the Conservatives put pressure on MacDonald to call a general election and ask for a mandate to take whatever emergency measure might be necessary. Having been expelled from the Labour Party the previous month, MacDonald felt he had to agree.

The result, on 27 October, was a landslide victory, with the National grouping winning a massive 67 per cent of the votes and a staggering 90 per cent of the seats. Labour was reduced to a rump of only 52 MPs. Before this many Labour figures had been glad to see the back of MacDonald, and also to let the National Government make unpopular cuts. But now their catastrophic performance demanded a scapegoat, and MacDonald, depicted as a latter-day Judas, fitted the bill nicely.

MacDonald remained Prime Minister until June 1935, but more and more it was the Conservatives who dominated both the policies and the Cabinet of the National Government. When Neville Chamberlain at the Exchequer introduced protection, towards the end of 1932, the Prime Minister could only plead in vain with Herbert Samuel and the other Liberal free-traders to remain on the government benches. He insisted, all too correctly, that on their departure his own position would become 'more and more degraded ... I should be regarded as a limpet in office'.[20] Perhaps as a refuge he immersed himself in foreign affairs. He was an important figure at two conferences in 1932–33: the Lausanne Conference, which effectively ended German reparations, and the Geneva Disarmament Conference, in which Britain tried to square the circle of German demands for equality of armaments with France's wish to ensure its own security. The advent to power of Adolf Hitler in 1933 meant that its proceedings became even more futile than they already were.

It was soon clear to observers that the Prime Minister's mental powers were diminishing as the length of his sentences increased. Devotees of Marcel Proust would surely have taken them in their stride, while fans of Henry James might possibly have understood them. Most listeners, however, were none the wiser. He had always, as Churchill said, packed the smallest amount of meaning into the largest number of words. Now the amount of sense in his sentences became so homeopathic that some wondered if there was any there at all.

His insomnia became worse than ever. By the end of 1932 he described himself as suffering from 'a complete breakdown from top to toe, inside and out'.[21] Operations for glaucoma on both eyes were only partially successful, and there came a time when he could only read documents by holding them a few inches from his face. By 1935 he was a pathetic figure in the Commons, losing the thread of his argument, laughed at by Conservatives, jeered by Labour. 'He slowly faded away,' wrote Malcolm Muggeridge, 'existing at last in a kind of twilight; there and not there ... sometimes speaking, certainly moving, smiling, shaking hands and otherwise indicating that he was alive and in possession of what faculties he had, yet difficult to believe in.'[22] He should have resigned, or been manoeuvred out of office, long before 1935. That the Conservatives accepted him as Prime Minister was due, above all, to the fact that he embodied the electorally important fiction that in 1933–35 the National Government was more than a Conservative façade.

MacDonald resigned as Prime Minister on 7 June 1935, taking Baldwin's place as Lord President of the Council. He failed to be elected in the general election of November 1935, but was then found a seat for the Scottish Universities and continued as Lord President, though taking little part in government. He died of heart failure on 9 November 1937, a few months after finally retiring from the government, while cruising in the Caribbean.

Conclusion

Ramsay MacDonald had a truly amazing career. No Prime Minister has ever overcome so many early disadvantages, and none has ever followed such a wide political trajectory, from left to right, and from the heights to the depths.

That he made a highly significant contribution to the Labour Party is incontestable. Indeed he did much to create the party and to make it electorally viable. MacDonald had many fine qualities. He worked extremely hard and his emphasis on foreign and imperial affairs did much to widen Labour's political scope. He was also a great speaker, and provided an appealing political vision of a socialist future that rallied support. He alone of Labour's leading figures had some charisma. Admittedly the achievements of the first two Labour governments were only minor, but there are vital mitigating factors. MacDonald was at a major disadvantage in having served no ministerial apprenticeship and each government was a minority administration, while in 1929 he had to face truly formidable challenges – on a scale that no other democratic government, in Europe or America, managed to survive for long. MacDonald was surely in an impossible position in 1931, when he decided, as in 1914, to take what he considered the principled course of action, even at the cost of the enmity of the party to which he had given his life.

It can easily be argued that, in happier circumstances, MacDonald's type of Labour Party might have prospered. MacDonald can be seen as a progenitor of the majority Labour governments of 1945–51, though it must be said that Attlee was at pains to be a party leader and Prime Minister as unlike MacDonald as possible. Or perhaps he was a forerunner of New Labour, which repudiated socialism altogether? Certainly both MacDonald and Blair at times seemed to be prima donnas, and 'word-spinning',[23] a term a contemporary applied to MacDonald's political style, was no inconspicuous feature of New Labour.

To portray MacDonald as the blameless martyr is to accept him at his own valuation. It is no more than a caricature. The man undoubtedly had his faults. He was neither the servant of the party, in the sense of willingly carrying out majority decisions, nor its leader, in the sense of convincing people and taking them with him. He was too conscious of his own superiority and of the inferiority of his 'comrades'. If he could have talked freely with Labour colleagues in August 1931, appreciating their point of view and helping them to appreciate his, the crisis of that month might have ended very differently. Furthermore, his socialism was too theoretical. It did not furnish him with positive policies – and there were positive policies available. Ernest Bevin, of the Transport and General Workers' Union, had written no books, but he for one realized the importance of leaving the gold standard at the earliest opportunity. Nor, despite his humble background, did MacDonald's socialism give him empathy with the poor. He did not feel that they were *his* people or appreciate their problems. There is truth in the judgement of a German observer in 1930 that MacDonald's temperament was at odds with his avowed political faith: the socialist was essentially a Conservative.[24] It was this temperament that made him all the more likely to accept the need for a National Government in 1931.

By no stretch of the imagination can MacDonald be considered a great Prime Minister. He had the wrong psychological make-up, sleeping poorly and seeming perpetually on the verge of a nervous breakdown. The civil servant Thomas Jones made an effective comparison between three premiers: Ramsay MacDonald 'disliked admitting his ignorance of a problem even to the expert whom he had summoned to unravel it – in contrast with Lloyd George, who wanted to understand the problem quickly, and with

Baldwin, who was content that the expert should understand it'.[25] This may well show the suspicion and vanity for which MacDonald was notorious. More profoundly, it reveals a lack of true self-confidence at the core of his being.

On his death in 1937 Beatrice Webb wrote that MacDonald had been born into the wrong class and joined the wrong party. He became 'a simple careerist, singularly mean in his methods'.[26] This was a harsh and one-sided verdict, but with a grain of truth. His motives in August 1931 may have been consciously patriotic, but the Labour Party under his leadership was ceasing to be any sort of moral crusade. Afterwards, once MacDonald had entered the National Government, he undoubtedly lost his way, appallingly bad health adding to personal failings. Few prime ministerial careers have ended so wretchedly. Yet the pathos and the bathos of his final years should not lead us to forget his major contribution to British political history from 1900 to 1932.

Notes

1 Kenneth Rose, *King George V*, London: Weidenfeld and Nicolson, 1983, p. 326.

2 M. Foot, 'Ramsay MacDonald', *Bulletin of the Society for the Study of Labour History*, 35, 1977. p.70.

3 Rodney Barker, 'Political Myth: Ramsay MacDonald and the Labour Party', *History*, Feb. 1976, 46–56.

4 Robert Skidelsky, *Politicians and the Slump*, Harmondsworth: Penguin, 1970, p. 81.

5 Greg Rosen, *Old Labour to New*, London: Politico's, 2005, p. 61.

6 Trevor Wilson (ed.), *The Political Diaries of C.P. Scott 1911–1928*, London: Collins, p. 460, entry for 15 July 1924.

7 Austen Morgan, *J. Ramsay MacDonald*, Manchester: Manchester University Press, 1987, p. 104.

8 Wilson (ed.), *Political Diaries*, p. 464, entry for 6 Sept. 1924.

9 Ibid., pp. 462–3, entry for 22 July 1924.

10 Ibid., p. 478, entry for 4 Mar. 1925.

11 R. Pearce, *Britain: Domestic Politics 1918–39*, London: Hodder, 2000, p. 54.

12 Ibid., p.72.

13 C.L. Mowat, *Britain Between the Wars*, London: Methuen, 1968, p. 356.

14 Greg Rosen, *Old Labour to New*, p. 76.

15 Harold Nicolson, *Diary and Letters 1930–39*, London: Fontana, 1969, p. 54, entry for 5 Oct. 1930.
16 Tony Wright and Matt Carter, *The People's Party*, London: Thames and Hudson, 1997, p. 50.
17 A. Morgan, *Ramsay MacDonald*, p. 90.
18 N. and J. MacKenzie (eds), *The Diary of Beatrice Webb*, vol. 4, London: Virago, p. 92, entry for 2 Aug. 1926; p. 217, entry for 29 May 1930.
19 Malcolm Muggeridge, *The Thirties*, London: Fontana, 1971, p. 114.
20 Pearce, *Britain*, p. 92.
21 Marquand, *MacDonald*, p. 695.
22 Muggeridge, *Thirties,* p. 214.
23 MacKenzie and MacKenzie (eds), *Diary of Beatrice Webb*, p. 24, Easter Week 1924.
24 Kevin Jefferys (ed.), *Leading Labour*, London: Tauris, 1999, p. 35. The observer, Egon Wertheimer, also judged that Baldwin was essentially a Liberal and Lloyd George a socialist!
25 Thomas Jones, *A Diary with Letters, 1931–1950*, London: OUP, 1954, p. xxxi.
26 MacKenzie and MacKenzie (eds), *Diary of Beatrice Webb*, p. 397, entry for 11 Nov. 1937.

Further reading

David Marquand, *Ramsay MacDonald,* London: Richard Cohen, 1997
Austen Morgan, *J. Ramsay MacDonald,* Manchester: Manchester University Press, 1987
Kevin Morgan, *Ramsay MacDonald*, London: Haus, 2006

8 Neville Chamberlain (1869–1940)

Prime Minister: May 1937–May 1940

'Neville Chamberlain acted with perfect sincerity according to his lights and strove with the utmost of his capacity and authority, which were powerful, to save the world from the awful, devastating struggle in which we are now engaged.'

Winston Churchill in the House of Commons, 12 November 1940.[1]

'Praise be to God and to Mr Chamberlain. I find no sacrilege ... in coupling those two names.'[2] Surely no victor with the spoils of war ever returned home to a more rapturous welcome than that accorded to Neville Chamberlain with the laurels of peace. The nation had held its breath during the Munich Conference at the end of September 1938, and now it sang forth his praises. Cheering crowds lined the Mall as he drove to Buckingham Palace, 'shouting themselves hoarse, leaping on the running board, banging on the windows & thrusting their hands into the car to be shaken'.[3] It was, of course, all too good to last. It was not peace 'for our time', as Chamberlain had promised, but only until September 1939, and soon Britain was suffering in a war for which, it seemed, he had prepared poorly. Now, anyone jumping on the running board of his car, and thrusting hands through the window, would have done so with the intention not of shaking his hand but his neck. The literary equivalent of throttling Chamberlain appeared in July 1940 with the publication of *Guilty Men*, a brilliant piece of sustained invective. Fifteen appeasers were put in the dock and condemned, but Chamberlain stood out as the real villain of the piece.

We can see, in the sober light of history, that neither the extreme praise nor the extreme blame was justified. Nevertheless most accounts are still 'pro' or 'anti' Chamberlain, and his appeasement policy remains a passionately contested issue. Paradoxically, a man whose career in government had focused largely on domestic issues had, as Prime Minister, to grapple with the aggression of Adolf Hitler.

The rise to the premiership

Neville Chamberlain was not meant for politics. His father, Joseph Chamberlain, had decided that his elder son, Austen, should have a political career. Educated at Trinity College, Cambridge, he became an MP in 1892 and a cabinet minister half a dozen years later. In sharp contrast, Austen's younger half-brother, Neville, was sent to study metallurgy at Mason College in Birmingham, and was expected to emulate his father's early career in business. The only problem was that he showed no aptitude for such a life. Indeed his attempts in 1890–97 to grow sisal on the island of Andros resulted in losses, in today's terms, of over £3.5 million. Instead, he found a niche in Birmingham local government. He became a councillor in 1911, at the age of 42, and served as mayor in 1915–16. Critics were later to say that municipal affairs were a poor training for international diplomacy: he looked at foreign affairs through the wrong end of a municipal drain pipe. But he was considered a successful mayor at the time, and Lloyd George made him Director-General of National Service in 1917. His subsequent dismissal after only seven months might have ended the career of someone less determined to emerge from the shadow of his father and brother. Instead, Neville Chamberlain became MP for Ladywood in Birmingham in December 1918, at the age of almost 50, and began a truly meteoric rise in the Conservative Party.

The Lloyd George coalition collapsed in October 1922. While Austen refused to return to the Conservative fold until later, Neville was appointed Postmaster-General and then Minister of Health in Bonar Law's government of the 'second eleven'. Under Stanley Baldwin, he was briefly Chancellor of the Exchequer and then, in 1924–29, a highly successful Minister of Health, establishing a reputation not only as a competent administrator but as a reformer. He was largely responsible for the Baldwin government's claim to be a progressive administration. During 1929–31 he was Chairman of the party and also head of the Conservative Research Department. He seemed likely to replace Baldwin as leader, and his claims were reinforced by a long spell as Chancellor of the Exchequer from 1931 to 1937, during which Britain successfully, if slowly, pulled out of economic depression. Few believed that Baldwin would stay on so long, and there were clear signs that Chamberlain was champing at the bit. 'I am more and more carrying this government on my back', he complained in March 1935; Prime Minister MacDonald was 'ill and tired', Conservative leader Baldwin was 'tired and won't apply his mind to problems. It is certainly time there was a change'.[4]

Few doubted that Neville Chamberlain was the best person to take over in May 1937. Admittedly he was 68 and suffered from occasional bouts of severe gout, but he was still mentally and physically vigorous. The real drawback was that people found it hard to warm to him. He seemed too conscious of his own strengths and of others' weaknesses. To some, he seemed to have been 'weaned on a pickle'.[5] Baldwin urged him to avoid giving the impression that he looked upon Labour MPs 'as dirt', unsuccessfully it must be said, for Chamberlain was adamant that 'intellectually ... they *are* dirt'.[6]

The record in government

As expected, the Chamberlain administration saw the enactment of several progressive, tidy-minded reforms. These, after all, were his forte. The 1937 Factory Act improved safety standards at work, and added four million workers to the seven million already covered by its provisions. The scope of state pensions was increased, a new slum clearance programme begun, and the government encouraged an extension of paid holidays in industry. In 1938 the Coal Mines Act nationalized mining royalties, and the following year a new public corporation was set up, the British Overseas Airways Corporation, which dominated British civil aviation. Perhaps, in more peaceable days, Chamberlain might have become a model premier.

Having replaced German democracy with a Nazi dictatorship, Adolf Hitler had already left the League of Nations, imposed conscription, and sent troops into the Rhineland despite Germany's earlier acceptance that it was to be permanently demilitarized. He had other demands too. That the dictator had to be appeased was not Chamberlain's initiative; it was a commonplace and accepted idea. The consensus in its favour stemmed from several obvious facts. The first was that Hitler's grievances seemed legitimate. Very few people now believed that Germany had deliberately started the First World War. Lloyd George, one of the authors of the 'War Guilt' clause in the Treaty of Versailles, wrote in his *War Memoirs* in 1934 that no statesman had wanted a major war in 1914. 'The nations backed their machines over the precipice.'[7] According to the conventional wisdom of the 1930s, the conflict had been a senseless accident. It followed that Versailles lacked moral legitimacy, that Germany had been treated unfairly, and that Hitler's grievances should be rectified. The second key fact was that Hitler was such a fanatic that, if he did not get his way, he would be prepared to fight. The most obvious fact of all, however, was simply that another major war would be even more destructive than the Great War of 1914–18. There seemed to be no antidote to the bombers and the mass destruction they could wreak. If the British public had not read about their awful potential impact in books such as *The Shape of Things to Come* (1933) by H.G. Wells, they had seen it with their own eyes on cinema newsreel reports from Manchuria or Spain. There were obvious signs that public opinion was verging on the pacifist. It was vital, therefore, that war be avoided. Chamberlain said that it was part of his nature 'that I cannot contemplate any problem without trying to find a solution for it'.[8] What could he do to solve the problem of Hitler's revisionism?

Chamberlain brought a new vigour to government and, as a man who detested humbug, a new determination to face uncomfortable facts. He would see the situation as it really was, not as he might like it to be. No one doubted that he was the master in his Cabinet. When Anthony Eden at the Foreign Office objected that Chamberlain was acting, in effect, as his own Foreign Secretary, his resignation was promptly accepted in February 1938. The Prime Minister saw with clear-eyed certainty that war would be a catastrophe. Nor was Britain economically strong enough for war. The British Empire might seem to wield enormous power, but it was over-extended and therefore a liability rather than a source of strength. In particular Japan, the new aggressive power in the Far East, might find Britain's colonies tempting prey. Whereas Britain had too many potential enemies – including Germany, Italy and Japan – it had too few possible allies. France was Britain's closest ally, but then the French, in Chamberlain's eyes, were unreliable at keeping either secrets or governments. The Americans had retreated into isolation and therefore it was 'best and safest to count on nothing from the Americans but words'; and on another occasion he called them 'a nation of cads'.[9] Russia had been Britain's ally in 1914, but the Soviets were a different proposition. Stalin and Communism were as bad, if not worse, than Hitler and Nazism. Clearly, therefore, only diplomacy could prevent calamity.

Rearmament was under way before May 1937, and Chamberlain increased its scope. He had to prepare for the worst. Defence expenditure increased from 15 to 26 per cent of total spending, from 1935 to 1937. But diplomacy could prevent the worst happening. The Prime Minister received a jolt in March 1938 when German troops occupied Austria, which soon became a province of the German Reich. It was not the *Anschluss* itself that shocked Chamberlain. Why shouldn't the Germans in Austria join with the Germans in Germany? The problem was the means Hitler had used. By taking unilateral action, and sending in troops, instead of arranging international agreement, he was risking a wider conflagration. Hence when, later that year, Hitler made it clear that he was prepared to wage war against Czechoslovakia in order that the Germans in the Sudetenland should join Germany, Chamberlain decided he must act. After all, France had foolishly guaranteed the Czech state, so that a problem 'in a far-away country between people of whom we know nothing',[10] could result in a major war involving Britain. He flew to meet Hitler twice without success but, not to be deterred, appealed to Mussolini to intervene and, at the eleventh hour, a third meeting was arranged at Munich. This time Chamberlain was successful. The Sudetenland was ceded to Germany without war. In Chamberlain's own words, he had saved the Czechs from destruction and Europe from Armageddon. In doing so, he won not only the plaudits of the public, but the approbation of the Chief of the Imperial General Staff, William Ironside: 'Chamberlain is, of course, right,' he noted in his diary. 'We have not the means of defending ourselves and he knows it. He is a realist ... *We cannot expose ourselves now to a German attack. We simply commit suicide if we do.*'[11]

Having proclaimed 'peace for our time', Chamberlain must have reeled at the events of 15 March 1939: Hitler marched into Prague and annexed the rump of Czechoslovakia, territory to which he had no legitimate claim. Appeasement was predicated on the idea that Hitler was a reasonable statesman who would cease to menace the peace of Europe once his genuine grievances had been redressed. Henceforth, appeasement could no longer be considered a reasonable policy, and therefore Chamberlain, ever the realist, reoriented British policy. At the end of the month he issued a guarantee to Hitler's next likely victim, Poland. Deterrence replaced appeasement, and British rearmament was stepped up. When even this did not deter the Führer, however, and he invaded Poland on 1 September, Britain and France declared war on Germany two days later.

Clearly Chamberlain's efforts to keep the peace had failed, and he felt acutely that everything he had worked for had 'crashed into ruins'. Many agreed with a critic in the Commons who decided that Chamberlain had 'eaten dirt in vain'; but arguably it had been correct to labour for peace, even by attempting and failing to appease Hitler. The British ambassador in Berlin, Sir Nevile Henderson, certainly thought so. He was convinced that it had been right to make the attempt to appease Hitler, 'that nothing was lost by making it, but that, on the contrary, we should never have entered upon this war as a united Empire and nation, with the moral support of neutral opinion behind us, if the attempt had not been made'.[12] Henderson's points were cogent, and they amount to a powerful case for the defence. Britain was united on the outbreak of war, much more so than in 1914, and no one could doubt that Britain was fighting a moral war. Even so, the notion that Chamberlain's polices were always correct is a fanciful one.

There were weaknesses in Chamberlain's strategy, as there are in the arguments of those historians who defend him to the hilt.

At Munich he was not the clear-eyed, realistic statesman. He thought that Mussolini was acting as honest broker, whereas the Fascist dictator was really Hitler's minion; and although Italian Foreign Minister Ciano considered Chamberlain a decent, if simple, old man, Mussolini felt only contempt for him. Earlier Chamberlain had decided that Hitler was 'half mad' and 'the commonest little dog';[13] but at Munich Hitler's opening sentences were 'so moderate and reasonable, that I felt instant relief'.[14] Emotion got the better of him. It was completely unrealistic of him to repeat the words Disraeli had coined after the Congress of Berlin in 1878 and to describe the Munich agreement as 'peace with honour': the sacrifice of the Czechs might be expedient, even necessary, but it was in no sense honourable.

Admittedly Britain did guarantee Poland in April 1939, but this was largely at the instigation of the British Foreign Secretary, Lord Halifax. Chamberlain merely acquiesced. Rearmament was stepped up, and in effect Munich had bought Britain time to rearm, but the pace was at a slower tempo than many wanted. Ironside was adamant that the spoils of Munich significantly increased German strength and that, therefore, Britain must increase its forces 'at full speed'.[15] Yet Chamberlain was convinced that Munich made war less likely and that there should be no all-out rearmament. The economy, he believed, was the 'fourth arm of defence', and nothing should put Britain's carefully nurtured prosperity at risk. To calls that Winston Churchill should enter the government as Minister of Supply, he gave a flat negative: Hitler would regard it as a provocative move.

Also to Chamberlain's discredit is that he, and his agent in the 'dirty tricks' department of the Conservative Party, Joseph Ball, interfered with the media in Britain in an attempt to foster a favourable – which means less horrific – image of Nazi Germany. Rather than public opinion restraining the government, the government restrained public opinion, or tried to. (Such effort to control the press, Richard Cockett has judged, 'not only subverts democracy, but eventually corrodes the mind'.)[16] Furthermore, Chamberlain was still trying to use Mussolini to moderate the Führer's ambitions, but without success. Mussolini instructed the British ambassador to tell Chamberlain in July 1939 that 'if England is ready to fight in defence of Poland, Italy will take up arms with her ally Germany'.[17] The fact is that appeasement was not dead. To this extent, *Guilty Men* underestimated the charge against Chamberlain. Even the guarantee to Poland was equivocal. Britain had agreed to fight to preserve Polish 'independence', but surely if Germany merely demanded territorial concessions from Poland, such as a strip across the Polish corridor or the annexation of Danzig, that would not threaten Polish independence as such? Unknown to the British public, Chamberlain put strong pressure on Poland's Josef Beck to comply with Hitler's wishes in the summer of 1939.

The fact is that Chamberlain never really got to grips with the mentality of Hitler. Hitler skilfully stressed that his grievances were reasonable and legitimate, but the creation of a 'Greater Germany' was no more than a first step towards the territorial expansion of the superior Aryan race, as he had proclaimed in *Mein Kampf* in the early 1920s. Chamberlain's very reasonable attempts to give Hitler what he wanted without recourse to war were interpreted as a sign of British decadence. 'Our enemies,' Hitler decided, 'are small worms. I saw them in Munich.'[18] That Chamberlain persisted in trying to appease Hitler after March 1939 shows that he had succumbed to wishful thinking. He had faith in appeasement, and faith, as Nietzsche once wrote, can mean 'not wanting to know what is true'. The consequences were serious. Chamberlain bowed to Cabinet pressure to explore the possibility of a British alliance with the Soviet Union in order to deter Hitler from attacking Poland. But in reality he made only half-hearted efforts, via the mission of Admiral Drax. He was simply stringing Stalin along, in order to prevent a German–Soviet agreement. Perhaps sensing this, Stalin signed the Nazi–Soviet pact on 23 August 1939.

Neville Chamberlain informed the House of Commons that Britain was at war with Germany in a calm and dignified, but totally uninspiring, manner. Many thought he would not have the stomach for war, and so it proved. He had no real choice but to find places in the Cabinet for Churchill and Eden, but he also chose obviously unsuitable men for key posts, for instance at Shipping and Information. He failed to form a coalition or to put the economy on a proper war footing. There was in fact an air of complacency about the government, as the public was told that

Hitler had 'missed the bus' or that Germany was in dire economic straits. When the 'Phoney War' did hot up, with the April 1940 Norwegian campaign in which Britain did badly, Chamberlain was unseated. Ironically it was Churchill who was primarily responsible for Britain's failure in Norway, but a two-day debate in the Commons, on 7–8 May, saw the whole of Chamberlain's conduct of the war come under a barrage of criticism, especially from his political enemies – and he had political enemies in plenty in the House of Commons. His government survived by 281 votes to 200, but it was clear that he could not carry on much longer. It is to his credit that he resigned with little fuss, paving the way for Churchill's wartime premiership from 10 May. He also agreed to stay on in government, giving valuable help to Churchill. In particular he supported him in his determination to defy Lord Halifax, who advocated talks with Hitler about a possible compromise peace in late May. Cancer forced Chamberlain to resign at the end of September, and he died in early November. Churchill and the Cabinet acted as pallbearers at his burial in Westminster Abbey.

Conclusion

There were some people who actually liked Neville Chamberlain. Conservative MP Henry 'Chips' Channon, for instance, discerned his 'shy charm' and gushed that he was 'so simple and so unspoilt'.[19] To many observers, however, he was too often prissy, egotistical, overbearing and unattractive. In his private correspondence, while congratulating himself at almost every opportunity, he was all too fond of criticizing other people. Lloyd George was 'a degraded little skunk', while Churchill was a 'wayward child', Baldwin 'lacks the qualities of a leader' and Attlee was 'a cowardly cur'. Even the great British public was not up to the mark: the electorate contained 'an immense number of very ignorant voters ... whose intelligence is low'.[20] How tempting, therefore, for historians to mete out similarly harsh judgements on Chamberlain himself. Yet it is a temptation we must resist.

Chamberlain deserves credit for working tirelessly for peace. He said he could 'gladly stand up ... and be shot if only I could prevent war'.[21] Alas, it was not that easy. He was up against intractable realities, not least the nature of Adolf Hitler. Nevertheless, Chamberlain's appeasement was at first a sensible policy. Only later did this seemingly clear-eyed, unsentimental man see things as he wished them to be, not as they really were. He was hoping against hope for the best; but perhaps the key issue is his preparation for the worst – rearmament.

Defence spending had been pushed up to a massive 38 per cent of government expenditure in 1938. Could more have been done? The poor state of the army was partly due to his planning. Hence he must take some share of the blame for its early defeat in France in May–June 1940. But the Royal Air Force was significantly stronger in 1939 than 1938 – monthly production of aircraft having grown from an average of 240 in 1938 to 660 in September 1939, and in addition a chain of 21 radar stations circled Britain's coastline from the Isle of Wight to the Orkneys. Chamberlain is therefore due a share of the praise for victory in the Battle of Britain in the late summer of 1940. Even so, a different strategy might have served Britain better. There was certainly little that was truly collective about Chamberlain's search for British security. Would Churchill's 'grand alliance' – of Britain, France and the Soviet Union, with the support of the USA – have got off the ground in the 1930s? Possibly, but not necessarily. Chamberlain's premiership was certainly not a disaster. Bad as things were in September 1939, war at another time might have been even worse.

Notes

1 R.R. James (ed.), *Churchill Speaks 1897–1963*, Leicester: Windward, 1981, p. 735.
2 C.L. Mowat, *Britain Between the Wars*, London: Methuen, 1972, p. 619.
3 Robert Self (ed.), *The Neville Chamberlain Diary Letters*, vol. 4, Aldershot: Ashgate, 2005, p. 351.
4 Keith Feiling, *Life of Neville Chamberlain*, London: Macmillan, 1946, p. 242
5 R. Self, *Neville Chamberlain*, Aldershot: Ashgate, 2006, p. 7.
6 Ibid., p. 115.
7 *War Memoirs of David Lloyd George*, vol. I, London: Odhams, n.d., p. 34.

112   *British Prime Ministers from Balfour to Brown*

8 Feiling, *Life of Chamberlain*, p. 258.
9 Self, *Neville Chamberlain*, p. 190.
10 Ibid., p. 321.
11 *The Ironside Diaries 1937–1940*, London: Constable, 1962, p. 62.
12 Sir Nevile Henderson, *Failure of a Mission*, London: Hodder and Stoughton, 1940, pp. vi–vii.
13 Feiling, *Life of Chamberlain*, p. 357; Self, *Neville Chamberlain*, p. 312.
14 Feiling, *Life of Chamberlain*, p. 376.
15 *Ironside Diaries*, p. 64.
16 Richard Cockett, *Twilight of Truth*, London: Weidenfeld and Nicolson, 1989, p. 191.
17 G. Ciano, *Diary 1937–1943*, London: Phoenix Press, 2002, p. 251.
18 Ian Kershaw, *Hitler 1936–1945: Nemesis*, London: Allen Lane/Penguin, 2000, p. 123.
19 *Chips: The Diaries of Sir Henry Channon*, ed R.R. James, Harmondsworth: Penguin, 1970, pp. 147, 186.
20 Self, *Neville Chamberlain*, pp. 50, 121, 137, 97.
21 Ibid., p. 322.

Further reading

Richard Cockett, *Twilight of Truth: Chamberlain, Appeasement and the Manipulation of the Press*, London: Weidenfeld and Nicolson, 1989
R.A.C. Parker, *Chamberlain and Appeasement*, London: Macmillan, 1993
Robert Self, *Neville Chamberlain*, Aldershot: Ashgate, 2006
Nick Smart, *Neville Chamberlain*, London: Routledge, 2010
Graham Stewart, *Burying Caesar*, London: Weidenfeld and Nicholson, 1999

9 Winston Churchill (1874–1965)

Prime Minister: May 1940–July 1945, October 1951–April 1955

'I have seen him take a lot of punishment, and not once did he look like a loser. Not once did he give me the feeling that he was in any way worried or anxious as to the outcome of the fight. Gradually I have come to think of him as invincible.'

Diary of Churchill's doctor, Lord Moran,
20 August 1943.[1]

In 2002 Winston Churchill was voted the 'greatest Briton' in a BBC poll. He is certainly the most celebrated: more books have been written about him than about any other person in British history. He is highly regarded for many aspects of his career, including his 'wit and wisdom': surely everyone knows at least one of his, often politically incorrect, jokes. But it is for his wartime leadership, from 1940 to 1945, that he is especially remembered. A.J.P. Taylor, an iconoclastic left-wing historian who delighted in mocking the political establishment in general and pretentious premiers in particular, nevertheless described Churchill – albeit hidden away in a footnote – as 'the saviour of his country'.[2] Yet in fact there is no consensus view. Churchill is a highly controversial figure. The spectrum of verdicts stretches, at the one end, from the glowing, almost filial endorsement of the official multi-volume biographer Martin Gilbert, to, at the other, the intense, unremitting criticisms voiced by Clive Ponting and John Charmley, the latter significantly entitling his 700-page study *Churchill: The End of Glory*.

The rise to the premiership

Winston Churchill felt enormous exhilaration on becoming Prime Minister on 10 May 1940. At last he had the authority he craved. 'I felt as if I were talking with destiny, and that all my past life had been but a preparation for this hour and for this trial.'[3] But exactly what aspects of his life had prepared him for the premiership?

First, he was a Churchill, the descendant of John Churchill, the first Duke of Marlborough, the victor at Blenheim, Oudenarde and Malplaquet in the War of the Spanish Succession against the forces of Louis XIV. Born at the ancestral seat, Blenheim Palace, in 1874, Winston came to believe that the blood of his illustrious ancestor coursed through his veins too. After Sandhurst, he had gained practical experience of warfare in India with the Fourth Hussars in 1886–97; in the Sudan, where in 1898 he took part in the cavalry charge at Omdurman; and with the 6th Royal Scots Fusiliers on the Western Front during the first half of 1916. He was confident that he understood the nature of warfare. No matter that many blamed him for the disastrous Gallipoli campaign in 1915, or indeed that the failure of the Norwegian campaign of April–May 1940 owed far more to him than Prime Minister Neville Chamberlain.

Second, Churchill had served a long apprenticeship in politics. His father had been Chancellor of the Exchequer in 1886, and the young Winston had heard the great figures of the day talking intimately at his home. Elected an MP in 1900, Churchill was Home Secretary in 1910–11, First Lord of the Admiralty in 1911–15, and Chancellor of the Exchequer in 1924–29. In fact, he had held almost a dozen offices of state. Politics were in his blood: he even talked politics, with the equally incorrigible Lloyd George, at his wedding to Clementine Hosier in September 1908. No matter that many believed his undoubted brilliance and eloquence were marred by grievous faults. Herbert Asquith, for instance, thought he would never reach the top in politics: 'To speak with the tongue of men and angels, and to spend laborious days and nights in administration, is no good if a man does not inspire trust.'[4]

Third, Churchill throughout his life had been learning to use words powerfully and effectively. At Harrow he had 'got into my bones the essential structure of the ordinary British sentence – which is a noble thing',[5] and in numerous books and newspaper articles and in countless speeches he had learned to move hearts by the grandeur of his language. No matter that, by 1935, in the era of the Baldwinesque broadcast, his rotund, epithet-laden, oratorical cadences seemed stuffy, old-fashioned, pre-Victorian. He was shouted down during a speech on the abdication crisis on 7 December 1936, receiving the worst rebuff of his parliamentary career. His son Randolph even began coaching him in how to speak and write like a normal person.

Churchill's career seemed over by the mid-1930s. There had been no place for him in the National Government. His attitude to Indian self-government seemed viciously racist; he had backed Edward VIII, who tamely abdicated in favour of his younger brother; and now he was making alarmist noises about the foreign policy of Germany's leader Adolf Hitler. His constituency association at Epping was on the verge of disowning him.

In fact, Hitler turned out to be Churchill's saviour. Winston had always believed that life should be a crusade, with himself playing the hero, and now he found a villain worthy of his mettle. Whereas most politicians thought they could appease Hitler by satisfying his legitimate aspirations, Churchill was one of the first to realize – albeit more slowly than he later claimed – that Hitler wanted far more than merely self-determination for Germans and that he had to be opposed. Admittedly Churchill ascribed far greater clarity to German foreign policy than was really the case, and his own call for a grand alliance of Britain, France and the Soviet Union, with the backing of the USA, may have been no more than a pipedream; but his warnings seemed like accurate predictions when Hitler occupied Bohemia and Moravia in March 1939 and then attacked Poland on 1 September 1939. There were press calls for him to be given a Cabinet post, the *Daily Mirror* even calling him 'the most trusted statesman in Britain',[6] and on 3 September, as Britain declared war on Germany, Churchill was back at the Admiralty. When Chamberlain proved a poor war leader and the Norwegian campaign failed, the choice of premier lay between Churchill and the Foreign Secretary, Lord Halifax. The latter was preferred by Chamberlain, King George VI and the bulk of Conservative MPs. The Labour Party would have been equally happy with Halifax. That Churchill was chosen instead was due to the simple fact that Halifax turned the position down. The thought of being wartime Prime Minister, with terrier Churchill snapping at his heels, made his stomach ache.

Yet Churchill relished the chance to lead the nation, despite what many saw as the glaring political and military mistakes of his past. Indeed some were aghast at his appointment. According to R.A. Butler, Under-Secretary of State at the Foreign Office, 'the good clean tradition of English politics ... has been sold to the greatest adventurer in modern political history ... a half-breed American'.[7] Only Winston had no qualms. The most important quality that life had given Churchill was not any particular expertise, in politics or war or language, but a resolute, unreasonable self-confidence. He had suffered grievous disappointments and defeats, and moments of black despair, but to him they were merely setbacks. He believed in his star. Though having no religious convictions, he really did believe in providence. (Wasn't that why a series of merest chances had several times saved him from being blown to smithereens on the Western Front?) Philosophers must deplore the muddled nature of his thinking, but Churchill's belief was not a matter of logic: it was unreasoning egotism and unbridled self-assertion.

First premiership

Domestic affairs

Churchill's first crucial task as Prime Minister, from 10 May 1940, was to determine Britain's policy towards Germany. His first speech in the Commons as premier, three days later, seemed to make this clear enough. Churchill – who said he had nothing to offer but 'blood, toil, tears and sweat' – defined Britain's aim in a single word, *victory*: 'victory at all costs, victory in spite of all terror, victory, however long and hard the road may be; for without victory, there is no survival'.[8] Yet Churchill's position was far from unassailable and his words were not accepted as definitive. There were members of the government who doubted that Britain could ever achieve victory. Even Churchill had momentary doubts in private, telling his bodyguard that perhaps the task was too great, adding 'We can only do our best'.[9] Events very soon made Britain's task look even more daunting. On the very day of Churchill's appointment Germany's fast-moving forces invaded the Netherlands and Belgium. On 15 May the Dutch surrendered and, as the German forces broke through Belgium, British and French forces were cut off. Only the evacuation from the beaches of Dunkirk of around 330,000 men between 26 May and 3 June prevented the destruction of the entire British Expeditionary Force. As it was, over 50,000 British troops were killed or captured and all their equipment and transport lost. The head of the Foreign Office had noted in his diary on 21 May that 'A miracle may save us; otherwise we're done',[10] and since then things had got worse. Would it be possible to stem the tide? Some members of the Cabinet thought not.

Lord Halifax had been an appeaser of Hitler in earlier times. Meeting him in 1936, he compared *Mein Kampf* to Magna Carta and called the Führer 'the resurrection and the way' for Germany.[11] Yet he had taken the initiative in guaranteeing Poland in 1939, and now looked at Britain's situation in a pragmatic way. Churchill's determination to fight on come what may was, to Halifax, 'the most dreadful rot': he himself thought that British policy should be based on 'common sense and not bravado'.[12] When Hitler put out peace feelers, therefore, Halifax argued that Britain should explore the possibility of a compromise peace. It became clear that Churchill would have to bend some way before the storm.

Churchill told his Cabinet that 'if we could get out of this jam by giving up Malta & Gibraltar & some African colonies he would jump at it'.[13] Yet he argued that the odds against Britain getting good terms from Germany at that time were a thousand to one. Much better to fight and show that Britain could not be defeated: then, possibly, peace might be considered. To the objection that Britain might well be beaten, Churchill responded that 'nations which went down fighting rose again, but those which surrendered tamely were finished'.[14] This was the line that won the Cabinet's approval, thanks not only to Churchill's romantic reasoning but to the support of Neville Chamberlain, who was still leader of the Conservative Party, and of Labour's leader, Clement Attlee. Later Churchill spoke more openly with the junior ministers: 'If this long island story of ours is to end at last, let it end only when each one of us lies choking in his own blood upon the ground.'[15]

A few days later, on 4 June, Churchill was at his best in the Commons. He used no oratory, said a commentator: no frills, no tricks, just 'a direct urgency such as I have never before heard in that House'.[16] In fact, Churchill was using all his oratorical skills, which were all the more effective for being unrecognized. He drew on words that Georges Clemenceau had used in the First World War – 'I will fight in front of Paris; I will fight in Paris; I will fight behind Paris'[17] – but transformed them into art. He pledged that Britons would fight 'in France, we shall fight on the seas and oceans, we shall fight with growing confidence and growing strength in the air, we shall defend our Island, whatever the cost may be, we shall fight on the beaches, we shall fight on the landing grounds, we shall fight in the fields and in the streets, we shall fight in the hills; we shall never surrender'.[18]

Yet Churchill was not merely voicing stern resolution – that would have been comparatively easy. At a critical juncture in the war, he had to walk a tightrope. On the one hand, he had to convince the nation that they would win and therefore should have confidence, and yet he also had to bring home the perilous gravity of the situation, so that no one should be complacent. He achieved both aims brilliantly, partly with a series of conditional clauses ('if all do their duty, if nothing is neglected, and if the best arrangements are made'), partly by suggesting that Britain might have to fight on for years and alone, and also by considering that Britain might be 'subjugated and starving'. In this worst case scenario, the British Empire would carry on the struggle until eventually 'the New World, with all its power and might, steps forth to the rescue and liberation of the Old'. The language was undoubtedly old-fashioned – and on another occasion he even got away with saying 'Be ye men of valour' – but this gave a sense of the historic importance of what was happening. Fond of allusions to Agincourt and Crécy and the Armada, all English victories, he made specific references to Napoleon's inability to invade Britain. Churchill considered that 1940 was not merely the present: it was, rather, history happening in the present moment. Yet all the glorious episodes of the past, even the Knights of the Round Table and the Crusaders, could not compare with the heroism that would be forthcoming at this apogee of Britain's story. An MP, Harold Nicolson, wrote to his wife that this was 'the finest speech that I have ever heard'. She replied that even hearing the words repeated by an announcer on the radio sent shivers down her spine.[19]

Mussolini was not impressed. Judging that the war was all but over, he declared war on Britain and France on 10 June. A week later France had fallen. But on 18 June Churchill delivered another defiant message. It was clear that 'the whole fury and might of the enemy' would soon fall upon Britain, and therefore he called upon Britons to brace themselves to their duties, so that if the Empire and Commonwealth lasted for a thousand years, men would still say 'This was their finest hour'.[20] It was clearly a desperate time, and yet Churchill made it plain that Britons were not fighting for any selfish national survival, 'for Hitler knows that he will have to break us in the Island or lose the war'. In fact, Hitler knew nothing of the kind, and there was no logical reason why he could not win the war while Britain remained independent. But Churchill's oratorical sleight of hand sent a message to potential allies across the Atlantic. If Britain fell, the whole world, including the USA, would 'sink into the abyss of a new Dark Age'. It was therefore a time of destiny. He had prepared the way for the Battle of Britain that would be waged in the skies over Britain over the next months.

What effect did this oratory have? It was only to be expected that some listeners would be immune to mere words. To newspaperman Cecil King, Churchill's message was often contradictory: 'the situation was disastrous, but all right'; to historian John Charmley, Churchill's perorations were simply 'sublime nonsense'.[21] Furthermore Churchill had to be cajoled into broadcasting to the nation on the radio, and some of his most famous orations may have been delivered by an actor, Norman Shelley, mimicking his voice. It is also true that Spitfires and Hurricanes, rather than words, produced survival in the Battle of Britain. Yet there is much evidence that Churchill's words did have a major effect. They certainly killed any idea of a compromise peace, and Halifax was soon exiled to Washington as Ambassador. In addition, huge numbers were affected emotionally and psychologically.

The American broadcaster Ed Murrow said that Churchill 'mobilized the English language and sent it into battle'; it took him until November 1954 to express himself so succinctly, but it was a line well worth waiting for.[22] The philosopher Isaiah Berlin worked out his views more quickly. He wrote that Churchill was not a lens reflecting and concentrating the feeling of British people. On the contrary: 'So hypnotic was the force of his speeches, so strong his faith, that by the sheer intensity of his eloquence he bound his spell upon them ... They went forward into battle transformed by his words.'[23] Churchill lived a life divorced from the mass of the British people, but he felt he was speaking for ordinary Britons. They in turn, or at least a good many them, believed he was voicing what was in their hearts. Many Britons in 1940 accepted the Churchillian choice: better to die on their feet than live on their knees.

A British premier, though leading a party that generally secures less than half of the votes cast at a general election, is also a national leader and is supposed to speak with the authority of the nation. This is an ideal that is seldom achieved. Yet Churchill, who was not a party leader at all in May–October 1940, really did seem, even if only briefly, the spokesman not of a party or a class but of a whole people.

Churchill's oratory was vital in 1940: vital for himself, in that he had to play the indomitable leader, but also for the nation, for those who would have to do the fighting, the killing and dying – and 30,000 died in 76 days of consecutive bombing in 1940 – and also for those who would have to work harder than ever before, to suffer and carry on. They had to believe that their efforts were part of a larger whole: any sign of defeatism at the top and morale might well have collapsed. Churchill's appeals for self-sacrifice would have carried no conviction if the British people had not believed he was prepared to sacrifice himself. In essence, Churchill was saying that there are things worth dying for. It is a message that can sound like romantic piffle and bring forth cynical jeers, or it can appear the most profound truth and elicit endless effort. George Orwell had, in the past, joked about 'Winston Churchill posing as a democrat', but now he believed that he was a guarantee against treachery.[24] Later he gave the name Winston Smith to the hero of *Nineteen Eighty-Four*.

The pilots of the RAF knew the historic importance of their efforts partly because of Churchill's broadcasts.

During the Second World War Winston Churchill exercised more power than any other British Prime Minister, before or since, and it is often said, not without some truth, than there was something of the dictator about him. If crossed, he often reacted petulantly, and he almost always treated his staff and associates with scant respect, to the embarrassment of his wife. He had always considered himself the protagonist in his own drama, and now he was the hub around which everyone else revolved, the key figure in the unfolding history of the world. He loved the theatricality of the wartime premiership and its power.

Churchill took immediate political action on becoming Prime Minister in May 1940. He set up a five-man War Cabinet, following the precedent established by Lloyd George in 1916, and like his predecessor he too appointed outsiders to government, including businessmen and civil servants, and had a clutch of unofficial advisers. He undoubtedly infused new energy and determination into government. John Colville, who became Churchill's Private Secretary, observed a rapid transformation of the tempo at which Whitehall's business was conducted: 'A sense of urgency was created in the course of a very few days and respectable civil servants were actually to be seen running along the corridors. No delays were condoned ... regular office hours ceased to exist and weekends disappeared with them.'[25] Churchill placed 'Action This Day' stickers on important files, short-circuiting the often leisurely pace at which business was traditionally transacted.

No one doubted that he was the master of his government. As he himself put it, 'All I wanted was compliance with my wishes, after reasonable discussion' – but he himself would do all, or almost all, of the discussing. He did not speak, he orated; he did not talk, he held forth; he did not converse or debate, he expounded or insisted. It had always been difficult to shut him up, so that once he had been reported as making 'a political speech that lasted without intermission for 8 days',[26] and now it was impossible. Here was no ordinary Prime Minister. In January 1941 President Roosevelt's special adviser Harry Hopkins came to Britain. He reported back that '*Churchill* is the gov't in every sense of the word ... I cannot emphasize too strongly that he is the one and only person over here with whom you need to have a full meeting of minds'.[27] Yet the idea that the British government during the Second World War was a one-man show is quite false.

There was an electoral truce between the parties and it was agreed that no general election would be held while war raged, but the normal machinery of democratic government continued to operate. Hundreds of MPs were in the armed forces or away from Westminster on special government work, but Parliament still functioned, even though its sessions were shorter, and individual MPs, including Aneurin Bevan for Labour and Lord Winterton for the Conservatives, acted as an unofficial and sometimes troublesome opposition. In addition, ministers were no mere ciphers.

Though interfering at times with questions or advice, Churchill was generally content to leave the home front to others. There is no doubt whatever that Churchill, like every other premier, owed a great deal to his ministers – to Clement Attlee, Deputy Prime Minister from 1942 and the only person besides Churchill to sit in the War Cabinet for the duration of the war in Europe; to Ernest Bevin, the Minister of Labour whose massive and constructive efforts helped Britain achieve a higher degree of mobilization of its resources, including the conscription of women, than Germany achieved, and with far more voluntary agreement from its workforce; to Lord Beaverbrook, whose intense, unorthodox methods as Minister of Aircraft Production helped produce fighter planes during the emergency of the Battle of Britain; to Sir John Anderson and Herbert Morrison, two men whose efforts and achievements as Lord President of the Council and Home Secretary respectively went far beyond the well-known eponymous air raid shelters.

Churchill also owed an enormous debt to special advisers, including the economist Maynard Keynes, who helped devise the means of paying for the war. He also utilized the work of the code-breakers at Bletchley Park, who decrypted top-secret German radio communications sent with the Enigma machine. These 'golden eggs' gave him valuable intelligence on the enemy's next moves. Mention must also be made of Churchill's Chief of the Imperial General Staff (CIGS), General Sir Alan Brooke, a rather dour Ulsterman who would fight his boss tooth and nail when he thought he was wrong.

Churchill's mind was squarely on the war and he often seemed uninterested in party political issues. Labour men began to dominate the home front in general and planning and reconstruction in particular, much to their advantage when a general election was fought in 1945. They realized the significance of the Beveridge Report of December 1942, which many citizens seized on as a symbol of the new world they believed they were fighting for. Churchill, on the other hand, gave only the most lukewarm response, and he dismissed Beveridge himself as 'an awful windbag and a dreamer'.[28]

It must also be said that, as the war proceeded, not only was Churchill's health suffering, but his vital powers were waning. Complaints from ministers began to multiply. In the emergency at the start of his premiership ministers accepted meetings late at night with a good grace, for Churchill was indispensable; but now many began to object at having to stay up half the night to suit his convenience. They had a full day's work, starting early the next day, while Churchill would sleep until 10 or 11, and have an accustomed nap from 5 to 6 in the afternoon. He was also less well briefed and more inclined to waffle. Attlee brought him up sharp with the comment that 'a monologue does not necessarily spell agreement', and in January 1945 reprimanded him in a long letter for hampering the efficient despatch of business by long unnecessary disquisitions.[29] The following month, the civil servant Sir Alexander Cadogan noted wearily in his diary that Churchill was constitutionally incapable of just saying Yes or No: he wasted hours 'simply drivelling'.[30] Many breathed a sigh of relief when Attlee chaired the Cabinet. Decisions were reached promptly and efficiently, and everyone got to bed at a reasonable hour.

Foreign affairs

Churchill knew that the home front might lose Britain the war, but that it could not win it – and winning was his aim. In May 1940 he created, and filled himself, the new position of Minister of Defence. Though he was in almost daily touch with the three Chiefs of Staff, he was able to exclude them from the War Cabinet, which consequently he dominated. His main efforts during the war were devoted to winning allies and influencing strategy.

Churchill himself took key decisions. For instance, he decided, with agonizing reluctance, that only limited help would he given to the French in the first months of his leadership, the RAF being retained for home defence. Instead he offered words, in the form of joint Anglo-French sovereignty. Perhaps the French had reason to feel let down. Certainly the French objected when, on 3 July 1940, Churchill ordered the bombardment of the French fleet at Oran, with the deaths of 1,297 Frenchmen. France's armistice with Germany, signed on 25 June, included an agreement that all French warships would pass to German control, and when Admiral Gensoul had refused to surrender his vessels or take them to a neutral port, the fleet was sunk. It was a difficult decision to take. The three British admirals involved – North, Cunningham and Somerville – all believed that eventually negotiations would either have brought the French fleet to the allied cause or led to its immobilization, but an intercepted French naval signal told a different story, and Churchill acted decisively.

Churchill wanted his generals to be similarly decisive. He himself diverted large numbers of troops from North Africa to Greece, where they fared badly and had to withdraw from Crete in May 1941, but he became convinced that Archibald Wavell in North Africa was unrealistically delaying an attack until conditions became ideal. In July 1941 he replaced him by Claude Auchinleck but then made exactly the same criticisms. Auchinleck too was sacked, in August 1942. Churchill had no more confidence in the generals than Lloyd George had shown in 1914–18. Finally, in Bernard Montgomery, he found someone who could bring him victory, at El Alamein at the end of 1942. This was a crucial turning point in Churchill's war. Criticisms had been multiplying at home. Hong Kong had fallen in December 1941, Singapore and Malaya in February 1942 and Burma in March. Tobruk had been lost in June. The Prime Minister 'wins Debate after Debate,' complained Nye Bevan in the Commons, 'but loses battle after battle'.[31] Critics were urging him to appoint someone else as Minister of Defence. Even George VI advised this. Some even thought he should give up being premier. For a time Orwell hoped that Churchill would follow the example of Lord Kitchener in 1916 and conveniently drown at sea.

After El Alamein, Churchill was safe politically, but he was not immune from criticism. Shipping losses in the Atlantic were still appalling, reaching their height in March 1943. Also, some doubted the efficiency and morality of Britain's heavy bombing raids on German cities. At first the bombing campaign had constituted the only way of hitting back at Germany, but a change of tactics from 'precision' to 'area' bombing in 1942, exacerbated when cities were targeted rather than the Ruhr, produced casualties out of proportion to the amount of damage inflicted on the enemy war effort. Half a million German civilians died and 55,000 air crew perished. 'Are we beasts?' Churchill expostulated, after seeing film footage of the destruction.[32] Furthermore, it was only late in the war that long-range aircraft could be spared from these raids to safeguard convoys in the Atlantic.

Churchill's involvement with the war effort was total. He undoubtedly had some good ideas, as for instance when he promoted the development of floating piers, which made cross-Channel landings less dangerous, but some bad ones as well. Alan Brooke, who became his CIGS in December 1941 and worked closely with Churchill for the rest of the war, drew an unforgettable portrait in his diary, warts and all. He found Churchill intuitive rather than logical. He was always single-mindedly calling for an offensive in some particular area regardless of the requirements of overall strategy. Too often, when tired, he tried to 'recuperate with drink'.[33] He could also be vindictive, rude, ungrateful and offensive. Several times, as Churchill talked absurdities, Brooke was on the verge of resignation because of this 'peevish temperamental prima donna of a Prime Minister'.[34] Yet the two men shared the same basic strategy, that the second front should be opened as late as possible, and Brooke also acknowledged that Churchill had the 'most marvellous qualities and superhuman genius'.[35] 'Never have I admired and despised a man simultaneously to the same extent.'[36] With victory assured, and the stress levels of both men under control, Brooke admitted on 8 May 1945: 'I would not have missed the last 3½ years of struggle and endeavour for anything on earth.'[37]

Churchill was a British patriot to his core, but this did not blind him to the need for allies; indeed it made his search for allies the more intense, for only with outside help could Britain survive and carry on the fight. In searching for allies, and then in conferring with them, Churchill travelled more than 125,000 miles, spending over 800 hours at sea and 350 in the air (generally lying uncomfortably on a mattress in the back of a bomber). It was a tough schedule and a punishing one for someone his age and in his health. In December 1941, in the White House, his pulse was up to 105 and he suffered a heart attack. In February 1943 he caught pneumonia. Such incidents owed a good deal to his frenzied wartime work load. He sacrificed his own health to victory, much to the dismay of his doctor. Lord Moran wrote in May 1943 that for three years Churchill had been doing everyone else's job as well as his own. 'It is easy to get into the way of thinking of him as different from other people, someone unique, a law to himself. But I know better.' A price had to be paid for flouting nature.[38] Yet it must also be said that Churchill took no exercise, smoked and chewed an average of sixteen cigars a day, and ate and drank not wisely but far too well. During the war he generally drank champagne and brandy at lunchtime, followed by two or three glasses of whisky and soda before dinner, with more champagne and brandy during the meal.

Churchill's first ally, quite unexpectedly, was the Soviet Union, invaded by Germany in June 1941. Churchill put aside his previous detestation of Bolshevism, and immediately sent what little aid he could, weakening the defences of Malaya in the process. But he believed that the 'New World' was far more powerful and would, in the long run, be more important in winning the war. His aim was to win first the moral support, then the economic aid and finally the actual participation of the USA. No lover, he insisted, ever wooed his mistress more attentively than he wooed President Roosevelt. He sent him around 1,300 telegrams during the war, and soon overcame the adverse reports Roosevelt received from his ambassador in London, Joseph Kennedy, that Churchill was 'a fine two-handed drinker' whose 'judgement has never proven to be good'.[39]

Early in 1941 the two men signed the Lend-Lease agreement, whereby Britain would receive military equipment with deferred payment, but only after selling off its assets in the USA at rock bottom prices. Britain was in effect mortgaging itself to the USA, but the price had to be paid. Then, at Placentia Bay off the coast of Newfoundland in August 1941, they met. Churchill was convinced that Roosevelt would act more and more provocatively until the Germans attacked. It is quite possible, however, that Roosevelt had duped the Prime Minister and never had any intention of declaring war on Germany. As with Russia, it was enemy action that brought the United States into the war. On 7 December the Japanese, whom Churchill always underrated, bombed the American fleet at Pearl Harbor. Britain managed to declare war on Japan even before the Americans. The nightmare scenario, that Japan would attack the British in the Far East and leave neutral Americans untouched, had been avoided. But it was only Hitler's declaration of war against the USA, three days later, that brought the Americans into the war in Europe.

Hitler had saved Churchill's career in the 1930s by his aggression, and now his egregious errors gave him the ally he most desired. Churchill realized that Britain would eventually be on the winning side. That night he 'slept the sleep of the saved and thankful'.[40] He even thought of resigning. Other people could now do his job – though not as well. He carried on. Within a month he had secured Roosevelt's agreement to a 'Europe First' strategy. Japan would be crushed only after Germany had been defeated. Churchill's aim was no longer survival: it was to influence the course of the war and help shape the peace.

Churchill enjoyed his wartime conferences. What he would later call summit diplomacy suited his self-image as the embodiment of Britain. Even meeting Stalin was fun at times, certainly when he was reported as drinking bucketfuls of Caucasian champagne and swapping toasts with the Russian dictator at Moscow in August 1942. He was acutely conscious that Britain's power was dwarfed by its two mighty allies, and this was reflected in the way he was sometimes treated. Yet he was confident that he had the answers. Describing the Tehran conference in November 1943 he wrote: 'There I sat with the great Russian bear on one side of me, with paws outstretched, and, on the other side the great American buffalo, and between the two sat the poor little English donkey, who was the only one ... who knew the right way home.'[41]

When the D-Day landings occurred in June 1944, America's General Eisenhower was the allied supremo. Churchill was pushed into the background. Yet it was due largely to him, and the backing he received from his military chiefs, that the Second Front had been postponed again and again – and there is plentiful evidence that he would have preferred it to take place even later, in 1945. It was he who directed the Americans into what they called sideshows, into North Africa at the end of 1942 and then into Sicily and Italy in 1943, both campaigns making a second front impossible in the immediate future. Perhaps Churchill prolonged the war unnecessarily by these means. More likely, it was his influence that ensured that, when the invasion of Europe did finally take place, it was successful. With his memories of the prolonged slaughter on the Western Front in 1914–18, he was more realistic in his assessment of the risks than the US and Soviet leaders.

On the postwar settlement his influence was of only limited significance. He signed the 'naughty document' with Stalin in October 1944, allocating spheres of influence, and the Russians did stick broadly to the agreement. But on the future of eastern Europe as a whole he had to accept Soviet domination. At times Churchill believed implicitly that Stalin would honour his pledges and allow free elections in Poland and elsewhere. At other times, he mused darkly that it might be said of him that he had been so blinded by the Nazi menace that he had neglected the perhaps greater threat from the Soviets.

It was during an interval in the Potsdam conference, in July 1945, that Churchill learned he had lost the general election in Britain. The crowds had cheered Churchill and valued his wartime work, but they voted for the party least associated with the unemployment of the 1930s and most likely to create a more equal and just society. Churchill had said there were two prevalent emotions: gratitude to him and 'this brave-new-world business'. He believed that the desire for a new world was 'nothing like universal ... the gratitude is'.[42] He may even have been right, but gratitude did not stop more people voting for the Labour Party, which promised to build houses and provide social security, than for the Conservatives, who downplayed positive promises, stressed that the war against Japan was still being fought, and vaunted Churchill as their leader. Furthermore, Labour had a real team of ministers, while the Conservatives seemed a one-man show. Winston could not but take defeat personally.

Second premiership

Churchill made a poor, and often absent, leader of the opposition after 1945. Yet in October 1951, after 50 years in Parliament and at the age of 76, this 'indestructible juvenile'[43] won his first general election – thanks to the vagaries of the electoral system. Labour polled more votes, but the Conservatives ended up with an overall majority of 17 seats. A Gallup Poll indicated that most Conservatives would have preferred Eden, and the result in Churchill's constituency of Woodford showed a swing to the right lower than the national average. It is not surprising therefore that most people thought that, ambition satisfied, the old man would preside as Prime Minister for a year or two before honourably bowing out. Yet most people were wrong: Churchill stuck limpet-like to office, defying colleagues who unanimously wished him to go.

Churchill tried very hard to recreate in 1951 the sort of government he had set up in 1940. Again, it was not a solely Conservative administration, and several figures from the war years were drafted into government. Churchill was once again his own Minister of Defence, and Anthony Eden, the successor designate, was again Foreign Secretary. It was a moderate government. Labour backbencher Richard Crossman noted that it was only slightly to the right of Attlee's cabinet, and *The Economist* soon invented 'Mr Butskell', an amalgam of Butler and the previous Labour Chancellor, Hugh Gaitskell, as the symbol of a new political consensus. Labour's Herbert Morrison had said towards the end of the 1940s that Britain needed a period not of fresh change but of consolidation. Churchill's second administration provided just that.

Initially there were economic problems, caused by the Korean War. Churchill said he had inherited a crown of thorns. By the end of 1952, however, there was a trade surplus of £300 million and the following year the Chancellor was able to reduce taxes and increase spending on welfare. To use a convenient shorthand, Britain was passing from the 'age of austerity' to the 'age of affluence'. Gross Domestic Product grew by an average of 2.9 per cent in 1951–55, slightly above the annual average for the whole 1948–73 period. Shares on the London stock market doubled between 1952 and 1955. The National Health Service was safe in Tory hands, and Harold Macmillan was able to exceed election promises by building over 300,000 houses a year in 1953 and 1954. There was also full employment, except in Northern Ireland, and industrial relations were relatively harmonious.

The real problem was Churchill's health. His Private Secretary, John Colville, noticed the differences in Churchill since 1940. He was less irascible and impatient, but increasingly deaf and had less energy. He was usually in bed by the relatively early hour of 1 a.m., and he did not eat or drink on quite the same scale as before, but hardly adopted an abstemious or healthy lifestyle. He would drink only very weak whisky and sodas between meals, but at meals 'he would still consume, without the smallest ill-effect, enough champagne and brandy ... to incapacitate any lesser man'.[44] His doctor, however, noted that alcohol 'fuddles what is left of his wits'.[45] He had to prescribe not only sleeping pills but also amphetamine stimulants.

It is not surprising that Churchill had a serious stroke in July 1952, and then, at the end of June 1953, a much worse one. He responded with all his tenacious will-power, and in three months was able to function again. If Churchill was just about fit to be Prime Minister before the second stroke, he was unfit after it. Yet he was a man with a mission. He had been the saviour of Britain in 1940. Now he would become the saviour of mankind.

The United States test-exploded the world's first hydrogen bomb on 1 November 1952 at Eniwetok Atoll. The new weapon was a thousand times more destructive than the atomic bomb dropped on Hiroshima in August 1945. When the Soviets followed suit the following August, it was clear that human beings had the capacity to destroy life on earth. Statesmanship of the highest order was needed to prevent Armageddon. Churchill sensed the possibility of *détente* after the death of Stalin in March 1953, and on 11 May, without consulting the United States or even his own Cabinet, he called for a 'meeting at the summit' between the Americans, the Soviets and the British.

Churchill's aim was laudable and he pursued it tenaciously, but he was overestimating his own standing and that of Great Britain in world affairs. He was up against hostility from both Americans and Soviets. The most President Eisenhower would agree to was a meeting of the western powers, which took place at Bermuda on 4–7 December 1953. It was not a success. Eisenhower insisted that, despite its superficial new look, Russia was the 'same whore underneath', while Churchill privately vented his spleen on the President, who was 'no more than a ventriloquist's dummy', and on 'this bastard' John Foster Dulles, the US Secretary of State, throwing in for good measure the opinion that the French were 'bloody frogs'.[46] But Churchill's invective was simply hot air. Nor was he himself impressive at the conference. A civil servant was shocked not only by how old he looked but that he was wrong on almost every issue. Churchill, in his egotism, decided that other people, including Eden, were simply fools: 'I can do it so much better than anyone else' – but this was after taking two sleeping pills the previous night which left a very agreeable 'drugged feeling'.[47]

Eisenhower met Churchill again in June 1954, in Washington. Here all Churchill could secure was the President's acceptance that a future Anglo-Russian meeting might pave the way for a summit. But the Russians were not interested. Churchill did not achieve anything substantial by his peacemaking efforts. Indeed the most important concrete decision he took in this period, in the summer of 1954, was in fact that Britain should manufacture its own hydrogen bomb. If the Cold War would not end, at least 'safety will be the sturdy child of terror, and survival the twin brother of annihilation'.[48] It is hard to avoid the conclusion that, in his last crusade, Churchill had been pursuing a chimera because he needed a cause to fight for. Deep down he was motivated by fear. He confided to his doctor that 'I think I shall die quickly once I retire. There would be no purpose in living when there is nothing to do'.[49]

In March 1954 his secretary, Jane Portal, confided in a friend that Churchill 'is getting senile and failing more and more each day'.[50] It was around this time that the press began calling for his resignation. Malcolm Muggeridge in *Punch* published a cartoon of a flaccid and despondent Winston slumped at his desk, with the caption 'Man goeth forth unto his work and to his labour until the evening'. Bowing to the inevitable, he formally relinquished office on 5 April 1955 at the age of 80. Civil servant Evelyn Shuckburgh voiced the opinion of many when he wrote: 'It is a relief that one can now revert to admiring W. for what he has done and been, and not worry about what he is doing or will do.'[51] The second administration had been an anti-climax, inevitably so – for how could it possibly compare with the glory days of 1940–45?

Conclusion

Reading Churchill's speeches, one sometimes forms an overwhelming impression of his mind as a glorious vista over rolling English countryside, marked by tranquil streams and magnificent mansions, but with a colossal storm brewing on the horizon. In contrast, most other politicians seem merely suburban streets, orderly but monotonous, dull and lacking in real character. Certainly no Prime Minister – not even those helped by a committee of speech-writers – has ever approached Churchill's verbal brilliance in set speeches. His doctor believed that his 'feeling for words' was his most important ability, as 'in judgement, in skill in administration, in knowledge of human nature, he does not at all excel'.[52] Strip away his grandiloquence, substitute for the orations his maxim KBO (Keep Buggering On), and how great a wartime Prime Minister was Winston Churchill?

Churchill rarely saw things in true perspective. The main theatre in the Second World War was the Eastern Front: 80 per cent of all German casualties were suffered in the East, while no more than a quarter of the Wehrmacht was stationed in the West. Yet Churchill never seemed to recognize this blatantly obvious fact, and in his six-volume history of the war he almost managed to airbrush it from history. Stalingrad paled into insignificance compared to El Alamein in his version. Similarly, uncertain of the morality of mass bombing of Germany, he failed to acknowledge the work of Bomber Command. It must also be pointed out that Churchill enjoyed several huge slices of luck, especially with Hitler's self-destructive mistakes. Furthermore, although Churchill was heroically prepared to die for the cause, and was easily moved to tears by the sufferings of others, he was at times just a little too willing to see others die. His caution in delaying the Second Front probably saved lives, but his invasion of Sicily and Italy, as well as his support for area bombing, caused needless deaths.

Possibly others might have guided Britain's fortunes equally well, if not better, in the period after Pearl Harbor. Yet it remains true that it was Churchill who insisted that Britain should fight on in 1940, and did so in unsurpassed and inspiring language. Without him, it was perfectly possible that Britain would have made some sort of compromise peace. The effects of that can only be guessed at; but there is no reason to suppose that Hitler would have stuck to any agreement, or that the Nazis and Soviets would have conveniently fought to mutual exhaustion, leaving a world in which Britain was free to flourish.

It is also hard to believe that another premier, agreeing to fight on, could have elicited the national unity that Churchill helped to inspire. In 1940 Churchill was in his element, helping to transform Britain's darkest hour into its finest. In this year, as the psychiatrist Anthony Storr has written, Britain at war needed 'not a shrewd, equable, balanced leader. She needed a prophet, a heroic visionary, a man who could dream dreams of victory when all seemed lost'.[53]

Churchill believed, rather simply, in 'great men'. He wrote of Clemenceau that he 'embodied and expressed France'.[54] No doubt he imagined that he filled the same role, but that was an error. Churchill was not the average Briton writ large. He was outstandingly different, and in 1940 he provided outstanding leadership and made a difference to the course of history. No wonder that Adolf Hitler, who was inclined to make fun of Baldwin and Chamberlain, saved his real venom for Churchill: 'He's an utterly amoral, repulsive creature ... the undisciplined swine who is drunk eight hours of every twenty-four ... the raddled old whore.'[55] Nor is it surprising that the more thoughtful Josef Goebbels exhibited a grudging respect in his diary: Churchill was a 'cunning old fox' whose speeches were 'insolent, but not without talent'; he was 'a shameless, bare-faced liar, but one with some style'. Above all, Goebbels judged that but for Churchill the Nazis would have won the war.[56]

To decide whether Churchill was a greater Briton than Shakespeare, or Newton or Florence Nightingale, is surely impossible. We have to compose our judgements with considerable care. Ed Murrow and Isaiah Berlin did so. The CBS broadcaster called Churchill 'perhaps the most considerable man to walk the stage of history in our time'.[57] The British philosopher called him 'the largest human being of our time'.[58] Churchill was indeed a man of his time. According to John Charmley, that limits his influence significantly, for Churchill was essentially a Whig-imperialist whose leadership, focusing on British nationalism and imperialism, was essentially barren: 'it led nowhere, and there were no heirs to his tradition'.[59] Yet such a judgement may be questioned on two grounds. First, although the British Empire has indeed disappeared, Churchill's stand in 1940, and his avoidance of a shameful compromise peace, has led directly – for good or ill – to the determination of later premiers that Britain should punch above its weight in international affairs. Second, ferocious and indomitable defiance of tyranny is surely a timeless value.

To call Churchill 'the saviour' of his country during the Second World War is a little like judging that, in the First, Lloyd George was 'the man who won the war'. Such exclusive verdicts disregard and so devalue the efforts of the countless others who contributed to victory. Nevertheless, and despite his many imperfections, which in fact make this self-conscious man of destiny a more endearing human being, Churchill surely won for himself in 1940, in the phrase he used about Alfred the Great, a 'deathless glory'.[60]

Notes

1 Lord Moran, *Churchill: The Struggle for Survival 1940–1965*, London: Sphere, 1968, p. 129.
2 A.J.P. Taylor, *English History 1914–1945*, London: OUP, 1965, p. 5n.
3 Winston S. Churchill, *The Second World War*, vol. I, *The Gathering Storm*, London: Cassell, 1949, p. 601.
4 Roy Jenkins, *Asquith*, London: Fontana, 1967, p. 380.
5 Winston S. Churchill, *My Early Life*, London: Fontana, 1959, p. 25.

6 R.R. James (ed.), *Churchill Speaks*, Leicester: Windward, 1980, p. 668.

7 John Colville, *The Fringes of Power: Downing Street Diaries 1939–1955*, London: Hodder & Stoughton, 1985, p. 122, entry for 10 May 1940.

8 James, *Churchill Speaks*, p. 705.

9 John Lukacs, *Five Days in London: May 1940*, New Haven: Yale University Press, 1999, p. 6.

10 *The Diaries of Sir Alexander Cadogan 1938–45*, ed. David Dilks, London: Cassell, 1971, p. 288.

11 Andrew Roberts, *The Holy Fox*, London: Papermac, 1991, p. 69.

12 Richard Overy, *The Battle of Britain*, Harmondsworth: Penguin, 2000, pp. 10–11.

13 Neville Chamberlain diary, 26 May 1940, Neville Chamberlain papers, University of Birmingham Library.

14 Lukacs, *Five Days*, pp. 182–3.

15 *The Second World War Diary of Hugh Dalton 1940–45*, ed. Ben Pimlott, London: Cape, 1986, p. 28.

16 Edward R. Murrow, *In Search of Light: The Broadcasts*, London: Macmillan, 1968, p. 27.

17 Winston S. Churchill, *Great Contemporaries*, London: Odhams, 1947, p. 246.

18 *Churchill Speaks*, p. 713.

19 Harold Nicholson, *Diaries and Letters 1939–1945*, London: Fontana, 1970, p. 90.

20 *Churchill Speaks*, p. 720.

21 John Charmley, *Churchill: The End of Glory*, London: Hodder & Stoughton, 1993, p. 411.

22 Murrow, *In Search of Light: The Broadcasts*, p. 237.

23 Isaiah Berlin, *Mr Churchill in 1940*, London: John Murray, 1949, pp. 26–7.

24 *The Collected Essays, Journalism and Letters of George Orwell*, Harmondsworth: Penguin, 1970, vol. 1, p. 434; vol. 2, p. 174.

25 J. Wheeler-Bennett (ed.), *Action This Day: Working with Churchill*, London: Macmillan, 1968, pp. 49–50.

26 Piers Brendon, *Winston Churchill*, London: Methuen, 1985, p. 42.

27 Martin Gilbert, *Finest Hour*, London: Heinemann, 1983, p. 988.

28 G.S. Harvie-Watt, *Most Of My Life*, London: Springwood Books, 1980, p. 117.

29 Robert Pearce, *Attlee*, London: Longman, 1997, p. 102.

30 David Dilks (ed.), *The Diaries of Sir Alexander Cadogan 1938–1945*, London: Cassell, 1971, pp. 719–20, entry for 22 Feb. 1945.

31 John Campbell, *Nye Bevan*, London: Hodder & Stoughton, 1987, p. 114.
32 Thomas Wilson, *Churchill and the Prof*, London: Cassell, 1995, p. 88.
33 Alex Danchev and Daniel Todman, *War Diaries 1939–1945: Field Marshal Lord Alanbrooke*, London: Weidenfeld and Nicolson, 2001, p. 566, entry for 6 July 1944.
34 Ibid., p. 447, entry for 28 Aug. 1943.
35 Ibid., p. 451, 30 Aug. 1943.
36 Ibid., p. 590, 10 Sept. 1944.
37 Ibid., p. 689, 8 May 1945.
38 Moran, *Churchill*, pp. 116–17, entry for 23 May 1943.
39 Charmley, *Churchill*, p. 429.
40 Max Hastings, *Finest Years: Churchill as Warlord 1940–45*, London: Harper Press, p. 213.
41 Ibid., p. 435.
42 Moran, *Churchill*, pp. 273–4, entry for 20 May 1945.
43 Murrow, *In Search of Light*, p. 177.
44 Colville, *Fringes of Power*, p. 635.
45 Moran, *Churchill*, 25 July 1953, p. 469.
46 Klaus Larres, *Churchill's Cold War*, New Haven: Yale University Press, 2002, pp. 308, 310.
47 Ibid., p. 343.
48 *Churchill Speaks*, p. 966.
49 Moran, *Churchill*, p. 828.
50 Evelyn Shuckburgh, *Descent to Suez: Diaries 1951–56*, London: Weidenfeld and Nicolson, 1986, p. 141, entry for 4 March 1954.
51 Ibid., *Descent to Suez*, p. 255, entry for 6 Apr. 1955.
52 Moran, *Churchill*, pp. 142–3, entry for 29 Oct. 1943.
53 A.J.P. Taylor, R.R. James, J.H. Plumb, B. Liddell Hart and Anthony Storr, *Churchill: Four Faces and the Man*, Harmondsworth: Penguin, 1973, p. 245.
54 Churchill, *Great Contemporaries*, p. 236
55 *Hitler's Table-Talk*, ed. Hugh Trevor-Roper, London: OUP, 1988, pp. 318, 369, 678.
56 Fred Taylor (ed.), *The Goebbels Diaries 1939–41*, London: 1982, pp. 71, 213, 330, 354, 417.
57 Murrow, *In Search of Light*, broadcast of 30 Nov. 1954, p. 236.
58 Berlin, *Mr Churchill*, p. 39.
59 Charmley, *Churchill*, p. 3.
60 Winston S. Churchill, *A History of the English-Speaking Peoples*, vol. 1, London: Cassell, 1956, p. 92.

Further reading

John Charmley, *Churchill: The End of Glory*, London: Hodder & Stoughton, 1993

Gordon Corrigan, *Blood, Sweat and Arrogance: the Myths of Churchill's War*, London: Weidenfeld & Nicolson, 2006

Alex Danchev and Daniel Todman (eds), *War Diaries 1939–1945: Field Marshal Lord Alanbrooke*, London: Weidenfeld & Nicolson, 2001

Martin Gilbert, *Churchill: A Life*, London: Heinemann, 1991

Max Hastings, *Finest Years: Churchill as Warlord 1940–45*, London: HarperPress, 2009

Roy Jenkins, *Churchill*, London: Macmillan, 2001

10 Clement Attlee (1883–1967)

Prime Minister: July 1945– October 1951

'People are ceasing to think of him as a "dear little man". They realise that he has vision and courage and integrity so compelling that it is a force in itself.'

Diary of Harold Nicolson, 27 April 1949.[1]

During the Second World War Conservative MP Walter Elliot remarked that there should be an 'Attlee Calendar', with every day of the year accompanied by one of Clement Attlee's huge store of platitudes, beginning on 1 January with 'Every avenue will be explored'.[2] One might cavil that this form of words was more hackneyed phrase or cliché than platitude, but it is easy to understand what Elliot meant. The Deputy Prime Minister was an exceedingly poor wordsmith. In one speech, he managed to include almost as many clichés as sentences, including 'socialism without tears', 'put first things first' and 'strike whilst the iron is hot'.[3] On other, more venturesome occasions he did indeed advance into the realm of platitudes. 'You don't keep a dog and bark yourself' was one of his favourites. When questioned about Christianity, he responded curtly that he could not believe in its mumbo-jumbo, but then added the well-used formulaic phrase that he nevertheless 'believed in the ethics of Christianity'.[4]

It is perhaps not surprising that an American journalist described Attlee in 1941 as 'the dullest man in English politics'.[5] As a speaker he compared to Churchill as 'a village fiddler after Paganini'.[6] At key moments during the war Attlee 'succeeded where lesser men would have failed' – in making dramatic episodes seem dull and victories sound like defeats.[7] If Churchill was 'the glittering bird of paradise', noted a colleague, Attlee was 'a sparrow',[8] though most observers thought of him merely as a mouse. Nevertheless Attlee and the Labour Party beat Churchill and the Conservatives in the 1945 election by a huge majority, and over the next six years Attlee's administration made fundamental changes in Britain's society, economy and external policy. Attlee was described in his *Times* obituary in 1967 as 'one of the least colourful and most effective of British Prime Ministers of this century'.[9] To the obituarist, there seemed a glaring paradox between a 'social revolution' that was smoothly effected and the qualities of the man who presided over it. Could dullness and effectiveness possibly go together? In fact, there was no paradox at all. Indeed Attlee's underwhelming personality goes a long way towards explaining his political success.

The rise to the premiership

Born on 3 January 1883, into an upper-middle-class family, Clement Attlee was educated at Haileybury and then University College, Oxford. He then studied law and became a barrister in 1906. Yet instead of predictably following in his father's legal footsteps, he fell back on the private income provided by his family and took a voluntary job as live-in manager of Haileybury House, a boys' club in the East End of London. It was the making of him. Though 'painfully shy',[10] he found fellowship with the East Enders and soon lost his prejudiced belief that the poor were poor because of moral failings. The fault lay not with them, but with society's dominant doctrine of *laissez-faire* capitalism. The only difference between the rich and poor was their wealth: as individuals, he now judged, they were equal. Attlee became an ethical socialist: as he put it, heart first, head afterwards.[11] When he later said that he believed in 'the ethics of Christianity', he meant this seriously. He valued other people, realized that they were as important as himself, and wished to promote social changes that would improve their lives. On the surface the most matter-of-fact and unemotional of men, at a deeper level Clement Attlee had a profound revulsion against poverty and a romantic vision of brotherhood.

Joining the Stepney branch of the Independent Labour Party, he combined social work with political activism at the grass roots. He worked hard organizing meetings, collecting subscriptions, selling pamphlets. Yet there seemed little hope of an important political career. In the first election he ever contested, as ILP candidate in 1908 for the Stepney borough council, he received only 69 votes, and he did little better in succeeding years. By 1914, when war started, the future of the 31-year-old was uncertain. He was technically too old to enlist, but string-pulling led to his appointment as a lieutenant in the South Lancashire regiment. He served with distinction in Gallipoli, Mesopotamia and France. He was severely wounded several times and ended with the rank of major.

After the war Attlee returned to the East End. He was co-opted as mayor of Stepney in 1919 as a compromise candidate acceptable to both of the two dominant but warring groups, the Irish and the Jews. Then, in 1922, he became the first Labour MP for Limehouse, winning the seat by 1,900 votes. The message in his first parliamentary speech was simple but clear: 'As the nation was organised for war and death, so it can be organised for peace and life, if we have the will for it.'[12] Seemingly unambitious, and all too easy to underrate, he rose rapidly. He served as Parliamentary Private Secretary to party leader Ramsay MacDonald in 1922–24; and then, during the first Labour government, he was Under Secretary of State for War. In 1927 he joined the Simon Commission examining the constitutional future of India. This gave him an expertise that was later to be invaluable, but it meant he was unavailable for office when MacDonald formed the second Labour government. Nevertheless he replaced Oswald Mosley as Chancellor of the Duchy of Lancaster in May 1930, and from March to August 1931 he was Postmaster-General.

The political crisis of August 1931, which resulted in the formation of the National Government, produced seismic shifts in the political landscape. Attlee was thrown out of office, but was a beneficiary nevertheless. Only 52 Labour MPs were returned in the general election in October, Attlee managing to scrape home in Limehouse by 551 votes. Immediately he jumped to the front ranks of the Labour opposition, serving as deputy leader to the septuagenarian George Lansbury. He gained valuable, if exhausting, experience of a whole range of issues. He became caretaker leader when Lansbury resigned in October 1935. In the snap general election called by Baldwin, Attlee led the party to defeat, but that was only to be expected, and most judged that he had done reasonably well. Labour's representation increased to 154 seats. In the leadership contest that followed, Attlee defeated Arthur Greenwood, who had a reputation for drinking so much that even Winston Churchill joked about his intake, and also Herbert Morrison, a more considerable and charismatic candidate but one who was detested by powerful trade union leader Ernest Bevin.

Attlee was still considered a caretaker leader by many, but over the following years they could not wrong-foot him. Temperamentally the undemonstrative Attlee was the polar opposite of the dominant Ramsay MacDonald, now a hate figure for Labour, and he made a virtue of lacking charisma by playing the part of the devoted party servant. He did not take the lead in formulating policy, but once a majority decision had been made he would humbly follow it. Even over the vexed issue of rearmament, Attlee would not give a lead. It was Hugh Dalton who convinced the party to cease voting against the arms estimates; only when this had been accepted, in 1937, did Attlee step nimbly into line. It was clearly impossible to chop off the head of someone who so meekly, but resolutely, refused to stick his neck out. Nevertheless, it was widely assumed that, when the party lost the next election, as it almost certainly would, Attlee would step down. That this did not happen was due to the outbreak of war in September 1939. The election was postponed for the duration, and Attlee's position was cemented. Indeed in May 1940, when Churchill formed a coalition, Labour's leader and deputy leader, Clement Attlee and Arthur Greenwood, were catapulted into a new five-man War Cabinet.

In the Commons, Attlee was a poor speaker, and on a personal level many found him deeply unimpressive. A Conservative backbencher, on meeting him for the first time, found that 'he shook and twitched, and generally seemed very nervous and fidgetty [*sic*]'.[13] Yet while Greenwood was sacked from the War Cabinet, Attlee kept his place on merit. He had no qualms about playing second fiddle to Churchill. It suited his temperament to do his work out of the limelight, and he did it very well.

Attlee was Lord Privy Seal in 1940–42, Deputy Prime Minister in 1942–45, Dominions Secretary 1942–43, and Lord President of the Council in 1943–45. In addition, he was the only member of the government to sit on all three key wartime committees: the War Cabinet itself, the Defence Committee and the Lord President's Committee. He himself had helped determine this committee structure in an early review of governmental machinery. A recent study of Attlee during the war concludes not only that he was 'a bureaucratic operator *par excellence*' but that his vast accumulation of authority paralleled that of Stalin in the USSR in the 1920s.[14] Certainly all but superficial or prejudiced observers found him highly competent, well prepared, and a bulwark of the government. In some ways he was its linchpin, pressing Labour policies in the Cabinet, and to the Labour Party putting the coalition point of view. He also chaired the Cabinet, during Churchill's absences, with consummate skill: he was better organized and despatched business far more efficiently. The public was more aware of the high-profile wartime work of Labour figures like Bevin, Morrison and Cripps, but Ismay, Churchill's wartime chief of staff, judged that Attlee was a brave man of absolute integrity who made 'an immense and self-effacing contribution to the victory'.[15]

After Germany's defeat in May 1945, Attlee had wanted to accept Churchill's invitation to carry on the coalition until victory against Japan. Yet when his party opted instead for an early election, Attlee had no hesitation in agreeing. In the campaign he acquitted himself well. When Churchill broadcast that socialism was inseparably interwoven with totalitarianism, and that Labour would use some form of Gestapo to enforce their will, Attlee gave a fine, caustic riposte:

> When I listened to the Prime Minister's speech last night, in which he gave such a travesty of the policy of the Labour Party, I realized at once what was his object. He wanted the electors to understand how great was the difference between Winston Churchill, the great leader in war of a united nation, and Mr Churchill, the party leader of the Conservatives.[16]

He then offered a vision of a improved Britain, with better housing and social security, through government planning. Attlee did not win the election for Labour. Their victory was already certain, given the electors' overwhelming concern with social reforms, but he had scored a palpable hit. Mass Observation diaries reveal that members of the public thought that this 'nonentity, without character' had 'walked rings round Churchill' and deserved to be given a chance to prove himself.[17] Some of his colleagues were not so generous. Morrison made a last-minute attempt to replace him as Labour leader, before he could kiss hands with the king; but Attlee, with the support of Bevin, batted him aside.

Governing style

According to his Parliamentary Private Secretary, Arthur Moyle, Attlee's epitaph should be: 'No Prime Minister in our Parliamentary history discharged his responsibilities with less fuss.' As premier, Attlee did everything with 'military precision' and 'personified economy'. He allowed himself twenty minutes 'to bath, shave, dress and present himself for breakfast'.[18] His working day then stretched from 8 a.m. to midnight. The duration of interviews was kept to a minimum and most time was spent reading, and succinctly annotating, a massive amount of paperwork. Attlee wanted no more than the minimum of public appearances, and for summit meetings he had no enthusiasm at all. After Potsdam, he met with President Truman only twice, on 10 November 1945 and 5 December 1950. Clearly Clement Attlee had no wish to be a presidential premier. Instead, he valued efficient administrative structures.

Attlee believed in committees. Such was his passion that their number mushroomed in the course of his premierships to a grand total of 148 standing committees and no fewer than 313 ad hoc ones. At their heart, and at the very centre of government, was the Cabinet. He chose its membership with real skill, and a noticeable lack of egotism. Heavyweights Herbert Morrison and Ernie Bevin would clearly have important roles, despite their mutual antagonism, and Attlee sensibly kept them as far apart as possible. The former became Lord President of the Council, overseeing the party's nationalization programme; the latter, briefly considered for the Exchequer, became Foreign Secretary. Morrison's well known skills as a political manager and Bevin's as a shrewd negotiator were utilized to the full. Key roles were also found for two more men whose prestige had grown due to their wartime offices. Hugh Dalton became Chancellor of the Exchequer and Stafford Cripps President of the Board of Trade. Attlee wanted the left of the party to be represented, and he found offices for two of his most outspoken wartime critics. Aneurin Bevan had in 1942 accused Attlee of betraying the party and of being a latter-day Ramsay MacDonald. Nevertheless he was made Minister of Health. The scarcely less critical and vituperative Ellen Wilkinson became Minister of Education. Attlee appointed them not so much to keep his enemies close but because he appreciated their energy and passion. Attlee had not served for over 20 years in Parliament to see the first majority Labour government merely gain experience of operating the system. He wanted to make real improvements in people's lives.

It was a highly talented Cabinet but a highly contrasting one, with a potentially explosive mix. Attlee was aware that there was 'nothing so dangerous as a Ministry of all the talents'.[19] The big names were also big egos – and over them presided the man often considered a little mouse. Yet, building on his experiences with the War Cabinet, Attlee proved himself highly capable. He knew that democracy meant government by discussion, but he was also aware that it could degenerate into discussion with no government. He expected his ministers to be well prepared, and if they were not he rapped them over the knuckles: 'It is no good your coming here so ill-prepared and wasting everyone's time.'[20] Indeed he criticized ministers in a far more magisterial fashion than ever Churchill had done. The result was the brisk despatch of business. The Parliament of 1945–50 was able to enact a record number of 347 Acts, and on this achievement Attlee's reputation must largely rest. That so much was done owed a good deal to his ruthless efficiency.

The secret of Attlee's success lay in his personality. He was not without emotion. He had real affection for Bevin, later writing that their relationship was 'the deepest of my political life'.[21] He also found Bevan 'both likeable and attractive',[22] and thought the fiery, silver-tongued Welshman might well succeed him as

Labour leader. Yet neither of them sensed any warmth. As a shy man, Attlee had always found it difficult to deal with emotion. It had become second nature to cover up his feelings and get on with the job. Hence in Cabinet he appeared distant, even cold. A civil servant observed that his habitual facial expression was one of 'mongolian impassivity'.[23] There was no 'inner' or 'kitchen' cabinet, no late-night gossiping sessions with a few favoured cronies. Indeed there were no friends – and no favouritism either. He was thus the ideal referee between opposing factions. It is certainly very unlikely that anyone else could have performed this function nearly as well. His brusqueness was also the result of his personality. He was not a naturally rude man, but he lacked social skills and had formed the habit over the years of expressing himself briefly. Thinking out loud was alien to his nature and might have led to his becoming tongue-tied: better to bark out opinions and conclusions staccato fashion. A backbencher, Richard Crossman, spotted that Attlee was 'shy to the point of incivility',[24] whereas most others simply found him intimidating. His reputation as a 'good butcher' also owed much to his inability to sugar the pill of ministerial dismissal with kind, insincere regrets.

First premiership

The atmosphere in the new Labour government was almost ecstatic in 1945. At last Labour had an overall majority, of no fewer than 146 seats. Bliss it was in that dawn to be alive, and to be a socialist was very heaven! Hugh Dalton wrote that Labour politicians felt 'exalted, dedicated, walking on air, walking with destiny'.[25] Yet Attlee's feet were firmly on the ground. Asked later whether he felt as if destiny had overtaken him, he responded 'No'.[26] He did not believe in providence, or any such nonsense. Attlee's caution was well advised for 1945 was an election that sensible politicians might well have preferred to lose.

The problems facing Labour in and after 1945 were daunting in the extreme. Having fought longer than any other combatant, Britain was bankrupt. It had accumulated debts larger than those of any other nation in history. Not only that, the very success with which the economy had been geared for war meant that it would be correspondingly difficult to return to peacetime trading patterns, especially now that foreign markets had been lost. In addition, Britain had intractable overseas commitments. Famine in India could no longer be ignored as it had been during the war, and British forces had occupied a zone of Germany that could not feed itself. In addition, ministers were themselves exhausted. Many of them had been in office since 1940 and had continuously overworked. Hugh Dalton wrote in his diary in August 1947 of his astonishment that 'a substantial number of my colleagues do not simply drop in their tracks', adding: 'What a good thing it would be if some of them did!'[27] Cripps and Bevin did not survive, the former resigning in October 1950 and dying within two years, the latter dying in office in April 1951; Morrison had two heart attacks in 1947; and Dalton himself was prey to chronic constipation and painful boils. Attlee himself was in hospital in 1948 and again in 1951 for the treatment of a duodenal ulcer, but he withstood the pressures better than most. He was described in 1945, at the age of 62, as looking younger and fitter than he had on joining Churchill's War Cabinet, at 57. He had an enviable capacity to sleep well at night and to switch off from the pressures of work. Reading was his main relaxation. He reread the whole of Gibbon, and much else besides, during visits to Chequers, while *The Times* crossword and Wisden were 'always good for settling the mind'.[28] When Attlee later referred to 'thousands of old friends', he meant his beloved books; and when he said that he was 'never alone', it was because of the poetry and prose he knew by heart.[29] He also had a happy family life. He had married Violet Millar in 1922, and had four children. His wife Vi became infamous in the press for her erratic driving skills, as she took Clem around the country during election campaigns, but her most important quality was being apolitical. She provided a refuge from the potentially overpowering demands of politics.

From the moment the Americans abruptly cancelled Lend-Lease in August 1945, precipitating what Keynes predicted would be a 'financial Dunkirk', the Labour government was battling to stay afloat. A US loan of $3.75 billion was negotiated, but there were strings attached, including the convertibility of sterling in July 1947, which itself produced a further crisis that some compared in its ferocity to August 1931. The year 1947 was indeed Labour's 'annus horrendus'. Even the weather conspired against the government, with a record period of sub-zero temperatures followed by floods, and a consequent loss of vital export production. Marshall Aid from 1948 provided vital relief, and Britain received $3 billion within the next three years, but in September 1949 the pound had to be devalued, and Britain's participation in the Korean War in 1950 produced not only massive defence spending but balance of payments problems, as the terms of trade turned decisively against Britain. It was no mean achievement that Labour managed to negotiate such high and hazardous hurdles, or that over the 1946–51 period as a whole Britain's output grew by one-third. By the end of the period Britain was paying its way. With the benefit of hindsight we can see that the prolonged period of postwar austerity helped pave the way for later affluence.

Yet if Britain survived and slowly began to prosper economically under Labour, what of the government's promised domestic reforms? After 1918, similarly expensive promises were jettisoned as Lloyd George's government turned to retrenchment, and after 1945 there were more than enough excuses, if not reasons, for a similar breaking of election pledges. Did Attlee, to quote his maiden speech, have 'the will for it', despite the sea of troubles that threatened to overwhelm him?

Having experienced wartime calamities, Attlee had a quiet confidence in the future. He did not strut, and he did not fret, he simply moved through his agenda with all possible despatch. The main planks of the welfare state were enacted: the National Insurance Act in 1946; the National Health Service Act also in 1946, though it did not become operative until 1948; and the National Assistance Act of 1948, as well as many second-tier reforms. Similarly the measures of nationalization specified in the party's manifesto were put on the statute book: the Bank of England, coal, civil aviation, the railways, gas and electricity. Significant costs were incurred, and there were some who doubted that Britain could afford them. The NHS, for instance, cost twice as much as expected in its first full year of operation, while compensation for the previous owners of industries totalled over £2.7 billion. But Attlee was adamant. He had faith in the future.

This is shown most clearly by a speech he made during a debate on the National Insurance Bill:

> The question is asked – can we afford it? Supposing the answer is 'No,' what does that mean? It really means that the sum total of the goods produced and the services rendered by the people of this country is not sufficient to provide for all our people at all times, in sickness, in health, in youth and in age, the very modest standard of life that is represented by the sums of money set out in the Second Schedule of this Bill. I cannot believe that our national productivity is so slow, that our willingness to work is so feeble or that we can submit to the world that the masses of our people must be condemned to penury.[30]

Generally Attlee was the consensus politician. He would take soundings in Cabinet and follow the majority view. He proceeded empirically and was willing to accept compromise. At the back of his mind was the belief that only reforms that commanded wide acceptance would survive a Conservative return to power, which was bound to come sooner or later. That is perhaps the reason why he was ambivalent over the nationalization of iron and steel, which Labour delayed and the Conservatives reversed. But at times Attlee was the conviction politician. He was determined that welfare reforms should be enacted, regardless of the high costs, and when there were clashes in Cabinet he was invariably on the radical side. He backed Bevan strongly in his clash with Morrison over the nationalization of local authority hospitals. Similarly, he stood foursquare with Ellen Wilkinson's measure to raise the school leaving age to 15 in 1947, despite its immediate cost of £100 million. Dalton, Cripps and Morrison were overruled by Attlee's decisive support.

Attlee was also vital for external policy. His commitment to Indian independence was absolute. It even drew from one observer in the Commons the perceptive comment that he 'burns with a hidden fire and is sustained by a certain spiritual integrity'.[31] Despite local politicians' inability to agree, and in the face of bloody Hindu–Muslim riots, Attlee sacked Wavell as Viceroy and appointed Lord Mountbatten in his place, with instructions that Britain must leave by June 1948. Later the date was moved forward to August 1947, when both India and Pakistan became independent. With the independence of Burma and Ceylon in 1948, and with an acceptance the following year that republics could be members, Attlee had helped to found the multi-racial Commonwealth.

In foreign affairs, Attlee would have scaled down Britain's overseas commitments more rapidly than Bevin, especially in the Middle East; but mostly he was in agreement with his Foreign Secretary. Both men took the decision in 1946 that Britain could not rely on the United States and must develop its own nuclear deterrent. Both were highly suspicious of the Soviets, and the North Atlantic Treaty Organization of 1949 represented the culmination of their strategic aims. Labour had a much more realistic foreign policy than in the 1930s, and the government's over-reaction to the Korean War, with a bloated defence budget that caused political havoc in its ranks, was perhaps an understandable response to the mistakes of the previous decade. The prospect of a third world war concentrated the minds of Attlee and Bevin on essentials.

Attlee as Cabinet chairman and determined decision-maker was undoubtedly an asset to the postwar Labour government. He even won occasional plaudits in the House of Commons. An acerbic debater, he was capable of delivering terse, barbed responses. Winston Churchill was sometimes the victim, pleading privately in mitigation, 'Feed a grub on royal jelly and it may turn out to be a queen'.[32] But Churchill's brilliance had never rubbed off on Attlee, and more generally he seemed the dull, but competent, figure of old. Sometimes this colourlessness was an asset, in that even radical and controversial policies, when presented in his accustomed low-key manner, seemed eminently sensible and respectable, if not downright dull.

There were several plots to unseat Attlee from the leadership after 1945, but all foundered on the rock of Bevin's support. His critics therefore changed tack. He should be given a public relations makeover. In 1949 the Society of Socialist Journalists decided that they really ought to try to present the diffident Attlee, who so patently lacked glamour, as a more popular figure. He resisted all such attempts. With image-making he would have nothing whatever to do. 'Public relations officers do not exist in order to build up the personalities of Ministers,' he insisted, in a chilling rebuke; they 'exist in order to explain Government policy ... Moreover I should be a sad subject for any publicity expert. I have none of the qualities which create publicity.'[33]

Was Attlee justified in this modest assessment? To an extent he was. He did not attract headlines, and had no wish to. But a growing number of people were beginning to see through the drab persona. Here, said the broadcaster Ed Murrow in 1951, was 'just a modest, steady little man doing his job' – yet he had no doubt that he was also a person 'of great integrity' with an enormous capacity for work.[34] Attlee had been growing on people for some time. A Mass Observation diarist, a housewife and part-time clerk in Sheffield, clearly liked him by July 1946: 'Sober, calm, dignified, just what we need for this time of pulling up our socks ... It always takes longer for unspectacular goodness to be appreciated. I've noticed that.'[35] By the end of the 1940s opinion polls showed that he was considerably more popular than the government he led.

Second premiership

Commentators were clear that, compared with 1945, there was less popular enthusiasm for Labour at the election of 1950 (which Labour won by a mere five seats) and 1951 (which the Conservatives won by 17). Yet Attlee found more enthusiasm at his political meetings than in 1945, and he privately expected to win in 1950 with a workable overall majority of around 20–30 seats. Paradoxically, when he won the election in 1945 he had little personal following, while in 1951, when he lost, he was more popular than ever. Nevertheless, we can see clearly that Attlee himself contributed to Labour's defeat. First and foremost, he mistimed the elections of both 1950 and 1951. On the former occasion, his instincts were for holding an election in May, but he allowed himself to be overruled by his Chancellor, Stafford Cripps, who priggishly threatened to resign rather than have a pre-election budget in April. Hence the vote took place in February. Opinion polls later suggested that a contest in May, after the de-rationing of petrol, would have resulted in a comfortable majority of 40–50 seats, not the unworkable majority that was achieved.

Similarly, Attlee's timing of the 1951 contest was politically crass. He called the election for October so that King George VI would not have to alter the dates of his trip to Australia. No matter that senior colleagues like Morrison and Gaitskell wanted a later contest or that opinion polls predicted a Tory victory in October. The following spring, with an upturn in the economy, Labour would probably have done much better. As it was, Attlee's period in office came to an end with the party polling almost 14 million votes, 48.8 per cent of the total – more than ever before in its history. Only the Liberals' inability to contest more than 109 seats and the quirks of the electoral system brought Attlee down.

Nevertheless, Attlee's grip seemed to be faltering. The party's 1945 programme had been implemented, and there was no consensus about the future. Morrison was calling for 'consolidation' while Bevan wanted further reforms, including more nationalization. Attlee failed to give a decisive lead. Similarly, he failed to secure a compromise between Nye Bevan and Hugh Gaitskell over the issue of NHS charges for false teeth and spectacles. Admittedly he was in hospital in April 1951 when Bevan resigned, taking Harold Wilson and John Freeman with him, but he was widely consulted. Expenditure cutbacks, to Attlee, meant a sensible pruning, to allow for later growth; and, in the end, he backed his Chancellor against the man who had set up the NHS. Attlee had the defects of his virtues. He had for so long been the distant, impartial umpire that he could not suddenly become the inspiring captain of the team. 'Too much ego in Nye's cosmos,' he wrote to his brother.[36] Yet a man with greater human understanding of his colleagues would have done more to assuage that ego. Attlee's cabinet reshuffles in 1950–51, with Gaitskell as Chancellor, Morrison as Foreign Secretary and Bevan as Minister of Labour, proved a fatal combination. Similarly, in opposition from 1951 until his retirement in 1955, Attlee failed to reunify the party, as the breach between the Bevanites and the Gaitskellites condemned Labour to fruitless opposition.

Conclusion

The Labour administration of 1945 proved to be one of the most significant in modern British history. Its welfare reforms, building

on the work of Beveridge and Keynes, its nationalization of
20 per cent of British industry, the independence of India, the
decision to construct a British atomic bomb, NATO – all these,
and other reforms too, were effected between 1945 and 1951.
Everyone agrees that this was a government that made a real
difference to people's lives in Britain and the wider world.
Whether the Conservatives would have enacted similar reforms
from 1945 is extremely unlikely. Yet coming to power in 1951
they acquiesced in them all except the nationalization of steel
and road haulage. Labour had set the contours of British political
economy for the next 30 years, until the Thatcher era undid some
of its work.

Margaret Thatcher herself professed admiration for Attlee: 'He
was a serious man and a patriot ... he was all substance and no
show. His was a genuinely radical and reforming government.'[37]
Attlee was indeed exceptional, so much so that all too often
commentators have not known what to make of him. His *Times*
obituarist felt ambivalent, for Attlee was 'devoid of those external
marks which Aristotle thought necessary for men of consequence'.
One should forgive Aristotle. Politicians like Attlee may well
have been even rarer in Athens in the fourth century BC than in
twentieth-century Britain.

There is really no mystery about Clement Attlee, for there is no
reason why ability should be twinned with flamboyance. Dullness
is no bar to achievement in many walks of life. It is rare in
democratic politics, but then Attlee achieved power in his own
party when there was a reaction against Ramsay MacDonald, that
'magnificent substitute for a leader';[38] and he achieved power
nationally, after there had been a revolution in expectations
during the People's War, because of the appeal of his party as an
instrument of social reform. Admittedly he seemed rather pathetic
to outsiders. Even after being Prime Minister for years he still
shook when making speeches, and his fingers and face would
twitch with nervousness. It was said that he had positively to
screw himself up to say Good Morning. His portrait in 1950 by
Sir James Gunn, now in the National Portrait Gallery, shows
a man totally ill at ease: the tension in the neck and temples is
achingly visible and the eyes, it seems, can scarcely bear to meet
ours. But that a man could overcome such a 'social phobia' and

put himself in the public arena required not merely stoicism but genuine courage. That he should, in addition, make his withdrawn personality into an asset in Cabinet required tremendous skill. Furthermore, despite appearances, Attlee had a large measure of intellectual self-confidence, though this never tipped over into arrogance.

Attlee was in many ways lucky to come to power, especially with the Labour débâcle of 1931 that removed rival figures. Nor was he a perfect Prime Minister. He had noticeable faults. He was certainly ignorant of economics, as was revealed all too clearly during the financial crisis in the summer of 1947, and as an aloof manager of his Cabinet he could not prevent the resignation of Bevan and Wilson in April 1951. Above all, he had not the vision or originality to enthuse his government after its original agenda, which had not been of his making, had been fulfilled. As a final disservice to Labour, he mishandled the timing of the elections of 1950 and 1951.

The fact is, of course, that no one is really fit to be Prime Minister. Yet many would prefer to be governed by Attlee than by any other premier of modern times. He lacked the tactical agility of Harold Wilson, he was not as popular as the avuncular James Callaghan, and he could not match the media-savvy Tony Blair when it came to winning elections; but many Labour supporters during these later premierships looked back nostalgically to the days of solid achievement under the unpretentious Clem Attlee.

'The object of power is power,' wrote Orwell in *Nineteen Eighty-Four*. All too often modern Prime Ministers have seemed to think so. No sooner is one election won than preparations are being made to win the next, even if principles have to be sacrificed in the process. Similarly, premiers have gloried in their position, often being corrupted – or at least made pompous – in the process. This was not Attlee's way. Power was won for a purpose, and that was to improve Britain. Power was for policies and policies were for people. That did not mean that the person of the Prime Minister did not matter. On the contrary, it took real grit, perseverance and determination not to succumb to the enormous difficulties that beset Britain and the Labour Government after 1945. Many mocked Attlee's dull personality, but the man had remarkable qualities of character.

Attlee loved poetry, though not the 'moderns'. For some reason he could not remember a single line of modernist verse. Yet there is a line from T.S. Eliot's 'East Coker' that encapsulates Attlee's no-nonsense political outlook. For him there was only the trying (in terms of brisk, efficient hard work, month after month, year after year): the rest (in terms of success or failure, the results, the political commentaries, his own historical reputation) was not his business. *The Times* decided, in his obituary, that he was 'a successful' but not 'a great' Prime Minister. Many historians disagree with this verdict. Attlee himself would surely have been supremely indifferent.

Notes

1 Harold Nicolson, *Diaries and Letters 1945–62*, London: Fontana, 1971, p. 159.
2 G.S. Harvie-Watt, *Most Of My Life*, London: Springwood Books, 1980, p. 91.
3 Greg Rosen, *Old Labour to New*, London: Politico's, 2005, p. 81.
4 Kenneth Harris, *Attlee*, London: Weidenfeld and Nicolson, 1995, p. 564.
5 William Golant, 'Mr Attlee', *History Today*, August 1983, 12.
6 Nicolson, *Diaries and Letters 1945–62*, p. 105.
7 Ibid., pp. 224, 296.
8 Max Hastings, *Finest Years*, London: HarperPress, 2009, p. 145.
9 *The Times*, 8 October 1967.
10 C.R. Attlee, *As It Happened*, London: Heinemann, 1954, p. 20.
11 Geoffrey Dellar (ed.), *Attlee As I Knew Him*, London Borough of Tower Hamlets, 1983, p. 54.
12 *Parliamentary Debates* (Commons), vol. 159, col. 92, 23 November 1922.
13 *Chips: The Diaries of Sir Henry Channon*, ed. R.R. James, Harmondsworth: Penguin, 1970, p. 322, entry for 7 Aug. 1940.
14 Robert Crowcroft, *Attlee's War*, London: Tauris, 2011. pp. 241, 231.
15 *The Memoirs of General the Lord Ismay*, London: Heinemann, 1960, pp. 133, 404.
16 Greg Rosen, *Old Labour to New*, p. 133.
17 Simon Garfield, *Our Hidden Lives: The Everyday Diaries of a Forgotten Britain, 1945–1938*, London: Ebury Press, 2004, pp. 37, 65.
18 Nicklaus Thomas-Symonds, *Attlee*, London: Tauris, 2010, p. 142–3.
19 Attlee, *As It Happened*, p. 163.

20 George Mallaby, *From My Level*, London: Hutchinson, 1965, p. 57.
21 Frank Field (ed.), *Attlee's Great Contemporaries*, London: Continuum, 2009, p. 129.
22 Ibid., p. 138.
23 Lord Salter, *Memoirs of a Public Servant*, London: Faber and Faber, 1961, p. 285.
24 Janet Morgan (ed.), *The Backbench Diaries of Richard Crossman*, London: Hamish Hamilton and Jonathan Cape, 1981, p. 68, entry for 31 Jan. 1952.
25 Hugh Dalton, *High Tide and After*, London: Muller, 1962, p. 3.
26 Field, *Attlee's Great Contemporaries*, p. 176.
27 Ben Pimlott (ed.), *The Political Diary of Hugh Dalton 1918–40, 1945–60*, London: Cape, 1986, p. 406, entry for 8 Aug. 1947.
28 Francis Williams (ed.), *A Prime Minister Remembers*, 1961, p. 103.
29 Field, *Attlee's Great Contemporaries*, pp. 15–21.
30 Peter Hennessy, *Never Again*, London: Cape, 1992, p. 119.
31 Alan Campbell-Johnson, *Mission with Mountbatten*, London: Hale, 1985, pp. 28–9.
32 *New Statesman Profiles*, London: Phoenix House, 1957, p. 71.
33 Nicolson, *Diaries and Letters*, p. 152, entry for 14 Jan. 1949.
34 Edward R. Murrow, *In Search of Light*, London: Macmillan, 1968, p. 177.
35 Garfield, *Our Hidden Lives*, p. 234.
36 Attlee to Tom Attlee, 25 Sept. 1950, C.R. Attlee papers, Bodleian Library.
37 Margaret Thatcher, *The Path to Power*, London: HarperCollins, 1995, p. 69.
38 N. and J. MacKenzie (eds), *The Diary of Beatrice Webb*, vol. 4, 1924–43, London: Virago, 1985, p. 92, entry for 2 Aug. 1926.

Further reading

Robert Crowcroft, *Attlee's War*, London: I.B. Tauris, 2011
Kenneth Harris, *Attlee*, London: Weidenfeld and Nicolson, 1995
Robert Pearce, *Attlee*, London: Longman, 1997
Nicklaus Thomas-Symonds, *Attlee: A Life in Politics*, London: I.B. Tauris, 2010

11 Anthony Eden (1897–1977)

Prime Minister April 1955–January 1957

'I don't believe Anthony can do it.'
> Winston Churchill to his private secretary, the night
> before his retirement as Prime Minister, 4 April 1955[1]

It is Anthony Eden's misfortune to be remembered almost solely for his association with the Suez crisis, which occupied less than six months in a political career lasting more than three decades. In the autumn of 1956 Eden faced, and by common consent failed, the decisive test of his premiership with his clumsy use of force in reaction to the Egyptian President Nasser's nationalization of the Suez Canal. Convinced that he had to face down a Middle Eastern version of the interwar Italian dictator, Benito Mussolini, Eden involved Britain in a military expedition in a bid to recover control of the waterway. The action aroused unprecedented international condemnation, led by Britain's most important ally, the United States, who refused to support the pound when it came under pressure on the international money markets. The outcome was a humiliating suspension of the operation and the premature termination of Eden's career as Prime Minister. Although ill health was the official reason for his resignation – and it undoubtedly played a part in the unfolding of the Suez drama – there was no doubt that his downfall was the result of a major failure of political judgement.

The rise to the premiership

It was ironic that Eden's downfall was caused by his failure to handle an international crisis successfully, since the greater part of his ministerial experience lay in foreign affairs. Appointed Foreign Secretary by Stanley Baldwin at the age of 38, he was retained in the post by Neville Chamberlain on his succession to the premiership in May 1937. Nine months later a policy disagreement over relations with fascist Italy, which overlay a deeper personality clash with the Prime Minister, led to Eden's resignation from the Cabinet. The episode gave him an exaggerated reputation for opposition to the appeasement policies of the National Government, which drew him into Churchill's orbit and led to his return to government following the outbreak of the Second World War. After a brief tenure of the Dominions Office and the War Office, Eden served for a second time as Foreign Secretary in 1940–45. Churchill nominated him as his preferred successor as early as June 1942. Eden's entitlement to the highest office was confirmed by his prominent role in opposition, following the Conservative defeat in the 1945 general election, and by a third term at the Foreign Office in 1951–55.

The length of Eden's apprenticeship was not necessarily an advantage for him. In the words of Harold Macmillan, 'the trouble with Anthony Eden was that he was trained to win the Derby in 1938; unfortunately, he was not let out of the starting stalls until 1955'.[2] Like another future Prime Minister, Gordon Brown, Eden had grown increasingly impatient, with a damaging effect on his nerves, as he endured the long wait for his inheritance. In both cases a Prime Minister took over, unchallenged from within his own party, in spite of persistent, privately expressed doubts on the part of a number of well-informed insiders. A senior Conservative, Lord Swinton, told Churchill early in 1955 that Eden 'would make the worst Prime Minister since Lord North. But you can't think like that now – it's too late. You announced him as your successor more than ten years ago'.[3] Another telling comment was made by a retired minister, Walter Elliot: 'He is a diplomat but Prime Ministers have to give orders.' Elliot also identified an area of vulnerability for Eden in describing the relationship between him and his two most senior colleagues, Harold Macmillan and R.A. Butler, as 'a triangle not a triumvirate'.[4] The suggestion was that the relationship between the three was one of uneasy rivalry rather than harmonious co-operation.

These comments were made by senior figures who had observed Eden at close quarters for up to three decades. Personal ill-feeling, of course, may explain Swinton's negative attitude; he was dropped as Commonwealth Relations Secretary in April 1955. Yet there had always been a school of thought which viewed Eden as a polished but superficial performer. Although popular with the public for his good looks and immaculate dress – the Homburg hat that he first favoured in the 1930s was widely known as an 'Anthony Eden' – there were suspicions in some quarters that these attributes concealed more fundamental weaknesses.

Governing style

Eden began his premiership with a personal success, raising the Conservative majority from 16 to 58 in the May 1955 general election. He deserves credit for seeking and winning a mandate from the electorate a month after entering Number 10, in contrast with other postwar premiers who took over midway through a Parliament. In reality, however, there was no scope for complacency. With the Labour opposition divided between left- and right-wing factions under the elderly Clement Attlee, it was unlikely that the Conservatives would lose. Butler's final budget as Chancellor in October 1955 was generally regarded as an inadequate response to emerging economic difficulties. The extension of purchase tax to new categories of household goods led it to being mockingly dubbed the 'pots and pans budget'. By delaying the reconstruction of his Cabinet until December, when Macmillan replaced Butler at the Treasury, Eden lost vital impetus. He gave the impression of lacking the capacity to stamp his own authority on the government. The restiveness of Conservative Party supporters was highlighted by an editorial in the normally loyal *Daily Telegraph* in January 1956, lamenting the absence of the 'smack of firm government'.

The situation was made more difficult by Eden's acute sensitivity to criticism. At one point he denied rumours that he was planning to resign, an unwise step since it suggested that his position really was in question. Although he was the first Prime Minister to appreciate the potential of television as a means of communication – in contrast with Churchill, who had treated it with disdain – he wanted this to be on his own terms, with the BBC acting as a channel for ministerial broadcasts rather than as a forum for political debate. Thus he clung to the 'fourteen day rule', which prohibited the discussion of any subject likely to come up in Parliament in the following fortnight, until it was swept away by the Suez crisis. Eden's relationship with the broadcasters was an unhappy one. He suspected 'those Communists at the BBC' of deliberately shining lights in his eyes when he spoke on television following Nasser's nationalization of the canal. He then clashed with the BBC over the right of the new Labour Party leader, Hugh Gaitskell, to respond to his broadcast calling for national solidarity in the wake of the Anglo-French attack on Egypt.[5]

Those who worked closely with Eden describe a man ill at ease with the burden of responsibility, impatient and frequently ill-tempered. Bill Deedes, who served in the Eden government as a junior Home Office minister, wrote that 'he lacked the broad shoulders which every occupant of No. 10 needs to have'. At that time ministers communicated by telephones made secure by scrambler devices, which took a little time to warm up. Deedes recalled a Cabinet minister who said of Eden, 'He will never wait, so you miss the first part of what he says, then have to ask him to repeat it and this irritates him'.[6] The stories of Eden's attempts to micro-manage government departments by making anxious telephone calls to colleagues are legion. He intended to be more businesslike than Churchill, whose Cabinet meetings had frequently dragged on without purpose. Instead Eden preferred to meet ministers for more focused, one-to-one conversations. In practice, however, he appeared aloof and inaccessible to his Cabinet colleagues and parliamentary supporters. As Macmillan noted in his diary shortly before the Suez crisis: 'Eden gives no real leadership in the House (for he is *not* a H of Commons man – he *never* enters the Smoking Room) altho' he is *popular* and respected in the country as a whole.'[7]

Although he was not yet 58 at the time of his appointment as Prime Minister, Eden suffered from poor health, which certainly affected his ability to project himself as a leader. He never fully recovered from three operations for a serious gall bladder condition in April 1953. Eden was hospitalized for three days with a high fever early in October 1956. After the ending of hostilities in the Canal Zone, he took a three-week break in Jamaica on medical advice – an interlude which destroyed any remaining prospect of his clinging to office. Evelyn Shuckburgh, who knew Eden well as his Private Secretary and then as a Middle Eastern specialist in the Foreign Office, noted in his diary: 'Is he on his way out, has he had a nervous breakdown, is he mad? The captain leaves the sinking ship which he has steered personally on to the rocks.'[8] Eden was dependent on a combination of prescription drugs from 1953 onwards, a fact to which he referred in his resignation statement. The side-effects of this medication may well have adversely affected his judgement and overall capability, although its importance should not be exaggerated as a factor in the miscalculations surrounding the Suez expedition. After all, the senior colleagues who shared responsibility with him in the autumn of 1956 did not have ill health as an excuse for their actions.

The record in government

The shortness of Eden's premiership made it unlikely that there would be significant achievements in home or overseas policy. Cabinet committees on two important subjects, the regulation of industrial relations and the question of legal controls on Commonwealth immigration, made no recommendations for action. The Prime Minister was unusual in the narrowness of his previous ministerial experience. It is true that he enthusiastically advocated the concept of a 'property owning democracy' – a term first outlined in the 1920s by the Conservative thinker, Noel Skelton, in an attempt to provide a constructive alternative to socialism by giving as many people as possible a stake in the country. Yet there is little evidence of an attempt to translate the slogan into actual policies. Eden's parliamentary private secretary, Robert Carr, later recalled his boss's regret that he had never had the opportunity to broaden his portfolio by serving at a junior level at, for example, the Board of Trade or the Ministry of Labour.[9] Yet Eden never seems to have pressed any of the Prime Ministers in whose governments he served for an opportunity to head a domestic department.

Eden also set in motion a reappraisal of Britain's global role, which was to have an influence on the defence review completed under his successor. An attempt was made to reduce Cold War tensions, with the visit of the Soviet leaders, Khrushchev and Bulganin, to Britain in April 1956. It was not Eden's fault, although he suffered embarrassment as a result, that the event was overshadowed by an ill-judged undercover security services operation. The disappearance of a former Royal Navy diver, Commander Lionel 'Buster' Crabb, apparently whilst inspecting the hull of the Soviet visitors' ship in Portsmouth harbour, suggested that the Prime Minister lacked control over the intelligence services.

In one policy area in particular, there is a danger of criticizing Eden with the benefit of hindsight. This is his unenthusiastic response to moves towards greater west European integration. His government played no part in the June 1955 Messina conference, at which the six members of the European Coal and Steel Community discussed plans to create a common market – the origin of the European Economic Community, created in January 1957, and forerunner of today's European Union. The government further distanced itself by dispatching a Board of Trade official, Russell Bretherton, rather than a minister, to represent Britain at the next round of discussions. It is easy to portray Eden as the bearer of outmoded imperial values, who failed to seize the opportunity to shape the making of a united Europe at an early stage, when Britain's voice might have counted. Yet in his refusal to pool British sovereignty in an untested experiment, and his reluctance to put his trust in a collection of continental countries, still fragile as a result of the Second World War, Eden was working with the grain of parliamentary and public opinion in the mid-1950s. At the time there was broad agreement that Britain stood at the centre of three circles in the international arena – the Empire-Commonwealth, the special relationship with the USA and Europe – and that its continuing influence depended on not becoming exclusively aligned with any one of these. Where Eden differed from most postwar British policy-makers was in his wish to act as independently as possible of the USA – an attitude which influenced his response to the Suez crisis.

Any assessment of Eden must reach a judgement on his handling of this defining episode. In some ways his conduct was out of character; as Foreign Secretary two years earlier, he had negotiated the withdrawal of British troops from the Suez Canal Zone. Moreover from July to October 1956 he showed a willingness to seek a diplomatic solution to the nationalization of the Canal. Ultimately, however, Eden was not prepared to submit to what he perceived as an act of aggression by the Egyptian government. In mid-October he accepted a French proposal for joint military action in collaboration with Israel. Following an Israeli invasion of Egypt, Britain and France would launch an attack under the guise of 'separating the combatants' and secure control of the Canal Zone. The full details of the plan were not disclosed to the Cabinet. Eden raised the issue of military co-operation with Israel in a hypothetical sense at a meeting on 25 October but the Cabinet did not probe for further details or push for a collective decision on the deployment of troops.[10] For military reasons secrecy had to be maintained in advance of the operation but it is harder to defend Eden's handling of the collusion charge after British troops had been withdrawn. Addressing the Commons on 20 December, he denied that there had been foreknowledge of the Israeli attack. He also ordered the British copy of the secret agreement, signed on 24 October in the Paris suburb of Sèvres, to be destroyed, and maintained the pretence that there had been no secret deal in his memoirs.

How are Eden's actions in the Suez crisis to be explained? Undoubtedly he feared the economic consequences of allowing a triumphant Egyptian regime to control the flow of oil to the West. Eden has been widely criticized for drawing an unjustified parallel between Nasser's Arab nationalism and the actions of the fascist dictators two decades earlier which, in the absence of firm resistance by the Western democracies, had led to the Second World War. A key theme of Eden's memoirs was 'the lessons of the 'thirties and their application to the 'fifties'.[11] Perhaps he felt that he had to live up to his pre-war reputation as an anti-appeaser. The need to emerge from Churchill's shadow by means of some bold stroke may have played a part. Within the Cabinet, Macmillan was known to be contemplating resignation if the military option was excluded. This would have left Eden gravely isolated in his own party, which demonstrated its hostility to Nasser's action at its annual conference in October.[12] Although the Cabinet contained a number of 'doubters', including Butler and the Minister of Defence, Walter Monckton, who was moved to another post shortly before the attack began, only two junior ministers actually resigned in protest. In his memoirs Edward Heath revealed his horror when the Prime Minister confided in him that the planned military action was 'the highest form of statesmanship'. Yet Heath did not resign, citing his obligation as Chief Whip to maintain the unity and discipline of the parliamentary Conservative Party.[13] Those who had reservations were balanced by ministers who saw the defeat of Nasser as a vital objective for Britain. The Colonial Secretary, Alan Lennox-Boyd, wrote to Eden in August that 'if Nasser wins, or even appears to win, we might as well as a government (and indeed as a country) go out of business'. He viewed the seizure of the Canal as 'a step in a careful plan to drive us out of the Eastern Mediterranean and the Middle East'.[14]

The crisis had dire consequences for Britain. It left Nasser in control of the Canal, with his prestige in the Arab world enhanced, and interrupted Britain's oil supply. As the future Foreign Secretary, Douglas Hurd, at that time a diplomat in New York, demonstrates in his memoirs, Britain was isolated at the United Nations.[15] Its international prestige was tarnished and its relationship with the USA, whose disapproval Eden had failed to foresee, was damaged. Eden allowed his judgement to be seriously affected by personal animosity towards Nasser and he had no clear idea of how stability in the region could be guaranteed, had he succeeded in removing the Egyptian leader. At home the crisis proved deeply divisive. The intervention in Egypt temporarily identified Eden with the right of the Conservative Party, with whom he had little in common, and who turned against him once the decision to abandon the operation had been taken. Macmillan, who possibly exaggerated the threat to sterling caused by the crisis, using this to support a case for immediate withdrawal, was able to position himself for the succession. By going into Egypt Eden had undermined his credentials as a moral, statesmanlike figure; by coming out, without achieving any substantial objective, he had confirmed the suspicions of those who already doubted his capacity for leadership. Although he was far from solely responsible for the fiasco, as head of government he paid the heaviest price in terms of his career and ultimate reputation. What remained for him after leaving Number 10 was ennoblement as the Earl of Avon and two decades in retirement as an observer of politics rather than a participant. It was a sad fate for one who had once promised so much.

Notes

1 John Colville, *The Churchillians,* London: Weidenfeld and Nicolson, 1981, p. 171.
2 D.R. Thorpe, *Eden: The Life and Times of Anthony Eden, First Earl of Avon, 1897–1977,* London: Chatto and Windus, 2003, p. 430.
3 John Ramsden, *The Age of Churchill and Eden, 1940–1957,* London: Longman, 1995, p. 274.
4 Janet Morgan (ed.), *The Backbench Diaries of Richard Crossman,* London: Hamish Hamilton and Jonathan Cape, 1981, p. 416, entry for 7 April 1955. Macmillan served as Foreign Secretary from April to December 1955 and then as Chancellor, succeeding Eden as Prime Minister in January 1957. Butler was Chancellor from October 1951 to December 1955, then Leader of the Commons and deputy Prime Minister.
5 Michael Cockerell, *Live from Number Ten: The Inside Story of Prime Ministers and Television,* London: Faber and Faber, 1988, pp. 44–50.
6 W.F. Deedes, *Brief Lives,* London: Macmillan, 2004, pp. 81–2.
7 Peter Catterall (ed.), *The Macmillan Diaries: The Cabinet Years, 1950–1957,* London: Macmillan, 2003, p. 576, entry for 21 July 1956. The Smoking Room was the part of the House of Commons where MPs usually met to socialize.
8 Evelyn Shuckburgh, *Descent to Suez: Diaries, 1951–56,* London: Weidenfeld and Nicolson, 1986, p. 365.
9 Peter Hennessy, *Muddling Through: Power, Politics and the Quality of Government in Postwar Britain,* London: Indigo edition, 1997, p. 207.
10 Peter Hennessy, *The Prime Minister: The Office and its Holders since 1945,* London: Allen Lane/Penguin, 2000, pp. 222–3.
11 Sir Anthony Eden, *Full Circle,* London: Cassell, 1960, foreword.
12 David Carlton, *Anthony Eden: A Biography,* London: Allen Lane, 1981, p. 425.

13 Edward Heath, *The Course of My Life*, London: Hodder and Stoughton, 1998, pp. 169–72.
14 Lennox-Boyd to Eden, 24 August 1956, quoted in Philip Murphy, *Alan Lennox-Boyd: A Biography*, London: I.B. Tauris, 1999, pp. 162–3.
15 Douglas Hurd, *Memoirs*, London: Little, Brown, 2003, pp. 136–8.

Further reading

David Carlton, *Anthony Eden: A Biography*, London: Allen Lane, 1981
David Dutton, *Anthony Eden: A Life and Reputation*, London: Arnold, 1997
Robert Rhodes James, *Anthony Eden*, London: Weidenfeld and Nicolson, 1986
D.R. Thorpe, *Eden: The Life and Times of Anthony Eden, First Earl of Avon, 1897–1977*, London: Chatto and Windus, 2003

12 Harold Macmillan (1894–1986)

Prime Minister: January 1957–
October 1963

'He understood ... the art of serious political acting. He of all
men knew the necessity and the potency of the mask ... He
built himself his Edwardian facade and it provided him with
enough cover to get on with a strictly contemporary job.'

Norman Shrapnel, parliamentary correspondent of
the *Guardian*, on Harold Macmillan, 1978.[1]

Harold Macmillan's enigmatic personality remains a challenge
to the biographer. As Prime Minister he projected a languid,
mannered persona: his drooping moustache, dated clothes and
urbane wit made him an irresistible magnet for the media. Yet
behind the 'Edwardian' mask lurked a thoroughly professional
politician who was capable of considerable ruthlessness. The
paradoxes were many. A cynical man of the world, he was also
a devout Anglican with a deeply felt sense of responsibility in
public life, a legacy of his good fortune in surviving the horror
of the Great War. At home in the world of the country house and
the upper-class London club, he adopted modern advertising
and public relations techniques for electoral purposes. Chosen by
his party essentially as the candidate of the right, who offered
reassurance after the failure of Anthony Eden's 1956 Suez expedition, in office Macmillan pursued unexpectedly radical policies.
He connected with the aspirations of an electorate emerging from
postwar austerity, promoting an agenda of economic expansion
and almost doubling his party's majority in the October 1959
general election. At the same time he was the first Prime Minister
seriously to confront the issues raised by Britain's decline as a

world power, accelerating the process of disengagement from empire and pointing towards a European destiny.

The rise to the premiership

Macmillan was born into a privileged, upper-middle-class background, the beneficiary of his grandfather's remarkable ascent from Scottish crofter to founder of a leading London publishing firm. Education at Eton and Oxford was followed by enrolment as an army officer following the outbreak of the First World War. Macmillan's service on the Western Front left him with a deep feeling for the loyalty and courage of the ordinary soldier, and a belief that in peacetime more should be done for the welfare of the class from which his men came. His paternalistic social philosophy was confirmed by his election in 1924 as Conservative MP for Stockton-on-Tees, which he held, with a short interval, until the 1945 Labour landslide. Macmillan's association with a depressed industrial constituency helped to persuade him of the need for greater state intervention in the economy, a case which he argued in his best known book, *The Middle Way*, published in 1938. Although arguments for managed capitalism were to find favour in the postwar years, in the era of Baldwin and Chamberlain he occupied an isolated position on the left of the Conservative Party.

On the eve of the Second World War Macmillan was a politically marginal figure. His private life offered little consolation: his marriage to Lady Dorothy Cavendish, daughter of the Duke of Devonshire, gave him access to a highly congenial upper-class world but his wife had embarked on an affair with another Conservative MP, Robert Boothby, which was to last until her death in 1966. Perhaps, however, personal disappointment drove Macmillan to dedicate himself single-mindedly to seek political advancement. The first step on the ladder came as a result of his opposition to the National Government's policy of appeasement, which drew him into Winston Churchill's orbit. The latter's appointment as Prime Minister in May 1940 enabled Macmillan to progress, via a series of junior ministerial appointments, to a position of real influence as the government's representative in North Africa and subsequently in the wider Mediterranean world.

After being defeated at Stockton in 1945, he found a more conventional Conservative seat in Bromley, a middle-class suburb
on the outskirts of London, which he held for the rest of his
political career. Churchill's patronage brought Macmillan a high-
profile role in the years of opposition and, after the Conservatives
returned to office in October 1951, he gained the opportunity to
make a national reputation as Minister of Housing. This he
achieved by fulfilling an electoral pledge to build 300,000 houses
a year, a target which he met by extracting subsidies from the
Treasury and securing scarce raw materials. Success at Housing
was Macmillan's passport to promotion as Minister of Defence in
October 1954, a post which he held until Churchill's retirement
the following April.

It was Anthony Eden's troubled 19-month premiership which
gave Macmillan a platform from which to seize the ultimate prize.
Eden moved him in quick succession to two of the great offices of
state, first to the Foreign Office and then, in December 1955, to
the Exchequer. This did not, however, indicate a real closeness
between the two men. Eden mistrusted his colleague's ambition,
later commenting that 'he should have been a cardinal in the
Middle Ages, under a strong Pope'.[2] This rueful observation was
made in the light of the Suez affair of October–November 1956,
which shattered Eden's health and reputation and propelled
Macmillan into his place. Macmillan was among the most enthusiastic Cabinet supporters of military action against Egypt after
President Nasser's nationalization of the Suez Canal. His intervention was also decisive in halting the operation, once it became
clear that this would be the price of abating international condemnation and securing American support for the deteriorating
position of sterling. Such a rapid *volte-face* earned Macmillan
Harold Wilson's gibe, 'first in, first out'. It also exposed him to
later allegations that he had deliberately misled his colleagues
about the seriousness of Britain's financial position in order to
bring about a humiliating retreat, the consequence of which
would be Eden's downfall and his own elevation. This interpretation seems excessively Machiavellian. It is, however, likely that
Macmillan exaggerated the figures in order to ensure that the
Cabinet backed the conclusion which he had already reached,
that withdrawal was the only way to avoid a devastating run on

the pound and to give hope of rebuilding Britain's relationship with the USA.

Whatever Macmillan's motivation may have been, there is no doubt that he moved swiftly, in the aftermath of the crisis, to outmanoeuvre his main rival, R.A. Butler, in the competition to succeed Eden. Butler was fatally damaged in Conservative circles by the knowledge that he had misgivings about the action. Moreover, as Eden's deputy he had the unenviable task of supervising the withdrawal from Egypt. By contrast Macmillan projected an upbeat, defiant image in a crucial meeting with backbenchers in late November. Enoch Powell, a partisan of Butler, recalled with distaste the way in which Macmillan, exhibiting 'the skill of the old actor manager, succeeded in false-footing' his less assertive rival.[3] Most Conservative MPs, however, relished Macmillan's ebullient performance, which was remembered when Eden resigned in January 1957. In the absence of a formal leadership election procedure, soundings were taken by the Cabinet's elder statesmen, the leader of the upper house, Lord Salisbury, and the Lord Chancellor, Lord Kilmuir. Macmillan was the overwhelming choice of his colleagues as the individual best placed to restore unity and purpose to a bruised and leaderless party.

Governing style

The task confronting Macmillan as Prime Minister was formidable. In the words of Lord Kilmuir: 'Suez had shaken the party to its foundations.'[4] A minority of liberal Conservatives had opposed the operation, whilst the bulk of the party had supported the use of force and were angered by the abrupt withdrawal. Macmillan proved more than equal to the task of restoring his party's confidence, refusing to apologize for Suez and exuding a sense of optimism and decisiveness. Colleagues noted with approval the businesslike way in which he conducted Cabinet meetings. In contrast to Eden's restlessness, he largely left his colleagues to get on with their own departmental business, although he was capable of intervening when he considered it necessary. The Defence Minister, Duncan Sandys, for example, observed that 'Eden had no gift for leadership; under Macmillan as PM everything better,

Cabinet meetings quite transformed'.[5] Macmillan could be entertaining as well as authoritative, employing a range of historical and literary allusions to make a point. Charles Hill, who was sacked as Housing Minister in July 1962, admired his natural dominance in Cabinet: 'it was done by sheer superiority of mind and of judgement'.[6] There was no inner Cabinet; instead Macmillan governed through a series of individual relationships with key figures. His principal rival, Butler, was occupied with a number of senior responsibilities, including deputizing for the Prime Minister during his frequent absences abroad. Selwyn Lloyd, who served successively as Foreign Secretary and Chancellor of the Exchequer, considered that Macmillan acted as a presidential figure, treating a favoured few as intimates but regarding most ministers as 'junior officers in a unit which he commanded'. The resignation of Lord Salisbury in March 1957, following a dispute over the handling of policy towards Cyprus, removed the last senior member of the premier's own generation. According to Lloyd, Macmillan 'regarded the Cabinet as an instrument for him to play upon, a body to be moulded to his will ... very rarely did he fail to get his own way'.[7] He departed from traditional practice in his use of his Private Secretaries, Freddie Bishop, Tim Bligh and Philip de Zulueta, for policy advice, something which Eden had scrupulously avoided. These civil servants formed an informal 'think-tank', whose influence with the Prime Minister sometimes disconcerted ministers. As Foreign Secretary in May 1960, Lloyd was understandably irritated to find himself marginalized when Macmillan, accompanied only by Bishop and de Zulueta, made an approach to the Soviet leader, Khrushchev, during the Paris summit meeting. 'This is government by private secretary,' he complained, to which Bishop retorted: 'Well, the only alternative is government by politician.'[8]

Macmillan's easy dominance of the Cabinet was replicated in the Commons. A prominent opposition MP and diarist, Richard Crossman, testified in March 1959 to the premier's ascendancy over the Labour leader: 'I don't think there has been a single occasion on which Gaitskell has got the better of Macmillan and it has been depressing to watch how, in debate after debate, our Front Bench has been outmanoeuvred.'[9] In the country at large Macmillan's assured, patrician style went down well in the early years of his premiership. The left-wing cartoonist, Vicky, caricatured him as 'Supermac' in a bid to depict him as an ageing leader with delusions of superhero status; in fact the image rebounded to its subject's advantage. The official Downing Street spokesman, Harold Evans, wrote of Macmillan's 'instinctive feel for public relations': 'he was always completely alert to the niceties of presentation, whether in content, style or timing'.[10] This manifested itself in Macmillan's ability to come to terms with the new medium of television. In the run-up to the 1959 election, for example, he cleverly used a televized discussion with President Eisenhower, who was visiting Britain, to portray himself as an experienced world statesman.

Central to Macmillan's success was the impression he conveyed of 'unflappability'. Although belied by his diary entries, in which he privately admitted his anxieties, in public the mask could not be allowed to slip. This facet of Macmillan's personality was displayed in January 1958 when his first Chancellor, Peter Thorneycroft, and the two junior Treasury ministers, Nigel Birch and Enoch Powell, resigned in protest at Macmillan's refusal to countenance a more stringent approach to public spending. Departing for an extended overseas tour, Macmillan breezily announced that he intended to 'settle up these little local difficulties and then to turn to the wider vision of the Commonwealth'.[11] This apparently throw-away line was in fact carefully prepared and concealed his private concern that the government was in jeopardy. He feared that the resignations were part of a 'deep plot' to unseat him, confiding to his diary his suspicion that Thorneycroft intended to use another sterling crisis as the occasion for a leadership bid.[12] The one major occasion on which Macmillan appeared to give way to panic was his dismissal, in the space of 24 hours in July 1962, of seven Cabinet ministers in the so-called 'night of the long knives'. The most prominent victim was the Chancellor, Selwyn Lloyd, whose downfall was caused mainly by his inability to deliver a dynamic and politically appealing economic policy. Although a case could be made for revitalizing the government by promoting younger, more effective communicators, the episode smacked of panic in the face of adverse by-election results. This clumsy act of butchery left Macmillan open to mockery; one backbencher congratulated him because 'he had kept his head, when all about were losing theirs'.[13]

The record in government

Domestic policy

The ageing 'Supermacbeth' figure of 1962 was far removed from the assured manager of government and party who had taken over five years earlier. The most common charge against Macmillan, in his early years as Prime Minister, was that he was pre-occupied, for reasons of short-term popularity, with the selfish pursuit of prosperity. As Chancellor in 1956 he had already struck a populist note with his introduction of Premium Bonds – a move denounced at the time by puritanical critics on both left and right, but one which the general public appreciated. The phrase which is most often taken to encapsulate Macmillan's allegedly shameless materialism is his declaration, at a public meeting at Bedford in July 1957, that 'most of our people have never had it so good'. In a less frequently noted section of the speech he warned of the difficulty of maintaining full employment in an expanding economy, whilst also restraining the growth of prices: 'What is beginning to worry some of us is "Is it too good to be true?" or perhaps I should say "Is it too good to last?"'[14] Nonetheless it is the case that, partly as a legacy of his time as MP for Stockton, Macmillan feared unemployment more than inflation and he recoiled from the electoral consequences of unpopular economic measures. This helps to explain his refusal to give in to Peter Thorneycroft and his Treasury team's demands for additional savings in public expenditure, in the dispute which led to their departure from government in January 1958. The argument was not over the principle of spending reductions but over the proposed level. Backed by a majority of the Cabinet, Macmillan turned down the Treasury demands for an additional £50 million of cuts, equivalent to 1 per cent of the total budget, which would have affected sensitive areas such as family allowances. Under a new and more compliant Chancellor, Derick Heathcoat Amory, there was a marked shift towards the expansion of economic demand. The tax-cutting 1959 budget, combined with relaxed credit controls and wage increases, helped to generate a consumer boom which helped Macmillan to win the general election later that year, his majority increasing from 54 to 100 seats. The party's election slogan, 'Life's better with the Conservatives. Don't let Labour ruin it' was echoed by a newspaper cartoon showing a victorious Macmillan in a sitting room surrounded by a fridge, washing machine, television set and car, with the caption: 'Well gentlemen, I think we all fought a good fight.'[15]

The economic disadvantages of the government's expansionist approach became apparent within months of the election, as rising demand sucked in foreign imports, damaging the balance of payments position. Selwyn Lloyd, who became Chancellor in July 1960, grappled unsuccessfully with the problem of inflation unaccompanied by sustainable growth. His 'pay pause' of July 1961 and its successor, the so-called 'guiding light', represented an attempt to restrain wage increases for public sector workers. The strategy proved politically inept since it had a practical effect only on vulnerable groups such as nurses. At the same time there was a move in the direction of economic planning with the creation of the National Economic Development Council ('Neddy'), which brought together representatives of government, employers and trade unions to propose targets for production and wage levels. This was in keeping with Macmillan's pre-war advocacy of a greater measure of state intervention in the economy.

Macmillan was one of a series of postwar premiers who struggled to reconcile the main aims of economic policy: full employment, stable prices, a strong pound and expansionary growth. He likened these goals to 'four balls in one of those puzzles we had as children – you can get three into the holes and when you get the fourth in, out pops one of the others'.[16] Selwyn Lloyd's dismissal and his replacement by a more naturally expansionist Chancellor, Reginald Maudling, was intended to mark a bold re-launch of policy, designed to revive the government's deteriorating electoral fortunes. There is little evidence that the government's leading figures were lifting their eyes above the pursuit of short-term political advantage in order to tackle the fundamental problems posed by Britain's relative economic decline. Their chosen device for controlling inflation, the National Incomes Commission, was undermined by trade union hostility, and a workable incomes policy proved elusive. Maudling's 1963 budget, which cut taxes by £269 million, initiated a 'dash for growth' which encouraged another rise in imports. In his last months as Prime Minister Macmillan's fertile brain was formulating plans for floating the pound or introducing import controls, so that a pre-election boom could be engineered without causing a balance of payments crisis. It remains an open question whether this would have been enough to secure a Conservative victory in 1964, since Macmillan was no longer in office by then and his successor chose not to take up his ideas.

In other areas of national life Macmillan became a perhaps unlikely promoter of modernization. By the end of his government a unified Ministry of Defence had replaced the previous division of responsibility between three separate service departments. The introduction of life peerages in 1958 marked a first tentative step towards reform of the House of Lords, which until then had largely consisted of holders of hereditary titles. The 1963 Robbins report on higher education paved the way for a significant expansion of university places. In the field of transport, Britain took a decisive step towards what Margaret Thatcher would later call 'the great car economy' with the start of a national motorway building programme; Macmillan, himself a non-driver, opened the first stretch, the Preston bypass, in December 1958. With more questionable forethought, the government endorsed the recommendations of the 1963 Beeching report, which axed almost one-third of Britain's railway network on narrow grounds of profitability. Britain was clearly moving away from the austerity of the immediate postwar years.

Overseas policy

Macmillan's contribution to the reorientation of Britain's overseas position was no less significant. His overriding objective was to maximize Britain's international influence at a time when its declining economic strength increasingly constrained its ability to make a difference. The first requirement, following the damage done by the Suez crisis, was to rebuild relations with the US administration. In this Macmillan was outstandingly successful.

At a meeting in Bermuda only two months after he became Prime Minister, he persuaded President Eisenhower to resume the sharing of nuclear technology, a practice which had been abandoned by the USA in 1946. This was vital to the government's defence policy, as outlined in Duncan Sandys' April 1957 White Paper, the thrust of which was to reduce spending on conventional weaponry and to rely mainly on the nuclear deterrent. For Macmillan the maintenance of Britain's atomic capability was vital to the preservation of its status. To this end he used his diplomatic skill with Eisenhower's successor, John F. Kennedy, at the December 1962 Nassau meeting, to secure the Polaris missile system from the Americans. Underlying Macmillan's strategy was the conviction that without nuclear weapons 'we would be in no position to take an independent line on all the other issues in which we became involved round the world'.[17] The reality, however, was that Kennedy was persuaded, against the wishes of his defence advisers, to give Macmillan what he wanted for the sake of the latter's domestic political credibility. The ironic price of maintaining Britain's 'great power' role was its transformation into a technological client of the USA.

Macmillan devoted a great deal of energy to acting as a broker between the USA and the USSR in the Cold War. His visit to the Soviet Union in February 1959 was a bold stroke of imagination. In May 1960 he achieved his goal of a summit meeting of the superpower leaders in Paris, only to see the conference dissolve in acrimony, following a row about the shooting down of a US spy plane over the USSR. The episode cruelly demonstrated Britain's marginal status in the global rivalry of the two giants. This was further underlined by the Cuban missile crisis of October 1962, when Kennedy confronted the Soviet Union over its attempt to turn the Caribbean island into a strategic base. The President kept in contact with Macmillan by telephone during the crisis but the latter's role was essentially one of support for decisions already taken in the White House. Macmillan's influence with Kennedy did, however, produce one substantial success in the form of the Test Ban Treaty, concluded with the Soviets in July 1963 after Macmillan had overcome initial American scepticism. By securing an agreement to restrict the testing of nuclear weapons Macmillan helped to slow the growth of the Cold War arms race whilst vindicating his determination to keep Britain at the 'top table' in international diplomacy.

Macmillan also displayed his pragmatism in his decision to push ahead with the liquidation of Britain's colonial commitments in Africa, a process which gathered pace from 1959. Decolonization was already under way in West Africa by the mid-1950s but it had not thus far affected British possessions elsewhere on the continent. Here the presence of significant white settler communities made it more difficult to withdraw. Although Macmillan favoured a more measured pace than his two Colonial Secretaries, Iain Macleod (1959–61) and Reginald Maudling (1961–62), he was in no doubt of the need to accommodate the growing African nationalist movement, famously urging white populations to recognize the 'wind of change' in a speech in Cape Town in February 1960.[18] The most difficult situation was the one that confronted Britain in the three territories of Northern Rhodesia, Southern Rhodesia and Nyasaland (modern Zambia, Zimbabwe and Malawi respectively), which had been combined into the Central African Federation in 1953. The federation was presented as establishing a multi-racial partnership between the inhabitants of the region, which would prevent its assimilation into white-run South Africa. With good reason, the black population saw it primarily as a device to strengthen the privileged position of the settler community. Matters came to a head with the Devlin commission's investigation into nationalist disturbances in Nyasaland in July 1959, which likened the imperial authorities' response to that of a 'police state'. The report followed hard on the heels of the adverse publicity surrounding the mistreatment of prisoners at Hola Camp in another important colony, Kenya. The negative image that these events gave Britain in the international community was particularly damaging at a time when the French and Belgian colonial empires were unravelling. If Britain alone sought to maintain its position by force, the outcome would be bloody insurrection, the alienation of Afro-Asian opinion and isolation in the United Nations. Macmillan was also concerned, against the backdrop of the Cold War, that prolonged instability would invite Soviet involvement in central Africa. Of the turmoil that followed the collapse of Belgian authority in the Congo, he later wrote that this was 'an arena in which the rival concepts of life and politics nurtured by the Communist and the Free World were being fought out, and in which there was a growing danger that the great Powers representing these rival principles might be drawn into direct intervention and perhaps open war'.[19] These considerations made it imperative to hand over power to nationalist leaders with whom Britain could work, and who commanded broad support from the indigenous populations. It was a concern that underpinned Macmillan's thinking on the end of empire in other parts of the world. During his 1958 Commonwealth tour, for example, he noted that in Ceylon (modern Sri Lanka), which had gained its independence ten years earlier, 'the danger here (as elsewhere throughout the East) is the collapse of the agreeable, educated, Liberal, North Oxford society to whom we have transferred power, in the face of the dynamism of Communism, with all the strength of Russian imperialism behind it'.[20]

Macmillan showed a degree of skill and persistence in shedding British responsibilities, appointing R.A. Butler as a trouble-shooting minister to oversee the break-up of the Federation by the end of 1963. It was a role which earned him the enmity of the hardline settler leadership and its allies in Britain, headed by the embittered Lord Salisbury on the Conservative Party's right wing. The Prime Minister of the doomed Federation, Sir Roy Welensky, paid Macmillan a grudging tribute, describing him as 'soothing as cream and as sharp as a razor' and his mind as 'the most complicated I have encountered in my political life'.[21] By the time Macmillan left office Britain's only remaining liability in the continent was Southern Rhodesia, where an unusually determined white government was to declare independence two years later, rather than surrender power to the African majority. Elsewhere Macmillan proved much less willing to cede power, maintaining the 'east of Suez' military commitment in Singapore and Malaya, and seeking to consolidate Britain's presence in southern Arabia. Both commitments would prove unsustainable by the end of the decade. He can also be criticized for placing too much faith in the potential of the Commonwealth to replace formal empire as a vehicle for global British influence. By contrast, however, with the violence which attended the French withdrawal from Algeria, or that of Belgium from the Congo, he deserves credit for the relatively orderly manner in which his government managed the transition to African successor regimes.

The counterpart of imperial retreat was a hesitant movement towards closer links with Western Europe. Although Macmillan was more favourable than his two Conservative predecessors to the concept of greater integration with Europe, he was not at first willing to join the European Economic Community, which was established by the Treaty of Rome in March 1957. Membership of a continental bloc, which aimed to raise a common external tariff against the outside world, was not readily compatible with Britain's Commonwealth trading links. Nor was there an appetite in government for the surrender of British sovereignty to untried European institutions with supranational pretensions. In the first three years of his premiership, Macmillan sought to foster a European free trade area as a commercially successful counter-weight to the EEC. As the latter outstripped its rival as an economic force, however, it became a more attractive proposition. Macmillan was also becoming concerned that a successful EEC might replace Britain as the USA's chief ally. A report by Sir Frank Lee, head of the Treasury, in April 1960 painted a discouraging picture of Britain isolated and disadvantaged in a world dominated by three powerful blocs: the USA, the USSR and the EEC. For these reasons Macmillan announced in July 1961 that Britain would seek to join the 'Common Market', provided that satisfactory terms could be negotiated with the six founding members.

Macmillan's diaries confirm that he approached the talks with 'the Six' in response to the narrowing of options for Britain, against a background of relative economic decline. 'Shall we be caught between a hostile (or at least less and less friendly) America and a boastful, powerful "Empire of Charlemagne" – now under French but later bound to come under German control ... It's a grim choice ... '.[22] Concerns about the political difficulties of selling a European destiny to the Conservative Party, the farming community, and the powerful pro-imperial section of the press controlled by Lord Beaverbrook, also weighed with Macmillan. The need to secure special terms for Britain's food imports from the Commonwealth complicated the negotiations and perhaps confirmed suspicions on the part of the existing members that

Britain's commitment was not wholehearted. Crucially, Macmillan failed to overcome the implacable hostility of the French President, Charles de Gaulle, to British entry. With West Germany as a subordinate ally, the French leader enjoyed his role as the Community's senior statesman and feared Britain as a potential rival. As Macmillan noted in his diary, British membership would disturb Europe's character as 'a nice little club, not too big, not too small, under French hegemony'. He also commented that de Gaulle 'thinks that, apart from our loyalty to the Commonwealth, we shall always be too intimately tied up with the Americans'.[23] When Macmillan negotiated independently with Kennedy to obtain Polaris, he inadvertently underlined the perception that Britain would always put the Atlantic alliance before its European links. This provided de Gaulle with the necessary pretext to veto Britain's application in January 1963, a decision which wrecked Macmillan's strategy for reviving British economic fortunes and giving the country a new international role. It was to take another decade before Britain gained entry to Europe. The Prime Minister who finally overcame French resistance was Edward Heath, who had conducted the ill-fated first negotiations as a member of Macmillan's government.

Decline and fall

The failure of Macmillan's European bid was a blow to a premiership which was already weakening under the impact of a series of adverse events. It was unfortunate for Macmillan that the early 1960s saw the growth of an aggressive brand of 'anti-establishment' satire, typified by the television show *That Was the Week That Was* and the magazine *Private Eye*, which exploited his difficulties and portrayed him as doddery and out of date. Another challenge for the 69-year-old premier was the Labour Party's election of a new leader in February 1963, Harold Wilson, whose hallmark was a self-conscious appeal to modernity. Richard Crossman noted the reversal of fortune in his diary: 'as long as he has Macmillan opposite him, old, effete, worn out, a cynical dilettante, the contrast between Harold [Wilson]'s character and Macmillan's is an overwhelming advantage to Harold and the Labour Party'.[24] The point was highlighted by the Prime

Minister's uncertain response to two serious scandals. The first was the imprisonment in October 1962 of an Admiralty clerk, John Vassall, for passing secrets to the Soviet Union. More sustained media and parliamentary interest was aroused by the events which culminated in the resignation of the War Minister, John Profumo, in June 1963. Profumo's admission that he had lied to the Commons about his relationship with a call-girl, Christine Keeler, who had also extended her favours to a Soviet naval attaché, led to an intense if rather spurious debate about issues of national security and the morals of the ruling class. Macmillan himself appeared to have lost control of events. His public transformation, from experienced statesman to failing representative of a decadent elite, was an object lesson in the power of image in modern politics.

It was, however, Macmillan's health which brought his premiership to an end. After dithering for several months over whether he should continue in office, the sudden onset of prostate trouble, on the eve of the Conservative Party conference in October 1963, forced a decision. It has been claimed that Macmillan concluded at the time that his condition was malignant and that when he later discovered that it was less serious, he regretted his unnecessary resignation. The testimony of the medical consultant, however, demonstrates that this was not the case. Instead the unexpected illness, which Macmillan saw as an 'act of God', provided him with an opportunity to resign gracefully, rather than being forced out by political pressure. In this way Macmillan's prolonged indecision over his future was resolved. From his hospital bed, he orchestrated a consultation of senior party figures which, in the absence of a formal leadership election procedure, produced as his successor an authentic representative of the party's old-fashioned 'grouse moor' element, the aristocratic Foreign Secretary, Lord Home. This was a more formal and elaborate version of the process which had followed Eden's decision to resign in January 1957. A crucial difference was that the latter had made no recommendation as to his successor. Macmillan's critics, such as Iain Macleod, argued that he had colluded with a 'magic circle' of Tory grandees to block the succession of his deputy, Butler. This interpretation ignores the widespread misgivings within the party over Butler's fitness to lead and over the capacity of other candidates, notably the flamboyant Lord Hailsham, who was Macmillan's first preference. Home was the second choice of a surprising number of senior Conservatives and as such earned the outgoing premier's endorsement as the person best equipped to unite the party.

Conclusion

Macmillan's legacy has been reassessed more than once since his departure from office. By the time of his death in December 1986, at the age of 92, he was widely seen as a premier who had ducked the hard choices posed by Britain's relative economic decline. In the Thatcher era he was condemned for having failed to curb the twin challenges of rising inflation and over-mighty trade unions, with which his successors were then grappling. When, in extreme old age, he criticized their privatization of public utilities as a policy of 'selling the family silver', he was attacked for trying to revive the discredited expansionist economic thinking of the postwar consensus era. The phrase did, however, cause damage by depicting the government as a set of unscrupulous asset-strippers. More recently, however, Macmillan has experienced a partial rehabilitation in Conservative circles. It is significant that David Cameron, who became party leader in December 2005, is known to keep a photograph of his fellow Old Etonian predecessor in his office.

This may indicate a renewed appreciation of the virtues of flexibility and pragmatism, which Macmillan so triumphantly exhibited. He used his talents as a showman to revive his party's morale and keep it united, leading it in directions which it would not have been expected to take. James Margach, a leading commentator, wrote that 'his skill lay in the fact that he appeared to be charting to the Right whilst in reality he was steering hard to the Left'.[25] By managing the retreat from empire, and using his close relationship with the USA to the full on the world stage, Macmillan enabled Britain to punch above its weight in the international arena. If this was in large part an illusion, the great political impresario would perhaps have been content. More than most Prime Ministers, he understood that appearance may be no less important than reality in making the most of a country's diminishing room for manoeuvre.

Notes

1 Alistair Horne, *Macmillan 1957–1986*, London: Macmillan, 1989, p. 154.
2 Robert Rhodes James, *Anthony Eden*, London: Weidenfeld and Nicolson, 1986, p. 617.
3 Anthony Howard, *RAB: The Life of R.A. Butler*, London: Jonathan Cape, 1987, p. 241.
4 Lord Kilmuir, *Political Adventure*, London: Weidenfeld and Nicolson, p. 288.
5 Malcolm Muggeridge, *Like it Was: A Selection from the Diaries of Malcolm Muggeridge*, London: Collins, 1981, p. 479, entry for 8 April 1957.
6 Lord Hill of Luton, *Both Sides of the Hill: The Memoirs of Charles Hill*, London: Heinemann, 1964, p. 235.
7 D.R. Thorpe, *Selwyn Lloyd,* London: Jonathan Cape, 1989, p. 279.
8 Ibid., p. 304.
9 Janet Morgan (ed.), *The Backbench Diaries of Richard Crossman*, London: Hamish Hamilton and Jonathan Cape, 1981, p. 742, entry for 19 March 1959.
10 Harold Evans, *Downing Street Diary: The Macmillan Years 1957–1963*, London: Hodder and Stoughton, 1981, p.27.
11 Harold Macmillan, *Riding the Storm 1956–1959*, London: Macmillan, 1971, p. 373.
12 Peter Catterall (ed.), *The Macmillan Diaries Vol. II: Prime Minister and After 1957–1966*, London: Macmillan, 2011, p. 94, entry for 31 January 1958.
13 Douglas Jay, *Change and Fortune: A Political Record*, London: Hutchinson, 1980, p. 291.
14 Harold Macmillan, *Riding the Storm*, p. 350.
15 *The Spectator,* 16 October 1959.
16 Kevin Jefferys, *Retreat from New Jerusalem: British Politics, 1951–64*, London: Macmillan, 1997, pp. 93–4.
17 Harold Evans, *Downing Street Diary*, p. 239.
18 D.R. Thorpe, *Supermac: The Life of Harold Macmillan*, London: Chatto and Windus, 2010, p. 457.
19 Harold Macmillan, *Pointing the Way, 1959–1961*, London: Macmillan, 1972, p. 435.
20 Peter Catterall (ed.), *The Macmillan Diaries Vol. II*, pp. 91–2, entry for 19 January 1958.
21 Roy Welensky, *4000 Days: The Life and Death of the Federation of Rhodesia and Nyasaland*, London: Collins, 1964, pp. 144, 361.

22 Peter Catterall (ed.), *The Macmillan Diaries Vol. II*, p. 313, entry for 9 July 1960. Macmillan compares modern French domination of the EEC to the power of the medieval ruler, Charlemagne, who established the Holy Roman Empire in the heart of Europe.

23 Ibid., p. 475, entry for 3 June 1962.

24 Janet Morgan (ed.), *The Backbench Diaries of Richard Crossman*, p. 1005, entry for 22 June 1963.

25 James Margach, *The Abuse of Power: The War Between Downing Street and the Media from Lloyd George to Callaghan*, London: W.H. Allen, 1978, p. 116.

Further reading

Peter Catterall (ed.), *The Macmillan Diaries Vol. II: Prime Minister and After 1957–1966*, London: Macmillan, 2011

Alistair Horne, *Macmillan*, 2 vols, London: Macmillan, 1988–89

Richard Lamb, *The Macmillan Years, 1957–1963: The Emerging Truth*, London: John Murray, 1995

Harold Macmillan, *Riding the Storm, 1956–1959*, London: Macmillan, 1971; *Pointing the Way, 1959–1961*, London: Macmillan, 1972; *At the End of the Day, 1961–1963*, London: Macmillan, 1973

D.R. Thorpe, *Supermac: The Life of Harold Macmillan*, London: Chatto and Windus, 2010

John Turner, *Macmillan*, London: Longman, 1994

13 Alec Douglas-Home (1903–95)

Prime Minister: October 1963–October 1964

> 'Lord Home is clearly a man who represents the old, governing class at its best ... He is not ambitious in the sense of wanting to scheme for power, although not foolish enough to resist honour when it comes to him.'
>
> Harold Macmillan, memorandum on his successor, 15 October 1963.[1]

With the solitary exception of Arthur Balfour, Sir Alec Douglas-Home was the only twentieth-century Prime Minister to occupy a more junior Cabinet post after leaving Number 10. He served as Foreign Secretary in 1970–74 under Edward Heath, who had once been a member of his own Cabinet. Heath later recalled inviting Douglas-Home to attend the funeral of the former French President, Charles de Gaulle, along with Anthony Eden, Harold Macmillan and Harold Wilson. '"Oh, I don't think so, thank you," he replied. "With all those former Prime Ministers you won't need your Foreign Secretary." "But you are a former Prime Minister yourself, you know," I reminded him. He laughed, almost giggled, as he said: "Oh, so I am. I'd quite forgotten."'[2] Although there is no need to take Douglas-Home's apparent memory lapse seriously, the story illustrates his essential modesty and charm. It also hints at the brevity of his premiership – just two days short of a year – and the unexpected nature of his elevation to the highest office. He was the most surprising post-war occupant of Downing Street: an aristocrat who, according to the discontented former minister, Iain Macleod, reached Number 10 as the result of shadowy manipulation by a tightly knit 'magic circle' of Old Etonian Tory grandees. Widely derided as out of touch with the modern world, Douglas-Home's overriding concern was with preparations for the 1964 general election, in which he was narrowly defeated by Harold Wilson's Labour Party.

The rise to the premiership

Douglas-Home was the heir to substantial estates in the Scottish border country. The son of the thirteenth Earl of Home, he held the courtesy title of Lord Dunglass until his father's death in July 1951. Under the rules of the time he was then compelled to give up his seat in the Commons in order to assume his father's place in the House of Lords. His aristocratic connections had earlier helped to advance his career, by bringing him into contact with a series of influential figures in the Conservative Party hierarchy. First elected to Parliament in October 1931, the young Dunglass was chosen by Neville Chamberlain as his parliamentary private secretary, the lowest rung on the ministerial ladder. In this capacity he was present at the negotiation of the Munich agreement with Hitler in September 1938. The patronage of the senior Scottish Conservative MP, James Stuart, brought him a junior post in the Scottish Office in Churchill's postwar government. Entry to the Cabinet as Commonwealth Secretary followed in April 1955. In this role Home acquired a reputation as a safe pair of hands, earning promotion five years later to the Foreign Office.

It seems unlikely that Home would have climbed higher than this without the accident of Harold Macmillan's sudden illness and decision to resign the premiership in October 1963, which threw the Conservative Party into turmoil on the eve of its annual conference. Although a recent change in the law made it possible for a hereditary peer to disclaim his title and stand for election to the Commons, Home does not appear to have considered this option until persuaded by others to put his name forward for the succession. Little known at the time outside Westminster, he benefited from a combination of luck and the personality flaws of the more obvious contenders. As president of the National Union, the organization responsible for running the party conference, it fell to him to announce Macmillan's resignation, which put him centre stage at a crucial moment. Lord Hailsham, who was the outgoing Prime Minister's initial first choice, spoiled his chances by a too obvious display of ambition. Macmillan's deputy, R.A. Butler, the best qualified on grounds of experience, was unacceptable to many Conservative MPs. Long mistrusted by right-wingers for his progressive policy track record, his subtle intelligence and penchant for detached irony came across as a fatal lack of decisiveness.

The way in which soundings of Conservative Party opinion were taken also favoured Home's appointment. In the absence of a formal procedure for electing a leader, Macmillan authorized various senior figures to canvass the views of ministers, MPs, peers and constituency organizations, on the basis of which he recommended a name to the Queen. This consultation process gave undue weight to second preferences, enabling Home to come through as the compromise candidate who was best placed to unite the party. Once Home had been invited to try to form a government, it was up to a handful of key figures to decide whether they were willing to serve under him. Although he commanded the support of a number of Cabinet colleagues, Butler was not prepared to cause a party split by refusing office for reasons of personal ambition. Meanwhile the willingness of a recently adopted candidate to stand aside in the safe Conservative seat of Kinross and West Perthshire enabled the Prime Minister, who was now to be known as Sir Alec Douglas-Home, to move smoothly from the Lords to the Commons.

The record in government

Douglas-Home was not an innovator by nature, even if he had been permitted to stay long enough in Downing Street to make a permanent mark on the machinery of government. He was, however, noted for the cool dispatch with which he chaired Cabinet meetings. He rationalized the mushrooming number of Cabinet committees and formalized arrangements for the Leader of the Opposition to hold talks with senior civil servants in the run-up to a general election, thus facilitating a more orderly transfer of power. Burke Trend, who served four Prime Ministers as Cabinet Secretary from 1963–73, considered Douglas-Home the most orderly and efficient in his transaction of government business. All those who came into contact with him were struck by his integrity and lack of interest in what nowadays would be called 'spin'.

These virtues were, however, of limited utility in an increasingly abrasive, media-driven political environment. After 12 years in the more genteel world of the upper house, Douglas-Home seemed ill at ease with the partisan cut and thrust of the Commons, where Harold Wilson as Leader of the Opposition enjoyed a clear ascendancy. Apart from his time as a junior Scottish Office minister a decade earlier, Douglas-Home's governmental experience had been restricted to overseas affairs. In his memoirs he expressed regret that 'by reason of the fact that I never dreamed of holding the position [of Prime Minister], I had taken no particular steps to prepare myself for it. Had I done so I would have soaked myself more thoroughly in domestic issues, rather than specialising so completely in the foreign field'.[3] Yet ironically he did not distinguish himself in the policy area in which he claimed expertise. The only overseas success was Britain's contribution to the United Nations peace-keeping force sent in March 1964 to contain the civil war which had broken out in Cyprus between the Greek and Turkish communities. After the assassination of John F. Kennedy in November 1963 Douglas-Home struggled to develop a harmonious relationship with the new US President, Lyndon Johnson, who condemned Britain's willingness to continue trading with Communist Cuba.

More serious was Douglas-Home's unfamiliarity with economic issues, highlighted in an interview in which he admitted to doing sums with matchsticks. This left him dependent on the judgement of his Chancellor, Reginald Maudling, who had presided over increases in public spending in the final months of the Macmillan government, inadvertently encouraging an inflow of imports. This necessitated the introduction of a mildly deflationary, tax-raising budget in April 1964. Sluggish export growth, combined with failure to agree an incomes policy with the trade unions, made the Chancellor vulnerable to opposition attack. By the autumn it was evident that the government would bequeath a major balance of payments problem to its successor.

The only major domestic policy initiative of Douglas-Home's premiership was the abolition of resale price maintenance, which had allowed manufacturers to fix the prices of goods in shops. The removal of this system was the work of the dynamic President of the Board of Trade, Edward Heath, who saw it as a symbol of the government's commitment to ending inefficient restrictive practices and widening consumer choice. The move provoked a major rebellion within the parliamentary Conservative Party since many MPs were responsive to the interests of small shopkeepers, who feared abolition as a threat to their livelihoods. Douglas-Home's support for Heath within the Cabinet was crucial to the passage of the measure. The political consequences of abolition are unclear. The historians of the 1964 election considered that it had no impact on the outcome[4] but Douglas-Home later cited it as one of several factors which might have contributed to the Conservative defeat.[5] An unrepentant Heath, on the other hand, argued that had other government departments emulated his modernizing zeal, the party might have won.[6]

The closeness of the 1964 result – Labour secured a bare majority of four seats – necessarily overshadows any evaluation of Douglas-Home's premiership. His defenders point to his success in turning around the unfavourable situation that he inherited, with Labour's lead over the Conservatives in the opinion polls cut from 11 to 5 percentage points in the 12 months from October 1963. They also argue that he was simply unlucky: had news of the downfall of the Soviet leader, Khrushchev, or of China's decision to test an atomic bomb arrived earlier, voters might have decided to stick with Douglas-Home, the experienced statesman who emphasized the importance of the British nuclear deterrent.

To make the case against Douglas-Home's leadership it is not necessary to agree with his disappointed rivals within the Conservative Party, such as Lord Hailsham, who asserted in his memoirs that either he or Butler could have won the election.[7] Undoubtedly Douglas-Home was at a disadvantage in a contest dominated by the relatively new medium of television. In a bid to counter the charge that he was remote from ordinary people, he undertook an arduous cross-country tour, addressing numerous gatherings, rather than trying to master the potential of television as Wilson had so triumphantly done. Another problem was the filming of Douglas-Home's encounters with aggressive heckling, the worst instance of which was in Birmingham. 'Who exhumed you?' read one banner on which the cameras lingered. The victim later acknowledged the damage done by these images: 'I looked rather hunted and that had a bad effect. I blame myself for not studying the techniques of television more than I did.'[8]

Douglas-Home performed as well as might have been expected in the circumstances. After 13 years of Conservative rule it was natural that desire for change would play a part in the election. Any Tory leader who took over at that point, with economic difficulties tarnishing the party's association with popular affluence, would have struggled against Labour's beguiling message of modernization. Douglas-Home's was an honourable failure but it was one which the party would strive not to repeat. It was fitting that, shortly before his resignation as Leader of the Opposition in July 1965, he devised the rules under which his successor would be elected by a ballot of Conservative MPs. In this way Douglas-Home ensured that there would be no repetition of the way in which he had been chosen as leader. It was not the least of the services that he performed for his party and country.

Notes

1 D.R. Thorpe, *Alec Douglas-Home*, London: Sinclair-Stevenson, 1996, p. 301.
2 Edward Heath, *The Course of My Life: My Autobiography*, London: Hodder and Stoughton, 1998, p. 468.
3 Lord Home, *The Way the Wind Blows: An Autobiography*, London: Collins, 1976, p. 216.
4 David Butler and Anthony King, *The British General Election of 1964*, London: Macmillan, 1965, p. 23.
5 Lord Home, *The Way the Wind Blows*, p. 215.
6 Edward Heath, *The Course of My Life*, p. 267.
7 Lord Hailsham, *A Sparrow's Flight: Memoirs*, London: Collins, 1990, p. 358.
8 Michael Cockerell, *Live from Number Ten: The Inside Story of Prime Ministers and Television*, London: Faber and Faber, 1988, p. 107.

Further reading

Lord Home, *The Way the Wind Blows*, London: Collins, 1976
D.R. Thorpe, *Alec Douglas-Home*, London: Sinclair-Stevenson, 1996
Kenneth Young, *Sir Alec Douglas-Home*, London: Dent, 1970

14 Harold Wilson (1916–1995)

Prime Minister: October 1964–June 1970; March 1974–April 1976

'I am accused of being a tactician ... But the truth is I think very long term indeed. Nobody knows what my current long-term strategic thought is.'

> Harold Wilson in conversation with the journalist
> Hugo Young, 26 November 1975.[1]

Few Prime Ministers have experienced so rapid or complete a fall in reputation as Harold Wilson. Attaining the highest office for the first time in 1964, for a relatively short period he was widely taken at his own evaluation, as a dynamic, modernizing force, who would equip Britain for the challenges of a new era. By contrast with his privileged Conservative predecessors in Number 10, Wilson came across as a classless, meritocratic individual who had risen to power through his own abilities: a breath of fresh air after the so-called 'thirteen wasted years' of Tory rule. By winning a total of four general elections, Wilson set a record unequalled by any other twentieth-century premier. He was the only Prime Minister of the century, apart from Stanley Baldwin, to retire at a time of his own choosing rather than being forced from office by electoral defeat, party rebellion or ill health.

On closer examination, however, Wilson's achievements appear less impressive. He rarely possessed a secure parliamentary majority. In the October 1964 general election Wilson replaced the lacklustre Alec Douglas-Home by a bare margin of four seats. Although he increased this to an impressive majority of 97 in March 1966, he lost to Edward Heath in June 1970. When he returned to Number 10 in March 1974, it was as the head of a minority government; the following October he scraped a wafer-thin majority of three seats. Not surprisingly, therefore, Wilson had little opportunity to implement a programme which might have established him as a great reforming Prime Minister. Even had the political circumstances been more favourable, however, his critics doubt that Wilson would have bequeathed a more substantial legacy. Although often commended for his effectiveness as a party manager and a communicator, he has also been accused of thinking in an exclusively short-term, self-interested manner, with his famous statement that 'a week is a long time in politics'.[2] Bernard Donoughue, who created the Downing Street Policy Unit for Wilson in his 1974–76 administration, regarded him as much shallower than his successor, James Callaghan, for whom he also worked. According to Donoughue, Wilson's personality possessed just two layers: on the surface, 'Tricky Harold, the clever and devious political manipulator' and beneath that merely 'a kindly, weak and insecure man'.[3] Even the publication of two scholarly biographies, by Philip Ziegler and Ben Pimlott, has not succeeded in rescuing Wilson's popular reputation.

The rise to the premiership

In terms of his social background the postwar premiers whom Wilson most closely resembled were his Conservative rivals, Edward Heath and Margaret Thatcher. Born into a lower-middle-class Yorkshire family, he won a scholarship to grammar school and then progressed to Oxford University. Politically Wilson was not attracted by the well-to-do Marxist intellectuals who typified university Labour politics in the 1930s, finding the Liberal club more congenial. His allegiance to socialism was based upon an ill-defined but deeply felt ethical sense, rather than a doctrinaire ideological commitment. His family's experience of the interwar slump, in which his industrial chemist father lost his job, helped to move him emotionally towards the left. At Oxford, however, academic achievement was his main priority. After gaining a first class degree in Politics, Philosophy and Economics, a research appointment at University College drew him into the orbit of Sir William Beveridge, author of the celebrated wartime report on welfare services. Wilson's credentials as an economist drew him into specialized work in wartime Whitehall, where he worked in the Ministry of Fuel and Power before being appointed as secretary of an inquiry into the coal mining industry. The resulting study of coal nationalization confirmed Wilson's attachment to Labour. It also helped in his selection to fight the safe Lancashire seat of Ormskirk at the 1945 general election. He was to remain as the town's MP until 1950, when a redistribution of seats led him to relocate to nearby Huyton on Merseyside, which he held for the rest of his political career.

Wilson was untypical of his political generation in a number of ways. Unlike many of his contemporaries, such as James Callaghan, Roy Jenkins and Denis Healey, all of whom were to hold senior posts in Wilson's Cabinets, he had no experience of the armed services. More completely than Jenkins or Healey, he masked his credentials as an academic with a reassuring, ordinary image. He retained his homely Northern manner of speech and social habits, famously declaring that 'if I had the choice between smoked salmon and tinned salmon, I'd have it tinned. With vinegar'.[4] He was unusual in the rapidity of his promotion at Westminster, being given junior office on the formation of the Attlee government. In October 1947 he became the youngest member of the Cabinet at the age of 31, when he was appointed President of the Board of Trade. Over the next three years he gained a reputation as a competent minister, identified with no particular faction in the Labour Party. His well-publicized removal of wartime restrictions on a range of consumer goods – the so-called 'bonfire of controls' in November 1948 – led some to detect an early sign of his lukewarm commitment to socialism. The left-wing MP Ian Mikardo, for example, described him as 'a man looking for popularity; and a pragmatist looking for popularity is going to let you down in the end, isn't he?'[5] Wilson's reputation as a man of the left was based largely upon his resignation, along with Aneurin Bevan, in April 1951. He seems to have felt deeply about the government's commitment to fund rearmament for the Korean War, the price of which was the imposition of NHS charges. Yet committed members of the party's left continued to have reservations about Wilson's sincerity, which were confirmed when he took Bevan's place in the

shadow cabinet three years later. In 1960 he revived his association with the left by unsuccessfully challenging the party's right-
wing leader, Hugh Gaitskell, after the latter had been defeated at
the Labour conference by supporters of nuclear disarmament.

The episode earned Wilson the lasting enmity of the Labour
right, who venerated Gaitskell as a man of principle as well as
an enormously talented Prime Minister in waiting. The latter's
sudden death in January 1963 gave Wilson the opportunity for
a second, successful attempt at the leadership. To some extent he
was lucky in his opponents. The official candidate of the right,
the deputy leader, George Brown, was widely regarded as brilliant
but erratic, his judgement compromised by heavy drinking.
Callaghan's intervention in the contest helped to split the centre-
right vote. With the support of former adherents of Bevan, who
had died in 1960, Wilson was able to emerge as the unexpected
victor. Yet he was far from secure in a parliamentary party whose
upper echelons were still dominated by MPs who deeply regretted
Gaitskell's premature passing. In order to maintain party unity
the right, headed by the two defeated leadership candidates,
had to be conciliated with key posts. Bevanites such as Richard
Crossman and Barbara Castle, who had supported Wilson's candidature, were allocated subordinate roles.

In one important respect, however, circumstances favoured
Wilson's prospects. His election to the leadership coincided with
the beginning of the Conservative government's visible decline.
Harold Macmillan, from whose political flexibility Wilson had
learned a great deal, was past his best. His aristocratic successor,
Sir Alec Douglas-Home, appeared remote from everyday issues
and ignorant of economics. Wilson clearly out-performed him
in the House of Commons and was much more at ease with the
relatively new medium of television. The contrast between the
Labour leader and his out-of-touch opponent was highlighted
by Wilson's decision to place the notion of state-directed modernization at the heart of his preparation for the forthcoming general
election. In his address to Labour's Scarborough conference in
October 1963, Wilson identified the party with technological
progress, energetic central planning and the sweeping away of
outdated class distinctions: 'the Britain that is going to be forged
in the white heat of this revolution will be no place for restrictive

practices or for outdated methods on either side of industry'.[6] The speech struck a chord with many, both in the Labour Party and beyond, who were impatient with the outdated 'grouse-moor' image of the Conservative leadership. It also enabled Wilson to re-focus his party on the pursuit of victory. The theme of dynamic change, at once inspiring and imprecise, was sustained throughout the election campaign, enthusing Labour supporters and drawing left and right away from the factional struggles which had kept the party in opposition in the preceding decade. It was not enough, however, to counter the effects of a pre-election consumer boom, stimulated by the outgoing government's final, tax-cutting budget, which helped to deny Labour a decisive majority in October 1964. Nonetheless the Conservatives' ejection from office was a significant achievement, for which Wilson deserves a considerable share of the credit.

Governing style

The rhetoric of 1964 encouraged a widespread sense that Wilson's election would herald a new beginning. The new Prime Minister spoke of turning Number 10 into a policy-making 'powerhouse'. Self-consciously modelling himself on the glamorous former US President Kennedy, he promised a 'first hundred days' of dynamic action. In his first government he was an active Prime Minister, reluctant to delegate and liable to intervene in various policy areas. This reflected Wilson's awareness of his colleagues' lack of governmental experience. Only two, the Foreign Secretary, Patrick Gordon Walker, and the Welsh Secretary, James Griffiths, had served in the Attlee Cabinet, and few ministers had held even junior rank before 1964. Increasingly, however, colleagues accused him of failing to give a firm lead. Denis Healey, who served as Defence Secretary in 1964–70 and Chancellor of the Exchequer in 1974–79, later described him as 'curiously reluctant to lay down the law in Cabinet', suspicious of conspiracies and conducting frequent reshuffles in order to prevent the growth of power-bases, from which ambitious rivals might mount a challenge.[7]

A closer examination of Wilson's premierships, however, suggests that his style of management varied over time and according to the particular circumstances in which the government found itself. Decisions on sensitive issues, such as that to continue the previous Conservative government's building of the Polaris nuclear force, in defiance of the 1964 Labour manifesto, were often taken in small groups of reliable ministers rather than in full Cabinet. In chairing Cabinets in the early years, Wilson tended to sum up the general view of the meeting, frequently giving greater weight to the ministers whose views accorded with his own preferences. Shirley Williams, who served as Prices and Consumer Affairs Secretary in 1974–76, recalled his management of the Cabinet as 'low-key' but 'masterly': 'I once challenged his conclusion, busily counting heads myself. The Prime Minister abruptly reminded me that summing up was his prerogative.'[8] Under pressure, however, when it became vital to maintain unity, he paid closer attention to the exact number of votes for or against a course of action. A good example is the controversial decision in January 1968 to accelerate Britain's military withdrawal from its bases in Singapore and Malaysia, an episode which saw Wilson execute a U-turn in Cabinet. Wilson switched his support from the powerful 'junta' of right-wing ministers who continued to defend the 'east of Suez' position, headed by Brown and Healey, mobilizing a combination of left-wingers and the uncommitted to get the new policy through Cabinet. In his diary Richard Crossman registered the new balance of power as Wilson moved from 'Prime Ministerial government' to 'Cabinet government': 'when I asked Harold the other day why he is now regularly counting votes he said that if he didn't insist on doing so his position would be challenged by the junta ... Six months ago he could take the voices and interpret the voices as he liked.'[9]

Undoubtedly a great deal of Wilson's energy was absorbed by the need to neutralize potential threats to his position. Thus on taking office in 1964, he played his two most dangerous rivals off against each other by giving them control of departments with overlapping responsibilities. Callaghan was appointed Chancellor of the Exchequer whilst Brown headed a new ministry with a brief to drive forward economic growth, the Department of Economic Affairs. After Callaghan was moved from the Treasury to the Home Office in November 1967, Wilson replaced him with the rising star of the Labour right, Roy Jenkins, with whom he forged an effective partnership in the last two years of the government. As his difficulties mounted, the Prime Minister created an inner group of advisers, the so-called Parliamentary Committee, whose purpose was to shore up his position rather than to act as a vehicle for strategic policy planning. By the time of his return to office in March 1974 Wilson was more tired and also more relaxed in his dealings with colleagues. With a more experienced team, using an analogy from soccer, he no longer felt the need to occupy almost every position on the field but would now play the part of a 'deep-lying centre half, not scoring all the goals'.[10] As in 1964–70, Wilson continued to maintain the balance between left and right within the government, on which party unity depended. Thus Jenkins' leadership ambitions were deliberately hampered by Wilson's decision to deny him a second term at the Treasury, whilst the rising champion of the hard left, Tony Benn, was frustrated by a move from Industry to the less influential Energy Department in June 1975.

Wilson's long-term impact on the machinery of government was limited. His first government witnessed the creation of a number of new Whitehall departments: not only the Department of Economic Affairs but also Ministries of Land and Natural Resources, Technology and Overseas Development, and the Welsh Office. Only the last two survived beyond 1970 and the Ministry of Overseas Development did not carry Cabinet rank after the departure of its first head, Barbara Castle, at the end of 1965. The number of Downing Street staff was increased and the influence of the civil service was balanced by the introduction of advisers whose loyalty was to the Labour Party. Yet it was not until Wilson's 1974–76 administration that he introduced an enduring governmental innovation, the Downing Street Policy Unit. Its purpose was to provide the Prime Minister with an independent source of advice and to co-ordinate initiatives which cut across Whitehall departments. It proved useful in several areas, for example in developing the government's incomes policy in 1975, but not all its radical ideas were realized. The opposition of the Environment Secretary, Tony Crosland, for example, led to the shelving of the unit's proposals for the sale of council houses to tenants.

Greater public interest was aroused by a more ephemeral feature of Wilson's premierships, his cultivation of an informal group of cronies popularly known as the 'kitchen cabinet'. This was a collection of intimate associates, some drawn from the left of the party, in whose company Wilson indulged his liking for political intrigue and gossip. The composition of the group changed constantly; in Wilson's first administration it included his economic adviser, Thomas Balogh, and several middle-ranking ministers including Richard Crossman and the Paymaster-General, George Wigg, who acted as the Prime Minister's adviser on security matters. The most important member was Wilson's 'Personal and Political Secretary', Marcia Williams, who had worked for him since 1956. Her closeness to Wilson and abiding influence on him invited gossip regarding the nature of their relationship; in 1974 he took the unusual step of elevating her to the Lords as Baroness Falkender. She acted as a link between Wilson and the party machine and controlled access to him. In his final administration she seems to have been engaged in an unending series of struggles on minor matters with other Downing Street officials. Bernard Donoughue's diaries portray Wilson as distracted and drained by the constant need to pacify his mercurial assistant. Writing in June 1974, he described Wilson as reduced to a 'tragic and pathetic dependence' on her: 'she drags him down, diverts his mind on to the paranoid trivia which obsess her'.[11] In terms of influence over policy-making, however, it is hard to discern any tangible contribution by Marcia Williams or other members of the 'kitchen cabinet'.

The record in government

Domestic policy

An important reason for the disappointing performance of the Wilson governments was the unenviable economic inheritance with which they had to grapple in both 1964 and 1974. On taking office for the first time Wilson found that his Conservative predecessors had allowed imports to exceed exports, producing a massive balance of payments deficit of £800 million. The new government's economic policies were to be overshadowed by the vulnerability of the pound on the money markets. The rate at which it exchanged with other currencies became a constant preoccupation. Devaluation, which might have restored the competitiveness of British exports, was ruled out, even after a major sterling crisis in July 1966. Wilson's success in keeping discussion of the devaluation option off the Cabinet agenda testifies to his dominance in his first years as Prime Minister. He believed that the defence of sterling was essential for a variety of reasons, even though it forced the government to implement a policy of deflation – a combination of tax increases and public spending cuts which was particularly unpopular with Labour supporters. A veteran of the Attlee government's 1949 decision to devalue, Wilson was convinced that a further reduction in the value of the pound would be disastrous for Labour's electoral fortunes and for national prestige. As a strong supporter of the Atlantic alliance, he wanted to avoid a course of action which the USA feared would adversely affect its own trade. Eventually the government was forced into devaluation in November 1967. Further spending cuts failed to reassure the markets until the new Chancellor, Roy Jenkins, announced the biggest single set of tax increases since the Second World War in his March 1968 budget. Gradually the balance of payments came back into surplus, although an inflation rate of 5.4 per cent on the eve of the 1970 general election weakened Labour's position. The main political casualty of devaluation was the Prime Minister himself. His mistake was his attempt to rationalize the U-turn with a broadcast in which he proclaimed that 'from now on the pound abroad is worth 14 per cent less in terms of other currencies. This does not mean the pound here in Britain in your pocket or purse or bank has been devalued'. His attempt to present devaluation as a positive outcome seemed unconvincing. From the spring of 1968 dated the cruel joke in a television comedy programme, 'What's the piece of body language to look for to tell if he [Wilson]'s lying?' 'When you see his lips move.'[12]

The hopes of Labour supporters were disappointed by the Wilson government's inability to deliver centrally planned economic growth. The intended creative tension between the newly-created Department of Economic Affairs and the well-established Treasury failed to produce concrete results. Moreover the government never created the administrative machinery or, arguably, possessed the political will to implement its much vaunted National Plan. The average annual growth rate for 1964–70 fell well short of the projected 3.8 per cent and was actually lower than that achieved by the Conservatives in 1951–64. Expansion consistently took a lower priority than the government's attempts to control wage inflation. Although something was done to promote regional development outside the prosperous South East, the government joined a series of postwar administrations in its failure to tackle the underlying problems of British industry: low productivity, an insufficiently trained workforce, weak management and the financial sector's reluctance to invest in manufacturing.

Ironically, for a Prime Minister often seen as the embodiment of principle-free compromise, Wilson's greatest domestic failure occurred in the one area where he attempted to make a decisive stand, that of trade union reform. Frustrated by the unions' failure to co-operate with the government's efforts to induce wage restraint, and by the impact on production of unofficial 'wildcat' strikes, Wilson and his Employment Secretary, Barbara Castle, brought forward a radical set of proposals in the 1969 White Paper, *In Place of Strife*. The document's recommendations for legal sanctions were deeply unpopular within the Labour Party. The Secretary of State was to be empowered to order a 28-day 'conciliation pause' before a strike could be held and to direct unions to ballot their members before industrial action. A Cabinet rebellion, led by the Home Secretary, Callaghan and supported by a significant section of the party, resisted any attempt to regulate the status of the unions. Wilson and Castle were obliged to abandon the White Paper in favour of a meaningless 'solemn and binding' undertaking, whereby unions promised to follow the TUC's guidelines on regulating unofficial stoppages of work. It was a humiliating climb-down which contributed to Labour's electoral defeat the following year. With an uncharacteristic loss of his political touch, Wilson had failed to prepare the ground and had left it too late in the Parliament to launch such a controversial initiative. Nonetheless, with hindsight, some commentators praised *In Place of Strife* as a last chance to avert the more far-reaching and divisive measures imposed on the union movement by the Conservative governments of the 1980s. The experienced political journalist Geoffrey Goodman, for example, argued that the White Paper 'did contain the ingredients of a programme that, if it had been possible for it to succeed, then not only would the 1970 election result have been different, but we would not have had Thatcherism'.[13]

Perhaps the most significant achievements of the 1964–70 governments lay in the field of social reform. The period saw some modest improvements in the welfare state, even if the spending cuts of the late 1960s compelled the abandonment of some cherished party goals, such as the raising of the school leaving age to 16. More significant, however, was the relaxation of legal restrictions in matters of personal morality and social behaviour: the abolition of capital punishment, the liberalization of the divorce laws and the legalization of adult male homosexual acts and of abortion. Most of these measures originated in private members' bills, for which the government found parliamentary time without overtly taking a lead. Wilson was personally unenthusiastic about some of them; one of his more socially progressive colleagues, Richard Crossman, described him as 'a perfectly sincere Sunday Methodist; he's against the legal reforms to deal with homosexuality or abortion'.[14] A visible sign of the modernization of Britain, the 1966 decision to introduce decimal currency, was in fact the realization of proposals mooted by the Halsbury committee under the Macmillan government. Another reforming measure, the 1965 Department of Education circular requesting local authorities to press ahead with the introduction of non-selective comprehensive schools, merely accelerated a process which had been spearheaded by individual councils for a decade. The innovation closest to Wilson's own heart was the establishment of the Open University, which used distance learning methods to extend educational opportunity to those who had missed out in later life.

Wilson also deserves credit for some steps in the direction of a more egalitarian society. The 1968 Race Relations Act was the first significant legal measure designed to make racial discrimination unacceptable. 1969 saw the lowering of the voting age from 21 to 18. The 1970 Equal Pay Act was an attempt to address a situation in which women were paid on average 25 per cent less than men for the same work. Northern Ireland, where civil rights protests by the Catholic minority led to conflict with the

Protestant Unionist government in 1968–69, was stabilized by the introduction of British troops as peace-keepers. It can be plausibly argued that Britain was a more tolerant and democratic country, if a no more economically efficient one, by the time that Wilson's first administration left office.

Wilson lost the 1970 election unexpectedly, his energetic 'meet the people' campaigning style failing to compensate for last-minute adverse trade figures and a relentless focus by the Conservatives on rising prices. He returned to Number 10 in March 1974, following the destruction of the Heath government through a combination of a four-fold increase in oil prices and growing industrial unrest. As the head of a minority government Wilson's priorities were to settle the miners' strike, which Heath had proved unable to resolve, and to contain the growth of inflation, so that he stood a chance of winning a parliamentary majority. Labour's solution was the 'social contract', whereby the trade unions offered restraint in wage bargaining in return for extended welfare benefits. The deal was enough to see the government through the October 1974 election but it offered no solution to the growing problem of 'stagflation', a compound of sluggish economic growth, rising unemployment and inflation, which peaked at 26 per cent the following year. In practice, for those who belonged to an assertive trade union, wage increases were not held below the level of price rises. As the Treasury minister Joel Barnett wryly recalled, 'the only give and take in the contract was that the Government gave and the unions took'.[15] In response to the failure of the social contract the government turned to a policy of deflation, with a voluntary pay policy alongside the introduction of 'cash limits' on public expenditure and tax increases. The political price was the alienation of the Labour left, whose Cabinet representative, Tony Benn, also found his proposals for a National Enterprise Board to lead economic recovery watered down. Instead the government sponsored piece-meal rescue operations for selected 'lame-duck' industries, such as the Chrysler car-making firm. By the time of Wilson's retirement, inflation had come down to 21 per cent although unemployment remained worryingly high at 6 per cent of the workforce. By contrast with the ambitious talk of a national plan a decade earlier, this was a disappointingly limited agenda, which underlined the narrowing of government options in an increasingly inauspicious economic environment.

Overseas policy

Wilson's pragmatism was displayed most fully in his approach to foreign and post-imperial policy. Although he was not opposed to the loss of empire, which had become irreversible by the time he became Prime Minister, he took it for granted that Britain would continue to play a world role. Speaking in June 1965, he declared dramatically that 'Britain's frontiers are on the Himalayas'.[16] Inertia, combined with a desire to maintain national prestige, shaped this stance. A 'patriotic' foreign policy would also expose Labour less starkly to Conservative attack. Wilson sought to maximize Britain's influence on the world stage, much as Harold Macmillan had done, by exploiting the 'special relationship' with the USA and his country's place at the heart of the Commonwealth. Private resentment that he had lost the goodwill of progressive opinion by becoming 'the tail-end Charlie in an American bomber'[17] was outweighed for Wilson by the strategic and economic advantages of the Atlantic alliance. Thus he endured the opprobrium of the Labour left for his refusal to condemn America's highly controversial involvement in the Vietnam War, even though he was careful to turn down US President Lyndon Johnson's appeals for a British military commitment to the struggle. In retrospect, in contrast with Tony Blair's uninhibited support for a later American administration's intervention in Iraq, Wilson's circumspect stance has much to commend it.

The Prime Minister's commitment to the American alliance was one of the reasons for the most controversial aspect of his overseas policy, the commitment to a British military presence east of Suez. In the mid-1960s the US government put strong pressure on Britain to share the burden of resistance to the Communist threat in the Far East and agreed in return to support the value of sterling. Britain's direct interest in the region was never subjected to rigorous analysis, to the dismay of two important groups in the Labour government, the anti-imperial left and those who wanted to re-orientate foreign policy towards closer links with the

European Economic Community. Nor did the sudden announcement in January 1968, that the east of Suez commitment would come to an end three years later, reflect a cool reappraisal of British interests. The decision was taken in haste, as it became clear that the November 1967 devaluation had failed to stabilize sterling's value, necessitating the introduction of substantial spending cuts. The Chancellor, Roy Jenkins, was the key figure in the decision to withdraw the garrisons. For political reasons it was necessary to give prominence to defence cuts, in order to ensure acceptance by the Cabinet of unpalatable economies in social expenditure. The decision caused a temporary rift in Anglo-American relations but it secured the necessary economies, pleased the Labour left and proved acceptable to public opinion. Indeed a consensus tacitly developed around the ensuing readjustment of Britain's overseas role. It was significant that although they criticized the decision at the time, the Conservatives did not attempt to slow the pace of withdrawal on regaining office in June 1970.

Wilson also found himself grappling with one of the most contentious legacies of empire, the long-running crisis over Rhodesia. The problem arose from the determination of the white settler regime to decide its own future, ignoring the wishes of the African majority. Such an outcome was unthinkable to a British government which was committed to the advancement of black political rights as part of the process of decolonization in Africa. Matters were brought to a head by the decision of the Rhodesian Prime Minister, Ian Smith, to make a unilateral declaration of independence (UDI) in November 1965. Wilson's government faced an irreconcilable set of pressures. Labour Party opinion, together with the Afro-Asian majority in the Commonwealth, favoured strong action to end what they perceived as an illegal rebellion by a racialist government. On the other hand the cost of military intervention, combined with the practical difficulties of intervention in a land-locked state, ruled out the use of military force. In addition Wilson knew that such an option would meet strong opposition from important sections of British society, including the armed services and elements in the Conservative Party, which viewed the white minority as their own 'kith and kin'. Wilson has been criticized for weakening Britain's bargaining power by renouncing the use of force in a broadcast before the announcement of UDI, quashing hopes in some quarters of 'a thunderbolt in the form of the Royal Air Force' descending on the settler regime. He was also wildly over-optimistic about the potential of economic sanctions to resolve the situation, stating in January 1966 that they 'might well bring the rebellion to an end within a matter of weeks rather than months'.[18] Yet he also deserves credit for his efforts to play a very weak hand with persistence and some skill. Talks with Smith on board two Royal Navy warships, HMS *Tiger* in December 1966 and HMS *Fearless* in October 1968, aimed at finding a compromise formula, were doomed by the Rhodesian leader's unwillingness to agree to meaningful concessions at a time when his country's position remained strong. Wilson's was not the only British government to have its impotence exposed by a problem which was not resolved until the transformation of Rhodesia into black-ruled Zimbabwe in 1980. Resolution was ultimately achieved as a result of Smith's growing isolation, as South Africa withdrew its help for sanctions-busting, and the newly-independent neighbouring countries of Angola and Mozambique provided bases for increasingly effective black guerrilla raids into Rhodesia.

Wilson had more success in his handling of an issue with much greater long-term importance for Britain: its relationship with the European Economic Community. His own attitude towards Europe was determined more by his perception of its impact on the Labour Party than by its intrinsic merits. Thus in 1967 he attempted to take Britain into the Community, only to be rebuffed by the French President, de Gaulle. In opposition, as Labour Party opinion moved against Europe, he opposed the terms on which Edward Heath secured Britain's entry in January 1973. Wilson's position at the time of his return to office was described by Bernard Donoughue as 'agnostic, mentally ... accepting the arguments that it was on balance better to stay in'.[19] His solution was to renegotiate the terms of British membership and then to allow the people to decide using the device of a referendum – a constitutional novelty which would compel both Labour's pro and anti factions to accept the outcome. In the run-up to the popular vote in June 1975, Wilson allowed his Cabinet colleagues to argue their respective cases in public, temporarily suspending the doctrine of collective responsibility with the so-called 'agreement to differ'. The success of the 'yes' campaign in the referendum achieved the result preferred by Wilson whilst holding the party and government together.

Conclusion

Anchoring Britain in Europe was one of the few substantive achievements of Wilson's final term. Those closest to him noticed a marked deterioration of his mental and physical powers in the second half of 1975. He was increasingly obsessed in private with the suspicion that members of the security services were engaged in intrigues designed to undermine his government. The damning verdict of MI5's official historian is that 'conspiracy theorists are inherently unfitted for the ultimate responsibility which fell to Wilson as prime minister for the management of the British intelligence community'.[20] Although Wilson's fears are generally now regarded as unfounded, it is true that some of his friends attracted the attention of MI5 for their business links with Iron Curtain countries. They included Sir Joseph Kagan, manufacturer of the Gannex mackintosh favoured by Wilson, who featured on the Prime Minister's resignation honours list, and who was to be imprisoned for fraud four years later. Wilson's association with such characters certainly calls in question his judgement. It was hardly surprising that rumours of impending scandal circulated in explanation of Wilson's relatively early retirement, shortly after his sixtieth birthday in March 1976. The truth behind his decision to quit the political scene was more prosaic. Wilson was visibly tiring of confronting the same political and economic problems, and had in fact told his inner circle that he would serve only two years after returning to Downing Street in 1974.

Wilson has left the memory of an exponent of short-term manoeuvre who failed to tackle Britain's underlying problems. One colleague recalled that a favourite Wilson saying was 'a decision deferred is a decision made'.[21] Wilson himself told the Cabinet during discussions of the 'agreement to differ' over Europe that 'I'm at my best in a messy middle-of-the-road muddle'.[22] His concern with the preservation of Labour Party unity delayed rather than averted the conflict between left and right which proved so damaging under his successors. Yet had Wilson not striven so hard to reconcile the competing factions it is unlikely that his party could have wrested the title of the 'natural party of government' from the Conservatives in 1964–79. He proved more successful than his great rival, Heath, in generating a sense of reassurance at a time of great turbulence. Wilson's dedication to keeping the show on the road and his 'extraordinary rubber-ball capacity of bouncing back'[23] are reminiscent of Stanley Baldwin in the interwar period. In his final term, stressing the advantages of a quiet life after the industrial strife of Heath's government, Wilson most resembled his interwar Conservative predecessor of whom he was to write approvingly that he was 'a healer, one who sought to build bridges'.[24] This was a modest record, which contrasted sharply with the technocratic aspirations of more than a decade earlier. In the circumstances of the time, however, it was perhaps as much as could be expected.

Notes

1 Ion Trewin (ed.), *The Hugo Young Papers: Thirty Years of British Politics – Off the Record*, London: Allen Lane, 2008, p. 59.
2 Words attributed to Wilson in a briefing of parliamentary lobby journalists during the 1964 sterling crisis. Antony Jay (ed.), *The Oxford Dictionary of Political Quotations*, Oxford: Oxford University Press, 1996, p. 390.
3 Bernard Donoughue, *The Heat of the Kitchen*, London: Politico's, 2004, p. 272.
4 Interview with the *Daily Express,* 8 November 1962, quoted in Ben Pimlott, *Harold Wilson*, London: HarperCollins, 1992, p. 267.
5 Peter Hennessy, *Muddling Through: Power, Politics and the Quality of Government in Post-war Britain*, London: Indigo, 1997, p. 247.
6 Pimlott, *Harold Wilson*, p. 304.
7 Denis Healey, *The Time of My Life*, London: Michael Joseph, 1989, p. 331.
8 Shirley Williams, *Climbing the Bookshelves*, London: Virago, 2009, p. 200.
9 Anthony Howard (ed.), *The Crossman Diaries: Selections from the Diaries of a Cabinet Minister 1964–1970*, London: Hamish Hamilton and Jonathan Cape, 1979, pp. 439–40, entry for 7 January 1968.

10 Harold Wilson, *Final Term: The Labour Government 1974–76*, London: Weidenfeld and Nicolson and Michael Joseph, 1979, p. 17.

11 Bernard Donoughue, *Downing Street Diary: With Harold Wilson in No. 10*, London: Jonathan Cape, 2005, p. 140, entry for 15 June 1974.

12 Michael Cockerell, *Live from Number Ten*, London: Faber and Faber, 1988, pp. 140–1.

13 John Schwartz, 'In Place of Strife: Labour History Debate, 12 November 2003' in *Labour History*, 2, Spring 2004, 6.

14 Howard, *Crossman Diaries*, p. 282, entry for 11 December 1966.

15 Joel Barnett, *Inside the Treasury*: London: Deutsch, 1982, p. 49.

16 John Darwin, *Britain and Decolonisation: The Retreat from Empire in the Post-war World*, London: Macmillan, 1988, p. 291.

17 Philip Ziegler, *Wilson: The Authorised Life of Lord Wilson of Rievaulx*, London: Weidenfeld and Nicolson, 1993, p. 223. The reference is to the vulnerable rear-gunner in a bombing aircraft.

18 Pimlott, *Harold Wilson,* pp. 371, 377.

19 Donoughue, *Heat of the Kitchen*, p. 178.

20 Christopher Andrew, *The Defence of the Realm: The Authorized History of MI5*, London: Penguin, 2010, p. 635.

21 Barnett, *Inside the Treasury,* p. 42.

22 Tony Benn, *Against the Tide: Diaries 1973–76*, London: Arrow, 1990, p. 305, entry for 21 January 1975.

23 Labour Cabinet minister Peter Shore, quoted in Hennessy, *Muddling Through*, p. 257.

24 Harold Wilson, *A Prime Minister on Prime Ministers*, London: Weidenfeld and Nicolson and Michael Joseph, 1977, p. 167.

Further reading

Bernard Donoughue, *The Heat of the Kitchen: An Autobiography*, London: Politico's, second edition, 2004

Anthony Howard (ed.), *The Crossman Diaries: Selections from the Diaries of a Cabinet Minister 1964–1970*, London: Hamish Hamilton and Jonathan Cape, 1979

Ben Pimlott, *Harold Wilson*, London: HarperCollins, 1992

Harold Wilson, *The Labour Government 1964–70*, London: Weidenfeld and Nicolson, 1971

Harold Wilson, *Final Term: The Labour Government 1974–76*, London: Weidenfeld and Nicolson and Michael Joseph, 1979

Philip Ziegler, *Wilson: The Authorised Life of Lord Wilson of Rievaulx*, London: Weidenfeld and Nicolson, 1993

15 Edward Heath (1916–2005)

Prime Minister: June 1970–March 1974

'For those who choke on Europe, Ted's the villain. For the rest of us, I guess he deserves a sort of heroic status, pulling us over the line through sheer will-power and bloody-mindedness.'

Obituary of Heath by Chris Patten[1]

It is a truism that there is no friendship at the top in politics. Yet there often seems a certain insincerity about the ritual parliamentary jousting of Prime Minister and Leader of the Opposition. There is little doubt, however, that there was venom between Harold Wilson and Edward Heath, much more so than between any previous party leaders in the twentieth century. In particular, Heath's contempt for Wilson verged on hatred. He complained that Wilson's abrupt changes of policy, his insincerity and lack of scruple were debasing the standards of political life. He himself, on the other hand, would pursue policies in the true national interest and would do so consistently and honourably. The irony is that once in power himself, from 1970 to 1974, he too gained a reputation for U-turns. Wilson and Heath, like MacDonald and Baldwin in the 1920s and 1930s, can be seen as Tweedledum and Tweedledee, except that the telegenic and witty Wilson was the far more assured political performer. A 'man of the people', he won three out of the four general elections they fought against each other. His footwork, noted the TV journalist Robin Day on one occasion, 'was dazzling ... his twisting and turning was worthy of the Great Houdini'.[2] In sharp contrast, Heath seemed cold and humourless, and a condescending elitist, as well as politically flat-footed if not positively lame. Even so, Day classified premiers into two types – those who make a difference and those who do not – and he placed Heath into the first category, Wilson into the second. A case can be made that Edward Heath changed the course of British history.

The rise to the premiership

Many assumed that Heath had a typical Tory background. They were quite wrong. He was born on 9 July 1916 in Broadstairs in Kent, the son of a skilled carpenter and a former maid. There was little privilege in his background, and for a time his family had to take in lodgers to make ends meet. Yet neither was his upbringing in any way deprived. In particular, this rather solitary boy received an excellent education. At the age of ten he won a scholarship to a grammar school in Ramsgate, and in 1935 he won a place at Balliol College in Oxford. There he not only gained solid Second-Class Honours in PPE (Philosophy, Politics and Economics) but lost his Kentish burr and acquired a more acceptable accent for Oxford and the Conservative Party (complete with what his biographer John Campbell calls 'tortured and artificial vowel sounds').[3] He also became politically engaged, as an opponent of Neville Chamberlain's appeasement, and was elected President of the Oxford Union in November 1938.

Heath was intending to read for the bar, a traditional route into politics, but the Second World War interrupted his plans. He spent most of the war in England, his major enemy being tedium rather than Nazism, but he saw action after D-Day, was mentioned in despatches and won the MBE. His final rank was that of Colonel. What he consciously took from the war – having been surrounded in Germany 'by destruction, homelessness, hunger and despair'[4] – was a conviction that another European conflict must never happen again. He was not demobbed until 1946, and for the next few years had a variety of jobs, but in February 1950, at the age of 33, he was elected Conservative MP for Bexley, scraping home, after a recount, by 133 votes. He was a member of the 'class of "50"', a distinguished group which showed that the Tory Party had loosened the requirements of public school and wealth for its MPs.

Characteristically, Heath's maiden speech, in 1950, was in favour of European unity, calling for Britain to accept the Franco-German Schuman Plan, creating a common coal and steel community. But in fact this was the last speech he made in the Commons for nine years, as in 1951, when the Conservatives returned to power, he was made a Whip, and so by convention would not speak in the House. In 1952 he became Deputy Chief Whip and Chief Whip three years later. 'I have never known a better-equipped Chief Whip', Prime Minister Eden wrote of him.[5] It was deserved praise, especially since Heath not only kept his mouth loyally shut when he found the Cabinet Secretary destroying secret documents on Eden's orders during the Suez débâcle but he steadied the party at a time when it threatened to rip apart. He then forged a close relationship with Eden's successor, Harold Macmillan, whose verdict on him varied from 'admirable' to 'superb'.[6] In 1959 he became Minister of Labour and the following year was given the difficult, but welcome, job of negotiating Britain's entry into the European Economic Community (EEC), the forerunner of today's European Union.

That Heath failed in the task of securing Britain's entry is undeniable, for France's General de Gaulle issued his famous '*Non*' in January 1963, but everyone recognized that his efforts had been valiant. He certainly impressed with the sincerity and force of the impromptu speech he delivered on first hearing the French veto. 'We in Britain are not going to turn our backs on the mainland of Europe or on the countries of the Community. We are part of Europe: by geography, tradition, history, culture and civilisation. We shall continue to work with all our friends in Europe for the true unity and strength of this continent.'[7]

Harold Macmillan's shock resignation in October 1963 played nicely into the hands of Wilson's Labour Party. The new Tory leader, the Earl of Home, who hastily renounced his title and became plain Sir Alec Douglas-Home, had not been elected: instead he had 'emerged' as leader, chosen by the 'charmed circle' of Tory grandees. In October 1964 the Conservatives lost, and Harold Wilson formed a government with a tiny majority. It was only a matter of time before Douglas-Home resigned and the Conservatives, for the first time, held an election among MPs to decide on a new leader. The party needed a modern image and a meritocrat to face up to Wilson. Heath seemed to have the right credentials: he was combative, professional and tough. In July 1965 he became the first elected leader of the Conservative Party, beating rivals Reginald Maudling and Enoch Powell. He was also, at 49, the youngest.

It was not long before some Conservatives were regretting their choice. Heath seemed distant and aloof, and again and again Wilson got the better of him in Commons debates. In 1966 Labour increased their majority in the general election to almost a hundred seats. Heath, a rather awkward and solemn bachelor, was an easy target for critical journalists and TV satirists. How easy to mimic his too too determined laughter, with shoulders heaving and teeth flashing! TV pundit Robert Mackenzie compared him, when electioneering, with a sensitive man in a butcher's shop. Other journalists concluded that he was perennially 'buttoned-up' and unable to relax. They even tried to delve into his sex life, only to conclude that it was, and had always been, non-existent.

Yet in the general election of 1970 Heath confounded his critics and the pollsters. The Conservatives won a million more votes than Labour and gained an overall majority of 30 seats. The result owed a good deal to bad last-minute economic news for the Labour government, but it also reflected the popularity of Heath's message. Heath criticized Wilson's 'cheap and trivial' style of government in which short-term gain counted for everything. He himself would stick to his policies; and these would include entering the EEC, curbing inflation, though without an incomes policy, lowering taxes and cutting back on public expenditure. There would be less government, but it would be better government.

The premiership

Heath's number one priority was to enter the EEC, and in this he succeeded. His task was much easier than in the early 1960s, for de Gaulle had been replaced as French President by Georges Pompidou. All Heath had to do was move swiftly to calm French fears that Britain was too pro-American. His real difficulty was in securing the British parliament's acceptance of entry, for most members of the Labour Party were anti-Europe and his own party was split. There were a number of Conservatives who were implacable Euro-sceptics, including the formidable Enoch Powell. Whereas Powell insisted that 'to give away the independence and sovereignty of this House now and for the future is an unthinkable act', Heath judged that entry into the EEC 'does not entail a loss of national identity or an erosion of essential national sovereignty'.[8] For most MPs, however, the key issue was economic advantage. There were intense battles, and the vote on the second reading of the Bill achieved a majority of only nine. There were some who wondered whether Heath had actually achieved 'the full-hearted consent' of the British people laid down as a pre-condition for entry.[9] Nevertheless Britain formally entered the EEC on 1 January 1973.

Many of Heath's other polices were less successful, but they were certainly not failures. If he blundered in introducing internment in Ulster in August 1971, after Wilson had sent British troops into Northern Ireland in response to escalating violence between Catholics and Protestants, he was surely right to begin direct rule from Westminster in 1972. The power-sharing Sunningdale Agreement of December 1973, with its notion of a Council of Ireland, though it faltered, can be seen as a constructive forerunner of Blair's Good Friday Agreement of 1998. Heath has also been praised for standing strong against the anti-immigrant views of Enoch Powell and for allowing into Britain around 28,000 Ugandan Asians expelled by Idi Amin in 1972.

The key area for contemporaries, however, was the economy. There were economic problems even before war in the Middle East led to a rapid and destabilizing rise in the price of oil. (A barrel of oil, which had cost $2.40 in January 1973, had reached $11.65 by the end of the year – a rise of almost 500 per cent.) When unemployment reached a million early in 1972, Heath decided to intervene much more in the economy, propping up failing firms like Rolls-Royce aero-engines and Upper Clyde Shipbuilders. His Industry Act of 1972 was dubbed by critics the 'Lame Ducks (Unlimited) Bill'. Heath was providing more government – including an extra 400,000 officials – not less. Instead of accepting the operation of market forces, his Chancellor, Anthony Barber, attempted to reflate the economy and thereby absorb unemployment. In addition, rising inflation led Heath in

November 1972 to resort to a statutory prices and incomes policy, much to the dismay of many Conservatives. An incredulous Enoch Powell asked on 2 November 1972 whether, in going back on his previous pledge, Heath had 'taken leave of his senses'.[10]

Industrial relations deteriorated savagely, so that Heath declared five states of emergency during a premiership of less than four years. His attempt to regulate trade unions, with the Industrial Relations Act of 1971 which required strike ballots and a 'cooling off' period before industrial action could be initiated, became a dead letter when the TUC refused to accept it and a group of dockers ('the Pentonville five') contrived to get arrested under its provisions.

Was this a Prime Minister who U-turned, putting expediency above principle? Or, on the contrary, was it a Prime Minister with the sense to realize that circumstances not only alter cases but must alter policies? Both verdicts have been given by different commentators. The key question, however, was whether the new course would work or not. Unemployment certainly fell, standing at 500,000 in December 1973; but competitiveness in industry declined and inflation remained an intractable problem.

Conflict with the miners proved Heath's undoing. Not that Heath wanted confrontation. Jack Jones, the leader of the Transport and General Workers' Union, wrote that: 'No Prime Minister ... could compare with Ted Heath in the efforts he made to establish a spirit of camaraderie with trade unions and to offer an attractive package which might satisfy large numbers of work people ... He revealed the human face of Toryism.'[11] Heath genuinely felt that unregulated pay rises, fuelling inflation and harming the standard of living of vulnerable groups such as pensioners, had to be opposed. In 1972 the miners had won a strike by using 'flying pickets' to prevent coal reaching the power stations. Their leader Arthur Scargill commented, with an allusion to the General Strike, that: 'We ... were in a class war. We were not playing cricket on the village green, like they did in '26.'[12] Then, at the end of 1973, when the miners banned overtime, Heath put British industry on a three-day working week, to conserve power. Several colleagues wanted an immediate general election on the issue of 'Who Governs?', but Heath delayed.

Only when the miners voted for a strike did Heath call an election for 28 February.

Heath seemed infused with a new, vibrant energy, and dominated the campaign for his party. Yet not everyone liked Heath. Indeed he was not an easy man to like. The few who knew him were aware of a kindly, considerate person beneath the rigid exterior. Heath did not tell jokes, wrote Douglas Hurd, his political secretary in 1968–74: instead he would deliver an 'outrageous statement in a deadpan voice' or ask sardonic questions and then maintain a quizzical silence.[13] But it was a humour so dry as to be all too easily mistaken for pomposity, and many believed that he revelled 'in his own charmlessness'.[14] At this time several British politicians were asked to name their favourite dish for a new cook book. Wilson chose a Cornish pasty with brown sauce; Heath chose lobster thermidor with two wine sauces. The *Daily Mirror* was able to use details like this to portray the man as remote and elitist.

At first, everyone seemed to believe that the Tories would win, but Enoch Powell, in a dramatic gesture, refused to stand for the Conservative Party and advised his followers to vote Labour, as the party willing to hold a referendum on Britain's continued membership of the EEC. In Northern Ireland, those Unionists discontented with Sunningdale also turned against the Conservatives. For his part, Harold Wilson refused to allow the election to focus on the single issue selected by the Tories. He brought in economic issues, pointing out that the January trade figures showed the worst ever deficit, at £383 million (due to the rocketing price of oil), and that the retail price index had risen by 20 per cent over the past year. What is more, the question 'Who Governs?' was not necessarily a vote-winner. Just what would the Tories do to settle the miners' strike with a renewed mandate that they could not do with their already workable majority?

The result was extremely close. The Conservatives polled 230,000 more votes than Labour, but won four fewer seats. Heath tried but failed to win the support of the Liberal Party, and so Wilson became Prime Minister of a minority Labour government. A re-run of the election in October 1974 produced a small swing to the left, and Wilson secured an overall majority of three seats. Many now judged that Heath had to go. He had lost three out of four elections. He had also offended far too many Conservative backbenchers with his brusque, unfriendly manner. Heath was thus the first Conservative to be elected leader, and the first Conservative leader to lose a leadership contest. Margaret Thatcher took over in February 1975. It was not the end of Heath's career. That same year he took a leading, and impressive, role in the referendum over continued membership of the EEC. Yet when Mrs Thatcher refused to offer him the post of Foreign Secretary in 1979, he began what has been called 'the longest sulk in history'. He stood down as an MP in 2001, after 51 continuous years as Member of Parliament for Bexley. He died, aged 89, on 17 July 2005.

Conclusion

Many foolish things have been said about Ted Heath. In the *New Statesman*, Paul Johnson wrote that he hated the poor, while others on the left believed he was a hard-nosed reactionary out to increase unemployment and destroy the unions. It was even asserted that he instituted a three-day week to manufacture the sense of panic needed to win another general election. There were also outspoken critics on the right. That he tried, after the election of February 1974, to get the support of the Liberals seemed to the *Spectator* to be an example of his 'monomania'. He was described as a ludicrous figure clinging 'with grubby fingers to the crumbling precipices of power ... pathetic ... contemptible'. He spent nine years 'trying to ruin the Conservative Party, and three and a half trying to ruin the country'.[15]

Such views now seem not merely erroneous but positively preposterous. Heath was in fact a decent and sincere man, with more honesty and less guile than we are accustomed to from our image-conscious politicians. 'Ted Heath is not a smooth man. He is not a phoney man,' wrote Robin Day. 'Among all the leading politicians whom I have known, he is one of the most straight-forward.'[16] Yet he lacked the common touch, and this fatal flaw limited his electoral appeal. According to the obituary in *The Times*, 'He was a great lighthouse, indifferent to the waves of criticism, casting out strong and steady beams which flickered neither for convenience nor popularity' – a view which may account for some of his successes but which perhaps does more to explain his failures. Nevertheless Heath was not the one-dimensional man he sometimes seemed. He was not only a successful politician, he was also an expert musician, who conducted the London Symphony Orchestra in November 1971, and a world-class yachtsman, who captained the British team that won the prestigious Admiral's Cup, beating 15 other nations, also in 1971. John Campbell calls him 'the most multi-talented Prime Minister' of the twentieth century.[17]

Heath will long be remembered, in the words of Douglas Hurd, as having been broken by 'the brutal exercise of trade union power'.[18] Yet if he mishandled the unions, they too mishandled him. A more responsible attitude on their part would have spared them the catastrophic loss of power they suffered in the 1980s under Margaret Thatcher, the true union-basher. 'Thatcherism' was formed in reaction against the perceived failures of Heath's U-turns.

One feature of the 1970–74 premiership stands out: Heath's run of exceptionally bad luck. He had bad luck with the world economy, bad luck with militant miners' leaders, bad luck that his talented first Chancellor, Iain Macleod, died within five weeks of taking office in 1970, bad luck to lose the election in 1974 despite polling more votes than Labour, bad luck that his two areas of non-political expertise, classical music and yachting, were unfairly mocked as elitist in the press. Two further examples, coinciding with his greatest triumphs, may be taken as symptomatic. As his electoral victory in 1970 was announced, a Labour supporter stubbed out a cigarette on his neck; and at a ceremony heralding Britain's accession to the European Community, a woman hurled a bottle of ink that splashed all over his suit.

Yet outrageous fortune did not affect Britain's entry into the EEC. Would another Prime Minister have taken Britain into Europe at some point, if Heath had failed? Perhaps, but it is by no means certain. Heath's European success will have significance long after his other policies have become mere historical curiosities. Will Britain's entry be perceived by future historians as a blessing or a disaster – or something in between? Upon the answer to this question depends Heath's true historical legacy. He would have wanted no less.

Notes

1 Chris Patten, *Balliol Record*, 2006, p. 31.
2 Robin Day, *Grand Inquisitor*, London: Pan, 1989, p. 262.
3 John Campbell, *Edward Heath*, London: Cape, 1993, p. 18.
4 Ibid., p. 49.
5 Ibid., p. 91.
6 Ibid., p. 100.
7 Ibid., p. 131.
8 Ibid., p. 360.
9 Ibid., p. 401.
10 Robert Shepherd, *Enoch Powell*, London: Pimlico, 1996, p. 427.
11 Jack Jones, *Union Man*, London: HarperCollins, 1986, p. 259.
12 Paul Routledge, *Scargill*, London: HarperCollins, 1993, p. 70
13 Campbell, *Heath*, p. 488.
14 Patten, *Balliol Record*, p. 29.
15 *Spectator*, 9 March 1974, pp. 281, 283.
16 Day, *Grand Inquisitor*, p. 266.
17 Campbell, *Heath*, p. xv.
18 Stuart Ball and Antony Seldon (eds), *The Heath Government 1970–74*, Harlow: Longman, 1996, p. 189.

Further reading

Stuart Ball and Anthony Seldon (eds), *The Heath Government 1970–74: A Reappraisal*, Harlow: Longman, 1996

John Campbell, *Edward Heath: A Biography*, London: Jonathan Cape, 1993

Edward Heath, *The Course of My Life*, London: Hodder & Stoughton, 1998

Philip Ziegler, *Edward Heath: the Authorised Biography*, London: HarperPress, 2010

16 James Callaghan (1912–2005)

Prime Minister: April 1976–May 1979

'We can win the [1979] election if … people will say, "Jim Callaghan is the Prime Minister of this country, he's the able seaman, he's a man who understands the common man."'

James Callaghan on himself, quoted by his Minister of Transport, William Rodgers.[1]

James Callaghan was the only Prime Minister to have held all four great offices of state, serving as Chancellor of the Exchequer (1964–67), Home Secretary (1967–70) and Foreign Secretary (1974–76) before attaining the premiership in April 1976. Yet Callaghan's formidable experience did not make him proof against the relentless pressure of events. His three-year premiership was dogged by economic and industrial difficulties, and the disappearance of his slender parliamentary majority, within months of his entering Number 10, compelled him to struggle continually for political survival. In his first autumn as Prime Minister he was driven to seek financial support from the International Monetary Fund. Two years later the government faced a wave of strikes which it proved unable to control, causing the final months of 1978 and the opening ones of 1979 to enter political mythology as 'the winter of discontent'. In May 1979 Callaghan joined a small group of Prime Ministers in our period – the others are Sir Alec Douglas-Home and Gordon Brown – who lost the only general election that they called.

The rise to the premiership

Callaghan's ultimate failure should not be allowed to detract from his remarkable rise to prominence. He had progressed from a disadvantaged upbringing in Portsmouth, through a career as a tax officer and civil service union official – the beginning of a long and important association with the trade union movement – before joining the Navy in the Second World War. Unlike his three predecessors as Labour Party leader, he had not had the benefit of a university education, a lack of opportunity to which he often referred in later life. Callaghan was elected as Labour MP for Cardiff South in 1945 and attained junior office in the Attlee government. During the party's 13-year stint in opposition he rose steadily through its ranks and was a contender for the leadership when Hugh Gaitskell died in January 1963.

Callaghan was a key figure in the Wilson governments without ever truly distinguishing himself in any of the senior posts he held. He never seemed comfortable as Chancellor and his period at the Treasury was terminated by the politically damaging U-turn of sterling's devaluation in November 1967. The episode almost destroyed his ministerial career; he was rescued when Wilson arranged for him to exchange places with the Home Secretary, Roy Jenkins. As one of his colleagues, Bill Rodgers, told the journalist Hugo Young during the IMF crisis in September 1976, the experience had been a traumatic one for Callaghan, leaving him with a deeply felt need to avoid a second failure of economic policy.[2] As Home Secretary he appeared out of step with the progressive social movements of the late 1960s; it was Jenkins who had taken the lead in facilitating liberal reforms such as changes to the divorce laws and the legalization of abortion. Only in Northern Ireland, which came under the remit of the Home Secretary until 1972, did he reveal real flair, showing sensitivity towards the Catholic minority whilst rigorously upholding the rule of law. He also led the opposition in Cabinet to the 1969 White Paper, *In Place of Strife*, the attempt by Wilson and his Employment Secretary, Barbara Castle, to reform the laws governing trade unions. The episode gave him a lasting reputation as 'the keeper of the cloth cap', the trade union movement's most highly placed spokesman at governmental level.

By the time that Harold Wilson announced his retirement in March 1976, Callaghan had spent two unremarkable years as Foreign Secretary. As he later admitted in his memoirs, by this stage he had come to accept that promotion to the highest office was unlikely.[3] Yet he defeated five other contenders for the succession. In so doing he became the first – and so far the only – Labour Prime Minister to enter Number 10 by fighting and winning a leadership contest whilst the party was in government. At 64 he was not only four years his predecessor's senior but also the oldest of the leadership candidates. His rivals were experienced, heavyweight figures reflecting a cross-section of the party – Michael Foot and Tony Benn on the left, Tony Crosland in the centre, Roy Jenkins and Denis Healey on the right. Callaghan was Wilson's preferred successor, having forged a trusting relationship as Foreign Secretary and overcome memories of the rift caused by *In Place of Strife*; alone of the contenders he had been given advance knowledge of the contest, which gave him time to prepare mentally. With Labour increasingly divided, he seemed best placed to guarantee unity. Although Callaghan came from Labour's centre-right, he commanded support from all strands of party opinion, with the exception of the far left.

Governing style

The outwardly relaxed but also businesslike manner in which Callaghan discharged his prime ministerial duties made a welcome change for those who had experienced Wilson's declining years. Many senior figures had lost patience with the outgoing premier's wheeler-dealing, his disorganized working habits and paranoid suspicion of plots. By contrast Callaghan exuded a quiet, dignified authority. The Cabinet Secretary, John Hunt, who had served Heath and Wilson, and who was to retire during Thatcher's first term, recalled him as 'the best manager of government business he had known in a premier'.[4] Taking account of the formidable range of problems that confronted his government, Callaghan's Chancellor, Denis Healey, considered him 'for most of the time, the best of Britain's post-war Prime Ministers after Attlee'.[5]

Callaghan consciously set aside factionalism, working as effectively with a left-winger like Michael Foot as he did with Healey. His close working relationship with Foot was vital because the latter, as Leader of the Commons, was primarily responsible for striking parliamentary deals with smaller parties to ensure the government's survival. Callaghan was assiduous in his attendance at the Commons, making himself accessible to Labour MPs as part of his strategy to maintain parliamentary support. His colleagues testified to his effectiveness as chairman of the Cabinet. In her memoirs the Education Secretary, Shirley Williams, recalled how Callaghan kept in touch with ministers without seeking to micro-manage their departments, as some of his successors sought to do.[6] A disinclination to meddle may, in part, have been a consequence of Callaghan's age. Less positively, close advisers also recalled his tendency to retreat into himself when under pressure, and his preference for handling one problem at a time, characteristics which counted against him in the crisis of the winter of discontent.[7]

Callaghan's public image as an avuncular 'Sunny Jim' figure was misleading. Roy Jenkins, who left the Cabinet in September 1976 to become President of the European Commission, after Callaghan had denied him the succession to the Foreign Office, later described him as 'a bit of a bully'. He reflected, however, that 'after the very easy-going regime of Wilson's final days a bit of bullying might do the Government no harm'.[8] Callaghan could be ruthless in his dealings with Cabinet colleagues. On taking office he dispatched Barbara Castle, a long-standing adversary, to the backbenches. She was not fooled by his claim that the reason was the need to lower the average age of the Cabinet.[9] Even an ideological ally like Roy Mason, who viewed Callaghan as a friend and mentor, was taken aback on being told over the telephone that he must decide at once whether he would accept a move from Defence to Northern Ireland in the September 1976 Cabinet changes. Mason recalled that, after being accustomed to face-to-face job offers from Wilson: 'I didn't reckon much to being shuffled at the end of a telephone.'[10]

Nor was there an equivalent of Wilson's 'kitchen cabinet' of trusted confidants. Callaghan was a practised user of the Whitehall machine who respected the civil service and saw no need for institutional reform. He retained the Policy Unit, which had been created by Wilson to provide personal and political advice on policy matters. Callaghan employed it to garner background knowledge of a number of issues and to assist him in his dealings with government departments. A good example was the preparation for his speech at Ruskin College in Oxford in October 1976, in which he tried to stimulate a 'great debate' on education – one of the few original initiatives of his premiership.[11] In this and other matters, Callaghan retained his independence, using others' expertise but making his own decisions.

The record in government

Callaghan's premiership was dominated by two closely linked imperatives: the need to overcome the country's grave economic problems and to secure the government's survival. Inflation stood at 21 per cent when Callaghan became Prime Minister, whilst unemployment had passed the one million mark the previous summer. The government's strategy for bringing inflation down depended precariously on persuading the trade unions to restrain their members' demands for wage increases. The Labour left would not readily accept any erosion of working-class living standards and would continue to demand increases in public expenditure. The parliamentary situation was also extremely discouraging. The bare overall majority of three seats, won by Wilson in the October 1974 General Election, was soon dissipated by defections and by-election losses. Simply to stay in office, the government had to conclude an electoral pact with the 13 Liberal MPs in March 1977. When the arrangement came to an end 15 months later, Callaghan had to strike deals with other small parties to prop up the government. This meant that it was almost impossible to do much more than react to events.

The Callaghan government's reputation has been largely determined by its response to two key events: the International Monetary Fund crisis and the winter of discontent. At the root of the former was relentless pressure on the value of sterling, as the international money markets reacted adversely to the government's slowness in bringing inflation and wage settlements under control. Between June and September 1976 the exchange rate for the pound fell from $1.85 to $1.63. The crisis was heightened by the fact that this occurred whilst the Labour Party's annual conference was taking place at Blackpool. Callaghan demonstrated courage in telling the conference that the country needed to face up to economic reality. In his address he warned that the postwar consensus idea, that governments could spend their way out of recession, no longer held true. It had led to inflation, whose consequence was growing unemployment. The speech was intended as a wake-up call to the Labour left and as a signal to the country and the IMF that the government would approach the sterling crisis in a responsible manner.

The ensuing negotiations with the IMF revealed Callaghan's political skills at their best. In order to secure a loan he had to demonstrate a willingness to prune public expenditure. This would, however, be bitterly resented by a party whose priority was to defend public services and the living standards of working people. Callaghan faced a difficult task in securing united Cabinet acceptance of the IMF's terms in November–December 1976. He did so, in a marathon 13 hours of discussions, by allowing opponents as well as supporters of Denis Healey's package of spending cuts to have their say so that, in the words of Shirley Williams, 'no one could claim afterwards to have been bounced, silenced or misinformed'.[12] By giving the Energy Secretary, Tony Benn, an opportunity to expound the case for a socialist 'siege economy' strategy, and then letting others expose its weaknesses, he built consensus around the Cabinet table. In so doing he averted a split comparable to the one that had destroyed Ramsay MacDonald's Labour government in August 1931 – an eventuality which seemed a real possibility in the late autumn of 1976.

From an economic point of view, however, the exercise was unnecessary. As Healey ruefully noted in his memoirs, the Treasury's Public Sector Borrowing Requirement forecast had been seriously overestimated; only half of the IMF loan was actually needed and the whole was paid back by May 1979.[13] Politically, however, Callaghan had carried out a successful piece of damage limitation, securing more favourable terms than those originally demanded by the IMF. The latter had originally demanded cuts of £3 billion in 1977–78 and a further £4 billion in 1978–79, but eventually agreed to £1 billion in 1977–78 and the sale of £500 million of government-owned British Petroleum shares, followed by another £1 billion of cuts in 1978–79. Although many later commentators portrayed the episode as a humiliation, which saw Britain going 'cap in hand' for financial relief, this view was less prevalent at the time. The economy steadied, with the public finances assisted by revenues from North Sea oil and inflation falling to 8 per cent by the summer of 1978 as the level of wage increases temporarily slowed. Unemployment experienced a modest drop, from 1,522,000 in the third quarter of 1977 to 1,306,300 in the final quarter of 1978. Living standards experienced a general improvement, although the position of the low paid remained weak as inflation began to rise again to double figures. In addition the government passed some undramatic but worthwhile social reforms, such as the extension of child benefit payments to first and only children from 1977.

With hindsight Callaghan would have done better to call a general election in the autumn of 1978, as many of his supporters wanted and expected him to do. Opinion polls showed that in terms of personal popularity he was consistently ahead of the Conservative leader, Margaret Thatcher. The latter, who was still far from acquiring unchallenged authority over her party, failed to impress in Parliament and there was a good chance that the electorate would have preferred the experienced, reassuring figure of 'Sunny Jim' in a contest held at that stage. The most likely explanation of Callaghan's decision to delay the election is his belief that it would deliver a hung parliament at best. Some Downing Street insiders considered that, with an eye to the history books, he simply wanted to complete three years as Prime Minister. After all, given his age – he would turn 67 in the spring of 1979 – this was likely to be his one chance to fight a general election. Perhaps he wanted more time to see the fruits of his counter-inflationary strategy. He had negotiated the support of the Ulster Unionists and believed that other parties, including the Liberals, would sustain him in office in the coming parliamentary session.[14] Whatever the reason, the delay proved to be a grave miscalculation.

The events of the following winter were shaped by the government's attempt to impose a 5 per cent limit to pay increases.

This was an arbitrary and unsustainable figure, on which Callaghan insisted, despite the reservations of more pragmatic colleagues and the opposition of the TUC. Over the coming months it was rejected by a range of groups, from comparatively affluent Ford car workers and lorry drivers to much more badly paid public sector workers. The media focused on strikes by health service employees, refuse collectors and (in Merseyside) grave diggers, whose actions directly affected the public. The tabloid press carried a series of emotive headlines – 'No Mercy', 'The Road to Ruin' – whilst the television news showed disturbing images of picket lines outside hospitals and piles of rubbish building up in public spaces.

Callaghan's background in the trade union movement inclined him towards conciliation. He may have been right to reject calls to declare a state of emergency; it is doubtful whether there were enough troops to run public services, and such a move would have created divisions within the government and the Labour Party. He did not, however, appear to have a grip on the situation. The tradition of class solidarity, in which the historic Labour movement was steeped, had been replaced by a much more aggressive, individualistic spirit, with groups of workers out to advance their own claims without concern for the wider public good – a phenomenon which the Environment Secretary, Peter Shore, termed 'occupational tribal warfare'.[15] The disputes were driven by shop-floor activists, who were not as amenable as the older trade union bosses to ministerial appeals to reason. Symbolic of this shift was the retirement in April 1978 of Jack Jones, leader of the largest union, the Transport and General Workers, who had once been offered a Labour Cabinet post. His replacement, Moss Evans, was a far less commanding figure and more inclined to approve the actions of grass-roots militants. Another problem was that Callaghan now seemed out of touch with public opinion. It was unfortunate that he was pictured on TV in January, relaxing with other world leaders at a summit on the Caribbean island of Guadeloupe. On his return he compounded the problem by responding in an inappropriately dismissive way when challenged by a reporter about the 'mounting chaos'. Although he did not use the actual words, *the Sun* reduced his message to a damning headline, 'Crisis? What Crisis?' By now

Callaghan's popular image, as the 'able seaman' who understood the common man, had worn thin.

The government's industrial troubles paved the way for its downfall, but its actual collapse was brought about by the failure of its attempt to appease nationalist feeling by granting devolution to Scotland and Wales. The prospects for success were undermined by a wrecking amendment to the legislation, introduced by a hostile backbench MP, George Cunningham. This required a 'yes' vote in a referendum to win the support, not only of a majority of those who took part, but also of at least 40 per cent of those entitled to vote. When the referenda predictably failed to clear this hurdle, nationalist support for the government evaporated. Eventually, following defeat by a margin of just one, in a vote of no confidence in March 1979, Callaghan called a general election in which the government went down to defeat. The Conservatives took 51 seats from Labour, winning 43.9 per cent of the popular vote against Labour's 36.9 and bringing Callaghan's premiership to a close.

Could Callaghan have done better, given the circumstances facing his government? Bernard Donoughue, the head of the Policy Unit, considered that with some outstanding exceptions such as Denis Healey, he was not well supported by his Cabinet colleagues. He accused his former boss of thinking in terms of internal Labour Party politics and personalities, rather than choosing the most able people for the job.[16] Observers perceived him as sunk in depression during the winter, at the mercy of events and deeply conscious of a sense of personal failure.[17] He seems to have fallen prey to a sense of fatalism, as indicated by his private remark, shortly before polling day, that 'there are times, perhaps once every thirty years, when there is a sea-change in politics ... I suspect there is now such a sea-change – and it is for Mrs Thatcher'.[18]

As the Labour Party moved to the left in the aftermath of defeat, Callaghan's reputation declined. Conservative perceptions of him were typified by Thatcher's description of him as 'a sort of moderate disguise for his left-wing party and its backers'. Although his gift for short-term manoeuvre kept the government afloat for a time, 'in the Winter of Discontent the entire house of cards that was Labour moderation collapsed'.[19] The Labour left regarded the Callaghan government as a time of missed opportunities, when hopes for a full-blooded socialist transformation of the economy and society had been betrayed. Tony Benn, who was to become the leader of the hard left in opposition, looked forward to a future in which the party and the unions were 'free to represent their interests and to campaign for socialist policies', which had been sidetracked under Callaghan's leadership.[20] Nor did Tony Blair's revival of Labour's fortunes usher in a graceful rehabilitation, notwithstanding the publication of a generally favourable reappraisal in 1997, in the shape of Kenneth Morgan's official biography. Blair was at pains to distance himself from Callaghan's collegiate style of Cabinet management. He accused his predecessor of failing to take decisions, asserting that government business went 'through umpteen committees which meant things never got done at all'.[21] In the longer run, it is likely that Callaghan will be remembered for his valiant but doomed attempt to defend the postwar consensus. Governments since 1979 have moved away from the mixed economy; the concept of a partnership between government, business and trade unions has all but vanished; and the concept of a 'cradle to grave' welfare state has been severely eroded. Callaghan's defeat signalled the beginning of that process, which saw Britain start to turn its back on the world of 1945.

Notes

1 Phillip Whitehead, *The Writing on the Wall: Britain in the Seventies*, London: Michael Joseph, 1985, p. 256.
2 Ion Trewin (ed.), *The Hugo Young Papers: Thirty Years of British Politics: off the record*, London: Allen Lane, 2008, p. 100.
3 James Callaghan, *Time and Chance*, London: Collins, 1987, p. 387.
4 Dennis Kavanagh and Anthony Seldon, *The Powers Behind the Prime Minister: The Hidden Influence of Number Ten*, London: HarperCollins, 1999, p. 141.
5 Denis Healey, *The Time of My Life*, London: Michael Joseph, 1989, p. 447.
6 Shirley Williams, *Climbing the Bookshelves*, London: Virago, 2009, p. 226.
7 Bernard Donoughue, *Downing Street Diary, Volume Two: With James Callaghan in No. 10*, London: Jonathan Cape, 2008, p. 3.

8 Roy Jenkins, *A Life at the Centre*, London: Macmillan, 1991, p. 441.
9 Barbara Castle, *The Castle Diaries 1974–76*, London: Weidenfeld and Nicolson, 1980, pp. 724–5, entry for 8 April 1976.
10 Roy Mason, *Paying the Price*, London: Robert Hale, 1999, p. 160.
11 Donoughue, *Downing Street Diary*, p. 82, entry for 13 October 1976.
12 Williams, *Climbing the Bookshelves*, p. 241.
13 Healey, *Time of My Life*, pp. 432–3.
14 Bernard Donoughue, *The Heat of the Kitchen: An Autobiography*, London: Politico's, 2004, pp. 302–3.
15 Whitehead, *Writing on the Wall*, p. 284.
16 Donoughue, *Heat of the Kitchen*, pp. 272–3.
17 Kenneth O. Morgan, *Callaghan: A Life*, Oxford: Oxford University Press, p. 665.
18 Bernard Donoughue, *Prime Minister: The Conduct of Policy under Harold Wilson and James Callaghan*, London: Jonathan Cape, 1987, p. 191.
19 Margaret Thatcher, *The Path to Power*, London: HarperCollins, 1995, p. 313.
20 Tony Benn, *Conflicts of Interest: Diaries 1977–80*, London: Hutchinson, 1990, pp. 492–3, entry for 2 May 1979.
21 Morgan, *Callaghan*, p. 485.

Further reading

James Callaghan, *Time and Chance*, London: Collins, 1987
Bernard Donoughue, *Downing Street Diary, Volume Two: With James Callaghan in No. 10*, London: Jonathan Cape, 2008
Denis Healey, *The Time of My Life*, London: Michael Joseph, 1989
Kenneth Morgan, *Callaghan: A Life,* Oxford: Oxford University Press, 1997

17 Margaret Thatcher (1925–)

Prime Minister: May 1979– November 1990

'Her tragedy is that she may be remembered less for the brilliance of her many achievements than for the tenacity, the recklessness, with which she later defended her own, increasingly uncompromising, views. The insistence on the undivided sovereignty of her own opinion – dressed up as the nation's sovereignty – was her undoing.'

Sir Geoffrey Howe in the *Financial Times*, 24 October 1993[1]

Margaret Thatcher was Britain's first female Prime Minister, indeed the first in the western world. She was also Britain's longest-serving premier of the twentieth century, occupying 10 Downing Street for a total of eleven and a half years and winning three successive general elections in the process. Yet, remarkably, what is truly outstanding about Thatcher is neither her gender nor duration: it is her agenda and the sustained, passionate energy with which she sought to implement it. She was a strong leader, even an intimidating one: 'There's not much point in being a weak floppy thing in the chair, is there?'[2] She did not believe in *consensus* ('a soft wishy washy word ... something you reach when you cannot agree'),[3] she believed in deeply held *convictions*.

'I can't bear to see Britain in decline. I just can't.'[4] Margaret Thatcher may have doubted the existence of 'society', arguing that in reality there were only individuals and families, but she had no trouble with the equally abstract concept of 'Britain'. She would not manage decline, the timid ambition of so many 'realists'; instead she demanded recovery. The economy, she decided, needed a reinvigorating dose of free-market capitalism, so that wealth could be created and not merely redistributed. But economic revival was only the method: 'The object is to change the soul.'[5] The moral flabbiness engendered by a dependency culture must end, the false values of 1960s' permissiveness must be replaced by traditional values. Eventually Britain would resume its historic role as a leader of mankind. Such was the strength of these convictions, and such her dominance of the political system and her high profile in the media, that friend and foe alike actually began to believe she embodied the 1980s – as Britain's saviour or tormentor, according to taste.

The rise to the premiership

If we ask what, in Margaret Roberts' childhood, prepared her for the premiership, the simple answer is her father, Alfred Roberts. A successful grocer and also a Methodist lay preacher, he practised thrift, self-denial and hard work. He believed in a hard-edged capitalism but also in public service, becoming a local councillor and eventually mayor of Grantham. Having no son, he inculcated ambition into his favourite daughter. She too believed in dedicated service, patriotism and personal responsibility. 'Never do things just because other people do them,' her father counselled.[6] It was advice all the easier to take because, known at school as 'Snobby Roberts', she was conscious of being different from the crowd.

When another candidate dropped out in 1943, she secured a place at Somerville College, Oxford, where, unique among British premiers, she studied science, winning a second-class degree in chemistry. But by this time her consuming interest was politics. Churchill's wartime speeches had given her a sense that 'there was almost nothing that the British people could not do';[7] and in 1946 she became President of the Oxford University Conservative Association. Soon she was employed as a research chemist and then as a lawyer, but politics was her consuming passion. In 1950 and 1951 she contested Dartford for the Conservatives, each time reducing the safe Labour majority; and in 1959, at the age of 34, she was elected MP for Finchley, in North London.

There were 25 female MPs in the House of Commons in 1959, more than ever before, but a tiny minority in a House of 630 Members. The position was generally considered too onerous for a woman, especially a wife and mother. But hers was no ordinary family. In 1951 she had married Denis Thatcher, an affluent businessman ten years her senior; and two years later, with the production of twins, childbirth was conveniently over. The babies were cared for first by a nurse and then a nanny; and at eight and nine respectively Mark and Carol were sent to boarding schools. The latter wrote that her mother was an extraordinary person but not an extraordinary parent: she 'rarely interfered' in the upbringing of her children.[8] The political reward was that, after only two years in Parliament, Thatcher became a junior minister; and after Labour's election victory in 1964 she entered Edward Heath's Shadow Cabinet as spokesman first for Fuel and Power, then Transport and finally Education. In 1970 the Conservatives under Heath won the 1970 general election and Thatcher duly became Education Secretary.

When, under pressure from the Chancellor, she removed free milk from 8–11-year-olds, she became notorious as 'Margaret Thatcher, Milk Snatcher'. But soon adverse publicity shifted to the government as a whole. Economic and industrial problems overwhelmed Heath's administration (see Chapter 15). When the Conservatives narrowly lost the general election of February 1974, and then a re-run in October, a leadership contest was held. The heir-apparent, William Whitelaw, believed that Heath should go, but would not stand, at this stage. Right-wing maverick Enoch Powell was out of the running, having urged electors to vote Labour to secure a referendum on British membership of the European Economic Community. The right of the party therefore pinned their hopes on Keith Joseph, but his candidature was undone when he made an incautiously worded speech implying that the lower classes should be discouraged from breeding so rapidly. Only then did Margaret Thatcher decide to stand as party leader.

Thatcher was a rank outsider. She was a woman in a male-dominated party, she was relatively inexperienced, and not many actually liked her. She seemed too distant and too abrasive – too much, in fact, like Edward Heath. Confident of an easy victory,

Heath would not exert himself. Thatcher's campaign, on the other hand, was masterminded with positively Machiavellian skill by Conservative MP and war hero Airey Neave, whose tactics included the disingenuous advice to Whitelaw's supporters that a vote for Thatcher would allow Willie to come into the second round. As a result, Heath gained 119 votes to Thatcher's 130. The momentum lay with her, and in the second ballot Whitelaw was trounced by 79 votes to Thatcher's 146. Powell judged that she was simply 'opposite the spot on the roulette wheel at the right time', adding that she 'didn't funk it'.[9]

The Conservatives had their first female leader. It was far from certain, however, that she could hold on to the leadership, let alone become Prime Minister. It would be all over by Christmas, judged her hopeful critics. Certainly the odds seemed stacked against her. Thatcher proved no match in the Commons for the wily Harold Wilson. Nor did she fare much better when the avuncular James Callaghan took over as Prime Minister in April 1976. It was fortunate that another general election was several years off, allowing her time to grow in stature.

Thatcher gained valuable publicity from a speech attacking the Russians as 'bent on world dominance'. When the *Red Star* then criticized her as the 'Iron Lady' she cashed in on the propaganda value of the description.[10] Her message that the state was stifling personal initiative, and had to be rolled back, also appealed to many. In particular, she insisted, government should allow a return to free collective bargaining, while controlling inflation by limiting the money supply, as monetarists like Milton Friedman in the USA and Enoch Powell in Britain had been arguing. In short, Britain should return to 'good housekeeping', even if this meant defying the trade unions. She also benefited from the slick advertising of Saatchi & Saatchi, especially from their poster containing the words 'Labour Isn't Working' below a lengthy dole queue (which in fact consisted of Young Conservatives). The most crucial work for the Tories, however, was done by the Labour government and their inability to avert a 'winter of discontent' (see Chapter 16). As a result, in the general election of May 1979, the Conservatives gained a majority of 43 seats, with a swing of 5.6 per cent from Labour to Tory. Margaret Thatcher became Prime Minister, at the age of 53.

Governing style

Margaret Thatcher was unlike any previous Prime Minister in that the spotlight was constantly upon her, and on her appearance as much as her pronouncements. She used this publicity to superb effect, becoming a consummate media politician – with more than a little help from the experts.

One of these was Gordon Reece, a TV producer who became director of publicity at Tory Central Office in 1978. He found her a willing and malleable pupil. Her hair was restyled, being 'backcombed and sprayed into immovable shape'.[11] She also became a power-dresser. Her fashion apotheosis came in 1987 with a trip to Moscow. She alighted from the plane, to a reception of TV cameras and flash photography, in a regally magnificent black fur coat and hat. Nothing was left to chance, as she had been coached on the need to walk slowly and on no account to look down at her feet. Her voice was also remodulated to overcome the effects of childhood elocution lessons. She learned to speak more slowly, and to vary her intonation; and the pitch was lowered, acquiring a huskier quality, and then lowered again – in total, according to the experts, by a full 46 hertz. (On occasions, especially when 'fighting mad' in the Commons, the Thatcher voice would become deeper still, and far more loud and manly. In such tones, one imagines, would Lady Macbeth castigate her husband for infirmity of purpose and call for the daggers!) She was coached to improve her TV performances. She also became adept at delivering 'sound-bites' for news programmes and always made the most of 'photo-opportunities', for instance holding a new-born calf during the 1979 election campaign – for a full 14 minutes, to allow the paparazzi their fill – and later being filmed riding in a tank, or, more mundanely, enquiring concernedly of busy shoppers about the price of food.

In 1978 Reece had engaged Saatchi and Saatchi, whose managing director, Tim Bell, became one of Thatcher's closest advisers. Negative campaigning was used more than ever before. Bell targeted working-class women and skilled manual workers; and rather than explaining issues he attempted to evoke emotional responses. He organized youth rallies, with pop stars and celebrities, and arranged that Thatcher would speak not just on serious radio discussions but on the Jimmy Young Show and other popular programmes. Later Bell organized 'focus-groups' of 'ordinary' people to provide feedback on political presentation. Newspaper editors were assiduously cultivated, especially Larry Lamb of the *Sun* and David English of the *Daily Mail*. A media-friendly 'Maggie' emerged from the remodelled Margaret Thatcher.

Thatcher's assistants were in fact legion. Particularly important were her speech-writers, the most important of whom was the playwright Ronald Millar. A huge amount of hard work went into the construction of her major speeches: ideas would be debated, drafts written, corrected, re-written, often abandoned altogether, begun again, reconstructed and then fine-tuned. Millar insisted that Thatcher was the 'driving force' behind her speeches,[12] even though he, and others, almost always provided their key phrases and jokes.

Thatcher was not the creation or mouthpiece of other people. Her image was moulded and remoulded, but she was in charge of the process. She was simply doing what was necessary to achieve victory. She represented the triumph of the Nietzschean principle: there were stronger and more creative intellects among her advisors, but hers was the strongest will. Certainly no one worked harder than Margaret Thatcher. She worked seven days a week, and sleep was limited to four or five hours a night. Characteristically, when the IRA detonated a bomb in the Brighton hotel in October 1984, just before 3 a.m., she was still working – a fact that may have saved her life. She enjoyed work, glorying in detail as well as overall plans. Food was merely fuel: 'It was a case of fill up the tank and get back to work.'[13] Holidays were detested, and she could bear no more than ten days a year without the stimulation of work. Nor did she have any passionate interests outside politics. She paid the price for this single-minded intensity with a lack of perspective, but clearly Margaret Thatcher was amazingly tough and resilient.

It is often pointed out, quite correctly, that Thatcher was a successful politician – and therefore flexible, pragmatic and at times unscrupulous. Yet at the core of her being were inflexible ideas. One such belief was patriotism, at white heat during Britain's struggle during the Second World War and simmering, and occasionally boiling over, thereafter. Another was capitalism.

She was a capitalist to the core, and several times wished she had entered a more lucrative profession than politics. She believed that capitalism had religious sanction. In her first major interview as premier, she explained that the Good Samaritan did not just have good intentions: he had money as well. She actually believed that the Parable of the Talents was to be taken literally, as Christ's call for an entrepreneurial society.

On a personal level, Thatcher was responsible for many small, almost nameless acts of kindness to friends and acquaintances. But on a larger scale she was remorseless. 'Compassion?' she once insisted, 'That's not a word I use.'[14] On TV she criticized those who 'drooled and drivelled about the poor',[15] and an observer judged she had 'no sentimental or guilty feelings about underdogs'.[16] Others might be too full of the milk of human kindness to press on with ultimately beneficial policies, but not Thatcher.

As premier, Margaret Thatcher was remarkably forceful and dominant. In a term coined to encapsulate her political style, she would give people a good 'handbagging' – an image that preserved her femininity while still conjuring up the grievous bodily harm she regularly inflicted. TV viewers found the regular battle of wills between the premier and Robin Day, the most fearsome political interviewer of the day, compulsive viewing. After one encounter the *Sun* bore the headline: 'Maggie Beats Sir Robin in Big Telly Battle'. It was grist to Day's after-dinner speeches, however, as he joked about beginning an interview with the words: 'Prime Minister, what is the answer to my first question?' Among those who laughed loudest were members of the Cabinet.[17]

Clearly Thatcher was not of a temperament to be merely *prima inter pares* in Cabinet. Furthermore, there were very good reasons why relations were unlikely to be harmonious with her colleagues. She was, after all, an outsider. Not only was she a woman but, in a party containing more than its fair share of toffs and snobs, she was the girl brought up above the family's grocery shop in Grantham, in a flat without an inside toilet or hot water. Old Etonian Francis Pym decided that the basic problem for the Conservatives was that 'we've got a corporal at the top, not a cavalry officer'.[18] She also wanted to bring about changes in policy of which most traditional Conservatives, with their traditions of paternalism, viscerally disapproved.

It is not true that all Cabinet members found her rude and overbearing. Nor did she stifle all discussion or disagreement. During her first administration, according to the usually critical James Prior, there was plenty of argument. Nor is it true that she announced Cabinet conclusions at the start of a meeting. Although she would give her viewpoint and defend it forcefully against opposing voices, she rather liked debate and respected those with the courage to stand up against her. She would even accept being told that she was wrong. Once Nigel Lawson interrupted her interruptions of another minister with the words 'Shut up, Prime Minister, just occasionally let someone get a word in edgeways' – at which Thatcher blushed and remained silent for a full 20 minutes.[19] It remains true, however, that many ministers felt browbeaten. She was harsh on those who were poorly prepared and had little regard for those too gentlemanly to argue with her. She did not cavil at sacking ministers or forcing their resignations, and her loyal and long-serving press secretary, Bernard Ingham, was quite prepared to brief against those not in her favour, making their position untenable.

Those whom she sacked were particularly bitter, complaining that she governed through cliques and had ended collective decision-making and thus collective responsibility, or that she wanted to run every department herself. Kenneth Baker, who in fact survived, later wrote that Mrs Thatcher 'categorised her ministers into those she could put down, those she could break down, and those she could wear down'.[20] She was particularly determined that budgets should be presented to the full Cabinet only as *faits accomplis*. Proper discussion, on economic policy and other key areas, was limited to ad hoc committees whose composition she decided.

Thatcher played the game of politics to win, with deadly seriousness. *She* was the Prime Minister, in charge of *her* government, and it was *her* duty to run the country. In her view of Britain's largely unwritten and therefore infinitely malleable constitution, the Cabinet like the civil service was merely there to assist the Prime Minister, and at times she was better off relying on personal advisers. From another point of view, however, she was simply bad at man-management. Thatcher undoubtedly underestimated the abilities of many colleagues, especially the milder-mannered ones, and government suffered accordingly. As Labour's Denis Healey once said, 'she was not a tree under whose shadowing branches much else was encouraged to grow'.[21]

Thatcher's failings were exacerbated the longer she was in office. She described the Cabinet in 1987, to a group of new Under Secretaries, as 'a load of moaning minnies', adding 'They said they were tired but I told them they weren't'![22] A dominant Prime Minister was becoming a domineering one, wholesome self-belief transmuted into a towering egotism. More and more she succumbed to the delusion of indispensability. She may even have believed that her role was preordained. On being elected Conservative leader, she had mused that there might be a destiny that shapes our ends; and during the election campaign of 1979 she felt with mystical intensity that she 'was instinctively speaking and feeling in harmony with the great majority of the population. Such moments are ... unforgettable'.[23] No matter that only 43.9 per cent of the 76 per cent who registered a vote cast it for the Conservatives, or that Callaghan was more popular in the country than she was – the intuition was all. The feeling grew in succeeding years, even though her party received only 42.4 and 42.3 per cent of votes in the general elections of 1983 and 1987. While some considered her more presidential than prime ministerial, others began to think of her as a monarch, and not of the constitutional type. She herself announced to the press in May 1989 that 'We are a grandmother.'[24] A haughty spirit came before Thatcher's destruction in 1990.

First premiership

'Where there is discord may we bring harmony ... where there is despair may we bring hope.'[25] In retrospect, Margaret Thatcher's use of words generally attributed to St Francis of Assisi as she entered 10 Downing Street seems dramatically ironic, for she brought not peace but a sword. Yet they symbolize that, in May 1979, she was not yet the 'Iron Lady' of legend. Indeed in many ways she was hesitant and uncertain, to the dismay of some of her more right-wing advisers.

The composition of her cabinet inevitably put her on the defensive. She made her mentor Sir Keith Joseph Secretary of State for Industry, while Sir Geoffrey Howe, awarded the imprimatur 'one of us' (a true believer or 'dry', rather than a 'wet'), became Chancellor of the Exchequer. In addition, Whitelaw proved a tower of strength as Deputy Prime Minister. But there were few others she felt she could rely on wholeheartedly. Perhaps for this reason she allowed Lord Carrington a free hand at the Foreign Office, and with beneficial results. He helped to break the impasse in Rhodesia, striking a deal that resulted in elections in April 1980 and victory for Robert Mugabe's ZANU party, which henceforth controlled Zimbabwe. It was not the result Thatcher had wanted, but she acquiesced.

Similarly, under pressure in her Cabinet in 1979–80, she gave some financial help to ailing industries like British Leyland. Yet in macro-economic strategy Thatcher, egged on by Howe, was remorseless. Tough medicine had to be accepted, they believed, if Britain's spiral of decline was to be halted. In Howe's first budget, in June 1979, direct taxes were reduced, the standard rate falling from 33 to 30 per cent and the top rate from 83 to 60. At the same time the rate of Value Added Tax rose from 8 to 15 per cent, a higher rate than Thatcher had initially favoured, while public expenditure was cut by £4 billion. In the succeeding budgets of March 1980 and 1981, further cuts were made, while government borrowing was also reduced. The Medium Term Financial Strategy, announced in 1980, set tough targets for the restriction of the money supply: Howe persuaded Thatcher that its growth had to fall by 50 per cent by 1983–84. It was thought that this realistic monetarism would end the scourge of inflation and put Britain's finances on a sound and sustainable footing.

In fact, the rise in VAT and a general fall in government subsidies pushed inflation significantly higher. Standing at 10.3 per cent when Thatcher came to power, it reached 21.9 per cent a year later, necessitating rises in interest rates that harmed industry and mortgage holders. Yet at least VAT hike fell out of the equation a year later. Indeed by 1983 inflation was down to 4 per cent. Unemployment, however, was a far more intractable problem. From 1.5 million in 1979 it reached 3 million in 1982, and privately ministers admitted that only changes to the methods of calculation kept the official figure from rising still higher. Britain lost about a quarter of its manufacturing capacity in 1979–82.

These were not the results of their economic strategy that Thatcher and Howe had expected. They had assumed that unemployment would rise, but not to the extent that it did. Thatcher believed in Darwinian economics: the fittest companies, producing what people wanted to buy at a price they could afford to pay, would thrive, while the inefficient would perish. But the former were proving far too few, the latter far too numerous. It seemed to many that the economy was becoming not leaner but more emaciated. Crucially, the cuts were being made at a time when the world economy was going into recession, while the fact that sterling was now a 'petro-currency', due to the flow of North Sea oil, kept the pound high and so made British exports less competitive and imported manufactured goods cheaper. A surplus on trade in manufactures of £5 billion in 1980 became a deficit of £4 billion by 1985.

Crisis arose in April 1981 when riots took place in Brixton, followed by similar disturbances elsewhere in the summer. To some, Britain's social fabric was being torn apart by government austerity. To the Prime Minister, however, the violence was sheer criminality: individuals had free will – it was almost as if, as in existentialist thought, they were *condemned* to freedom – and therefore were responsible for their actions. Many ministers considered her viewpoint extremely limited, believing, as did senior judge Lord Scarman in his official report on the riots, that poor living standards had created 'a predisposition towards violent protest' and that there was a good case for social and economic aid from the government.[26] Yet, as Thatcher made crystal clear at the 1980 Party Conference, her face was turned against fundamental changes in strategy: 'To those waiting with bated breath for that favourite media catch-phrase, the U-turn, I have only one thing to say: "You turn if you want to. The lady's not for turning."' No matter that in 1981, after bitter wrangles, she had to reshuffle her Cabinet, sacking several ministers (Christopher Soames, Ian Gilmour, Mark Carlisle), moving others (so that Prior went to Northern Ireland), and drafting in new supporters (including Lawson, Cecil Parkinson and Norman Tebbit). No matter either that Thatcher feared she might be forced from office, or that in the winter of that year her popularity rating slumped to a record low of 23 per cent. As a *Sunday Times* profile judged: 'The Thatcherite universe is designed to give birth to a new world – or end with a big bang, rather than steady decline into whimpering moderation.'[27]

Certainly it mattered not that after the 1981 budget no fewer than 364 economists wrote to *The Times* calling for extra government spending to create jobs. In his memoirs, Howe mocked their advice, for the very next quarter the fall in national output came to an end, and over the next eight years there was uninterrupted growth, with Gross Domestic Product growing by an average of 3.2 per cent a year. Perhaps the medicine was beginning to have beneficial effects, or perhaps, as critics believed, growth after 1981 was achieved despite the government. Certainly the Chancellor soon dropped all talk of monetarism as, with the growth of credit card purchases and other forms of credit, it was proving quite impossible to control the money supply. What is indisputable, however, is that the Conservatives would almost certainly have lost the next election had it not been for the 'Falklands factor'.

On 2 April 1982 Britons were bemused by news that Argentina's dictator, General Galtieri, had invaded the little-known Falkland Islands, with their 1,800 British inhabitants, 8,000 miles away from Britain and 300 miles off the South American coast. Then came anger, as it was realized that the withdrawal of HMS *Endurance* had given the invaders a free hand, a fact that led to the resignation of Carrington as Foreign Secretary. Soon, however, as Britain launched a task force to retake the islands, many Britons gave way to an upsurge of triumphant nationalism. In the process, Margaret Thatcher's popularity soared: her approval rating reached 80 per cent while, in the middle of the conflict, a little known Labour candidate, Anthony Charles Lynton Blair, lost his deposit in the Beaconsfield by-election.

Thatcher's significance during the conflict was, first, that she refused to listen to the majority view that it would be impossible to reconquer the Islands. Instead, she accepted the advice of Sir Henry Leach, the Chief of Naval Staff, that, with sufficient political will, they could be wrested from the Argentines. Second, she used all her powers to secure sufficient logistical help from

President Reagan of the USA to enable success, despise important presidential advisers who wanted no such thing. Third, she backed the judgements of the military commanders on the spot, even when they wanted to sink the *General Belgrano* – an attack that cost 360 lives – when it was sailing away from the exclusion zone the British had established. Her tactics bore fruit when, on 14 June 1982, Britain regained control of the Falkland Islands. Few stopped to count the cost: not only around 750 Argentine and 255 British deaths but an expenditure of £5 billion and a large ongoing liability to maintain 'fortress Falklands'.

Failure, Thatcher believed, would have been the final death-knell of Britain as an important nation. It would certainly have signalled her political demise. As it was, many now agreed with Enoch Powell's encomium in the Commons: the Iron Lady was constructed of 'ferrous matter of the highest quality ... of exceptional tensile strength ... highly resistant to wear and tear and to stress, and may be used with advantage for all national purposes'.[28] She herself basked in the post-Falklands limelight. Britain had ceased to be a nation in retreat, she averred. 'The lesson of the Falklands is that Britain has not changed and that this nation still has those sterling qualities which shine through our history.' Furthermore, domestic problems would henceforth be tackled with the 'spirit of the South Atlantic – the real spirit of Britain'.[29] Yet, if her rhetoric verged on the Churchillian, her spirit in victory lacked his magnanimity. She could not, for instance, forgive the Archbishop of Canterbury for urging that the dead on both sides be remembered. Undoubtedly victory in war changed Thatcher psychologically: she became more confident and resolute, less concerned with accommodating waverers and fainthearts in her own party.

That she would be given another period in office was a foregone conclusion in June 1983. Not only was Thatcher considered by many a great national hero, not only was the economy showing signs of picking up, but Labour's manifesto, which included a commitment to unilateral nuclear disarmament, seemed even to many of its own supporters 'the longest suicide note in history'. Furthermore Labour's 69-year-old leader, Michael Foot, who scorned modern methods of presentation, was a public relations disaster. Labour secured only 27.6 per cent of the popular vote, its lowest share since 1918. The centre-left had been split ever since the breakaway Social Democratic Party had been formed in 1981, and as a result Thatcher's Conservatives, though with only 42.4 per cent of the vote, romped home with 397 seats and an overall majority of 144.

Second premiership

The years from 1983 to 1987 constituted a period of sustained economic growth, with Nigel Lawson occupying 11 Downing Street for the whole of the period, Howe being moved to the Foreign Office. It was a period of affluence, as real wages grew by as much as 15 per cent, the Tories insisting that their policies were responsible, their critics believing, probably with more justification, that the upturn in the world economy and an increase in consumer credit were the more likely causes. But if most people were better off, unemployment dipped below 3 million only after the 1987 election.

It was an era of popular capitalism. An important start had been made in Thatcher's first government, when council tenants were given the 'right to buy' their homes, a popular policy because prices were considerably lower than market valuations, and beneficial for the government as many former tenants decided to vote Conservative as a result. The policy proceeded apace during the second government and beyond. In total, 1.5 million council houses and flats were bought, and £15 billion was raised.

Privatization, or de-nationalization, was another plank in the Conservative strategy. Supporters believed that industries would prosper far more in the market-oriented private sector, that government would be spared the running costs and subsidies expended in the past and, furthermore, that large sums would be raised from the sales. In her first administration, government-owned shares in British Petroleum and British Aerospace were purchased by institutional investors. Now shares were sold direct to the public, first with the privatization of British Telecom and then with British Gas, British Airways, Rolls-Royce and the British Airports Authority (and, in the third Thatcher administration, British Steel, Rover Group and the water companies were sold, with the sale of the electricity companies being almost finalized). In total, from 1979 to 1990, almost £34 billion was raised. Admittedly many investors sold for a quick profit, but the number of shareholders nevertheless grew from 3 million in 1979 to 11 million in 1990. By the latter date shareholders outnumbered trade union members by 1 million. Thatcher's vision of a property-owning and share-owning democracy was coming to pass, providing a vested interest among the beneficiaries of this process in voting Conservative, as Labour at first pledged itself to renationalization. Yet not only was Mrs Thatcher initially cautious about privatization, she knew where to draw the line. It was her successor who undertook the more problematic privatisation of the railways and nuclear energy.

There were changes in finance too. The 1986 Building Societies Act allowed for the conversion of mutually-owned institutions into banks. Most important of all was the 'Big Bang' of October 1986 when the City of London was deregulated. 'Yuppies' (young urban professionals) became the symbols of the new affluence, while vast shopping centres sprang up and regenerated dock areas became enormous retail parks. Few troubled about old-fashioned notions of equality, as house prices increased to record levels, giving millions of owners the 'feel-good' factor that their wealth was increasing.

Yet despite this affluent economic and financial background, Thatcher's second government suffered major problems. The most significant was the miners' strike of 1984. Thatcher had bowed to pressure back in 1980 and withdrawn pit closures, but at that time coal stocks were low and a strike might have been successful. She was adamant that, eventually, uneconomic pits had to close; and she was determined that, in any conflict with the National Union of Mineworkers, the government must emerge victorious. The NUM President, Arthur Scargill, on the other hand, insisted that there was no such thing as an uneconomic pit, and in his campaign to preserve the coal industry he wanted to bring down the Thatcher government.

When in March 1984 the National Coal Board announced pit closures, with the loss of 20,000 jobs, Scargill announced a national strike. It was the beginning of an epic struggle. Thatcher threw the full weight of the state behind the Coal Board. Money was no object, and as much as £5 billion may have been expended to achieve victory. In 1973 the police had stood by passively as pickets paralysed the country, but in 1984 the police were mobilized as never before to ensure there were no power cuts. If pickets were often intimidating and sometimes brutal, so were the police. As a result, the strike – and especially the confrontation outside the Orgreave coke plant in Yorkshire, with 5,000 arrayed on each side – at times looked remarkably like a civil war. Furthermore, the government used MI5 and Special Branch to discredit the miners in general and Scargill in particular.

Thatcher did everything possible to defeat 'the enemy within'. Even so, the miners were undone partly by their own tactics. Scargill refused to ballot miners on the strike, fearing that he would lose. Instead he relied on article 41 of the NUM constitution, specifying that each area could call out its men without a vote. 'Flying pickets' then used violence and intimidation to coerce those who wanted to work. This division in the miners' ranks, especially strong in Nottinghamshire, profoundly weakened Scargill's cause, losing him support not only from the Labour Party but the general public too. Often has it been said, with justification, that Mrs Thatcher was lucky in the choice of her enemies. Eventually there was a drift back to work, and in March 1985 the strike was over.

Thatcher was victorious, but she paid the price of victory. On the left she was hated as never before. Many Britons had been repelled by the manner of victory, and by Thatcher's reaction to it. People had told her not to gloat: 'Well, I am gloating. I am gloating.'[30] Opinion polls now gave Labour a lead, their first since 1981. Furthermore, the nation suffered economically, as Britain was reduced to importing coal.

There are, however, mitigating facts. First, Thatcher had shown some moderation. Not only was the government side more willing to negotiate than the miners' leaders, but she had wisely refrained from using troops. Second, it was not she, but her successor John Major, who authorized the closure of the Nottinghamshire pits whose men had kept on working in 1984. Finally, it must be said that a victory for Scargill in 1984 would have been problematic, if not catastrophic, for democratic politics. By its series of employment and trade union laws, which banned secondary picketing and provided for compulsory pre-strike postal ballots, and more importantly by defeating Scargill and the miners in 1984–85, Thatcher's government had weakened the trade unions, whose membership fell from 13.5 million in 1979 to under 10 million in 1990, and tackled the problem of over-mighty trade unions barons – even if, some said, at the cost of producing an over-mighty Prime Minister.

The second major problem of this period was the continuing campaign of violence waged by the Irish Republican Army. In fact, violence as a whole was in decline, as several key IRA captives became 'supergrasses', but in October 1984 Thatcher and her Cabinet almost became victims. A bomb containing between 20 and 30 pounds of explosives had been concealed behind a bath panel in room 629 of the Grand Hotel in Brighton, three weeks before it was due to explode during the Conservative Party Conference. Five people were killed, though Thatcher was unharmed, and she bravely addressed the conference on schedule later that morning, insisting that murderers would never extinguish democracy. It was also to her credit that, in November of the following year, she was flexible enough to sign the Anglo-Irish Agreement.

The Agreement, while insisting that there would be no change in the status of Northern Ireland without the consent of its people, nevertheless provided for an input from the South in the affairs of the North. Thatcher would have preferred to defeat the IRA, but her Northern Ireland Secretary, Douglas Hurd, and Irish Taoiseach, Garrett Fitzgerald, persuaded her to accept a constructive initiative. In the short term, it bore no fruit; but in the longer term both Major and Blair built upon it to help bring peace to Northern Ireland.

The third major problem was the Westland scandal in 1986. A relatively minor issue – whether a near-bankrupt British manufacturer of helicopters should be supported by a European consortium or by the American Sikorsky firm – assumed menacing proportions. Defence Secretary Michael Heseltine supported the former, Trade Secretary Leon Brittan the latter. Thatcher herself threw her weight decisively against Heseltine, whom she regarded as an ambitious rival. A letter from the Attorney-General criticizing Heseltine was, against the rules, published in the press, and Heseltine was not allowed to put his case in full Cabinet. Others had resigned before, but never with the publicity Heseltine attracted by storming out of Cabinet in January 1986. The fall-out included the resignations of Brittan and a civil servant from his department, Collette Bowe, who had supposedly taken the initiative and leaked the letter. But many felt that Thatcher and her press secretary, Bernard Ingham, were really responsible; and Bowe said as much. Thatcher herself might well have fallen, had not the Labour leader, Neil Kinnock, who had replaced Foot in 1983, performed poorly and mishandled a critical debate in the Commons. Even so, Thatcher was not unscathed. Many felt that she had become too isolated from her party and Cabinet and was too reliant on a small coterie of advisers. Some wanted the next general election to be her last.

The election of June 1987 saw a majority of 102 seats for Thatcher and the Conservatives. Kinnock was thought too inexperienced and perhaps too unreliable, and many wanted more Conservative affluence. In his 1986 budget Lawson had injected £5 billion into the economy and in 1987 he took another two pence off the standard rate of income tax. The Conservative manifesto insisted that 'the British economy has never been stronger or more productive', a message Thatcher reiterated with an insistence that 'Tory reforms have transformed a lame duck economy into a bulldog economy'.[31] Cynics were correct in assuming that this self-congratulatory chorus presaged the bursting of the Tory economic bubble. But Margaret Thatcher, at the age of 61, had won a momentous third general election in a row.

Third premiership

Thatcher's virtues of strength and determination were now beginning to turn into the vices of stubbornness and blindness. It was as if her face were taking on the contours of the iron mask. She became increasingly out of touch with the party and the public, listening only to her personal advisers, and they often told her what she wanted to hear. Crucially, she did not have a Willie any longer, Whitelaw having resigned in January 1988 after a stroke. She began to lecture and hector her Cabinet. 'Why do I have to do everything in this government?' she demanded,[32] and would not stay for an answer. As the BBC political correspondent John Cole put it, 'Margaret was on transmit, not receive'.[33]

Commentators now spoke openly of 'Thatcherism'. So did the lady herself, arguing, quasi-religiously, that it so 'strikes a chord in the hearts and minds of men and women that they say yes and believe it'.[34] One key component of the term was a nationalistic determination that Britain's voice should be heard on the world stage.

Thatcher had voted, as a member of Edward Heath's Cabinet, for entry into the European Economic Community. Yet almost from the beginning of her first premiership she had quarrelled with Europe's leading figures, for instance by stridently but successfully demanding a rebate on Britain's financial contribution in 1979–80. Now she set her face against greater integration. She was particularly determined to resist membership of the European Monetary System (EMS), an attempt to create stable interest rates between member states – and some thought a step on the road to a single currency. Her refusal led to intense friction with her Chancellor, Nigel Lawson, and her Foreign Secretary, Geoffrey Howe. Paradoxically, she conceded entry only in October 1990, after Lawson had resigned and Howe had been demoted, under pressure from their successors. Europe was a key battleground for power within the Thatcher administration.

Thatcher's view was that Britain should remain a nation state and not degenerate into part of a European federation. Her views were set out most clearly in her speech at Bruges in September 1988. 'We have not successfully rolled back the frontiers of the state in Britain only to see them reimposed at a European level, with a European super-state exercising a new dominance from Brussels.' She wanted active and willing co-operation between 'independent sovereign states', not the attempt to fit European nations 'into some sort of identikit European personality'.[35] When Jacques Delors, President of the European Commission, indicated that he wanted the European Parliament, Commission and Council of Ministers to develop into *supra*-national institutions, her response was an emphatic 'No, No, No'.[36] It was a message the *Sun* rendered two days later as 'Up Yours, Delors!'

Many found her position attractive, and it is quite possible that she intended to rally public opinion by a Eurosceptic crusade, with Delors cast as a new Galtieri or Scargill. But her remarks ran counter to the more nuanced words of her colleagues, and many suspected that she was doing the right things for the wrong reasons. Her off the cuff remarks about Europeans – using the words German and French almost as terms of abuse – seemed to reveal not a reasonable political position but arch prejudice. Soon the truth of this view was to be revealed.

In sharp contrast to her Euroscepticism, Thatcher wholeheartedly wished to secure harmonious relations with the United States. Her Cabinet had made the decision to purchase Trident nuclear missiles from the USA in December 1979, and after Reagan became President in 1981 Britain received an updated version at a bargain price. She and Reagan were ideological kindred spirits, both as capitalists and as implacable opponents of the 'evil empire' of the Soviet Union. Under their leadership the 'special relationship' began to flourish. US cruise missiles were stationed in Britain, Reagan proved helpful during the Falklands war, and in April 1986 Thatcher gave Reagan permission to use British bases for bombing attacks on Libya, as punishment for its support of terrorism – despite widespread criticism at home. To some commentators, the Prime Minister was acting as the tame poodle of the American President, but such was her personal dominance that few took the charges seriously. She was quite prepared to argue vigorously with Reagan when he seemed prepared to bargain away nuclear missiles and rely on the Strategic Defence Initiative, a series of laser anti-ballistic missiles in space. Yet, remarkably, Thatcher also took the initiative in trying to end the Cold War.

Key officials in the Foreign Office had believed Thatcher was too unbending in her hostility to the USSR. Yet, after reading a report by an academic, Professor Archie Brown, in September 1983, in which he insisted that change could come from within the Soviet power structure and identified a certain Mikhail Gorbachev as 'a likely, reform-minded leader',[37] her attitude began to change. She invited Gorbachev to London in December 1984 and found him 'the only Communist leader I can have a good argument with'.[38] When in March 1985 Gorbachev became

General Secretary of the Communist Party, Thatcher spoke with him after the funeral of his predecessor, a scheduled 15-minute talk that stretched to an hour. Five further meetings followed before her premiership ended. The Foreign Office was again unhappy, but this time that she was too optimistic about change in the USSR. Nevertheless Thatcher's voice was listened to with respect in the USA, as she facilitated contact between the leaders of the Superpowers. Once Reagan and Gorbachev began meeting, Thatcher was inevitably pushed into the background, a process further enhanced when George Bush replaced Reagan as President in January 1989; but as an intermediary in the period from December 1984 to November 1985 she had undoubtedly played an important – and entirely unpredictable – part in ending the Cold War.

The collapse of Communism in Europe in 1989 boosted Thatcher's standing in world affairs, for the successor states respected her as a Cold War Warrior and a champion of the free market. Yet the possibility of German reunification sent shivers down her spine. Quite simply, she feared that Germany would grow too strong. It was an obvious lesson of history, she believed, that an overmighty Germany would become dominant. The reason? – national character. She held a seminar with historians at Chequers in March 1990 in the hope of receiving support for her views. 'We've been through the war,' she had insisted, 'and we know what the Germans are like ... Once a German, always a German ... You can never trust them.'[39] Had not Hitler been elected, she asked rhetorically. It was pointed out that he had never received more than 43.9 per cent of the vote (in fact, the same proportion her Conservatives polled in 1979), but she persisted in her viewpoint. The historians were appalled at her gross national stereotyping.

In domestic affairs, too, Thatcher was becoming impervious to argument. Some right-wing Tories now wanted consolidation, but not so Thatcher. There were important reforms in education, with a national curriculum and the option for governors to take schools out of local authority control. Student loans were also introduced. In addition, NHS hospitals were allowed to opt out of local control and become self-governing trusts, while General Practitioners were encouraged to become budget holders shopping around for the most economical treatment for their patients. The civil service too was profoundly changed. Already over 100,000 posts had been cut, and now many departments were transformed into semi-autonomous agencies charged with meeting strict targets and with rigidly controlled budgets.

The main domestic problem was the economy. Already there were signs that it was over-heating, and now Nigel Lawson gambled by lowering interest rates and cutting taxes, the standard rate falling from 27 to 25 per cent and the higher rate from 60 to 40 per cent in 1988. He did this partly to combat what was perceived to be a stock market crash, though in reality it was no more than a correction, in October 1987. This policy, he believed, would prevent the sort of depression that had followed the 1929 crash. Yet inflation, which had been as low as 2.5 per cent in 1986, reached 8 per cent in 1989 and 10.9 per cent in October 1990. Interest rates had to be raised, eventually reaching 15 per cent, thus harming mortgage-holders, many of whose properties were now in 'negative equity', and alienating Conservative voters. Thatcher also quarrelled with Lawson because he was intervening in the markets to shadow the German Deutschmark, as an alternative to joining the EMS. She much preferred the floating pound advocated by her economics adviser, Alan Walters, and in October 1989 Lawson resigned. His legacy lived on, however, in his refusal to subsidize a new 'community charge'.

Few people in Britain approved of the rates as a means of financing local government. Less than half the population paid, and the sums assessed were not directly related to people's ability to pay. The Scots demanded reform before a new unpopular reassessment of rateable values was undertaken, and two junior ministers at the Environment Office, Kenneth Baker and William Waldegrave, worked out the details of a 'community charge', a flat-rate tax on almost every individual over the age of 18. Yet this 'poll tax' seemed to many even worse than the system it was designed to improve. Thatcher had long been unhappy with local government in Britain, 'capping' the amounts that could be charged in rates in 1984 and even going so far as to abolish the Greater London Council, and other metropolitan authorities, from 1986. At first she had seemed lukewarm towards the flat-rate charge, but now she unwisely made its acceptance a touchstone of her authority. There would be no U-turn, even though the bills turned out to be twice as high as anticipated.

The new tax was bitterly resented. The press reported that the Duke of Westminster, who had previously contributed £10,000 a year in rates, now paid £417, the same as his housekeeper. A protest march in London turned into a riot around Trafalgar Square on 31 March 1990. The fact that damage was done to cars and property, however, and that 350 were arrested, allowed Thatcher to argue that such actions could not possibly represent broad swathes of public opinion. Yet other Conservatives, fearful of losing their seats at the next election, were far more apprehensive.

The poll tax undoubtedly weakened Thatcher, but it did not bring her down. The Tories did badly in the May 1990 local elections, but over the summer Labour's lead in the opinion polls began to fall back, and in October Thatcher received a nine-minute standing ovation at the party conference. Her position was relatively secure until Geoffrey Howe resigned and, on 13 November, delivered a lethal resignation speech. Denis Healey had once likened being attacked by Howe in the Commons to being savaged by a dead sheep. But now, though the dead-pan delivery was typical of his understated style, the message was deadly. Howe had been a member of the Thatcher Cabinet from the very beginning, first as Chancellor, then as Foreign Secretary and finally, from July 1989, as Leader of the House of Commons. He had been treated, in Lawson's words, as a cross between a doormat and a punchbag. Now he had his revenge, attacking her unreasonable and strident attitude towards Europe and her unwillingness to work harmoniously with colleagues. His speech, in the words of the Chief Whip, was 'horribly good'.[40]

Events then moved rapidly. Heseltine stood against Thatcher in a leadership contest. Thatcher won, but by four votes short of the requisite majority. At first she intended to contest a second election, but a large majority of ministers advised that she would be defeated, indeed humiliated, if she did so. She decided to stand aside, and John Major, the rapidly promoted Chancellor of the Exchequer, beat both Foreign Secretary Douglas Hurd and Michael Heseltine to become Prime Minister.

Thatcher's fall in November 1990 was anything but certain. Had she deigned to canvass MPs in her contest with Heseltine, instead of refusing to grub for votes, or had her small team of campaigners been more energetic, she might well have retained the premiership. That her days at the top were numbered, however, was extremely likely. She had many enemies within her own party, and too many backbenchers believed they could not retain their seats under her leadership. Furthermore, there were obvious signs that the public wanted change. Thatcher had been defeated neither by the electorate nor by Conservative MPs, but her later description of her Cabinet colleagues as committing 'treachery with a smile on its face',[41] in refusing to give full support in a second ballot, is pure melodrama.

Conclusion

Margaret Thatcher excited strong and contradictory emotions, and among people who previously had taken relatively little interest in party politics. The poet Philip Larkin and the comedian Kenneth Williams, for instance, were profoundly pro-Thatcher, while the playwright Denis Potter and the philosopher A.C. Grayling were entirely anti. While some shed tears of joy at her resignation, others shed tears of bitter regret. Given such strong emotions, and the fact that her multi-faceted leadership lasted so long and in a period so recent as to be very imperfectly understood, the task of reaching overall conclusions is both difficult and hazardous.

What of Thatcher's determination to turn around Britain's economy? Admirers focus on the 1982–87 period, when Britain's recovery was longer and faster, and the growth of productivity and of real wages was higher, than in many competitor states. Yet if we take into account the early Thatcher years, the picture is far less rosy. The annual growth rate for 1979–89 was 2.25 per cent, significantly better than the 1.5 per cent average in1973–79, but worse than the 3 per cent annual growth figure for 1964–73. Britain's share of world manufacturing exports fell in the 1980s, while its overall share of world trade, even taking into account North Sea oil exports, was stationary. In addition, average household debt rose significantly and the savings ratio fell. Nor did the overall burden of taxation fall under Thatcher: in fact it rose slightly. Furthermore, the wealth created was not evenly spread. The rich got richer, if only because upper rate tax bands fell, but unemployment remained high. Wealth was expected to 'trickle down' to all sectors of society, but in practice it rarely did so. The term 'cardboard city' was coined in 1985 to describe the groups of rough sleepers in many of Britain's cities. In short, there had been no economic miracle, and Major argued in his memoirs that he inherited 'a sick economy',[42] but there had been economic modernization and the trend towards relative economic decline had been halted.

Nor did Thatcher succeed in rolling back the state and ending a dependency culture. In some ways the powers of the state were extended, with the curtailment of civil liberties and an extension of police powers; and, as unemployment grew, millions more people depended on the state for survival. Thatcher's enemies professed to believe that social services in general, and the NHS in particular, were unsafe in Tory hands, but in 1979–92 public spending grew by an average of 1.7 per cent every year, very similar to the average of 1.8 per cent under Labour in 1974–79. Certainly a graph showing expenditure on health from 1950 to 1990 shows a steady expansion, regardless of the political complexion of governments. If advisers advise and ministers decide, as Thatcher said on the resignation of Lawson, it is often trends that determine.

Nevertheless Thatcher and her governments produced real change. They broke the power of the unions; they sold 1.5 million council houses; and they vastly increased the number of shareholders in Britain, as the majority of industries taken into public ownership by Labour after the Second World War were privatized. The Prime Minister did not destroy all elements of the postwar consensus, but her governments had a more profound impact than any since Attlee's. Thatcher also, like Attlee before her, changed the political norms of her successors. Her influence on the Labour Party was particularly profound.

In their memoirs Howe and Lawson, despite their quarrels with Thatcher, decided that she had been a great premier. Far more surprising, however, is that Tony Blair also decided that 'she was undoubtedly a great prime minister'.[43] He disapproved of her Euroscepticism, but approved her determination to modernize Britain and combat trade union power, and also her pro-American foreign policy. It was because of her electoral success that Labour shifted its policies and moved to the right. Another key figure in New Labour, Peter Mandelson, summed up her success by announcing in June 2002 that, in economics: 'We are all Thatcherites now.'[44]

Thatcher clearly made the political weather. But did she fulfil her ambition of changing the soul of Britain? Her wish that Britain should turn its back on the permissive values of the 1960s was clearly not fulfilled. If she herself was generally old-fashioned, even puritanical, in terms of morality, most Britons, including several scandal-prone members of the Cabinet, certainly were not. Thatcher could not overturn well established social trends, with an inexorable rise in the number of divorces, abortions and of children born outside wedlock. Similarly, though Section 28 of the Local Government Act of 1988 prohibited local authorities from 'intentionally promoting homosexuality', this made little difference to the inexorable rise of gay rights.

Perhaps, with her emphasis of wealth-creation, Thatcher changed Britain's morality for the worse, so that the country became a 'brutopia of competitive individualism'.[45] It has been argued that she 'changed the mind-set of the nation'.[46] But did Thatcherism really transform Britain into 'a more grasping, greedy, mendacious and mean-spirited society'?[47] These are important charges, but not fully credible ones, as they assign too much influence to politicians. British society was, and is, anything but monolithic; and if some succumbed to the worship of the money-god, there were others who managed to lead decent lives and pay little heed to politics. Ordinary life for millions in the 1980s failed to mirror media images of selfish hedonism. Thatcher's Tory enemy Ian Gilmour believed that, just as most people did not vote for Thatcher, so most were impervious to her values: 'Unfettered individualism made little or no headway.'[48] Opinion polls at the end of the Thatcher era showed that a majority of people preferred extra spending on social services to further tax cuts and that attitudes to the poor and unemployed were softening. There was still a good deal of traditional sympathy with the underdog. Admittedly there were examples of gross materialism, but this was also the decade that saw the Live Aid concert in July 1985, with donations of over £150 million to alleviate starvation in Ethiopia, while Comic Relief began in the following year.

Thatcher did not embody the 1980s. 'When the history of the 1980s is written,' insisted the *Sun* on 23 November 1990, 'the name Margaret Thatcher will appear on every page.' But it is not so; and we must avoid the temptation to attribute too much to her influence. Who, for instance, can accept the judgement of the critic Sir Peter Hall that she spawned commercially successful but meretricious musicals, or of the playwright Alan Bennett that she was responsible for the bad manners exhibited on TV discussion programmes?

Nevertheless there was something about Margaret. She dominated British politics for a whole decade in a way that had no precedent in the twentieth century. Margaret Thatcher was such a powerful and passionate political protagonist that, to those who saw her in her prime, succeeding premiers appear not only monochrome, humdrum and bland but relatively innocuous in comparison.

Notes

1 Peter Hennessy, *The Prime Minister*, London: Allen Lane, 2000, p. 434.
2 'Thatcher: The Downing Street Years', BBC, 1993.
3 Ibid.
4 John Campbell, *Margaret Thatcher*, vol. 2: *The Iron Lady*, London: Cape, 2003, p. 3.
5 Campbell, *Margaret Thatcher*, p. 5.
6 Margaret Thatcher, *The Path to Power*, London: HarperCollins, 1995, p. 6.
7 Thatcher, *Path to Power*, p. 31.
8 Carol Thatcher, *My Story*, London: Headline Review, 2008, p. 128.
9 Robert Shepherd, *Enoch Powell*, London: Pimlico, 1996, p. 462.
10 Thatcher, *Path to Power*, pp. 361–2.
11 Brenda Maddox, *Maggie: The First Lady*, London: Hodder and Stoughton, 2003, p. 168.
12 Ronald Millar, *The View from the Wings*, London: Weidenfeld and Nicolson, 1993, p. 283.
13 Thatcher, *My Story*, p. 16.

14 Maddox, *Maggie*, p. 137

15 Iain Dale (ed.), *Memories of Maggie*, London: Politico's, 2000, p. 162.

16 Nicholas Henderson, *Mandarin*, London: Weidenfeld and Nicolson, 1995, p. 486.

17 Robin Day, *Grant Inquisitor*, London: Pan, 1989, pp. 230, 283.

18 Hugo Young, *One of Us*, London: Macmillan, 1989, p. 331.

19 Dale (ed.), *Memories of Maggie*, pp. 137–8.

20 Kenneth Baker, *The Turbulent Years*, London: Faber, 1993, p. 256.

21 Chris Patten, *Not Quite the Diplomat*, London: Allen Lane, 2005, p. 67.

22 Dale (ed.), *Memories of Maggie*, p. 69.

23 Thatcher, *Path to Power*, p. 430.

24 'Thatcher: Downing Street Years.'

25 Millar, *View*, p. 266.

26 *The Scarman Report: the Brixton Disorders*, Harmondsworth: Penguin, 1982, pp. 36 and 34.

27 *Sunday Times Magazine*, 27 April 1980, p. 37.

28 Simon Heffer, *Like the Roman*, London: Phoenix Giant, 1998, pp. 860–1.

29 Anthony Barnett, *Iron Britannia*, London: New Left Review, 1982, pp. 149–53.

30 Maddox, *Maggie*, p. 166.

31 Andrew Gamble, *Britain in Decline*, London: Macmillan, 1994, p. 188; Ian Gilmour, *Dancing with Dogma*, London: Pocket Books, 1993, p. 58.

32 Maddox, *Maggie*, p. 200.

33 John Cole, *As It Seemed To Me*, London: Weidenfeld and Nicolson, 1995, p. 315.

34 Jonathan Raban, *God, Man & Mrs Thatcher*, London: Chatto and Windus, 1989, p. 27.

35 Margaret Thatcher, *The Downing Street Years*, London: HarperCollins, 1993, pp. 744–5.

36 Campbell, *Iron Lady*, p. 713.

37 Wm. R. Louis (ed.), *Resurgent Adventures with Britannia*, London: I.B. Tauris, 2011, p. 265.

38 Ibid., p. 267.

39 George R. Urban, *Diplomacy and Disillusion at the Court of Margaret Thatcher*, London: I.B. Tauris, 1996, p. 104.

40 Tim Renton, *Chief Whip*, London: Politico's, 2004, p. 87.

41 Hennessy, *Prime Minister*, p. 403.

42 John Major, *The Autobiography*, London: HarperCollins, 2010, p. xxi.

43 Tony Blair, *A Journey*, London: Hutchinson, 2010, p. 533.

44 E.H.H. Green, *Thatcher*, London: Hodder Arnold, 2006, p. 189.
45 R. Eccleshall and G. Walker (eds), *Biographical Dictionary of British Prime Ministers*, London: Routledge, 1998, p. 380.
46 Eric. J. Evans, *Thatcher and Thatcherism*, London: Routledge, 2nd edn, 2004, p. 1.
47 Ibid., pp. 146–7.
48 Gilmour, *Dancing with Dogma*, p. 215.

Further reading

John Campbell, *Margaret Thatcher*, vol 2: *The Iron Lady*, London: Cape, 2003
Eric J. Evans, *Thatcher and Thatcherism*, London: Routledge, 2004
E.H.H. Green, *Thatcher*, London: Hodder Arnold, 2006
Margaret Thatcher, *The Downing Street Years*, London: HarperCollins, 1993
Richard Vinen, *Thatcher's Britain*, London: Pocket Books, 2010
Hugo Young, *One Of Us*, London: Macmillan, 1989

18 John Major (1943–)

Prime Minister: November 1990– May 1997

'Yes, he's an attractive man, intelligent and well-intentioned, but he doesn't frighten anybody, does he? When Margaret [Thatcher] came into the tea room the teacups rattled.'

Peter Tapsell, in conversation with Gyles Brandreth, a fellow Conservative MP, 29 June 1992[1]

John Major's period at the top of British politics was marked by a series of remarkable triumphs and reversals. He became Prime Minister unexpectedly in November 1990, as a result of Margaret Thatcher's dramatic downfall. The new premier had served less than four years in the Cabinet and was little known outside Westminster. In April 1992 he confounded the opinion polls, which had predicted a hung parliament at best, by winning a fourth consecutive general election for his party. In the next few years, however, Major's premiership unravelled amid internal party wrangles over Britain's relationship with Europe and a series of political scandals. As a result, the Prime Minister whose arrival had initially been welcomed as a relief from his predecessor's autocratic style, was widely derided for his lack of authority. In May 1997, facing a revitalized Labour opposition, he led a divided and demoralized Conservative Party to its heaviest twentieth-century electoral defeat. Exhausted by the struggle to hold his government together, he retired from front-line politics, whilst his party embarked on 13 years in the wilderness.

The rise to the premiership

The words with which John Major opened his first Cabinet – 'Who would have thought it?'[2] – reflected the widespread surprise which greeted his rapid political ascent. Although he was the third Conservative Prime Minister to emerge from a lower-middle-class, grammar school background, he was socially much less securely rooted than either Heath or Thatcher. His father had been a music hall performer and small businessman who fell on hard times, obliging the family to move from the relative affluence of Surrey to straitened domestic circumstances in Brixton – a development which the Conservative Party would use as evidence of Major's ability to connect with ordinary people in the 1992 election campaign. Leaving school with few qualifications, he found employment in banking and won election as a Conservative councillor in the south London borough of Lambeth in 1968 before seeking a parliamentary seat. Major's early struggles left him with a sense of inferiority over his lack of educational attainment but also bred a quiet determination and self-reliance.

In May 1979, aged 36, Major was elected MP for Huntingdon in the general election which brought the Thatcher government to power. His capacity for work, attention to detail and ability to get on with others won him a series of promotions. After a period as a whip and a junior Social Security minister, in 1987 he reached the Cabinet as Chief Secretary to the Treasury, the minister responsible for negotiating departmental budgets. Having proved himself as a 'safe pair of hands', he was unexpectedly appointed Foreign Secretary in July 1989, followed in October by a transfer to the more congenial post of Chancellor of the Exchequer.

Major owed this remarkable rise to the patronage of Thatcher, who persuaded herself, after other possible successors had fallen by the wayside, that he might be groomed for even higher things. Her faith in him survived the episode in October 1990 when he persuaded her to join the European Exchange Rate Mechanism (ERM). The forerunner of today's single currency, this was an attempt to create stable exchange rates between the member countries of the European Community in order to encourage the growth of a single market and to control inflation. Major was fortunate that Michael Heseltine challenged Thatcher for the Conservative leadership shortly afterwards, before it could become even clearer that he did not share her hardline Euro-sceptic instincts. Thatcher's withdrawal, following her failure to win convincingly in the first round of the contest, enabled two contenders from within the Cabinet, Major and Douglas Hurd, the Foreign Secretary, to come forward. Thatcher backed her Chancellor as the only plausible candidate of the right. Many years later, after she had become disillusioned with Major, Thatcher told Hurd privately, with an astonishing lack of tact, that 'he was the best of a *very* poor bunch'.[3] At the time, however, she used her considerable influence to encourage her natural supporters in the parliamentary party to vote for Major. He also benefited from the fact that, as someone with connections across the party, who was not identified with a particular faction, he was the candidate best equipped to unite the Conservatives at a difficult time. He possessed neither the flamboyance of Heseltine nor the outdated, patrician image of Hurd. Conservative MPs saw him as the best means of preserving the essential legacy of Thatcherism, whilst projecting a more appealing public image which would give them a better chance of victory at the next general election.

Governing style

Major's more collegial style of Cabinet management, particularly in the early months of his premiership, has been widely acknowledged. Heseltine, who had resigned from the Thatcher government in January 1986 over her autocratic conduct of Cabinet business, gave Major credit for the 'improved atmosphere', noting approvingly that 'arguments were countered by reason and not interrupted or shouted down'.[4] Whereas his predecessor had discouraged debate by stating her own views in advance, Major preferred to build consensus by allowing open discussion. Chris Patten, Major's first party chairman, described 'a climate in which there are no givens, no off-limit areas, few sensibilities in Downing Street that have to be taken account of'.[5] The disadvantage of Major's style was that he sometimes failed to give a clear lead. Malcolm Rifkind welcomed the disappearance of Thatcher's use of 'bilateral interrogations with nobody else allowed to intervene' whilst wishing that 'Major would come out with his own view, which he almost never does'.[6]

Yet one should not exaggerate the degree to which the role of Cabinet changed under Major. Like Thatcher he did not regard it as a supreme executive body, instead using committees to recommend decisions to the full Cabinet. He tried to keep controversial subjects, such as Britain's response to the development of a single European currency, off the Cabinet agenda and aimed to delay decisions until he could reconcile conflicting viewpoints. This was to some extent a consequence of Major's lack of deeply held ideological beliefs and of his desire to maintain unity, especially after the 1992 election, when his parliamentary majority was much reduced and Europe became an increasingly divisive issue. Critics viewed this as a sign of his weakness as a leader, which was highlighted by the growing number of 'leaks' from Cabinet, as ministers with opposing views sought to influence events through the media. One consequence was much less open discussion in Cabinet. As Kenneth Clarke, who served as Chancellor of the Exchequer from May 1993 recalled: 'John's great strength was collective Cabinet discussion. But by the end, Cabinet was not a place anyone wanted to bring business to because of the deep distrust of other colleagues and fear of leaks.'[7]

One difficulty that Major faced was a scarcity of close Cabinet allies. He depended heavily on Chris Patten until he lost his parliamentary seat at the 1992 election. Although Major developed a good working relationship with Hurd, the latter was absorbed by departmental responsibilities as Foreign Secretary and retired from government in July 1995. In his final two years Major relied heavily on Heseltine, who took on the position of Deputy Prime Minister, but by then the government's standing had irreversibly deteriorated. Inside Number Ten Major appointed a talented team of advisers, notably Sarah Hogg, an economics specialist who headed the Downing Street Policy Unit until January 1995. From 1992, however, the team was drawn increasingly into helping with crisis management rather than long-term policy planning.

Major participated in debates in the Commons more than Thatcher had done, and made more statements, yet seemed oddly isolated from the parliamentary Conservative Party and frequently appeared uncomfortable in the twice-weekly arena of Prime Minister's questions, preparation for which absorbed a disproportionate amount of his time. He seemed more at ease with the Conservative Party in the country and with popular audiences, whilst his ability to command respect at Westminster ebbed away from 1992. How are we to account for the dramatic shifts of fortune which characterized his premiership?

The record in government

Major himself felt that the opportunity to take the highest office had come too early. He would have preferred to have had more time to establish himself as Chancellor. As a consequence he had one of the shortest periods available to any twentieth-century premier to work out his own agenda. His own philosophy was not clearly defined at the time of his appointment. He spoke of creating a 'classless society' in which people would be able to enjoy wider opportunities, and in which state-run services would be more responsive to the needs of the public. With the economy in recession, it was essential to control inflation, which was running at more than 6 per cent at the end of 1990, and which he viewed as the root cause of Britain's lack of competitiveness. He also wanted to make an impact on unemployment, which was set to rise above two million over the next year.

Other aspects of the Thatcher legacy demanded more immediate attention. Abroad, British and US forces were preparing to drive Iraq's army of occupation out of Kuwait in the Gulf War of early 1991. On this issue Major made a generally favourable impression, working effectively with the Americans and uniting British public opinion behind the action. *The Times* journalist Robin Oakley described his style on a visit to troops in the Gulf as 'more fireside chat than Henry V ... unscripted, direct and unvarnished, it was all the more effective for its lack of artifice'.[8] The most pressing domestic matter was the need to find a replacement for the community charge or poll tax, whose unpopularity had contributed to Thatcher's downfall. A form of local taxation which applied to all adults, regardless of income or property values, this was widely regarded as untenable. Major was undoubtedly right to prioritize the search for a visibly fairer alternative. The result was the introduction of the council tax, graduated according to property values and with reductions for single domestic occupancy – essentially a retuned version of the old rating system which had preceded the poll tax – which was in place before the 1992 election.

None of this, however, amounted to a distinctive set of ideas or policies that could be associated with Major himself. The premier's 'big idea' in his first year was the 'Citizen's Charter', an attempt to make public services more accountable to their users, and to enable more effective measurement of their performance. Although the Charter laid down many worthwhile expectations, including the publication of comparative school statistics, agreed hospital waiting times and compensation for delays in rail travel, it failed to capture the public imagination. Mockery surrounded the motorway 'cones hotline', a response to motorists' frustration with road works, which was soon abandoned. The privatization of railways earned the government criticism for the complexity of the model adopted, and for the arguably unwise separation of responsibility for track from train operations.

More substantial was Major's achievement in taking forward the peace process in Northern Ireland. Personal experience of IRA violence – republican terrorists attacked Downing Street with mortar bombs in February 1991 – did not deter him from seeking a solution to a conflict which had scarred the province for over two decades. By making clear that the government would abide by the democratically expressed will of the people of Northern Ireland, and by reiterating a principle first enunciated in November 1990, that Britain had no selfish economic or strategic interest there, Major won the trust of moderate nationalists without alienating Unionists. The December 1993 Downing Street declaration, the outcome of patient negotiation with the Irish Republic, ruled out the imposition of a united Ireland solution whilst demonstrating Britain's respect for nationalist aspirations. This helped to secure the first sustained IRA ceasefire, announced in August 1994. Although there was a return to paramilitary violence in February 1996, Major had pointed the way towards an eventual settlement, laying foundations on which his successor was able to build.

A fundamental challenge facing Major was the need to differentiate himself from Thatcher, without being seen to abandon her legacy and thereby antagonizing a large section of the Conservative rank and file. Her throwaway line in November 1990, that 'I shan't be pulling the levers there, but I shall be a very good back-seat driver',[9] encapsulated the problem facing the new premier. Unreconciled to her own deposition, Thatcher became increasingly critical of a successor whom she viewed as departing from her policies. Her supporters ignored the inconvenient truth that her disappearance had rescued the Conservative Party from a catastrophic slide in the opinion polls, with the approval rating of the Prime Minister leaping from 26 to 49 per cent within one month of Major's arrival in Number Ten. His victory in the April 1992 election was an achievement which by common consent would have eluded her. The campaign saw Major at his most popular: an accessible individual who appeared at ease with the crowds, whom he addressed from an old-fashioned soapbox, yet a leader who seemed more statesman-like than Labour's Neil Kinnock. 'Call me a dull dog if you wish, he seemed to be saying', wrote the novelist and journalist Julian Barnes in January 1992, 'but that is what I am: self-made, hard-working, unspectacular, trustworthy, the very spirit of middle England.'[10] Even his opponents recognized his appeal. Paddy Ashdown, leader of the Liberal Democrats, described him as looking 'just like the man next door' but as 'effective in his own quiet way – the sort of suburban Baldwin of our times' and 'probably the most plainly decent man we have had in Downing Street this century'.[11] Also crucial to Major's victory was the argument that, in spite of the continuing recession, his opponents' proposals for increased taxation meant that they were not to be trusted with the economy. Electoral success gave Major his own mandate, independent of Thatcher. Unfortunately, the vagaries of the electoral system meant that in spite of winning more than 14 million votes – the largest total for any party in a UK general election, equivalent to just under 42 per cent of the popular vote – this translated into a disappointingly slim 21-seat majority.

In September 1992, however, the government's credibility was fatally undermined by the pound's forced ejection from the Exchange Rate Mechanism. As market pressure on sterling grew, and in spite of frantic interest rate rises by a government determined to support its flagship policy, it became clear that the pound could not be kept within the ERM's specified exchange rate limits. Although the economy slowly recovered, and the government should have been able to take credit for the steady reduction of both inflation and unemployment, the humiliation of 'Black Wednesday' was used by a reviving Labour Party as evidence of the Conservatives' incompetence. Major was unfortunate that, under Tony Blair and Gordon Brown from 1994, Labour successfully ditched its irresponsible 'tax and spend' image. They fashioned 'New Labour' as a disciplined machine, which expertly captured the electorally vital middle ground.

Meanwhile Major's attempts to recover the initiative backfired spectacularly. His so-called 'back to basics' campaign in October 1993, which was meant to focus on traditional values in law and order, education and other areas, was wrongly interpreted as a personal morality crusade. It was rendered risible by a series of scandals which involved a number of junior ministers and backbenchers in the ensuing months. In a bid to exorcise the charges of 'sleaze' – a media word for the combination of sexual and financial misconduct which seemed to dominate the news agenda – Major appointed a committee to examine standards in public life, headed by a senior judge, Lord Nolan. The resulting report failed to dispel public concerns yet antagonized Major's parliamentary supporters, who saw it as further evidence of his willingness to surrender to external pressure. The premier gained no more credit from his appointment of another judge, Sir Richard Scott, to hold an inquiry into charges that government ministers had helped businessmen to circumvent an embargo on arms sales to Saddam Hussein's Iraq. Although the government was cleared of the principal allegations of wrongdoing, it never rose above the aura of corruption which dogged its closing years.

Europe was the most divisive issue for Major's Conservative Party. Thatcher's opposition to further European integration commanded widespread support within the party and several ministers, notably Michael Howard, John Redwood and Michael Portillo, shared her instincts. They were balanced by a number of influential figures, including Heseltine, Hurd and Clarke, who saw constructive engagement with Europe as the best course for Britain. Major himself was keen to maximize British influence and to mend fences after Thatcher's confrontational approach. He was prepared to sacrifice some national sovereignty if compensating advantages could be secured. Yet he shared the Euro-sceptics' suspicion of moves towards political union. In his memoirs he described himself as 'a pragmatist, not an idealist ... To me, the European Union was far more than a trading relationship, but I did not want to see it become a federation'.[12]

Characteristic of his approach was his patient negotiation of the Maastricht Treaty in 1991–92, which transformed the Community into a European Union and set a timetable for the creation of economic and monetary union based upon a single currency. Major signed the treaty but opted out of the single currency until its merits could be demonstrated. He also excluded Britain from the Social Chapter, a section of the treaty which introduced new regulations on working conditions, which he regarded as imposing undesirable additional costs on employers. These opt-outs were insufficient to pacify his party's right, for whom the loss of national sovereignty was unacceptable. Maastricht was ratified by Parliament in July 1993, but only after 61 days of debate and the government's use of a confidence motion to bring Conservative opponents into line.

Major had achieved victory at the price of creating a core of determined Euro-sceptic rebels, who waged an unremitting parliamentary guerrilla war on the government's programme. A low point was reached in the winter of 1994–95, when an exasperated premier withdrew the Conservative whip from eight persistent malcontents, effectively suspending their membership of the parliamentary party. They were joined by a ninth MP in a reckless show of solidarity. It was a measure of Major's declining authority that the so-called 'whipless wonders' were neither cowed by this sanction nor quietened by their eventual readmission to the fold. Criticism of the Prime Minister extended well beyond this small hard core of opponents. Right-wing ideologues were reinforced by a growing number of disappointed office-seekers and ex-ministers – 'the dispossessed and the never-possessed'[13] as the premier dubbed them in an unguarded moment at the end of an interview in July 1993. In a desperate bid to end the internal strife, in June 1995 Major took the unprecedented step of resigning the party leadership and inviting his critics to put forward a rival candidate. Although he defeated the challenger, John Redwood – who resigned as Welsh Secretary to take on Major – by 218 to 89 votes, the infighting continued. Ian Lang, one of the ministers who managed Major's re-election campaign, sadly recalled that it was impossible to save a party which now lacked 'any spark of moral fibre or team spirit' and in which 'the traditional pillars of loyalty, unity and common sense' had been virtually destroyed.[14]

Major's efforts to deliver moderate, progressive Conservative policies were fatally overshadowed by his party's wanton disregard of its own electoral survival. He faced the additional disadvantages of a still active and hostile predecessor as a rival focus for loyalty, and of a Labour opposition confidently emerging from the political wilderness. Few premiers have had to contend with the mockery directed at Major from 1992. Whereas Thatcher had often aroused hatred, he attracted the politically much more damaging emotion of contempt. In the satirical TV puppet series *Spitting Image* he was depicted in monochrome grey. *Guardian* cartoonist Steve Bell portrayed him as a 'naff, underpowered Superman',[15] wearing Aertex underpants outside his clothes. Major's failure to project himself as a decisive Prime Minister contributed to his government's defeat in the May 1997 election, which saw Labour emerge with an overall majority of 179. Too often he seemed to be reacting to events, not shaping the agenda: well intentioned but unable to control a fractured, unmanageable party. Yet it is doubtful whether an alternative leader could have averted the catastrophe. Major's replacement by a more assertive pro-European, such as Heseltine, might have precipitated a worse split. Moreover, his survival in office had entrenched the economic and social changes of the previous 18 years and in so doing ensured that a future Labour government could not turn back the clock to 1979. In that sense Major's troubled premiership assumed an importance which was not perhaps clear at the time.

Notes

1 Gyles Brandreth, *Breaking the Code: Westminster Diaries, May 1990– May 1997*, London: Weidenfeld and Nicolson, 1999, p.107.

2 Anthony Seldon, *Major: A Political Life*, London: Weidenfeld and Nicolson, 1997, p.148.

3 Douglas Hurd, *Memoirs*, London: Little, Brown, 2003, p. 404.

4 Michael Heseltine, *Life in the Jungle: My Autobiography*, London: Hodder and Stoughton, 2000, p. 488.

5 Interview with Chris Patten, 8 January 1991, in Ion Trewin (ed.), *The Hugo Young Papers: Thirty Years of British Politics – Off the Record*, London: Allen Lane, 2008, p. 320.

6 Interview with Malcolm Rifkind, 26 November 1992, in Trewin (ed.), *Hugo Young Papers*, p. 352.

7 Seldon, *Major,* p. 210.

8 Sarah Hogg and Jonathan Hill, *Too Close to Call: Power and Politics – John Major in No. 10*, London: Little, Brown, 1995, p. 39.

9 John Major, *The Autobiography*, London: HarperCollins, 1999, p. 200.

10 Julian Barnes, *Letters from London*, London: Picador, 1995, p. 95.

11 Paddy Ashdown, *The Ashdown Diaries: Volume 1: 1988–1997*, London: Allen Lane, 2000, p. 106, entry for 10 January 1991.

12 Major, *Autobiography*, p. 581.

13 Seldon, *Major*, p. 390.

14 Ian Lang, *Blue Remembered Years: A Political Memoir*, London: Politico's, 2002, p. 246.

15 Seldon, *Major*, p. 204.

Further reading

Sarah Hogg and Jonathan Hill, *Too Close to Call: Power and Politics – John Major in No. 10*, London: Little, Brown, 1995

John Major, *The Autobiography*, London: HarperCollins, 1999

Anthony Seldon, *Major: A Political Life,* London: Weidenfeld and Nicolson, 1997

www.johnmajor.co.uk is a useful resource for the study of John Major and his government

19 Tony Blair (1953–)

Prime Minister: May 1997–June 2007

> 'I think most people who have dealt with me think I am a pretty
> straight sort of guy.'[1]
>
> Tony Blair in a BBC interview, 16 November 1997

Tony Blair was the only Prime Minister to win three successive
general elections for the Labour Party. His arrival in Downing
Street in 1997, with a post-1945 record majority of 179 seats,
brought to an end 18 years of Conservative rule and gave him
a remarkable ascendancy in British politics. At 43 he was the
youngest Prime Minister to take office since the Napoleonic Wars,
exuding a dynamic sense of purpose which contrasted starkly
with the aura of decline surrounding John Major's outgoing
administration. Although Blair's majority was to slip to 167 in
June 2001, and more seriously to 66 in May 2005, he retained
office for a full ten years. He projected a self-consciously modern,
informal image, associated with the spirit of 'cool Britannia' –
shorthand for the government's endorsement by various rock stars
and show business personalities in the late 1990s. He brought
with him an independent, professional wife and a young family,
becoming the first Prime Minister in 150 years to father a child
whilst in Number 10. Blair's description of himself as 'a pretty
straight sort of guy' was prompted by questions about his willingness to exempt Formula One from a ban on tobacco advertising
after Bernie Ecclestone, the head of the motor racing organization,
had made a sizeable donation to Labour Party funds. The remark
was a typical and, in the short term, successful attempt to project
himself as a trustworthy, accessible leader. He had an uncanny

ability, at least in the early years, to express the public mood; his tribute to Princess Diana as 'the people's princess',[2] after her death in a car accident in August 1997, is a classic example.

Yet Blair was also a ruthless re-shaper of central government, bent on making established institutions deliver results and frequently accused of creating a 'presidential' mode of leadership. In many respects he seemed more willing to build on the legacy of Thatcher than that of any previous Labour government, embracing the free market and an Atlanticist foreign policy with unabashed fervour. His period of office is indelibly linked with his decision, following the notorious attacks by Islamic extremists on the USA on 11 September 2001, to lead Britain into two protracted and controversial conflicts in Afghanistan and Iraq. By the time he left Number 10 the high hopes and goodwill which had greeted his ascent to power had largely evaporated. Although his memoirs were a bestseller when published in 2010, he was obliged to abandon a planned book signing event in London, following a noisy demonstration at an earlier event in Dublin. The fall from grace of a leader who had been welcomed into office on a wave of popular enthusiasm, little more than a decade before, was one of the most striking political reversals of modern times.

The rise to the premiership

In many ways Tony Blair was one of the least likely individuals to rise to the leadership of the Labour Party. His was a secure middle-class upbringing as the son of a Conservative-supporting law lecturer at Durham. After a mildly rebellious career at Fettes, a well-known Edinburgh public school, he read Law at Oxford. Acting and membership of a rock group were his main leisure pursuits, although his time at university also helped to develop his religious views. His most important contact was with a charismatic Australian Anglican priest, Peter Thomson, who introduced him to the writings of a little known Scottish philosopher, John Macmurray. From the latter's work Blair derived an understanding of the importance of community – the idea that individuals best realize their potential as part of strong, mutually supportive groups in society. This concept attracted Blair far more than the ideas of orthodox socialism; for him it 'proposed an answer to the eternal dilemma of the left in politics: how to ensure that active government is the friend rather than the enemy of individual fulfilment'.[3]

Blair's emerging philosophy of social action helped draw him towards a political career. Initially, however, political activity took second place to forging a career as a barrister in London. Here he trained in the chambers of Derry Irvine, a lawyer who was to serve as Lord Chancellor in Blair's government, and who also introduced him to his future wife, Cherie Booth. The latter not only provided him with a secure family life but also helped to reinforce his commitment to the Labour Party. In 1983, aged 30, he was fortunate to secure a safe seat at Sedgefield in County Durham. Although outwardly conforming to the left-wing agenda which characterized the party at the time, Blair was privately impatient with a hardline socialist ideology which he perceived as damaging to Labour's electoral prospects. After the party's 1987 defeat, he found common cause with two representatives of his generation who also regarded modernization of Labour's style and message as essential. One was a serious-minded Scottish MP, Gordon Brown; the other was Peter Mandelson, a former television producer who served as Labour's Director of Communications before finding himself a parliamentary seat in 1992. Of the three Blair was the most radical and determined in his wish to move the party towards the centre ground.

Blair believed that in order to win power, Labour had to accept much of the social and economic legacy of the Thatcher years. It had to recognize that many voters had been alienated by the party's apparent hostility to people's aspirations to property ownership and personal betterment. Promoted as Shadow Home Secretary, he tapped into a national mood of anxiety over rising crime in early 1993, promising – in a phrase borrowed from Gordon Brown – to be 'tough on crime and tough on the causes of crime'.[4] Behind the sound-bites lay a philosophy which came to be known as the 'third way', a term which originated in the interwar period, to be revived in the 1990s by an influential sociologist, Anthony Giddens. Hard to define, it went beyond the traditional categories of right and left, combining notions of personal responsibility and social cohesion. It linked the dynamism of the market with the social-democratic impulse to safeguard public services. It embraced the global economy whilst promising a more equal society.

The sudden death of Labour's leader, John Smith, in May 1994 enabled Blair to present himself as the most convincing modernizing candidate, with the fresh ideas and image needed to revive the party's fortunes. Party traditionalists had good reason to be sceptical, as in truth it was hard to be certain exactly what Blair stood for. After four successive defeats, however, most Labour Party members were willing to take a chance. Blair's ability to project an appealing, youthful public persona would enable the party to reach out beyond its core supporters to the uncommitted inhabitants of 'middle England', on whose support its prospects of regaining office depended. His path was smoothed by a pact with the only other credible challenger, Gordon Brown. The latter reluctantly gave his younger rival a clear run at the leadership in return for the post of Chancellor of the Exchequer in the next Labour government, combined with authority over a range of domestic policies. More controversially, Brown emerged with an expectation – never embodied in a precise agreement – that Blair would surrender the premiership at some point to give him an opportunity to serve in the highest post.

As leader Blair moved swiftly to complete the rebranding of the party as 'New Labour'. The most important symbolic step was taken at the 1994 conference, when Labour's historic commitment to the public ownership of industries and services, enshrined in Clause IV of the party's constitution, was abandoned in favour of a bland adherence to 'common endeavour' in pursuit of the realization of individual potential, and declared that power, wealth and opportunity should be 'in the hands of the many not the few'.[5] Another break with the past was a ruthless insistence on discipline, with party spokesmen expected to maintain a consistent message of reassurance and moderation. A talented and ruthless former tabloid editor, Alastair Campbell, was appointed Press Secretary to manage the party's relations with the media, and Blair himself visited Rupert Murdoch, boss of the influential News International organization, with a view to ensuring favourable press coverage. As John Major's government became increasingly divided and embroiled in scandal, Blair seized the opportunity to present himself as both trustworthy and authoritative.

He taunted the embattled Conservative premier with the wounding jibe, 'I lead my party, [you] follow yours'.[6]

Blair's projection of himself as a strong leader, linked with growing public recognition of Labour's new-found unity and confidence, played a vital role in the 1997 victory. Although the economy was recovering from the recession of the early nineties, the Conservatives gained no public credit for this. Building on the more tentative modernizing work of Neil Kinnock and John Smith as leaders over the previous decade, Blair successfully exorcised the 'Old Labour' ghosts of economic incompetence and subservience to the trade unions. Less important, perhaps, was Blair's insistence, over Brown's doubts, that the party seek to reassure 'middle England' by promising not to raise income tax rates, and by his pledge to keep to Conservative spending targets for the first two years of a Labour government. Analysis of opinion polls suggests that most voters expected taxes to rise, whichever party won, and that they would not mind, provided that the new revenues were spent on improving public services. Blair took office on a wave of popular goodwill, evoked by Labour's campaign song, 'Things can only get better'. Recalling his entry to Downing Street amid scenes of jubilation which are now known to have been carefully choreographed, Blair described himself as the focus for 'the pent-up expectations of a generation ... They wanted things to be different, to look, feel, have the attributes of a new era, and I was the leader of this sentiment'.[7]

Governing style

'We have been elected as New Labour,' Blair told the audience at his 1997 victory celebration, 'and we will govern as New Labour.'[8] This meant an emphasis on strengthening the centre of the government machine: in the words of a senior aide, Jonathan Powell, 'a change from a feudal system of barons to a more Napoleonic system'.[9] The Cabinet Office and the Downing Street Policy Unit were to work closely together to take the agenda forward. New bodies such as the Social Exclusion Unit, which addressed a range of issues affecting disadvantaged communities, were joined by 'task forces' and co-ordinators known as 'tsars', in a bid to tackle problems by breaking down traditional barriers between government departments. After the 2001 election a further impetus to the cause of 'joined-up government' was given with the creation of the Prime Minister's Delivery Unit, which sought to drive public sector reform across Whitehall. To provide a specifically political dimension, the number of special advisers – party appointees who worked alongside neutral civil servants – increased from 8 to 28. The White House was the model for a new post, that of chief of staff, held by Jonathan Powell, who was empowered to give orders to civil servants.

These developments led to accusations that New Labour was importing into government the techniques of tightly controlled campaigning that it had perfected in opposition. The key figure here was Alastair Campbell, who controlled the Downing Street Press Office until his departure in August 2003 and created a Strategic Communications Unit to respond to the pressures of the 24-hour news media. Some earlier Press Secretaries, such as Bernard Ingham under Thatcher, had been less than objective in their presentation of the official message, but Campbell was much more proactive, even aggressive in his approach. Blair was exceptionally sensitive to the way in which New Labour projected itself, using television appearances, links with favourable newspapers and the internet to get the message across. In July 2000, at a time when the government was in the doldrums, a leaked memo revealed the premier demanding that his staff provide him with 'headline grabbing initiatives' in order to 'change public perceptions of the government'.[10] This obsession with what became known as 'spin' – creating the impression that the presentation of policy was as important as the content – helped to damage Blair's public standing in the long run.

Another area in which Blair disregarded constitutional convention was in his approach to the Cabinet. He combined an informality of style – in contrast with the practice under Thatcher and Major, first names rather than official titles were used around the table – with a willingness to downgrade the role of Cabinet in favour of bilateral meetings with key individuals. The decision to hand control of interest rates to the Bank of England, announced within days of Labour taking office, was taken by Blair and Brown without reference to their colleagues. A majority of the Cabinet was opposed to the building of the Millennium Dome but, in a meeting chaired by Deputy Prime Minister John Prescott in Blair's absence, it was accepted that the premier would get his own way. Cabinet meetings were shorter than had been customary and ministers were provided with fewer official papers. A report by a former Cabinet Secretary, Lord Butler, on the decision-making process in the run-up to the Iraq conflict, highlighted Blair's preference for informal discussions in small groups, without minute-taking, for which the popular term 'sofa government' was coined. According to Butler, this practice made it harder for the wider Cabinet to influence policy and 'risks reducing the scope for informed collective political judgement'.[11] More direct criticism was offered by former International Development Secretary Clare Short, who resigned from the Cabinet in May 2003 to speak of 'a shocking collapse in proper government procedure, with a small unelected entourage in Downing Street making the decisions'.[12]

One should, however, be wary of exaggerating the extent to which Blair's government marked a discontinuity with earlier practice. Blair was not the first premier to take decisions, especially in foreign and defence policy, without full Cabinet involvement. Blair echoed Thatcher – a premier whose style of government he openly admired – in his strengthening of the sources of policy advice at Number 10 and his reduction of the opportunities for collective deliberation. In his attitude to Parliament, too, he was not so dissimilar from his immediate predecessors, limiting the time that he spent in the chamber and announcing policy directly to the media. He was bolder in curtailing parliamentary accountability, consolidating the twice-weekly slots for Prime Minister's Questions into one 30-minute session – a reform considered but not enacted under Major. Blair was by no means the first premier to aspire to a more 'presidential' style of leadership.

The record in government

Domestic policy

For a Prime Minister so determined to run policy-making from the centre, Blair took office with a remarkably ill-defined agenda.

Beyond a handful of specific, limited pledges, such as reducing primary school class sizes and hospital waiting lists, little detailed planning had been done. In domestic policy New Labour stood for the modernization of national institutions; increased investment and reform of public services, which had been neglected under the Conservatives; and ending the atmosphere of 'sleaze' which had tainted public life under the Major government. Unlike previous Labour governments, the Blair administration took office with the advantage of a buoyant economy, which made it much easier to carry out its plans. Until the election of David Cameron in December 2005, Blair also benefited from facing a series of Conservative leaders who lacked credibility with the electorate. What, then, did the government achieve on the domestic front?

The most prominent accomplishment of the first term was a far-reaching series of constitutional reforms: the removal of most hereditary peers from the House of Lords, which helped to end the Conservatives' historic domination of the upper house; the incorporation of the European Convention on Human Rights into UK law; a Freedom of Information Act which gave citizens greater access to data on the working of public bodies; elected mayors for London and other cities; and the creation of devolved legislative bodies in Scotland, Wales and Northern Ireland, each one endorsed by a regional referendum. Although the pace of change slowed in the second term, the constitutionally anomalous position of the Lord Chancellor, whose historic role combined headship of the judiciary, chairing debates in the Lords and membership of the Cabinet, was reformed. In 2007 the administration of law and order was rationalized with the creation of a continental-style Ministry of Justice to manage the courts and prison system, leaving the Home Office to focus on policing, counter-terrorism and immigration control. Another step towards the separation of legislative and judicial powers was taken with the creation of a Supreme Court, active from 2009, which replaced the Law Lords as the highest court in the land.

Blair's most significant personal achievement in the constitutional field was his contribution to brokering a workable settlement in the fraught arena of Northern Ireland. His starting point was that the British government must maintain strict neutrality between the unionist and nationalist factions, abiding by the democratically expressed wishes of the people. As he intimated in opposition, 'the most sensible role is for us to be facilitators, not persuaders in this, not trying to pressure or push people towards a particular objective'.[13] He inherited a fragile situation in the province. The IRA ceasefire, patiently negotiated by Major but broken in February 1996, had to be restored and unionist concerns about working with the political representatives of a terrorist organization addressed. Republicans had to be brought to accept that the consent of the people of Northern Ireland was a vital prerequisite for any future progress towards a united Ireland. A further dimension was the need to maintain the co-operation of the Irish Republic, whilst persuading its government to abandon the historic constitutional claim to Northern Ireland which so worried unionists. In such a complex situation Blair displayed his skills as a negotiator and problem solver, bringing the two sides together in the April 1998 Good Friday agreement without a definite resolution of the most contentious issue, the unionist demand for the scrapping of IRA arms. This was enough to make possible the creation of a devolved administration in which representatives of David Trimble's Ulster Unionist Party and the moderate nationalist Social Democratic and Labour Party participated in government.

The Good Friday agreement seemed perilously close to collapse on several occasions over the next nine years and the devolved institutions were suspended several times as trust between the two sides broke down. Trimble's failure to secure IRA disarmament was a source of deep anxiety to unionist opinion. The release of terrorist prisoners and reform of the police force were also difficult for unionists to accept but had to be swallowed as the price of republican engagement with the peace process. As a result unionist support switched to Ian Paisley's more hardline Democratic Unionist Party. At the same time the republican party, Sinn Fein, replaced the SDLP as the key player on the nationalist side. To bring these two extremes together in a new power-sharing arrangement, as Blair and the Irish Republic's Prime Minister, Bertie Ahern, contrived to do in May 2007 was a remarkable achievement. Key factors in this successful outcome were Blair's ruthless imposition of a deadline – the threat that the assembly would be finally wound up and unionists subjected to uncongenial policies imposed as part of direct rule from London – combined with his ability to build effective personal relationships across ideological divisions. Although sectarian tensions have by no means disappeared, few would seek to diminish the value of a settlement which has led historic sworn enemies from violent confrontation to political accommodation.

By any standards this was an impressive programme of reform. Taken as a whole, however, it lacked overall coherence and a number of issues were left unresolved. In the case of Lords reform, for example, Blair proved unable to resolve the contradiction between his own preference for a largely appointed second chamber and a growing desire in the House of Commons for an elected body. His centralizing instincts were further demonstrated in his ill-advised attempts to impose a New Labour loyalist, Alun Michael, as First Minister in Wales in preference to Welsh Labour's choice, Rhodri Morgan. He also tried to exclude the left-wing outsider, Ken Livingstone, from participation in the May 2000 London mayoral election. After Livingstone won the contest as an independent, a humbled Blair had little alternative but to readmit him to the Labour Party in time for his second successful campaign for the post in 2004. Scottish and Welsh devolution, introduced following referenda in September 1997, was a policy pledge inherited from Blair's predecessor, John Smith, about which the premier manifested little enthusiasm. There was little alternative to the creation of regional parliament in Scotland. By 1997 growing popular hostility to rule from London, combined with Labour's need to stem the electoral challenge posed by the Scottish National Party, made the transfer of some governmental powers and functions to Edinburgh unavoidable.

Electoral reform was an area where party political interests reinforced Blair's natural caution, to the disappointment of radical reformers who had looked to New Labour before the 1997 election. Although the devolved bodies were elected using forms of proportional representation, after securing his huge independent majority Blair declined to hold a referendum on replacing the 'first past the post' system for Westminster elections. In opposition Blair had improved his party's relations with the Liberal Democrats, and had spoken warmly of ending the historic divide on the centre-left of British politics, which had allowed the

Conservatives to dominate the politics of the twentieth century. In office, however, his priorities were to be found elsewhere. He appointed Roy Jenkins, a former Labour minister, now a senior Liberal Democrat, to chair an inquiry into electoral reform but shelved its findings. As the Liberal Democrat leader, Paddy Ashdown concluded, Blair was at heart a pragmatist who would not take risks with his party's current ascendancy: 'Blair never gives an ideological answer to anything. His first reaction is *always*, Will it work?'[14]

Perhaps more surprising is Blair's failure to achieve more in a field which he constantly presented as a much greater priority, that of public service reform. What was lacking in 1997 was a worked-out plan to deliver the desired outcomes of greater efficiency in service delivery and increased responsiveness to the needs of parents, pupils and patients. In part this was because a disproportionate amount of Blair's energy up to 2001 was directed towards securing a second full term for Labour, in defiance of the party's discouraging past electoral record. As Geoff Mulgan, a former director of strategy and policy at Number 10, later regretfully put it, 'because the communication and campaign side of New Labour was so strong, so dominant, the task of winning elections took precedence over the task of thinking through how to use power'.[15] Another problem was the fact that Blair was the first premier since Ramsay MacDonald to have had no prior ministerial experience. As Sir Richard Wilson, who served as Cabinet Secretary in 1997–2002, told the Prime Minister, 'neither you nor anyone in Number 10 has ever managed anything'.[16] Whereas Blair had led the Labour Party, Wilson explained that there was a great difference between running a complex organization and merely giving instructions to officials and announcing policy initiatives. This was confirmed by Peter Mandelson, who characterized Blair as good at establishing 'policy tone and momentum', and as responsive to new ideas, but lacking the time and perhaps the inclination to 'get a grip on the broader debate and planning needed to drive hard policy decisions'.[17]

Blair began to evolve clearer plans for reform in his second term but was frustrated by a number of factors. The events of 9/11 in America, the wars in Afghanistan and Iraq and the Islamic terrorist bombings of 7 July 2005 in London diverted Blair's attention and energy into issues of foreign and security policy. Personality problems constituted another obstacle to the fulfilment of a radical agenda. In an unusual move, after the 2001 election Blair assured four key ministers that he would leave them in post for the duration of the new parliament to complete their work: Alan Milburn (Health), Estelle Morris (Education), David Blunkett (Home Office) and Stephen Byers (Transport). For a variety of personal reasons, all four had resigned by the end of 2004. It was not merely a matter of finding the right people to take the policies forward. Some of the ways in which Blair sought to reform the running of public services were particularly difficult for a Labour Prime Minister to sell to his party. A key idea was to give the best performing schools and hospitals more freedom. This marked a departure from the socialist model of the state as monopoly provider and entailed a willingness to use the practices and resources of the private sector to improve standards. Many 'Old Labour' MPs criticized the proposal to establish self-governing 'foundation hospitals', whose managers would be granted additional powers and funding. They feared that this would create a 'two-tier' health service, with some hospitals gaining an unfair share of resources. The planned introduction of university 'top up fees' occasioned a tightly fought parliamentary vote in January 2004. Students had been first required to make a contribution towards the cost of their education under the first Blair government, and the prospect of increased payments aroused considerable anger. These measures were passed in the teeth of significant backbench opposition. Far from fulfilling the popular stereotype of docile support for government policy, Labour MPs rebelled in 21 per cent of divisions in the 2001–5 Parliament.

Another cause of frustration in policy-making was Blair's relationship with his most important colleague, Gordon Brown. The Chancellor acted on the assumption that the Treasury had a right to exercise unchallenged influence over the main domestic departments. A senior civil servant, Sir Richard Mottram, confided in the junior minister and diarist, Chris Mullin, that Brown was 'PM in all but name … Gordon thinks his writ runs everywhere'.[18] Brown also believed that he had an unwritten but morally binding undertaking from Blair to retire in his favour, and when it became clear that this would not happen before the end of Labour's second term, relations between the two became increasingly difficult. It was politically impossible for Blair to expose the extent of the conflict in public by sacking his Chancellor, as this would create an even more dangerous enemy on the backbenches. In any case Brown's management of the Treasury was associated with an exceptionally long period of economic prosperity, with high levels of employment, low interest rates and, at least up to 2006, low inflation providing the basis for a marked increase in public spending on health and education. Behind the scenes, however, the clash with Brown had a debilitating effect on the Prime Minister's morale and on his ability to push through his policies. It was a factor in Blair's decision to announce in September 2004 that the next general election would be his last as Labour leader – a move which ensured that as soon as the third term had been won, frenzied speculation on the precise date of the hand-over began. The secretive Chancellor was reluctant to pass budget details to the premier and opposed the implementation of several key policies, for example seeking to restrict the revenue-raising capacity of foundation hospitals. One Blairite minister compared the Treasury under Brown to Fallujah, the scene of particularly fierce resistance to American occupiers during the Iraq War: 'We have no idea what's going on in there, we have no control over it, and all we know is that it's full of fundamentalists who are fanatically loyal to their leader.'[19] The clash between Blair and Brown was neatly summed up by John Prescott, whose position as Deputy Prime Minister enabled him to play the role of conciliator in the relationship: 'One's concerned with his legacy. The other with his inheritance.'[20]

Blair was critical of his own record in the domestic sphere, confessing to the September 2005 party conference that 'every time I ever introduce a reform in government, I wish in retrospect I'd gone further'.[21] The government's legacy was mixed. In education there were some improvements, especially in standards of literacy and numeracy in primary schools. City academies – state schools directly funded by government and private sponsorship and with self-governing powers – were to be adopted by the Conservatives as a way of driving up educational standards. Yet evidence of wider progress at secondary level was unclear and the funding of higher education remained contentious. In the

NHS, the imposition of centrally set targets had some impact, for example in cutting hospital waiting lists. The massive injection of resources after 2000, however, was of uncertain value as increases in staff and a hospital rebuilding programme created a financial crisis for many NHS trusts. The first steps were taken towards reforming two areas of the welfare state, pensions and incapacity benefit, whose rising cost made the long-term provision of tax-payer-funded support a major challenge for government. Tax and benefit changes raised the incomes of the poorest fifth in society by 12 per cent. The most vulnerable pensioners gained from means-tested income support in the form of pension credit and from benefits such as winter fuel allowance. The introduction of a national minimum wage addressed the plight of the low paid. The provision of free nursery places and of Sure Start centres, designed to support parents in the upbringing of families in deprived areas, represented an attempt to improve the life chances of the poorest children.

Overall, the government halted the widening of the gap between rich and poor, which had been a feature of the Conservative years, but was less effective in putting it into reverse. A distinguishing feature of New Labour was its reluctance to confront the powerful in society. The City enjoyed a period of light regulation – a source of the banking sector crisis which occurred the year after Blair's resignation – and big business and media interests thrived, with Peter Mandelson famously declaring that: 'We are intensely relaxed about people becoming filthy rich, as long as they pay their taxes.'[22] The government promoted greater tolerance for minorities, with legislation to equalize the age of consent for homosexuals, civil partnerships for same-sex couples and the identification of racial harassment and racially motivated violence as new categories of crime. Yet liberal reforms of this kind were balanced by a creeping authoritarianism in the government's approach to law and order and the battle against terrorism. The anxieties of civil liberty groups were aroused by the widening of police powers to stop and search suspects, limitations on the right to protest in the vicinity of Westminster and the planned introduction of identity cards. Overall crime figures fell, yet the incidence of serious violent offences continued to rise, in spite of a significant increase in the prison population and numerous attempts to make the criminal justice system 'fit for purpose'. It is fair to say that Britain in 2007 was a more open and compassionate society than in 1997, but not necessarily a more secure or contented one. As falling party membership indicated, New Labour was also failing to enthuse its own supporters. It is worth noting that, after the initial enthusiasm of 1997, when electoral turn-out was 71 per cent, it fell to 59 per cent in 2001 and 61 per cent in 2005. Even the 1997 landslide was won on a less than impressive 43 per cent of the vote, and the equivalent figures for 2001 and 2005 were 40 per cent and 35 per cent respectively. In his memoirs Peter Hain, a long-serving minister, noted the detachment of party members from the government's activities, which he attributed in part to the fact that 'far too much of our language was technocratic and managerial; New Labour had drained us of passion and values'.[23]

Overseas policy

It was Blair's foreign policy that proved most damaging to his reputation as a progressive force in politics. Some of his achievements, such as an increase in Britain's overseas aid budget from 0.22 per cent of national income to 0.38 per cent, were widely applauded. He also used Britain's presidency of the G8 summit at Gleneagles in July 2005 to put climate change and the plight of Africa on the agenda of other world leaders. These achievements were, however, dwarfed by the implications of the Prime Minister's support for United States military intervention in the Middle East.

Blair believed that he had an original contribution to make to foreign policy, playing a more positive role in Europe than his Conservative predecessors whilst maintaining close relations with the United States. He saw Britain as an indispensable 'bridge' between the two, uniquely placed to exercise influence on both sides of the Atlantic. As Jonathan Powell put it: 'Heath chose Europe and turned his back on the US. Thatcher chose the US and turned her back on Europe. We are trying to avoid both those mistakes.'[24] This was in fact a caricature of the position taken by Blair's recent predecessors in Number 10. Where he differed from them was in the highly moralistic tone that he adopted in asserting a right to intervene in the internal affairs of other countries. In a speech in Chicago in April 1999, he outlined the principles of 'a new internationalism where the brutal repression of ethnic groups will not be tolerated',[25] which justified military action where diplomatic efforts to avert humanitarian disaster had failed. This doctrine was used to justify Britain's role in spearheading the use of NATO air strikes to protect the ethnic Albanian population of Kosovo against the aggression of neighbouring Serbia. Although generally supported in Britain, the Kosovo intervention saw the beginning of Blair's transformation in the public mind into a messianic leader, convinced of his own righteousness. *Guardian* cartoonist Steve Bell portrayed the premier in June 1999 as the God of the Old Testament, dispensing justice from the heavens.[26] Blair played up to this image with the dramatic language that he used, comparing the Serbian government's actions to the Nazi holocaust: 'it is time for my generation to reflect on the fight of our parents' generation against Hitler's regime'.[27]

The same moralism informed Blair's response to the al-Qaeda terrorist attacks on New York and Washington in September 2001. He was quick to interpret the events of 9/11 as presenting a broader challenge to the security and values of the democratic, capitalist West, and stood out among European leaders by the rapidity with which he demonstrated his solidarity with President George W Bush. He articulated the ideological basis of the 'war on terror' with a clarity which initially won him respect as a statesman of international stature: 'the kaleidoscope has been shaken,' he told the 2001 Labour conference, 'The pieces are in flux. Soon they will settle again. Before they do, let us reorder this world around us.'[28] Blair's belief in 'liberal intervention' seemed to be justified by the initial success of the ensuing Anglo-American military action in Afghanistan. The Taliban regime, which had been harbouring al-Qaeda, was overthrown before the end of 2001. It proved much harder, however, to achieve outright victory in the face of a persistent campaign of insurgency, and the losses endured by British troops in Afghanistan, long after Blair's departure from Downing Street, cast doubt on the feasibility of the operation.

Even more controversial was Blair's decision to support America's war against Saddam Hussein's Iraq in March 2003. Beyond his belief that Iraq was a rogue state, in possession of destructive weapons which made it a threat to the peace and security of the Middle East, Blair was convinced that participation in the invasion was vital for the maintenance of Britain's relationship with the US. Discussing the issue with his advisers in July 2002, he said that not to support US action 'would be the biggest shift in foreign policy for 50 years and I'm not sure it's very wise. On the tactical level ... maximum closeness publicly was the way to maximise influence privately'.[29] This argument failed to persuade many, not only in the Labour Party but across the political spectrum, who interpreted his stance as one of surrender to an American administration which seemed contemptuous of international opinion. Robin Cook, who resigned as Leader of the Commons in opposition to the war, spoke for many in his mistrust of the so-called 'neo-conservative' ideologues, whose doctrine of pre-emptive strikes against America's enemies had gained traction with the Bush administration after 9/11: 'the Neo-Cons around Bush often sound as if the only bridge they would welcome would be a drawbridge'.[30] Many on the left felt betrayed by the spectacle of a supposedly social democratic leader establishing such a close relationship with a right-wing American President. They found it hard to forgive him for failing to use his leverage with Bush to secure his practical support for progressive causes, such as action on climate change and a settlement of the Arab–Israeli conflict. Even the ultra-loyal John Prescott admitted in his memoirs to his disappointment: 'I believe that our relationship with Bush damaged Labour ... the Bush administration can only be described as a disaster.'[31]

Blair's uncritical support for the US government earned him deep disapproval. One million marched against the war in London in February 2003, shortly before British forces were committed. A record 139 Labour MPs voted against military action in the Commons. It is important to understand the reasons for the depth of feeling on this issue. There was widespread dismay as it became clear that the US and Britain had not worked out a plan for the reconstruction of Iraq after Saddam's regime had been toppled. Instead the country degenerated into violent chaos.

Most damaging politically was the revelation that Blair had taken the country to war on the basis of faulty intelligence material collected in the so-called 'dodgy dossier', not least the erroneous statement that Iraq was able to launch weapons of mass destruction within 45 minutes of an order being given. In a radio broadcast at the end of May 2003, BBC journalist Andrew Gilligan alleged that Downing Street had probably known that the claim was inaccurate before the war had begun. A tragic consequence was the suicide in July of a government weapons expert, Dr David Kelly, after he was named as the apparent source of the story. Blair and his advisers had not perpetrated a deliberate deception but they had failed to probe the veracity of the information supplied to them. A public inquiry headed by a senior judge, Lord Hutton, was more critical of the BBC's editorial policy than of the government. Nonetheless the episode caused huge damage to the Prime Minister's credibility, as the popular misspelling of his name as 'Bliar' by protestors demonstrated.

Another undesirable consequence was the disruption of Britain's relations with France and Germany, who opposed the Iraq intervention. This was a blow to a Prime Minister who had stated his desire to play a constructive role in Europe. Within a month of taking office Blair had demonstrated his credentials by abandoning Major's opt-out from the Social Chapter, thus enshrining in law a number of workers' rights that were accepted across the European Union. Another important contribution was the conclusion of the December 1998 St Malo defence agreement with France, which paved the way for the creation of a European 'rapid reaction force', capable of undertaking humanitarian and peacekeeping tasks without encroaching on NATO's established military functions. Blair also played a leading role in promoting the enlargement of the Union from 15 to 27 members by 2007, including a number of east European states who apparently preferred Britain's pro-market, Atlantic-oriented vision to the more protectionist, statist agenda of older west European members. The price was a renewal of demands by other states for Blair to give up the rebate negotiated by Margaret Thatcher in 1984 – effectively increasing Britain's contribution to the EU budget – in order to help meet the costs of admitting less economically developed nations. This led to acrimonious wrangling during Britain's chairmanship of the EU during the second half of 2005. The issue was finally resolved when Blair agreed to give up part of the rebate in return for a future review of EU spending, including the Common Agricultural Policy, whose cost was a standing concern for Britain. Although this was probably the best deal that could be gained in the circumstances, the Euro-sceptic lobby in Britain was quick to condemn what it saw as a surrender of national interests.

In two areas of European policy Blair was markedly less successful. His desire to take Britain into the euro was frustrated by the opposition of Brown, who insisted on the economy meeting five tests devised by the Treasury before he could recommend joining. When he ruled in June 2003 that Britain had made insufficient progress towards meeting the tests, it was clear that Blair would have to abandon his goal. In any case, the unspoken sixth test – the need to win the argument with a deeply sceptical public and press – was always likely to thwart British entry. Anxiety about public opinion was a factor in a second issue, the negotiations to create a European constitution establishing decision-making structures appropriate for the newly enlarged Union. Blair was perhaps fortunate when the constitution was rejected in referenda in France and the Netherlands in the early summer of 2005. This excused him from holding a popular vote which the government would probably have lost. It enabled him to persuade his European partners to concentrate on the more modest objective of a treaty and to insist on the retention of a British veto in the most contentious 'red line' areas, such as taxation and social security. The outcome was the Lisbon Treaty, which Brown was to sign as Prime Minister. In common with other British leaders, Blair found that engagement with his continental partners required a willingness to compromise and to live with a degree of frustration – a process which was hard to sell to a domestic audience which oscillated between apathy and hostility to the European project.

Conclusion

The gradual erosion of public trust was a key theme of Blair's decade in government. A man who had once seemed straightforward and modest came to appear increasingly self-seeking, pursuing an agenda that was in conflict with the priorities of many who had pinned their hopes on him. Robert Harris's 2007 novel *The Ghost*, which was later made into a successful film, contained a thinly veiled depiction of Blair as a beleaguered ex-premier living an isolated existence behind a tight curtain of security, still close to the Americans, who is pursued by vengeful protestors and eventually charged with war crimes. In his final year in office, Blair's image was tarnished by allegations that nominations to the House of Lords had been put forward in return for loans to the Labour Party. No charges were brought, but for Blair to become the first serving premier to be interviewed by the police was damaging enough.

Blair's legacy was an ambiguous one. Much of his time in government was spent in an attempt to find a middle position between competing pressures: between Thatcherism and social democracy; between his own centralizing impulses and the desire to modernize and liberalize Britain's institutional fabric; between Europe and America. Blair made Labour electable once again by refashioning its image and by compelling it to come to terms with the forces of economic globalization and consumer capitalism. Yet he left the party uncertain as to its future direction, under a successor who did not share the same instincts and about whom he harboured persistent doubts. In some ways his impact on the opposition was more positive, spurring them to find, in David Cameron, the professed 'heir to Blair'[32] who would move the Conservatives towards the political centre ground. In his bid to strengthen the reach of the premiership, Blair came up against the limits that confront all assertive occupants of Number 10. In retrospect, the gap between the language of change and renewal, and the reality of achievement on the ground, is probably the most enduring theme of the Blair decade in government.

Notes

1 Anthony Seldon, *Blair*, London: Simon and Schuster, 2004, p. 535.
2 Tony Blair, *A Journey*, London: Hutchinson, 2010, p. 140.
3 Philip Stephens, *Tony Blair: The Price of Leadership*, London: Politico's, 2004, p. 30.
4 Seldon, *Blair*, p. 150.

5 Stephen Driver and Luke Martell, *New Labour*, London: Polity Press, 2nd edn, 2006, p. 14.

6 John Major, *The Autobiography*, London: HarperCollins, 1999, pp. 606–7.

7 Blair, *A Journey*, p. 14.

8 Seldon, *Blair*, p. 260.

9 Ibid., p. 437.

10 David Butler and Dennis Kavanagh, *The British General Election of 2001*, Basingstoke: Palgrave, 2002, p. 27.

11 Lord Butler, *Review of Intelligence on Weapons of Mass Destruction: Report of a Committee of Privy Counsellors*, London: Stationery Office, 2004, paragraph 6.11, available at http://www.archive2.official-documents. co.uk/document/deps/hc/hc898/898.pdf

12 'Short: I was briefed on Blair's secret war pact', *Guardian*, 18 June 2003.

13 Jonathan Powell, *Great Hatred, Little Room: Making Peace in Northern Ireland*, London: Bodley Head, 2008, p. 312.

14 Paddy Ashdown, 10 March 1998, quoted in Ion Trewin (ed.), *The Hugo Young Papers: Thirty Years of British Politics – Off the Record*, London: Allen Lane, 2008, p. 531.

15 Andrew Rawnsley, *The End of the Party: The Rise and Fall of New Labour*, London: Penguin, 2010, p. 8.

16 Anthony Seldon with Peter Snowdon and Daniel Collings, *Blair Unbound*, London: Simon and Schuster, 2007, p. 41.

17 Peter Mandelson, *The Third Man: Life at the Heart of New Labour*, London: HarperPress, 2010, p. 228.

18 Ruth Winstone (ed.), *A View from the Foothills: The Diaries of Chris Mullin,* London: Profile Books, 2009, p. 45, entry for 10 November 1999.

19 Quoted in Simon Hoggart, review of *Gordon Brown* by Tom Bower, *Guardian*, 9 October 2004.

20 Winstone (ed.), *A View from the Foothills*, p. 415, entry for 5 June 2003.

21 Seldon, *Blair Unbound*, p. 388.

22 Mandelson, *The Third Man*, p. 265.

23 Peter Hain, *Outside In*, London: Biteback, 2012, p. 392.

24 Jonathan Powell, 6 July 2001, quoted in Trewin (ed.), *Hugo Young Papers*, p. 726.

25 Robert Self, *British Foreign and Defence Policy since 1945*, London: Palgrave Macmillan 2010, p. 244.

26 Reproduced in John Rentoul, *Tony Blair*, London: Little, Brown, 2001, plate number 36.

27 Stephens, *Tony Blair*, p. 228.

28 Blair, *A Journey*, p. 367.

29 Alastair Campbell and Richard Stott (eds), *The Blair Years: Extracts from the Alastair Campbell Diaries*, London: Hutchinson, 2007, p. 630, entry for 23 July 2002.

30 Robin Cook, *The Point of Departure*, London: Simon and Schuster, 2003, p. 133, entry for Easter recess, 2002.

31 John Prescott, *Docks to Downing Street: My Story*, London: Headline Review, 2009, p. 359.

32 Seldon, *Blair Unbound*, pp. 417–18.

Further reading

Tony Blair, *A Journey*, London: Hutchinson, 2010

John Rentoul, *Tony Blair: Prime Minister*, London: Little, Brown, 2nd edn, 2001

Peter Riddell, *The Unfulfilled Prime Minister: Tony Blair's Quest for a Legacy*, London: Politico's, 2006

Anthony Seldon, *Blair*, London: Simon and Schuster, 2004

Anthony Seldon with Peter Snowdon and Daniel Collings, *Blair Unbound*, London: Simon and Schuster, 2007

Philip Stephens, *Tony Blair: The Price of Leadership*, London: Politico's, 2004

Mick Temple, *Blair*, London: Haus, 2006

20 Gordon Brown (1951–)

Prime Minister: June 2007–May 2010

'The House has noticed the Prime Minister's remarkable transformation in the last few weeks from Stalin to Mr Bean.'
Vince Cable, acting leader of the Liberal Democrat Party,
in the House of Commons, 28 November 2007[1]

Few premiers have sought the highest office with the determination of Gordon Brown. As Chancellor for ten years he was the
indispensable co-architect, with Tony Blair, of the New Labour
project in government. He earned a reputation as a commanding
figure, whose grasp of economic policy was widely credited with
delivering continuous prosperity. At the same time stories of
his increasing impatience to move next door into Number 10, and
rumours of bitter conflicts with Blair behind the scenes, raised
doubts in some circles regarding his suitability for the premiership. Tragically for Brown and his party, his critics' misgivings
were borne out. A combination of his personal limitations, and of
adverse economic and political circumstances, rapidly undermined
his credibility as Prime Minister. The once dominant individual
appeared to be at the mercy of events, his premiership derailed by
constant speculation about possible challenges to his leadership.
Brown survived only to lose the general election of May 2010,
which brought his career as a front-ranking politician to a close
and ended the New Labour era in which he had played such a
crucial role.

The rise to the premiership

Brown's upbringing as the son of a Church of Scotland minister in Kirkcaldy, the town which he would later represent in Parliament, had a deep influence on his career. In later life he would often refer to the moral values instilled by his father, notably a sense of social justice which led him to join the Labour Party. He recalled that 'in our congregation, solidarity with those who have stumbled in the struggle of life was considered the most fundamental duty'.[2] Entering Edinburgh University at the early age of 16, Brown established himself as a serious academic. He also involved himself in university politics, securing the unusual distinction of being elected Rector, a post on the governing body, by his fellow students. After a brief career as a lecturer and journalist he entered the Commons at the 1983 election, soon forming a close friendship with another newly-elected MP, Tony Blair. With a shared belief in the need for Labour to modernize, the two rose together through the ranks of the Shadow Cabinet. Brown was the senior partner by virtue of his longer standing commitment to the party, and the seriousness with which he dedicated himself to policy-making as Shadow Chancellor from 1992. It was therefore a shock when the party swung behind Blair following the sudden death of Labour leader John Smith in May 1994. It was galling that Brown's greater experience was outweighed by the perception that the younger man was better placed to attract the votes of 'middle England' – aspiring middle-class people who might be won over by a modernized Labour Party. Although the details of their agreement remain unclear, it seems that Brown reluctantly stood aside to allow Blair an unopposed run at the leadership, in order to avoid splitting the pro-modernizing vote. In return Brown secured a promise, as Chancellor-designate, of an unusual degree of influence over the domestic policies of the next Labour government. He also expected that Blair would make way for him after serving no more than two terms as Prime Minister.

In office from May 1997, the two formed a publicly successful but privately uneasy relationship, with Brown sometimes described as the hard-working chief executive alongside the presidential figure of Blair. The Chancellor turned the Treasury into his private fiefdom, surrounding himself with a group of hand-picked advisers and exercising an iron control over New Labour's economic and social agenda. The key domestic policy decisions were all his: the transfer of the power to set interest rates from the Treasury to the Bank of England; reforms of the tax and benefit system designed to end the dependence of the poor on welfare; the indefinite postponement of Blair's hopes of taking Britain into the European single currency. He presided over a decade of stable, low-inflationary growth which was in part the product of favourable world trading conditions. It enabled him to claim that he had abolished the damaging cycle of 'boom and bust' which had bedevilled governments in recent decades. The slogan 'prudence with a purpose' indicated a determination to show the electorate that Labour could be trusted with the economy. By declining to raise income tax levels, and exercising public spending restraint in the early years, Brown prepared the ground for increasing levels of investment in the key public services of education, health and transport. These achievements, combined with a reputation for ruthlessly eliminating potential rivals, created a sense of entitlement to the premiership. Certainly none of his senior colleagues, whatever their private reservations about the driven, intense occupant of Number 11, dared to challenge Brown's claim when his predecessor finally retired in June 2007.

Governing style

Brown's style of leadership had an inward-looking and highly personalized quality which reminded his Chancellor, Alistair Darling, of 'an old-fashioned court: he was the centre around which trusted courtiers moved'.[3] It was a mark of his essential insecurity that he continued to rely on the support of a small clique whom he had known at the Treasury, who co-existed alongside the regular civil servants working in Number 10. Brown's former economic policy adviser, Ed Balls, remained a key presence in Downing Street after he had been given a Whitehall department of his own (Children, Schools and Families) to run. Brown seemed to prize loyalty above other attributes, causing him to tolerate for too long the sometimes misguided actions of those who acted on his behalf. Great damage was done by the activities of Damian McBride, a special adviser who was forced to resign in April 2009, following revelations of a plan to spread false rumours about Conservative politicians and their spouses.

Brown acquired a reputation among his Cabinet colleagues not only for attempting to micromanage their departments but also for indecisiveness, constantly seeking out new sources of advice and calling for more papers on a particular question before making up his mind. Peter Hain, who served as Work and Pensions Secretary and Welsh Secretary, contrasted Brown's working methods unfavourably with Blair's capacity to 'juggle dozens of issues at a time', writing in his memoirs that 'Gordon drilled down in forensic detail on the issue of the day, neglecting the many others competing for his attention'.[4] Peter Mandelson, who returned to the Cabinet at Brown's invitation in October 2008, considered that the lack of an effective Downing Street chief of staff was a key weakness, contributing to a disorderly style of working. Although Brown's conscientiousness was not in doubt, he never created a system to handle the 'disjointed, express-train flow of work'[5] which characterized the Prime Minister's daily routine. The Downing Street operation improved in Brown's final 21 months, with the adoption of a new 'horseshoe' office layout in Number 12, which placed the premier physically at the centre of his team of advisers. It did little, however, to correct his tendency to react to events rather than devising a longer-term strategy.

The record in government

Brown enjoyed a brief 'honeymoon' period in the summer of 2007 when he was seen to tackle outbreaks of terrorist violence, foot and mouth disease and flooding with quiet competence. He gained some credit for appearing plainer and more straightforward than the image-conscious Blair. Very soon, however, Brown's judgement was called in question. In October, having allowed speculation about an early general election to build, he abruptly shattered expectations that he would seek his own mandate. The main reason for the about-turn was an unexpectedly popular announcement by the Conservatives that they would raise the threshold for paying inheritance tax to £1 million. The Prime Minister's attempt to deny that he had been influenced by the opinion polls was not believed and he was widely ridiculed as 'bottler Brown' for avoiding a reckoning with the voters. The episode confirmed his reputation for indecisiveness and was a serious blow to his premiership. Labour MPs further questioned his judgement early in 2008 as evidence of the unpopularity of a measure announced by Brown as Chancellor, the abolition of the 10p income tax band for the lowest paid, began to accumulate.

At a deeper level Brown seemed unable to articulate a long-term vision for his government. On taking office he tried to present himself as representing a fresh start; 'and now let the work of change begin',[6] he told his audience in Downing Street. Yet this never seemed convincing from someone who had been virtually co-premier for a decade. After all the years of plotting his route to the top job, apparently he had no coherent strategy. Perhaps, after an unprecedented ten years as Chancellor, by 2007 he was suffering from exhaustion. Brown tried to establish himself as almost above partisan politics in his first few months, appointing non-party figures such as the eminent surgeon, Lord Darzi, as junior ministers. They became known as the 'GOATS' from the initial letters of the term 'Government of all the talents', yet few served for long. Brown also tried to distance himself from his predecessor's centralizing tendencies by announcing a raft of constitutional reform proposals, including an offer to surrender some of the Prime Minister's historic prerogative powers, but little was done. Proposals for an elected House of Lords and a referendum on changing the electoral system came only at the end of his premiership. He tried to emulate Blair's toughness on security issues by trying to extend the period of pre-charge detention for terror suspects from 28 to 42 days, only to be defeated in the Lords. It took until June 2009 before Brown announced, in the document *Building Britain's Future*, a coherent agenda for public service reform based on a series of entitlements. Many of the proposals – such as an entitlement to hospital treatment within a specified period, or to personal tuition for state school pupils – were laudable, but they came too late in the Parliament to be implemented.

In foreign policy, too, Brown seemed uncertain how far to differentiate himself from his predecessor. In December 2007 he signed the Lisbon Treaty on closer European integration, which had been negotiated by Blair, but offended pro-Europeans by turning up late, unconvincingly citing a prior appointment with a Westminster parliamentary committee as the reason. Brown created a more formal relationship with US President Bush than the bond established by Blair and sought to associate himself publicly with the popular and progressive Barack Obama after the latter's election in November 2008. British troops were withdrawn from Iraq but remained in Afghanistan. He placed greater emphasis than Blair on tackling climate change, committing the UK in 2008 to legally enforceable carbon dioxide emission targets. Disappointingly, he proved unable to secure a binding international agreement on global warming at the December 2009 Copenhagen conference.

The dominant story of Brown's government, however, was the onset of an unparalleled crisis in the banking sector, the first signs of which emerged in September 2007 with the near-collapse of the Northern Rock bank. As investors queued to withdraw their savings the government was forced to issue an unlimited guarantee of deposits and then – with understandable reluctance, because of its association with the era of 'Old Labour' – to nationalize the stricken bank. This was a foretaste of the much larger catastrophe which engulfed the international financial system in the autumn of 2008. At the root of the crisis was the collapse of the 'sub-prime' mortgage market in the USA. A number of banks had become over-extended during a decade or more of easy credit and had lent money to investors who had no prospect of being able to repay it. The banks had sold on debts in increasingly elaborate and confusing ways, leaving them exposed when confidence began to crumble. In the so-called 'credit crunch' they stopped lending to each other, creating a crisis of truly global proportions.

Brown rapidly concluded that a programme of recapitalization was essential to save the British banking system from imminent collapse. The package, announced in October 2008, comprised direct state investment in the banks, loans and guarantees of interbank lending, amounting to £500 billion of taxpayers' money. Some of Britain's largest banks, including Royal Bank of Scotland (RBS), Lloyds TSB and HBOS, were part-nationalized. Brown earned praise in April 2009 when, as chairman of the G20 group of advanced economies, he led them in devising a global economic stimulus to enhance the lending capacity of the International Monetary Fund and to shore up the world trading system. Brown argued that co-ordinated action of this kind was vital in what he called 'the first crisis of globalisation'. Conscious of the parallels with the interwar slump, he wrote that 'if the right decisions had not been taken by leaders across the world, we could have faced a worldwide depression, bringing with it a return to the protectionism, mass unemployment, extremism, and political instability of the 1930s'.[7]

Yet Brown received little domestic political credit for his actions. Labour backbencher Chris Mullin expressed dismay at the gulf between Brown's hostile portrayal in the UK media and the more favourable perception of him in the USA and Europe: 'while others dithered, he is seen as the one leader who knew what to do when the banking crisis struck ... but scarcely a word of this has reached the British electorate'.[8] The Conservative opposition under David Cameron focused on the growing size of the budget deficit under Labour, which had expanded as a result of the bank bail-out. By the end of 2008 it stood at £118 billion, which represented 8 per cent of the UK's gross domestic product, and it reached £175 billion by the time that Brown left office. The Conservatives were able to divert attention from their own lack of an alternative strategy for dealing with the banking crisis, and from the fact that in 2006–7 they had pledged to match Labour's levels of public spending. The government could, however, legitimately be accused of neglecting to set aside resources during the years of plenty and failing to 'fix the roof while the sun was shining'.[9] Chancellor Brown had left Britain with the fourth largest structural budget deficit among the world's largest industrial countries. His spending plans had been based on an unjustified assumption of continued growth, whose ending now left him vulnerable to accusations of a complacent lack of foresight. Equally damaging to his reputation was the inadequate regulation of the British banking sector, which could be traced to his 1997 decision to divide responsibility between the Bank of England, the Treasury and a new body, the Financial Services Authority. He was also slow to modify his desire to pitch his party's 2010 election appeal as a straightforward choice between continued Labour investment in the public sector and 'Tory cuts', when the need for retrenchment was becoming evident. With reluctance he adopted Darling's argument that public spending should be maintained in the short term in order to avoid a deepening recession, but that targeted spending cuts would be needed once the economy began to recover.

As the general election approached the flaws in Brown's personality and image, as well as his policy choices, were lambasted in the media. He suffered from comparison with Cameron, who was 15 years his junior and much more adept at self-presentation. A late yet happy marriage, and the birth of two sons, had made him appear more human but he never shook off his image as an intense workaholic who was ill at ease in social situations. The Conservative leader had highlighted the difference between the two men whilst Brown was still Chancellor, using an image drawn from television broadcasting to describe him as 'an analogue politician in a digital age'.[10] As Prime Minister Brown sought to overcome his limitations as a communicator by projecting himself as an experienced, statesmanlike figure in contrast to his rival's more superficial attractions: 'not flash – just Gordon'.[11] Too often, however, Brown appeared awkward and unable to get his message across. In the spring of 2010, as the first premier to agree to participate in televized election debates with his rivals, he appeared wooden and uninspiring. An incident in Rochdale, Lancashire, during the election campaign enabled hostile commentators to depict him as both short-tempered and out of touch. Unaware that he was still wearing a radio microphone, Brown was caught out blaming his staff for bringing him into contact with a Labour-voting pensioner, who had harangued him about immigration, and whom he dismissively described as a 'bigoted woman'.

The election was a mixed verdict on Brown. It was Labour's worst result since Michael Foot's defeat in 1983, with the party losing 91 seats and gaining just 29 per cent of the vote. Yet for all Cameron's efforts to make the Conservatives more attractive, and in spite of Brown's mistakes, the main opposition party failed to secure an overall majority. This led to five days of tortuous three-cornered negotiations between the main parties, which ended only when Brown accepted that the Liberal Democrats were more likely to do a deal with the Conservatives. He tried his best to create a majority for a progressive coalition, even indicating that he was willing to step aside as Prime Minister once such a government was established. Eventually he lost patience with the prevarications of the Liberal Democrat leader, Nick Clegg, and decided to salvage some dignity by resigning rather than clinging to office.

In the wake of the defeat, hostile commentators were able to argue that, had it not been for Brown's shortcomings as a leader, Labour might have scraped home. His tragedy was that he had never been able to show how his high ideals could be translated into practical policies. Of all premiers in our period, he most resembled Eden in his all-consuming ambition to reach the top and his inability to move successfully from running a major department of state to taking overall governing responsibility. This critical limitation helps to explain why his time in Number 10 was so frustrating and short-lived.

Notes

1 Anthony Seldon and Guy Lodge, *Brown at 10*, London: Biteback, 2010, p. 65.
2 Gordon Brown, *Beyond the Crash*, London: Simon and Schuster, 2010, p. 199.
3 Alistair Darling, *Back from the Brink*, London: Atlantic Books, 2011, p. 33.
4 Peter Hain, *Outside In*, London: Biteback, 2012, p. 417.
5 Peter Mandelson, *The Third Man*, London: HarperPress, 2010, p. 453.
6 Seldon and Lodge, *Brown at 10*, p. 4.
7 Brown, *Beyond the Crash*, pp. 2–3.
8 Chris Mullin, *Decline and Fall: Diaries 2005 – 2010*, London: Profile Books, 2010, p. 374, entry for 24 September 2009.
9 *Guardian*, 12 March 2008.
10 *Guardian*, 23 March 2006.
11 Andrew Rawnsley, *The End of the Party: The Rise and Fall of New Labour*, London: Penguin, 2010, p. 501.

Further reading

Gordon Brown, *Beyond the Crash*, London: Simon and Schuster, 2010

Alistair Darling, *Back from the Brink*, London: Atlantic Books, 2011

Andrew Rawnsley, *The End of the Party: The Rise and Fall of New Labour*, London: Penguin, 2010

Anthony Seldon and Guy Lodge, *Brown at 10*, London: Biteback, 2010

Index

SIGNPOST

SELECTED PREMIER HOTELS 2014

www.signpost.co.uk

Millstones at Stanage Edge, Peak District

Signpost 2014

Welcome to the 75th edition of Signpost, the UK's longest established annual hotel guide, founded in 1935.

Every Signpost hotel is visited and/or inspected annually by one of our team. All Signpost hotels have style, offer a personal welcome and provide exceptional cuisine. You will also find plenty to see and do in the area.

Find your perfect hotel using the indexes in the back of the book. You can search for your preferences, using the facilities index. If you have a particular area in mind for your holiday, use the regional index to choose your Signpost hotel. Or, if you have a hotel in mind, use the alphabetical index to find it in the book.

We know you'll love staying at our hotels and we'd love you to invite your friends and family to experience a break in a Signpost hotel. Contact us at enquiries@signpost.co.uk to purchase Gift Vouchers today. Vouchers are available in denominations of £50 and £100 and make a wonderful present.

Keep checking our website www.signpost.co.uk for more information on our luxury hotels. You can also register online to subscribe to our newsletter and receive special offers throughout the year.

Remember, wherever you are in the UK, look for the Signpost sign – your guarantee of a top quality hotel.

1. CITY OF DUNDEE
2. CLACKMANNANSHIRE
3. FALKIRK
4. EAST DUNBARTONSHIRE
5. WEST DUNBARTONSHIRE
6. INVERCLYDE
7. RENFREWSHIRE
8. CITY OF GLASGOW
9. NORTH LANARKSHIRE
10. WEST LOTHIAN
11. CITY OF EDINBURGH
12. MIDLOTHIAN
13. EAST RENFREWSHIRE
14. NORTH TYNESIDE
15. NEWCASTLE UPON TYNE
16. GATESHEAD
17. SOUTH TYNESIDE
18. SUNDERLAND
19. DARLINGTON
20. STOCKTON-ON-TEES

21. MIDDLESBROUGH
22. HARTLEPOOL
23. REDCAR & CLEVELAND
24. BRADFORD
25. CALDERDALE
26. KIRKLEES
27. WAKEFIELD
28. BARNSLEY
29. SHEFFIELD
30. ROTHERHAM
31. DONCASTER
32. CITY OF KINGSTON UPON HULL
33. NORTH LINCOLNSHIRE
34. NORTH EAST LINCOLNSHIRE
35. CONWY
36. DENBIGHSHIRE
37. FLINTSHIRE
38. WREXHAM
39. CITY OF STOKE-ON-TRENT
40. CITY OF DERBY

41. CITY OF NOTTINGHAM
42. TELFORD & WREKIN
43. CITY OF LEICESTER
44. CITY OF PETERBOROUGH
45. LUTON
46. SWANSEA
47. NEATH & PORT TALBOT
48. RHONDDA CYNON TAFF
49. MERTHYR TYDFIL
50. BLAENAU GWENT
51. TORFAEN
52. MONMOUTHSHIRE
53. BRIDGEND
54. VALE OF GLAMORGAN
55. CARDIFF
56. CAERPHILLY
57. NEWPORT
58. NORTH SOMERSET
59. CITY OF BRISTOL
60. SOUTH GLOUCESTERSHIRE

61. BATH & NORTH EAST SOMERSET
62. SWINDON
63. READING
64. WOKINGHAM
65. BRACKNELL FOREST
66. WINDSOR & MAIDENHEAD
67. SLOUGH
68. THURROCK
69. SOUTHEND-ON-SEA
70. MEDWAY
71. CITY OF PLYMOUTH
72. TORBAY
73. POOLE
74. BOURNEMOUTH
75. CITY OF SOUTHAMPTON
76. CITY OF PORTSMOUTH
77. CITY OF BRIGHTON & HOVE

Contents

Key to symbols

✈ airport pickup
◎ archery
🐾 baby listening service
🏸 badminton court
🏖 beach
💅 beauty salon
🎱 billiards/snooker
🦜 birdwatching
🚣 boating
⛳ boules, pétanque
🛶 canoeing
💍 civil wedding licence
🎠 childrens play area
👶 children welcome
🧗 climbing
🏢 conferences/meeting rooms
🔱 croquet
🚲 cycle hire
♿ disabled rooms available
👪 family room
☺ fax/modem points
🎣 fishing
🏋 fitness centre/gym/spa
🛏 four poster
❀ gardens
🏎 go karting
⛳ golf course
🚁 helicopter landing pad
🛁 hot tub
🎱 indoor games room
🏊 indoor swimming pool
🛀 jacuzzi
🧺 laundry/valet service
🛗 lift
⛺ lockable canvas/tents available
🍷 minibar
🚭 non-smoking hotel
🏊 outdoor swimming pool
🅿 parking (no)
🌳 parkland setting
🐕 pets welcome (+ fee)
🐕 pets not allowed
🎬 private cinema
⛳ putting green/pitch n putt
🍺 real ale
♨ riding
🏃 running track
🗝 safety deposit box
⛵ sailing
🧖 sauna
🏠 s/c cottage available
🔫 shooting
🚿 shower only
☀ solarium
🎾 squash
🦌 stalking
🏛 stately home/hotel
🎾 tennis
🛎 24-hr room service
🚶 walks
🎿 waterski-ing
🏄 watersports
📶 wi-fi
🐄 working farm

3

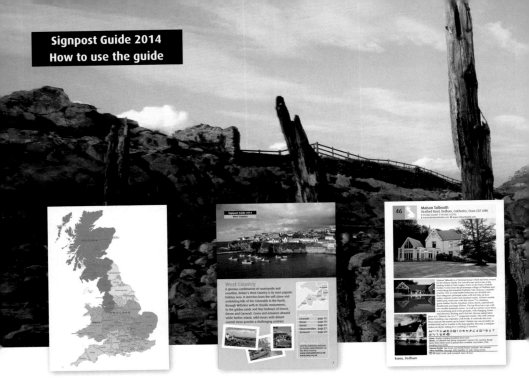

CHOOSE A REGION

You will find a map of regions on page 2. To browse the hotels in a particular region, simply turn to the matching colour coded section.

Alternatively, you can use the colour maps starting on page 167 to locate a specific hotel. Page numbers for each Signpost hotel in this book are shown on the maps.

HIGHLIGHTS

At the beginning of each regional section you will find a selection of historic houses, gardens and places of interest to visit during your stay at your Signpost hotel. These sites are recommended by Hudson's Historic Houses and Gardens. Visit Hudson's website at **www.hudsonsheritage.com** to find more places to enjoy on your holiday.

SELECT A HOTEL

Choose from a wide range of Signpost hotels in each region. Each page features a different hotel, with colour photographs and a description to help give you an idea of the hotel's character and its surrounding attractions. You will also find a handy box on each page, containing quick glance information on the hotel's facilities, room rates, number of bedrooms, dining options, leisure opportunities, opening times and special offers.

Rates Double including breakfast fr
Meals Le Talbooth fine dining restau
Rover from hotel; lunch & special die
breakfast from 0700.

Lindisfarne Castle, Northumberland

Stour and private rooms o
architectural sail or wand
makes an idyllic setting fo

🏤 12 (1 ⚑) ✂ 🚗 📻 📷
📻 🔍 🏃 🎣 🐾 📶

Rates Double including bre
Meals Le Talbooth fine dini
Rover from hotel; lunch & s
breakfast from 0700.

Leisure Breaks Spa breaks
Other facilities Massage, D

💷 All major credit cards ac

ONLINE:
Go to **www.signpost.co.uk**
to make a reservation at
your chosen Signpost hotel.
Remember to check the
Signpost website and
subscribe to our newsletter
for special offers from
Signpost hotels throughout
the year.

BY PHONE:
You can also book a room by
phoning the number on the
hotel's page.

HOTEL FACILITIES
Unless stated otherwise
ALL Signpost hotels have:

• direct dial telephones
• colour TV
• tea/coffee making
• en-suite bathrooms
• hairdryers
• laundry service

SYMBOLS are printed
where there are other
unique facilities at hotels.

Symbols for golf, fishing,
shooting or riding denote
that these activities can
be arranged near to the
Signpost hotel. Activities
that are not adjacent to,
or within the grounds of
the hotel are listed under
'Other Facilities'.

Port Isaac, Cornwall

SIGNPOST 2014

Signpost is the UK's longest established colour accommodation guide and is now in its 75th year of publication. The high standards set by the founders of Signpost, remain today. Every year, our inspectors personally visit each Signpost hotel to ensure that the expected standards are met. Each hotel is inspected according to the following criteria:

- Individual style,
- Good value, friendly service
- A personal welcome

Our inspectors expect the finest cuisine, using the best fresh produce. The bedrooms in a Signpost hotel must be furnished with style and offer all the comforts of a home from home. Signpost hotels are located in appealing, fascinating areas, with plenty of available sporting and leisure activities.

Most importantly, a Signpost hotel is a place you will want to visit again and again.

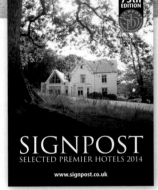

THE SIGNPOST SIGN YOUR GUARANTEE OF A TOP QUALITY HOTEL

Port Isaac, Cornwall

West Country

A glorious combination of countryside and coastline, Britain's West Country is its most popular holiday area. It stretches from the soft stone and undulating hills of the Cotswolds in the north, through Wiltshire with its Druidic monuments, to the golden sands and tiny harbours of Dorset, Devon and Cornwall. Coves and estuaries abound while further inland, wild moors with distant coastal views provide a challenging contrast.

GLOUCESTERSHIRE
BRISTOL
WILTSHIRE
SOMERSET
DEVON
DORSET
CORNWALL

Hotels guide

Further information:
Visit the following websites for further information on the West Country:
www.visitsouthwest.co.uk
www.swcp.org.uk

Portesham, Dorset

Weston-Super-Mare, Somerset

Bourton-on-the-Water, Cotswolds

Eden Project

CORNWALL AND THE SCILLY ISLES

The Scilly Isles form Britain's south-westerly bulwark against the potential invader and indeed the island's waters are littered with historic wrecks. Puffin and seal viewing trips can be arranged. The gardens on Tresco are sub-tropical and boast plants which are not seen in the rest of Europe. Access to the Scillies is either by boat from Penzance or by helicopter.

If imposing scenery, surfing and bracing cliff walks are for you, then make for **Cornwall's** rugged **north coast**. If the weather is fine, you can play golf. Overcast weather is usually a sign that the surf will be good. Be careful to observe the Red Flag limits as currents here can be very strong.

In addition to road and rail, internal flights mean that Cornwall is more accessible than ever before. The South Coast, by contrast to the capital, is another world, with palm trees and the picturesque Helford estuary and its tributary Gillian Creek. There are over 30 golf courses in the county and numerous little fishing ports to explore.

Above all Cornwall is an area steeped in history and legend, boasting tales of shipwrecks, smugglers and strange happenings in the tin mines. **Bodmin Moor**, with its hut circles, sacred sites and giant tors, has the county's highest hill, Brown Willy, at 315m, and was the setting for the atmospheric Jamaica Inn by Daphne du Maurier.

Cornwall's largest visitor attraction since 2001 has been the **Eden Project**, near St Austell, consisting of two huge biodomes. A great family day out!

Daymer Bay

DEVON

Devon is England's most visited county, largely due to its enduring beauty, excellent road, rail and air connections and its eclectic mix of city and countryside destinations.

Plymouth, its largest city, is a happy blend of holiday resort, historic centre and modern city. The famous Hoe has its associations with Francis Drake and the Barbican with the Pilgrim Fathers.

Exeter is the cultural capital of the county, with its university, theatre, medieval cathedral and Maritime Museum. The Quay House Interpretation Centre tells the story of the city from the Roman era (parts of Roman walls remain) to present day. 19th century dramatist Richard Ford wrote "This Exeter is quite a capital, abounding in all that London has, except the fog and smoke."

Exmoor

Inland are the two magnificent National Parks of **Dartmoor** and **Exmoor**. Dartmoor, in the South, has 365 square miles of great natural beauty and rugged grandeur with wild heather moorland and deep wooded valleys. From the sparkling streams of the lowlands to the starker granite tors of the 'high moor', new pleasures unfold. The dramatic moors and forested valleys are the home of red deer and the legendary Doones of RD Blackmore's novel. Exmoor, in the north, famous for its ponies, is a great place for walking or relaxation in one of its sleepy villages.

The **north coast** boasts the holiday resorts of **Ilfracombe**, **Woolacombe** and **Bideford** whereas the **south coast**, known as The English Riviera, features little inlets, harbours and fjords. **Torquay** is the 'capital' of the area and exudes a Mediterranean atmosphere with its stunning palm trees.

Paignton

Torquay

SOMERSET, BRISTOL AND BATH

Somerset is a county of contrasts, with rocky **Exmoor** to the west, together with the gentler **Quantocks**, **Brendon** and **Blackdown Hills** and the limestone **Mendip Hills** and **Cheddar Gorge** to the north east. In between are the wetlands around **Glastonbury**, ideal for apple growing, the resorts of **Burnham** and **Weston-super-Mare**, and the county town of **Taunton**, scene of bitter Civil War struggles.

Cheddar Gorge

Bath

Bristol

Bristol, the largest city in the West Country and a former capital of England, is steeped in history. You can stroll down King Street, famous for its Theatre Royal, Almshouses and sup in the Llandoger Trow. The city docks are of great interest, providing a home for the **SS Great Britain**, Brunel's famous iron ship, the Industrial Museum and the Watershed shopping area.

A few miles up the river Avon is Britain's only World Heritage City - **Bath**, whose Roman Baths are a must see. Bath's second great era was the Regency period, characterised by the Assembly Rooms and Royal Crescent. Don't miss taking tea in the Pump Room, accompanied by a string quartet.

Nearby **Wells** is England's smallest cathedral city. The west wall of Wells Cathedral dates from 1230 and the Bishop's palace is one of England's oldest inhabited houses.

Stonehenge

WILTSHIRE AND DORSET

Wiltshire is full of surprises. In the north, the **Marlborough Downs** sweep from the industrial and former railway town of **Swindon** down towards the **Vale of Pevensey**. Further south lies **Salisbury Plain** and the deserted village of Imber. At the edge of the Plain you will find **Stonehenge**, thought to have been built around 3000 BC, possibly for sun worship. **Avebury Stone Circle** predates Stonehenge by some 700 years and the **Long Barrow** at West Kennet dates from ca. 2700 BC.

Administrative centre of the county is **Trowbridge** in the west but its loveliest city is **Salisbury** to the south where the cathedral's 404 ft spire is the tallest in England. The Close, the quiet river gardens and specialist shops are amongst the city's attractions.

South west lies **Dorset**, Thomas Hardy's county, with the ancient cities of **Dorchester** (Roman remains) and **Casterbridge** (modern day Shaftesbury). In **Cerne Abbas** the infamous 180ft high Chalk Giant looks down on the village. There are several other prehistoric earthworks and chalk horses carved into hillsides in this area, including The Sanctuary, near Avebury, said to have been built around 3,000 BC.

Dorset also has the extraordinary **Jurassic Coast**, stretching from **Lyme Regis** to **Portland Bill** and including Chesil Beach, a 40ft bank of shingle stretching ten miles.

To the east is **Bournemouth**, a town with 2000 acres of parks and gardens, two piers and its own symphony orchestra.

Eastleach Turville

Cheltenham is the Centre for the Cotswolds and now hosts a respected annual Literary Festival as well as a Music Festival and the National Hunt Gold Cup held each March. Its stately colonnades and Regency terraces bring back the aura of a less hurried age. County town **Gloucester**, with its cathedral of Norman origins, co-hosts with **Hereford** and **Worcester** the Three Choirs Festival in rotation every three years, this year Worcester is hosting.

GLOUCESTERSHIRE

The **Cotswolds** is one of the most visited parts of the UK with its landscapes of rolling hills and stone cottages. Many of its villages have twinned names like **Lower and Upper Slaughter**, **Little and Great Rissington**, **Temple Guiting** and **Guiting Power**.

The magnificent churches at **Fairford**, **Cirencester** and **Chipping Campden** were built with the patronage of rich wool merchants, which brought the area its prosperity. Some of Britain's most celebrated country house hotels are in this area, which was the birthplace of the Signpost guide 75 years ago.

Chipping Campden

Fairfield

Athelhampton House and Gardens
(01305) 848363
www.athelhampton.co.uk
One of the finest 15th century Houses
in England nestled in the heart of the
picturesque Piddle Valley in the famous Hardy
county of rural Dorset.

Clovelly Village
(01237) 431781
www.clovelly.co.uk
Most visitors consider Clovelly to be unique.
Whatever your view, it is a world of
difference not to be missed.

Hartland Abbey & Gardens
(01237) 441496/234
www.hartlandabbey.com
Hartland Abbey is a family home full of
history in a beautiful valley leading to a wild
Atlantic cove.

St Michael's Mount
(01736) 710507
www.stmichaelsmount.co.uk
Explore the amazing island of St Michael's
Mount and discover legend, myth and over a
thousand years of incredible history.

Sudeley

Sudeley Castle
(01242) 602308
www.sudeleycastle.co.uk
The former home of Tudor Queen, Katherine
Parr. Fascinating exhibitions and award-winning
gardens. In 2014, the east Wing will be open
to the public for the first time in over decade.

Tintagel Castle

Tintagel Castle - English Heritage
(01840) 770328
www.english-heritage.org.uk/tintagel
Tintagel Castle is a magical day with its
wonderful location, set high on the rugged
north Cornwall coast.

Trerice
(01637) 875404
www.nationaltrust.org.uk/trerice
A grand manor on a Cornish scale.

Wilton House
(01722) 746714
www.wiltonhouse.com
Wilton House has one of the finest art
collections in Europe and is set in magnificent
landscaped parkland featuring the Palladian
Bridge.

Chavenage
(01666) 502329
www.chavenage.com
Elizabethan Manor Chavenage House, a TV/Film
location is still a family home, offers unique
experiences, with history, ghosts and more.

HUDSON's
HISTORIC HOUSES & GARDENS
MUSEUMS & HERITAGE SITES

For more suggestions
of great historic days
out across Britain visit
www.hudsonsheritage.com

Constantine Bay, Cornwall

WEST COUNTRY
WHERE TO STAY

Entries appear alphabetically by
town name in each county. A key
to symbols appeares on page 3.

Budock Vean Hotel
Helford, Mawnan Smith, Falmouth, Cornwall TR11 5LG
T (01326) 252100 **F** (01326) 250892
E relax@budockvean.co.uk **W** www.budockvean.co.uk

This privately owned, family run, luxury four-star hotel really does have it all! Budock Vean is the ideal base for visiting west Cornwall. The 32 acres of garden incorporate woodland, parkland, formal and informal areas, valley garden, pond and natural foreshore to the Helford river. Guests can also enjoy free, unlimited use of the well designed 9-hole golf course, which has 18 tees. Leisure facilities include a spectacular indoor pool, sauna, health spa, outdoor hot tub, tennis courts and snooker. Guests can be active or passive – simply relaxing in the tranquillity of this wonderful setting. Bedrooms have every modern comfort and facility. Self-catering cottages are also available. Head chef Darren Kelly and his team create menus featuring Cornish seafood, local fresh meat and vegetables, complimented by a good value wine list. Service and presentation are first class. It is a delight to relax in the sun lounge and enjoy the river views. From the jetty a ferry can take guests to a riverside pub or enjoy a private charter on the *Hannah-Molly* – splendid and unique. Falmouth and the Helford Estuary are near at hand with Glendurgan and Trebah gardens within walking distance.

Rates Single with breakfast from £76; double from £152.
Meals 4 course tdh dinner £39.95; alc, lunch & special diets available; last orders 2100; breakfast from 0800.

Leisure Breaks Check our website for special offers.
Other activities Hotel riverboat, fishing, sailing, riding, watersports nearby.

All major credit cards accepted. Open all year except 2–24 January.

Cornwall, Falmouth

Trevalsa Court Country House Hotel & Restaurant
Mevagissey, Cornwall PL26 6TH
T (01726) 842468 **F** (01726) 844482
E stay@trevalsa-hotel.co.uk **W** www.trevalsa-hotel.co.uk

Built as a private house in the arts and crafts style, Trevalsa Court embodies the elegance, comfort and informality of a country house. It stands high on the cliff tops, with most rooms enjoying fabulous sea views. It is an eclectic mix of ancient oak beams, mullioned windows and oak panelling with designer fabrics, leather sofas and modern art. Guests are encouraged to relax and make the hotel their holiday home. Our AA ® restaurant serves locally produced food, deliciously prepared and tastefully presented. Situated in an area of outstanding natural beauty at the start of the Roseland Peninsula, Trevalsa is the perfect location for a Cornish holiday. The many famous gardens, fishing villages and attractions of Cornwall, including the Eden Project are nearby and the Lost Gardens of Heligan are within walking distance. Golf, tennis, sea fishing, cycle and canoe hire are available locally. Or you may wish to relax in the hotel's own tranquil gardens, walk the coastal path, check out Mevagissey Harbour or venture down the cliff path to the secluded Polstreath Beach to swim in the turquoise waters or dabble in its rock pools. Whatever your Cornish dream, your stay in this unique house will be memorable.

🛏 15 ♪ 🐾 ⛰ 🏃 ↻ 🐕 🅿 14

Rates Single room with breakfast from £60; double from £110; luxury double from £175.
Meals Tdh dinner £30; bar lunches; special diets available; dinner from 1900–2100.

Leisure Breaks Please phone for details.
Other Facilities Golf, tennis, gym/fitness centre nearby.

💷 All major credit & debit cards accepted.

Cornwall, Mevagissey

The Abbey Hotel
Abbey Street, Penzance, Cornwall TR18 4AR
T (01736) 366906
E hotel@theabbeyonline.co.uk **W** www.theabbeyonline.co.uk

17

The building dates from the 17th century and was modernised in 1820 in Georgian Gothic style. It remained a private house until after WWII when it became an hotel. Set above Penzance harbour and overlooking Mounts Bay towards St Michaels Mount, the Abbey is one of the town's most important listed buildings. Its walled garden, courtyard and period features make it stand out from other hotels in the region. It is like staying in a private house. Bedrooms are exquisite, each one different. One has a *faux armoire* which opens onto a loo and basin area. Style is relaxed country house, with plush fabrics, lots of space for a town house, large comfortable beds with down pillows and modern bathrooms. Accommodation includes The Suite, with its own staircase approach and double aspect sitting room, and the self-catering 'apartment' which can sleep four. The hotel also owns *The Slipway* Restaurant, next door, which offers a delicious *a la carte* selection, including the freshest catch of the day with a lighter Street Food Selection alternative, serving all day Tapas-type dishes. This is a charming base from which to explore the many attractions of west Cornwall, including the Minack Theatre, Lands End, St Just, Zennor and St Ives, with the south west coastal path reprising at picturesque Mousehole nearby.

🛏 8 🅿 🐾 🐕 🕳 ⋮⋮⋮ 30 📶

Rates Single room with breakfast from £75; double from £100.

Meals Alc Menu available; Lunch available; Vegetarian & special diets available; Last orders 2200; Breakfast from 0730.

Other Facilities Colour TV; Hairdryer; Tea/coffee making facilities; Video/DVD players available.

💷 All major credit & debit cards accepted. Closed January & February.

Cornwall, Penzance

Penventon Park Hotel
Redruth, Cornwall TR15 1TE
T (01209) 203000 **F** (01209) 203001
E enquiries@penventon.com **W** www.penventon.co.uk

The luxury ★★★ privately run Penventon Park Hotel is a charming Georgian mansion set in acres of parkland. The hotel is centrally situated in Cornwall and is only 10–15 minutes from many landmarks, attractions, walks, gardens, beaches and historic places. There are 63 bedrooms which include the Junior Suites with marble bathroom and outside decking or for something a little special, why not try the romantic 4-poster Celebration Suite? The hotel restaurant *The Dining Galleries* offers breakfast, table d'hôte and light lunches and elaborate à la carte evening menus. The chefs use top quality local produce: fish, shellfish, meat and vegetables, to create a wide range of classic English, French and Italian cuisine to tempt any palate. The Spa has an indoor pool, spa bath, sauna and gymnasium as well as treatment rooms for that little bit of pampering. Nothing is too much trouble. Staff are friendly and professional. Pure Cornish hospitality at its best. Come and discover the Penventon experience.

🛏 63 (inc 20 suites) 🍴 ⚓ 🎐 ✳ 🐾 📖 🍸 ♨ ♨ 🎣 ☺ 🕺 ✒
👥 200 🅿 100 📶

Rates Single with breakfast from £69; double from £99.
Meals Dinner, lunch & special diets available; last orders 2130; breakfast from 0700.

Leisure Breaks 2–3 nights breaks available. Contact hotel.
Other activities Fishing, golf, riding, Cornish gardens, cliff walks nearby.

💷 Major credit cards (exc Diners) accepted. Open all year.

The Berry Head Hotel

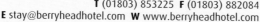

Berry Head Road, Brixham, Devon TQ5 9AJ
T (01803) 853225 **F** (01803) 882084
E stay@berryheadhotel.com **W** www.berryheadhotel.com

The Berry Head Hotel is set in a superb water's edge position in six acres of its own gardens and woodland, in the seclusion of the Berry Head Country Park, which is noted for its bird life and rare wild flowers. The hotel is steeped in history. It was built as a military hospital in the Napoleonic Wars and was later the home of the Reverend Francis Lyte, who wrote the famous hymn *Abide with Me* at the hotel, no doubt inspired by the glorious sunsets. The historic fishing port of Brixham, where William of Orange first landed to claim the English crown, is only a short walk away. The hotel offers relaxing accommodation and all rooms have up to date facilities as well as a baby listening service. The comfortable lounge and the restaurant, which overlooks the terrace, enjoy spectacular views of Torbay and the Devon coast. The emphasis here is upon good food, wine and company in a rather special setting. Set in national parkland with miles of coastal walks, fishing, birdwatching and sailing at hand, yet close to the major resort of Torquay, this is an ideal hideaway for a short break and the perfect location for any occasion, wedding or conference.

🛏 32   🅰   ✈   ⌖   ⊙   🐓   ░ 200   🐕   🅿 30   ✄

Rates Room & breakfast from £50 per pers; dinner, room & breakfast from £65 pppn.
Meals Last orders 2130; bar meals til 2130; special diets available children welcome.
Leisure Breaks Two nights, dinner, b&b from £99 per pers/3 nights from £145.
Other activities Boules. Outdoor (seawater) pool 200 yds, squash, sailing, boating, shooting, fishing, tennis and golf nearby.
💷 Visa, Mastercard, Switch & Solo accepted. Open all year.

Devon, Brixham

Dart Marina Hotel & Spa
Dartmouth, Devon TQ6 9PH
T (01803) 832580 **F** (01803) 835040
E reservations@dartmarina.com **W** www.dartmarina.com

Dart Marina Hotel, Dartmouth, is a luxury hotel situated on the banks of the River Dart, providing stylish hotel accommodation and self-catering apartments with stunning views over the river. Elegant hotel rooms with crisp white linen, deep, fluffy towels and bathrobes and amazing beds which offer rejuvenating sleep of the kind only experienced when breathing in fresh sea air! The health spa eases away stresses and strains with a range of luxury health spa treatments, aromatherapy products and holistic health spa therapies. With breath-taking scenery from every window, Dart Marina's River Restaurant is a fine dining restaurant which holds an AA ® recognising high standards of cuisine and a Strawberry icon for the hotel's commitment to using regional food. Menus combine the very best in seasonal ingredients with the light touch of an exceptional chef. Home of the Dartmouth Regatta, the Dart Marina is a perfect retreat for simply relaxing and an ideal base, both for local boating and more ambitious cruising. Historic Dartmouth, with its narrow winding streets, shops and galleries, is a short walk along the river embankment.

🛏 56 🐕 (£10 per day) ⚏ ⛵ 🍴 🎣 🎿 🅿 🏇 📶

Rates Single with breakfast from £95; double from £140.
Meals 3 course tdh dinner £45; alc, lunch & special diets available; last orders 2100; breakfast from 0730.

Leisure Breaks Stay five nights on the hotel's dinner, bed & breakfast tariff and only pay for four.
Other activities Fishing, golf, riding, walking nearby.

💳 Major credit cards accepted.

Devon, Dartmouth

Plantation House Hotel

Totnes Road, Ermington, Devon PL21 9NS

T (01548) 831100
E info@plantationhousehotel.co.uk **W** www.plantationhousehotel.co.uk

Formerly the parish rectory, this much loved restaurant with rooms now offers a harmonious blend of relaxed country tranquility and stylish sophistication, with a personal touch. A gently indulgent sanctuary on the very doorstep of river estuaries, soothing beaches, market towns and the wilderness of Dartmoor. Nestling on the green sunny bank of the river Erme valley, in an Area of Outstanding Natural Beauty, Plantation House provides understated comfort in the hands of a loyal, caring team. The kitchen boasts an experienced line up. John the expert fisherman and forager and Richard your chef/patron. Expect fine, locally sourced land and sea ingredients prepared and cooked with great care and expertise. Vegetables, fruits and eggs from the garden; breads, pastries and puddings from the kitchen; and there's a cracking wine list. Breakfasts are irresistible and as indulgent as you may wish. Modern bathrooms are stone clad with under floor heating, bathrobes, classy toiletries. Bedrooms all have comfy seating, sash windows, rural views and plenty of extras such as hot water bottles, fresh fruit, flowers, cafetiére coffee, in-room massage therapies.

Rates Single Room with breakfast from £60; double from £120 - £195; suite from £230.
Meals Dinner is £39 AA ★★★★★ restaurant with rooms. Lighter meals available.

Leisure Breaks Autumn and winter breaks a speciality. Exclusive use available.
Other activities In house massage therapies, guided fishing trips of all types, golf, riding, falconry, tennis, sailing, canoeing.

Major credit and debit cards accepted. Open all year.

Devon, Ermington

The Cottage Hotel
Hope Cove, Kingsbridge, Devon TQ7 3HJ
T (01548) 561555 **F** (01548) 561455
E info@hopecove.com **W** www.hopecove.com

Hope Cove is what the name implies: a beautiful village situated along the rugged south Devon coastline. The Cottage Hotel enjoys a superb position, overlooking the picturesque harbour and cove, set in two and a half acres of shrubs and lawns which lead, via sloping footpaths, to the largest of two beaches, where you can bathe in safety. The hotel has 31 en suite bedrooms. The Ireland family have run The Cottage since 1973 and provide a warm, personal service, whilst constantly updating the facilities. The Restaurant is renowned amongst visitors and locals alike. Locally caught crab, lobster and fish are on the menu and the house wines are truly special. The Cottage is popular with families – there is a games room and special high teas are available. Along this Heritage Coastline there are challenging walks affording superb views. The area is famous for its unique flora and fauna, including the Nature Reserve at Slapton Ley. Many sporting activities are available nearby with ten golf courses within easy reach – the hotel having concessions at Bigbury, Thurlestone and Dartmouth.

🛏 31 🔍 🏇 ⛰ 🐕 🛒 📷 ♨ 50

Rates Dinner, room & breakfast from £55–£95 per person.
Meals Bar meals 1200–1400; last orders 2030.

Leisure Breaks 1st Nov–17th April 2014 inc. 2-night stay £52.50–£69.40; 7-night stay £51.50–£68.40 acc. to room. Prices per person per night and include accommodation, breakfast & 5 course dinner + coffee & VAT.
Other activities Sailing 5 miles, golf 4 miles, tennis & squash 6 miles.

💳 Debit cards accepted. Open all year except 2nd Jan to 6th Feb inclusive.

Devon, Hope Cove

Ilsington Country House Hotel
Ilsington Village, Newton Abbot, Devon TQ13 9RR
T (01364) 661452 **F** (01364) 661307
E hotel@ilsington.co.uk **W** www.ilsington.co.uk

23

This peaceful country house hotel is situated in ten acres of the Dartmoor National Park and offers spectacular views over some of the most beautiful scenery in England. Bedrooms are well appointed and comfortable. They range from standard ground floor rooms through to deluxe rooms and suites. There are two lounges in which to relax, both with log fires in winter, and the conservatory offers a bright seating area from where to watch the world go by. The main restaurant has dramatic views over Dartmoor to Haytor Rocks. Head chef Mike O'Donnell has presided in this stunning setting for 15 years and is the proud holder of AA ◉◉. His contemporary cooking uses locally sourced produce, where possible. For less formal dining, the hotel has its own bistro *The Blue Tiger*, which resembles a traditional Dartmoor pub. The hotel has its own leisure facilities including indoor pool, spa, steam room, sauna and gymnasium. Ilsington Village is dominated by the 12th century St Michael's Church. Further afield are the riches of Dartmoor's tors, open moorland and dramatic wooded valleys to explore, fishing, golf and gardens to visit.

Rates Single with breakfast from £90; double from £115.
Meals Tdh 3 course dinner from £36; alc & special diets available. Last dinner orders 2100; breakfast from 0745.

Other activities Tennis, riding, golf, fishing nearby.

Major credit cards (exc. Amex) accepted.

24

Tides Reach Hotel
South Sands, Salcombe, South Devon TQ8 8LJ
T (01548) 843466 **F** (01548) 843954
E enquire@tidesreach.com **W** www.tidesreach.com

Tides Reach is a complete gem of a hotel, set just back from the famous South Sands beach. Here you will find everything you could possibly desire for a relaxing, invigorating break in Salcombe. The hotel has been run by the Edwards family for over forty years and their attention to each individual guest is second to none. Staff are courteous and good humoured. Whether you are in the hot tub, sauna, indoor pool, snooker room or conservatory overlooking the beach, someone is always at hand to provide a drink or a snack, or just to chat. The food is of a very high standard with wonderfully varied choices, like fillet of Salcombe sea bass served with aubergine caviar or char-grilled wild boar cutlet with crispy air dried ham and a balsamic jus, or roast pheasant on a pink peppercorn sauce with game chips. Starters and puddings are just as spoiling. If you can bear to venture outside the hotel, Overbecks Garden is within walking distance and the NT properties of Coleton Fishacre, Saltram, Buckland Abbey and Cotehele are just a short drive away.

📯 32 🦌 🔍 🎿 🎣 ⚓ ✏ 🎎 🏄 🃏 🍽 🔥 🐕 (£9.00) 🅿 100 📶

Rates Single with breakfast from £79; double from £140.

Meals Garden Room Restaurant tdh dinner £34.50; special diets available last orders 2100

Leisure Breaks Spa, Romantic, Indulgent, Bargain Breaks available all year.
Other activities Fishing 1 mile; golf & riding 6 miles; tennis ½ mile.

💶 Major credit cards accepted. Open all year.

Devon, Salcombe

Knoll House Hotel
Studland Bay, Dorset BH19 3AH
T (01929) 450450 **F** (01929) 450423
E info@knollhouse.co.uk **W** www.knollhouse.co.uk

This delightful hotel is situated on the finest stretch of Dorset heritage coastline, surrounded by some of the prettiest countryside in the west. It is within a National Trust Reserve and overlooks three miles of golden beach with first class swimming, fishing, boating and wind-surfing. Knoll House is an independent country house hotel under the personal management of its family owners and is set in pine trees with attractive gardens. Many of the bedrooms are arranged as suites, ideal for families. Log fires and an attractive cocktail bar add to the unique atmosphere of this efficiently run hotel. The quality, choice and presentation of menus is excellent. At lunchtime a superb hors d'oeuvres selection and buffet table laden with cold meats, pies and salads is a speciality, followed by delicious puddings and a good English cheese board. Young children are catered for in their own dining room and there are many and varied facilities to keep them amused all day. Sandbanks and Bournemouth are easily reached via the car ferry. Dorchester, Corfe Castle and the picturesque villages of Dorset are only a short drive away.

79 (inc 30) ⚐ △ ⚐ ⚐ ⚐ ⚐ ⚐ ⚐ ⚐ ⚐ ⚐ ⚐ ⚐ ⚐ (£5) (WiFi)

Rates Half board from £135 daily or full board (weekly) from £1020 (Apr) to £1250 (Aug). Generous full board terms for five nights out of season.

Special Breaks Family Five' (two adults, one or two children under 13) – five nights full board in low season £1050. Purbeck Five (single or twin rooms without private bathroom) – five nights full board in low season £400 per pers.

Other facilities Isle of Purbeck Golf Club (2 courses) 2 miles; Childrens' dining room; Studland Riding Stables 1 mile; childrens' playground.

Mastercard & Visa accepted. Hotel open Easter–January.

Dorset, Studland Bay

Plumber Manor
Sturminster Newton, Dorset DT10 2AF
T (01258) 472507 **F** (01258) 473370
E book@plumbermanor.com **W** www.plumbermanor.com

This imposing Jacobean manor house is set in idyllic countryside "far from the madding crowd". The Divelish stream weaves its way through delightful grounds, extensive lawns and fine old trees. Dating from the 17th century, the manor has been the home of the Prideaux-Brune family. Since 1973 the careful management of Richard, Alison and Brian (in the kitchen) has led to the creation of a first class hotel and restaurant. Richard knows many of his regular diners personally and is always on hand for advice, both about current dishes on the ever changing menu and about what to see in this charming part of Dorset. When we dined there recently we had the excellent 'medley of seafood' starter, followed by succulent *medallions de boeuf*. Remember to leave room for one of the excellent Plumber puddings! The wine list is of the same standard, well-chosen and with ever changing freshness. There are six elegant bedrooms within the main house and a further ten in the courtyard and converted barn. Plumber is welcoming, comfortable and has a charming atmosphere in which to relax and savour first class hospitality, cuisine and service.

🛏 16 ♿ 🅿 ♨ 16 ⚲ 🐕 (by arr't)

Rates Single room with breakfast from £115; double inc. breakfast from £150.
Meals 2 course tdh dinner £29/3 course £36. Alc, lunch & special diets available; last orders 2130.

Short breaks/special offers Nov–March 10% discount for 2 nts/15% discount. 3 nts+ exc. Xmas/New Year/Easter. See website for latest offers.
Other facilities Fishing, golf, riding, shooting nearby by arrangement.

💳 Major credit cards accepted. Hotel open early March–late January.

Dorset, Sturminster Newton

The White Hart Royal stands in the centre of this busy Cotswold market town. Built as a coaching inn in the 17th century and put on the map by King Charles I who stayed here on the eve of the Battle of Marston Moor nearby. The property has been cleverly refurbished whilst maintaining its period features. Bedrooms are some of the best in the area, with a number of ground floor Garden Rooms accessible via the courtyard. They are divided into singles, twins, doubles and Feature Bedrooms, like the King Charles Suite and the Four-Poster Rooms. The *Le Noir* Room has a double bathtub. The popular Courtyard Restaurant has been awarded an AA ◉ for cuisine. You can eat *al fresco* or enjoy the relaxed atmosphere of the Snug Bar with its inglenook fireplace. With a civil wedding licence this is the ideal place for a wedding or naming ceremony. Cuisine is contemporary English using local produce where possible, accompanied by a good selection of old and new world wines. Moreton-in-Marsh is blessed with good shops, a famous market and the Batsford Arboretum. Hidcote, Kiftsgate and Snowshill Gardens, and the rolling north Cotswolds are nearby.

🛏 29 (inc 🏠) 🐕 🐎 ♿ 👪 30 ♨ 🎠 📶

Rates Single with breakfast from £100; double from £125.
Meals Courtyard ◉ Restaurant alc starters from £5, mains from £10; lunch & special diets available; last orders 2100; breakfast from 0700.

Leisure Breaks 2 night breaks, dinner, b&b from £125 pp. Sunday Slumber 3 course lunch, b&b Sunday night from £49 per person.
Other activities Golf, walking, riding nearby.

💶 All major credit cards accepted. Open all year exc. 24 Dec–5 Jan.

Gloucestershire, Moreton-in-Marsh

Corse Lawn House Hotel
Corse Lawn, Nr. Tewkesbury, Gloucestershire GL19 4LZ
T (01452) 780771 **F** (01452) 780840
E enquiries@corselawn.com **W** www.corselawn.com

An elegant Grade II listed Queen Anne building, Corse Lawn House is set back from a quiet village green, standing in 12 acres of its own grounds, facing a pond which used to be a coach-wash. The house has belonged to the Hine family (of Cognac fame) since 1978 and since then has been carefully extended and refurbished to create a stunning country house hotel with individually decorated bedrooms. The AA ® ® restaurant, under the supervision of chef Martin Kinahan, is very much the heart of the hotel, with the emphasis on local and seasonal produce. Less formal dining takes place in the Bistro and a private dining/conference room is available. There are two comfortable drawing rooms, always busy with locals and residents taking tea in the summer and with the house labradors trying to make new friends! The atmosphere is happy and relaxed, the service attentive but unobtrusive.

Corse Lawn is in an unspoiled corner of Gloucestershire, near the Herefordshire and Worcestershire borders but is handy for visiting the Cotswolds, the Malvern Hills and the Forest of Dean. It is easily accessible from the motorway network.

🛏 18 ✿ 🜟 🎠 🐎 🔍 🎣 ⚓ 🚣 🐕 🅿 🎿 📶

Rates Single room with breakfast from £75; double from £120.
Meals 3 course tdh dinner ca £33.50; bistro £20; Lunch & special diets available.

Leisure Breaks B&B £120 for double room, providing dinner is taken in the restaurant or bistro; £110 two nights; £100 three nights.

Other facilities Satellite & SKY TV. Golf and riding nearby.

💷 All major credit cards accepted. Open all year exc. 3 days at Christmas.

Farthings Country House Hotel & Restaurant
Hatch Beauchamp, Taunton, Somerset TA3 6SG

T (01823) 480664 **F** (01823) 481118
E farthingshotel@yahoo.co.uk **W** www.farthingshotel.co.uk

Farthings is a charming Georgian country house hotel. Nestled in the historic village of Hatch Beauchamp, it is very close to both the M5 and A303. The rooms are all delightful, elegant and individually designed. The master bedrooms on the front, facing the village green, are particularly spacious with king size beds, a sitting area and larger bathrooms, one approached via a spiral staircase! There is also a cottage for longer stays. Downstairs there is a cosy lounge, with newspapers and magazines, a friendly bar and three dining rooms, one of which can be used for private parties or meetings. Log fires burn in winter but in summer guests can take advantage of the beautiful walled garden and terrace. Produce from the garden includes fresh free range eggs, guinea fowl and turkey in season and fresh herbs. The setting provides a warm welcome, great hospitality and delicious food in the award winning restaurant, with a good wine list. Farthings is perfect for short breaks, family gatherings, house parties and weddings. The delights of the Mendips, Quantocks and Blackdown Hills are near at hand.

🛏 12 🚪 ❄ 🐕 (£8 p.n) 🍽 20 🅿 🚲 📶

Rates Double/twin with breakfast from £130; master bedroom from £175; cottage from £225.
Meals AA ⓐ alc 3 course dinner from £35; Lunch & special diets available. Last orders 2100; breakfast from 0800.

Leisure Breaks Short break rates and multiple night discounts available.
Other activities Golf nearby.

💷 All major credit cards accepted. Open all year.

Somerset, Taunton

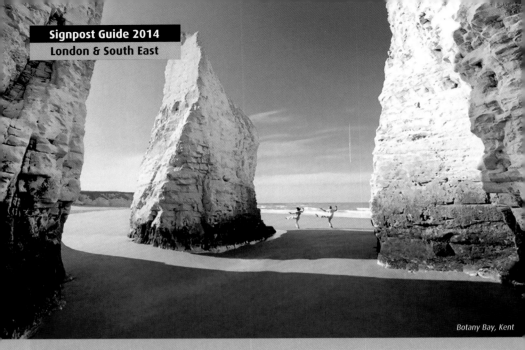

Botany Bay, Kent

London & South East

Fun-filled resorts along 257 miles of coastline, interesting harbours, glorious countryside, historic heritage, lovely gardens, hundreds of different places to visit and the capital's buzz and history - the South East has it all. With two of the country's main airports and the Channel Tunnel, the South East is gateway for most of the country's 28 million annual overseas visitors.

BUCKINGHAMSHIRE
OXFORDSHIRE
GREATER LONDON
BERKSHIRE
SURREY
KENT
HAMPSHIRE
WEST SUSSEX   EAST SUSSEX
ISLE OF WIGHT

Hotels guide

London	page 39
Hampshire/I.O.W.	page 45
Kent	page 47
East Sussex	page 49
West Sussex	page 55

Further information:
Visit London
Tel: 0870 1566 366
www.visitlondon.com

Tourism South East
02380 625400
www.visitsoutheastengland.com

Arundel Castle

Pett Village

Brighton

LONDON

London's treasures are well chronicled. Many visitors like to stay in the west/central Knightsbridge/Kensington areas which are handy for shopping, museums and quick access to the West End.

In the **Central/West End** area the most visited sights are the now public rooms of **Buckingham Palace**, the **National Gallery** in Trafalgar Square, **Tate Britain** on Millbank, **Westminster Abbey**, **Houses of Parliament** and **Cabinet War Rooms**. Westminster Abbey, nearly a thousand years old, has tombs of many English kings, queens, statesmen and writers. The **British Museum** in Bloomsbury houses one of the world's largest selections of antiquities, including the Magna Carta, the Elgin Marbles and the first edition of Alice in Wonderland. This entire area can be well viewed from **The London Eye** on the South Bank.

South Bank, London

Buckingham Palace, London

Further east, in the city of London, is **St Pauls Cathedral**, redesigned by Sir Christopher Wren. Nearby is the **Tower of London**, a medieval fortress dominated by the White Tower and dating from 1097. The Crown Jewels are kept here, guarded by the famous Beefeaters.

In north central London is **Madame Tussauds** featuring the 'Marvel Super heroes 4D attraction' which opened in 2010. Alternatively, if you fancy an historical fright, visit the **London Dungeon** near Tower Bridge and explore the streets of old London.

London's parks are its lungs. **St James**, the oldest, was founded by Henry VIII in 1532. **Hyde Park**, bordering Kensington, Mayfair and Marylebone, is the largest at 630 acres. **Regents Park**, with its zoo, lies north of Oxford Circus and was given to the nation by the Prince Regent.

To the **south east** of the capital, land has been reclaimed. **Canary Wharf** is one of Londons main financial centres and on the south bank opposite **Docklands** are the **Royal Greenwich Observatory**, the **National Maritime Museum** and the **O2 Arena**.

KENT

Kent is the Garden of England with hectares of hop growing fields and now over 70 vineyards, some open to visitors. The formidable **White Cliffs of Dover** have served as a bulwark against foreign invaders since time immemorial. Now they overlook some of the busiest shipping lanes in the world. The **Channel Tunnel** has replaced some ferries but hovercraft still ply between Dover/Folkestone and the French and Belgian coast.

Canterbury

Dover

Romney Marsh

Kent's oldest city, **Canterbury**, is the centre of the Anglican faith, brought to southern Britain by St Augustine landing in Sandwich Bay (in AD596) nearby. It is also the site of St Thomas a Becket's martyrdom. The flatland of **Romney Marsh** lies to the south, gradually reclaimed from the sea since Roman times. To the north is the **Weald of Kent** with its distinctive oast houses and orchards.

Royal Pavilion, Brighton

SURREY AND SUSSEX

A popular and beautiful commuter county. **Ashdown Forest**, now more of a heath, covers 6400 acres of upland, with a large deer, badger and rare bird population.

The heights of **Box Hill** and **Leith Hill** rise above the **North Downs** to overlook large tracts of richly wooded countryside, containing a string of well protected villages. **The Devil's Punchbowl**, near Hindhead, is a two mile long sandstone valley, overlooked by the 900-ft Gibbet Hill. **Farnham**, in the west of the country, has Tudor and Georgian houses flanking the 12th century castle. **Aldershot** nearby is the home of the British Army.

County town **Guildford** is a contemporary business and shopping centre with a modern cathedral and university. The north of the county borders Greater London and includes the 2400 acre **Richmond Park**, where deer roam, **Hampton Court Palace** and **Kew Gardens**.

Administratively divided into east and west 40 years ago, **Sussex** is a much visited county for those wanting a short break from the metropolis.

Brighton, must be named the capital of East Sussex, with its culture, boutique hotels, marina, shops and general 'buzz'. It was the Regency summer capital of Britain and has the eccentric **Royal Pavilion** as a monument to this era. Further west is the impressive **Arundel Castle**, seat of the Duke of Norfolk, and Chichester, with its famous drama festival and nearby popular marinas and Wittering sands. **Bognor Regis** was a favourite with the Prince of Wales, later Edward VIII.

Sussex has a plethora of historic houses and gardens and three of the historic cinque ports. **Rye** in particular, with its cobbled streets, transports the visitor back three centuries. The 1066 Story is told at **Battle**, near Hastings. Eastbourne has the impressive **Beachy Head** and **Seven Sisters** cliffs as backdrop.

Chilterns

BERKSHIRE, BUCKINGHAMSHIRE, HAMPSHIRE, AND OXFORDSHIRE

Much of Berkshire, Buckinghamshire and Oxfordshire serve as commuter territory, but the area is still one of great beauty, with many historic houses, gardens and parks. The Thames sweeps eastwards in broad graceful curves, cutting through the beeches of the Chiltern Hills.

Berkshire's most famous building is **Windsor Castle**. Built by Edward III in the 14th century and restored by later monarchs, most apartments are now open to the public after the 1992 fire. It is the largest and oldest occupied castle in the world and encapsulates more than 900 years of English history. **Cliveden**, former seat of the Astor family and now a famous hotel, is nearby.

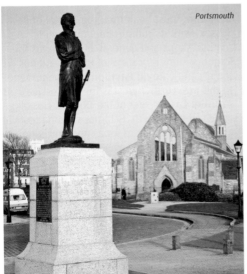
Portsmouth

Buckinghamshire to the north east contains the 'Capability Brown' landscape at **Stowe**, now a famous public school and also the city of **Milton Keynes**, with its famous concrete cows and longest (wet) ski slope in Britain.

Oxford's dreaming spires, echoing quads and cloistered college lawns have a timeless beauty. The **Ashmolean Museum**, Britain's oldest public museum, opened in 1683 and contains gold and jewellery believed to have belonged to King Alfred, the lantern carried by Guy Fawkes and riches from ancient Egypt and Greece. The **Bodleian Library**, founded in 1596, contains over one million volumes, including a copy of every book published in the UK since 1900.

Just north of Oxford at **Woodstock** sits **Blenheim Palace**, given to the first Duke of Marlborough by a grateful nation in 1705 after the eponymous victory and built between 1705 and 1722 by Sir John Vanburgh. It was the birthplace of Sir Winston Churchill and is one of Britain's most visited Great Houses.

Hampshire, with the **Solent**, **Southampton Water** and the **Isle of Wight**, is one of the sailing playgrounds of England. Nearby **Portsmouth Harbour** has Nelson's Victory, the Mary Rose and the ironclad HMS Warrior. **Winchester** has its 11-13th century cathedral and reputedly the remains of King Arthur's Round Table. **Beaulieu** and the **New Forest** are great family attractions.

Chiswick House
(020) 8742 3905
www.chgt.org.uk
Chiswick House is a magnificent neo-Palladian villa set in 65 acres of beautiful historic gardens.

Ham House and Garden
(020) 8940 1950
www.nationaltrust.org.uk/hamhouse
One of London's best kept secrets, this atmospheric Stuart mansion nestles on the banks of leafy Richmond-upon-Thames.

Houses of Parliament
(0844) 847 1672
www.parliament.uk/visiting
Inside one of London's most iconic buildings, tours of the Houses of Parliament offer visitors a unique combination of one thousand years of history, modernday politics, and stunning art and architecture.

Tower of London

Kensington Palace
(0844) 482 7777
www.hrp.org.uk/kensingtonpalace
Discover stories from Queen Victoria's life in her own words. Follow the footsteps of courtiers from the past. Explore the new landscaped gardens, inspired by the famous lawns that exited in the 18th century.

Osterley Park and House
(020) 8232 5050
www.nationaltrust.org.uk/osterley
Created in the late 18th century by architect Robert Adam, Osterley is one of the last surviving country estates in London.

Southside House

Southside House
(020) 8946 7643
www.southsidehouse.com
Described by connoisseurs as an unfortunate experience, Southside House provides an eccentric backdrop to the lives and loves of generations of the Pennington Mellor Munthe families.

Spencer House
(020) 7514 1958
www.spencerhouse.co.uk
London's most magnificent 18th century private palace.

Strawberry Hill House
(020) 8744 1241
www.strawberryhillhouse.org.uk
Strawberry Hill House is Britain's finest example of Gothic Revival architecture and interior decoration.

Tower of London
(0844) 482 7777
www.hrp.org.uk/toweroflondon
The ancient stones reverberate with dark secrets, priceless jewels glint in fortified vaults and pampered ravens strut the grounds.

HUDSON'S
HISTORIC HOUSES & GARDENS
MUSEUMS & HERITAGE SITES

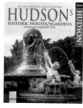

For more suggestions of great historic days out across Britain visit
www.hudsonsheritage.com

Hever Castle

Arundel Castle & Gardens
(01903) 882173
www.arundelcastle.org
Ancient Castle, Stately Home, Gardens & the Collector Earl's Garden.

Blenheim Palace
(0800) 8496500
www.blenheimpalace.com
Blenheim Palace is home to the 11th Duke and Duchess of Marlborough and the birthplace of Sir Winston Churchill.

Broughton Castle
(01295) 276070
www.broughtoncastle.com
"About the most beautiful castle in all England.... For sheer loveliness of the combination of water, woods and picturesque buildings." Sir Charles Oman (1898).

Dover Castle
(01304) 211067
www.english-heritage.org.uk/dovercastle
Explore over 2,000 years of history at Dover Castle.

Goodwood House
(01243) 755048
www.goodwood.com
Goodwood House, ancestral home of the Dukes of Richmond and Gordon with magnificent art collection.

Great Dixter Garden
(01797) 252878
www.greatdixter.co.uk
A very special garden with a great deal of character, planted with flair, always something to see, whatever the season.

Hever Castle & Gardens
(01732) 865224
www.hevercastle.co.uk
Experience 700 years of colourful history and spectacular award-wining gardens at the childhood home of Anne Boleyn.

Lancing College Chapel
(01273) 465949
www.lancingcollege.co.uk
"I know of no more spectacular post - Reformation ecclesiastical building in the kingdom." Evelyn Waugh, former pupil.

Leeds Castle

Penshurst Place

Hever Castle

Leeds Castle
(01622) 765400
www.leeds-castle.com
Set in 500 acres of beautiful Kent parkland, there's something to discover everyday at "The Loveliest Castle in the World".

Penshurst Place and Gardens
(01892) 870307
www.penshurstplace.com
One of Engalnd's greatest family-owned historic houses with a history spanning nearly seven centuries.

Hampton Court Palace
(0844) 482 7777
www.hrp.org.uk/
hamptoncourtpalace
Discover the magnificence of this former royal residence, once home to the flamboyant King Henry VIII.

Beaulieu Estate
(01590) 612345
www.beaulieu.co.uk
Voted 2013 Large Visitor Attraction Gold Winners in England for Exellence Awards, Beaulieu has been owned by the same family since 1538 and is still the private home of Lord Montagu.

Osborne House
(01983) 200022
www.english-heritage.org.uk/
osborne
Take an intimate glimpse into the family life of Britain's longest reigning monarch and the house Queen Vistoria loved to call home.

Chenies Manor House
(01494) 762888
www.cheniesmanorhouse.co.uk
The manor house is in the picturesque village of Chenies and lies in the beautiful Chiltern Hills.

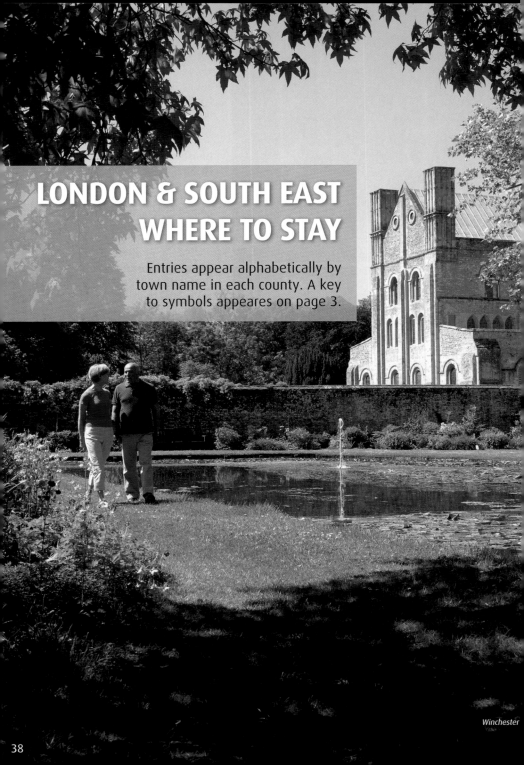

LONDON & SOUTH EAST
WHERE TO STAY

Entries appear alphabetically by
town name in each county. A key
to symbols appeares on page 3.

Winchester

Searcys Roof Garden Rooms

30 Pavilion Road, London SW1X 0HJ

T (0207) 584 4921 **F** (0207) 823 8694
E rgr@searcys.co.uk **W** www.searcys.co.uk/venues/30-pavilion-road/bed-breakfast

Searcys Roof Garden Rooms at 30 Pavilion Road provides a peaceful haven in the heart of Knightsbridge. It offers a relaxed atmosphere and friendly staff with a high level of personal and attentive service. After refurbishment in 2010, the beautiful new boutique bedrooms in this Georgian style townhouse boast an unusual breed of charm and character. All 11 rooms are individually designed to have a country house feel, now however with super king size beds, plasma TVs with a wide option of channels, plus the usual amenities – complimentary WIFI, air conditioning, tea or coffee brought automatically to your room once you have been checked in. Luxury touches continue in the bathroom with bathrobes and Molton Brown toiletries. The Roof Terrace is the ideal space to take breakfast on a sunny morning or to round off the day with a glass of chilled white wine. Searcys Roof Garden Rooms at 30 Pavilion Road is truly a hidden gem in the bustle of London, yet conveniently located for Knightsbridge, Hyde Park, museums and the theatre district. It is perfect for those seeking an alternative to large hotel chains.

🛏 11 AC ⊙ ✂ 🔲 ⤓ ⏻ 🅿 (NCP opposite) 👥 240 🍽 120 📶

Rates Single room, b&b from £144; double/twin room from £239.
Meals 24-hour room service.

Other facilities Lift. Banqueting Service.

💷 Amex, Visa, Mastercard, Maestro accepted. Closed Christmas.

London, SW1

40

San Domenico House
29–31 Draycott Place, Chelsea, London SW3 2SH

T (0207) 581 5757 **F** (0207) 584 1348
E info@sandomenicohouse.com **W** www.sandomenicohouse.com

San Domenico House is an intimate luxurious boutique townhouse hotel located just a few minutes from bustling Sloane Square and the fashionable heart of Chelsea. Behind its Victorian facade, San Domenico House enjoys all the luxuries of a small palace, preserving the charm and intimacy of its 17 rooms and suites. With easy access to the City and West End, it is ideally suited to business executive and leisure traveller alike. Each bedroom is individually themed and furnished with lovely antiques. They are all air-conditioned, have individually stocked mini bar, flat screen TV, DVD player and stylish bathroom facilities with Molton Brown toiletries, hand made Italian olive oil beauty products and fluffy bathrobes. An additional feature is the rooftop terrace with far reaching views across Chelsea.

Whether guests want an English or Continental start to the day in the charming breakfast room or wish to enjoy afternoon tea in the antiques-filled lounge, San Domenico House will provide them with the highest standard of service in a comfortable and relaxed atmosphere.

🛏 17 ♨ 🚗 📻 ☉ ⤬ ✢ ⚲ ∷ 15 ✈ 🐾 📶

Rates	Single from £230; doubles from £255; suite from £310 room only.
Meals	Breakfast only but room service available.

Special breaks Fitness Package – healthy breakfast and Daily Pass to local fitness centre with pool from £270 per couple per night. Theatre Experience – pair of theatre tickets + breakfast, afternoon tea, bottle of wine in room, from £355 per room per night exc VAT.

Other facilities Health club & gym nearby; airport pickup.

💷 All major credit cards accepted. Open all year.

London, SW3

The Mayflower Hotel & Apartments
26–28 Trebovir Road, Earls Court, London SW5 9NJ
T (0207) 370 0991 **F** (0207) 370 0994
E info@mayflower-group.co.uk **W** www.mayflowerhotel.co.uk

41

This well established, independently run, hotel is close to Earls Court Exhibition Centre, Olympia and the Underground, providing a fast link to the West End. There are many restaurants in the area, catering for every cuisine. The Mayflower is a sister hotel to Twenty Nevern Square *(see next page)* and has completed an extensive refurbishment to bring it up to 4-star standard. With the introduction of a lounge/coffee bar, a smart new reception area and an enhanced breakfast room, guests will immediately feel at home. Each of the 48 rooms, which range from singles to suites, is individually themed with dark polished wooden floors, climate controls and ceiling fans common to most. Four rooms have balconies. Marble bathrooms come with complimentary toiletries. Secure car parking can be arranged. The studios and apartments are for longer term occupation and come with daily maid service, fully equipped kitchen, bathrooms and entry phone system. We recommend The Mayflower as a homely place with friendly and attentive multi-lingual staff.

48+35 appts (from £25 per night 2pm-11am) WiFi

Rates Single room inc breakfast from £109; double from £120; suite from £220; family room from £275.

Special breaks Shopping, Conference, Valentines and Honeymoon breaks available.
Other facilities Satellite TV, lift. No restaurant.

All major credit cards accepted. Open all year.

London, SW5

Twenty Nevern Square
20 Nevern Square, London SW5 9PD

T (0207) 565 9555 **F** (0207) 565 9444
E hotel@twentynevernsquare.co.uk **W** www.twentynevernsquare.co.uk

Overlooking a quiet, tree-lined garden square, this is one of London's newest and, at the same time, most original and discreet boutique hotels. The mosaic patterned steps of the late 19th century mansion give a hint of the Eastern influences within, which are also apparent in the decor of the cosy ground floor lounge. The interior has been refurbished in exotic style. Most impressive are the carved oriental headboards and wardrobes and the silk curtains, found in, for example, The Grand Pasha Suite or the Chinese Room. The sleek marble bathrooms, too, imitate those found in designer hotels. The Eastern feel extends to the lounge and light, airy conservatory/breakfast room, which is filled with wicker furniture and greenery. The hotel overlooks an elegant square, which seems worlds away. The hotel is close to Earls Court and Olympia Exhibition Centres and has easy access to the West End, Kensington, Chelsea and Knightsbridge. To stay in this distinctive townhouse hotel is an experience not to be missed.

🛏 20 (inc 1 suite) ☺ ▾ **P** (charged) 📶

Rates Small double inc breakfast £120–£175; luxury double £120–£249; luxury 4-poster £149–£275; suite £220–£450.
Meals No restaurant but Cafe Twenty provides tea/coffee 24 hours.

Special breaks Special Christmas Break – 3 nights inc. lunch on Xmas Day.
Other facilities Airport transfer on request. Gymnasium nearby. Open 24 hours.

💷 All major credit cards accepted. Open all year.

London, SW5

The Gainsborough is located on the east side of Queensberry Place, facing its sister hotel, The Gallery, and close to the many good restaurants and shops of this exclusive area of London. The hotel is three minutes' walk from South Kensington Underground station, on the Piccadilly line to Heathrow and is within easy reach of London's museums, the Lycee Francais, the Royal Albert Hall, Harrods and the Olympia exhibition centre. The hotel is named after the celebrated artist and public areas are adorned with paintings, with the ground floor breakfast room displaying a cheerful array of cartoons and drawings. Adjacent to reception, there is a friendly and well stocked lounge bar for a leisurely drink or snack from the 24-hour light menu. There is a wide choice of accommodation, from family rooms and suites down to singles. Each room is

uniquely designed with colourful décor. Reception will be pleased to order a taxi, make a dinner or theatre reservation for guests. At most times of year, the hotel runs an Early Bird discount scheme, as well as free nights for those staying three, five or seven nights. Business and leisure travellers alike will want for nothing in this smartly kept, good value and well located hotel.

Rates Single room from £75; double from £85.

Meals In-room dining; Alc available; Lunch available; Vegetarian & special diets available.

Special breaks See our website for current special offers.

Other facilities Gym nearby.

£ All major credit & debit cards accepted. Open all year.

London, SW7

New Linden Hotel
59 Leinster Square, London W2 4PS
T (0207) 221 4321 **F** (020) 7727 3156
E newlindenhotel@mayflower-group.co.uk **W** www.hotelnewlinden.co.uk

The third hotel in the Mayflower Collection (*see pages 41–42*), the New Linden has undergone a major refurbishment to bring it up to the level of a top standard townhouse hotel. The display of seasonal flowers outside welcomes the hotel visitor, a recent winner of a *London in Bloom* award. There is the usual range of rooms of varying shapes and sizes, all attractively furnished and comfortable with gleaming bathroom or shower areas. Broad darkwood headboards add an original touch. Two strikingly unusual family rooms in terms of size and layout sleep up to five, one of these being on split levels with Doric columns dividing the upper and lower sections. A spacious breakfast room in the basement serves an extensive continental buffet to guests. The New Linden enjoys a quiet location in Leinster Square with Queensway and Bayswater underground stations both within five minutes' walk, and Paddington Station and the Heathrow express 15 minutes' walk away. The area is cosmopolitan with a varied choice of restaurants and Whiteleys, the indoor shopping mall, close by.

🛏 79 (inc 7 ⚏)   WiFi

Rates Single room with breakfast from £109; double inc. breakfast from £130; suites from £210; family room from £275.

Special breaks Discounted rates for Sun–Thurs specials, Valentines, Christmas, New Year, Honeymoon.
Other facilities Satellite TV. NCP nearby.

💷 Amex, Visa, Mastercard, Switch, Solo accepted. Open all year.

London, W2

The White Horse Hotel & Brasserie
Market Place, Romsey, Hampshire SO51 8ZJ
T (01794) 512431 **F** (01794) 517485
E reservations@silkshotels.com **W** www.silkshotels.com

45

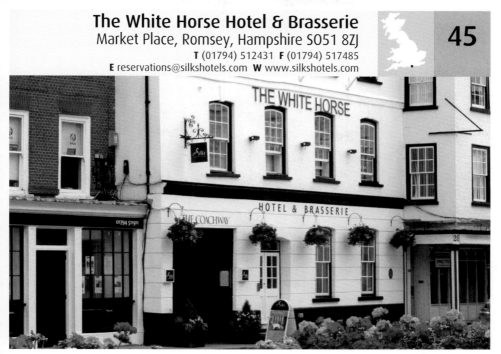

The White Horse Hotel, a grade II listed building, is one of only three late medieval structures in Hampshire which was purpose built as an Inn. Since the days of the stagecoach, for over 400 years the White Horse has extended hospitality to guests. This stunning historic Inn, situated in the heart of the market town of Romsey, is the main hotel for visiting this area of the New Forest and Hampshire, as well as being close to cathedral cities and coastal destinations. Standards are high throughout. Rooms are beautifully designed and luxury refinements provided. The Penthouse is sumptuous and the Loft Apartments have much character. The Brasserie is contemporary in style and serves acclaimed AA ◎◎ cuisine, sourced locally and presented with flair and attentive professionalism. In summer months, the picturesque courtyard is a must for dining and socialising. Public areas exude sophisticated style from Tudor influences up to today's modern yet classic elegance. The White Horse is the perfect spot for a weekend away to relax and savour the history, hospitality and charm of this fine ◇◇◇◇ hotel.

79 (24 only) (£10 p.n)

Rates Single with continental breakfast from £85; double from £115.

Meals Alc, lunch & special diets available; last orders 2200; breakfast from 0700.

Special breaks See our website for current special offers.

Other facilities Fishing, golf nearby.

All major credit cards (exc. Diners) accepted. Open all year.

Hampshire, Romsey

The Priory Bay Hotel
Priory Drive, Seaview, Isle of Wight PO34 5BU
T (01983) 613146 **F** (01983) 616539
E enquiries@priorybay.co.uk **W** www.priorybay.co.uk

This elegant Virginia creeper-clad country retreat has been built upon by medieval monks, Tudor farmers and Georgian gentry. It sits atop a small valley overlooking a stunning 70-acre estate, with spectacular views over its own private beach, six-hole golf course and the East Solent. Its restored buildings combine to create the unique *Country House by the Sea* – synonymous with fine dining, service and luxury. Superior rooms are in the main building whereas the converted tithe barns and self-catering cottages are more suitable for families. For an extra treat, guests can choose from a range of holistic therapy treatments in the comfort of their own rooms. The two restaurants (Regency-muralled and brasserie style with alfresco terrace) offer seasonal cuisine specialising in local and foraged produce plus an innovative wine list which focuses on organic and biodynamic wines. The estate is a haven for wildlife, including birds of prey, owls, red squirrels and orchids. The hotel is available for weddings and has a wedding pavilion on the beach. A fine family hotel with plenty for parents and children to do, and perfect for romantic getaways.

🛏30 ⏰ ♋ ✒ 🎵 🎿 🎠 ⛵ ⛰ ♨ 🎣 ∪ ✎ 🐕 (cottages only)
🅿 50 ♟ 50 🎾 🕴 📶

Rates Single room with breakfast from £90; double/twin from £160. Dinner, b&b from £125 single/£230 double.
Meals Tdh dinner £35. Lunch & special diets available; last orders 2115

Special breaks Reductions for 3–7 nights.
Other facilities Falconry courses, beach walks, watersports, historic houses nearby.

💷 Major credit cards (exc. Diners/Amex) accepted. Open all year.

Isle of Wight, Seaview

The Marquis at Alkham

Alkham Valley Road, Alkham, Dover, Kent CT15 7DF

T (01304) 873410 **F** (01304) 873418

E reception@themarquisatalkham.co.uk **W** www.themarquisatalkham.co.uk

The Marquis at Alkham is a strikingly contemporary boutique restaurant with rooms. Spacious and light with fine furnishings and beautiful fabrics - the opportunity to fine tune every detail hasn't been missed. The styling is contemporary. The décor is chic. But look outside the window, and you couldn't be anywhere but England. The ⊛ ⊛ ⊛ AA rosette restaurant is a revelation. Head Chef Charles Lakin's food is seasonally inspired and locally sourced. The constantly evolving menus are as fresh as they are imaginative and the elegant 21st century styling is exceptional. With a choice of a la carte and tasting menu's there is something for everyone. Located in the Alkham Valley, an Area of Outstanding Natural Beauty in the heart of the Kent Downs, this is the perfect resting place within a walkers paradise. Queen sized pocket sprung beds are swathed in the finest cotton. Sumptuous fabrics dress windows and chairs. An eclectic collection of art completes the mood, the mix and the personality that makes this place unique. A chic boutique hotel in the heart of the English countryside.

🛏 13 🛎 🛷 🐕 🅿 🚶 🎣 📶

Rates Single room with breakfast from £79; double/twin from £99.

Meals A la carte menu & Tasting menus available; breakfast from 0730 – 1000 Monday – Friday, 0800 – 1000 weekends and bank holidays.

Special breaks See our website for current special offers.

Other facilities Alkham walks, Vineyard.

💷 All major credit cards accepted. Open all year.

Kent, Dover

Romney Bay House Hotel
Coast Road, Littlestone, New Romney, Kent TN28 8QY
T (01797) 364747 **F** (01797) 367156
E romneybayhouse@aol.co.uk **W** www.romneybayhousehotel.co.uk

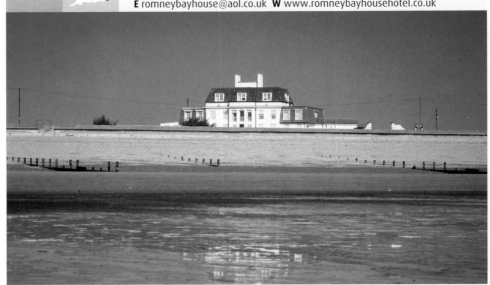

Built in the 1920s for the American actress Hedda Hopper and designed by Sir Clough Williams-Ellis of Portmeirion fame, Romney Bay House is owned by Clinton and Lisa Lovell, who are most welcoming hosts. The hotel is situated along a private road on a totally unspoiled stretch of coastline with spectacular sea views. The drawing room overlooks the terrace with the sea beyond and the first floor look-out room has a library and board games. The ten bedrooms, including two four-posters, are exceptionally well appointed with cheerful antique furniture. There is a croquet lawn and two golf courses immediately behind the hotel. Clinton cooks a four-course set dinner (different every night) which guests can meander through while watching the last golfers through the window of the conservatory restaurant. The freshest local produce is used and there is a select but fine wine list. Cream teas are also a speciality. The natural wildness of Romney Marsh and the proximity of the rolling Kent countryside and the historic Cinque Ports make this an ideal spot for a few days' relaxation.

🛏 10 (inc 2 🛏) 🚭 🔟 🐾 🚶 🔍 📶

Rates Single room including breakfast from £70; double from £95.
Meals 4 course set dinner £45 served at 2000 Tues, Wed, Fri & Sats; special diets available.

Winter Breaks Nov–Feb, Tues & Wed winter 2 night break, superior sea view double/twin, b&b + 3-cse set dinner = £320 per couple (exc Bank Hols, Xmas etc).
Winter Weekend Break Nov–Jan. Book 1 night dinner (4 courses) b&b and stay 2nd night for £25 per room b&b. Sorry, no children under 14 or pets.

💷 Major credit cards accepted. Open all year exc. one week over Xmas.

Kent, New Romney

Alfriston is a picture postcard village nestling in the South Downs, with the river Cuckmere running through it, just behind the hotel, antique and curio shops, a 14th century church, a 15th century pub and the Old Clergy House. The South Downs Way runs along beside the river and Drusilla's Zoo is just outside the village. Originally the centre of a large farming estate, Deans Place became a hotel at the beginning of the 20th century. This family run hotel has 36 indvidually styled bedrooms ranging from single through to four-poster, each with freeview TV and DVD player, luxury toiletries and complimentary WIFI. Cuisine has been awarded AA ◉◉ and Harcourts Restaurant has a monthly changing menu, reflecting the best of Sussex produce, according to season. The hotel offers a full events programme throughout the year with many themed evening and weekend break offers. It is also a favourite spot for exquisite weddings and conferences. Deans Place is handy for Glyndebourne Opera (picnic hampers can be made up), Brighton, Lewes, and the many attractions of the Sussex coast.

🛏36 ♿ 🏨 ▣ 🍴 🎵 ❄ ✓ 🏃 🐕 ⚓ 🐎 ⧉ 200 🅿 100 🚫 📶

Rates Single room including breakfast from £37.50; double from £90.

Meals 3 course alc dinner £35; lunch & special diets available; last orders 2130; breakfast from 0730.

Leisure Breaks Sunday night special, dinner, b&b from £120 per room. Winter Warmer from £119 dinner, b&b per room. Summer 4 Night Break, dinner, B&B £550 per room, per stay.

Other facilities Riding & tennis 400m; Golf 6 miles.

£ Major credit cards accepted. Open all year.

East Sussex, Alfriston

Drakes Hotel

44 Marine Parade, Brighton, East Sussex BN2 1PE
T (01273) 696934 **F** (01273) 684805
E info@drakesofbrighton.com **W** www.drakesofbrighton.com

When the stunning double-fronted Regency townhouse was sympathetically renovated to form Drakes, a luxurious boutique hotel, it immediately set standards for style and quality in Brighton and soon established an award winning fine dining restaurant. Drakes offers exceptional levels of service and comfort with just a hint of decadence. Most guest rooms boast impressive sea views and some have fabulous free standing baths. Hand made beds are draped in velvet throws with goose down duvets and pillows to ensure a perfect night's sleep. All rooms benefit from free WiFi, air-conditioning, plasma screen TV, i-pod docking, dvd/cd player and room service. With international experience and exceptional standards, *Restaurant at Drakes* has achieved several accolades, including the highest score of all Brighton restaurants in the 2014 Good Food Guide for the fifth year in succession. Modern European menus are created using only the finest seasonal ingredients complimented by a wine list of new and old world wines, as well as a selection of excellent Sussex wines. A private dining/meeting room is available. Reception will issue parking permits for off road parking spaces adjacent to the hotel.

🛏20 🍴 ♟ 🐕 ⛵ 🎰 15 **P** 14 - permit from rception 🚲 (WiFi)

Rates Single, room only, from £115; double from £135.

Meals 3 course tdh dinner £39.95; lunch & diets available; last orders 2145; breakfast from 0730.

Leisure Breaks Luxury Gourmet Break. 5 course dinner, b&b from £115 pppn.

Awards & accreditations Visit Britain ★★★★ Small Hotel – Silver Award.

💳 Major credit cards accepted. Open all year.

East Sussex, Brighton

Hotel Una
55–56 Regency Square, Brighton, East Sussex BN1 2FF
T (01273) 820464 **F** (01273) 724895
E reservation@hotel-una.co.uk **W** www.hotel-una.co.uk

51

Hotel Una stands out amongst the serried ranks of Regency guesthouses which line so many squares in Brighton today. Step inside and you are transported to a different, exotic world. The UNA sees itself as a river, with tributaries flowing off it into luxury bedrooms, bar and meeting facilities. Rooms are named after world rivers. *Aragon* and *Belice* each have a private sauna and whirlpool bath. Original artwork by local artists adorns the walls. Subtle lighting and *avant garde* furniture enhance the rooms, some of which have free standing baths. Each room has a combination of contrasting textures, organic wood and natural fabrics. Many overlook Regency Square. Physiotherapists are on hand for a variety of massages. Hotel Una is the result of passion, hard work and creativity on the part of the new family owners. Staff are young and helpful. Underground parking is available opposite the hotel. The hotel has a breakfast room, which also serves as a meeting room, and staff will be happy to recommend local eateries. Hotel Una is one of the leading lights of the accommodation scene in this buzzing seaside city.

🛏 19 🐕 ⛺ ⠿ 🅿 ⊡ 🏄 🔊 📶

Rates Single room with breakfast from £55; double from £115.

Meals Breakfast only from 0800.

Other facilities 24-hr reception, massage, satellite TV, DVD players.

💷 Major credit cards accepted except American Express. Open all year.

Stone House
Rushlake Green, Heathfield, East Sussex TN21 9RJ
T (01435) 830553 **F** (01435) 830726
E stonehousehotel@aol.com **W** www.stonehousesussex.com

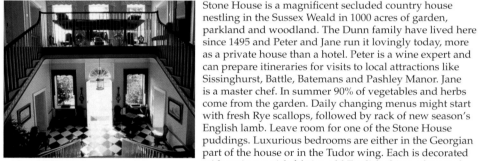

Stone House is a magnificent secluded country house nestling in the Sussex Weald in 1000 acres of garden, parkland and woodland. The Dunn family have lived here since 1495 and Peter and Jane run it lovingly today, more as a private house than a hotel. Peter is a wine expert and can prepare itineraries for visits to local attractions like Sissinghurst, Battle, Batemans and Pashley Manor. Jane is a master chef. In summer 90% of vegetables and herbs come from the garden. Daily changing menus might start with fresh Rye scallops, followed by rack of new season's English lamb. Leave room for one of the Stone House puddings. Luxurious bedrooms are either in the Georgian part of the house or in the Tudor wing. Each is decorated with antiques, rich fabrics, old English china, silver and embroidery. There are two four-posters and two suites with large baths and bidets. Stone House is convenient for Glyndebourne and the hotel can prepare picnic hampers with tables and chairs. Shooting and corporate entertaining can also be arranged. A splendid spot for a bit of old-fashioned self-indulgence!

🛏 7 (inc 2 🛏) 🍴 🎠 ❄ 🎣 🐴 🎱 🚶 ✒ 🐕 🅿 📶

Rates Single room including breakfast £107.50-£140; double from £148.
Meals 3 course tdh dinner for residents & their guests from £32; lunch (in summer) & special diets available; last orders 2030; breakfast from 0830.

Leisure Breaks Available Spring & Autumn. Contact hotel for details.

Other facilities Golf - 6 courses nearby; riding 9 miles.

💷 Mastercard & Visa accepted. Open all year exc. Xmas/New Year, & 17 February to 17 March.

East Sussex, Heathfield

Newick Park is a beautiful Georgian Grade II Listed country house set in 250 acres of landscaped gardens & parkland, with glorious views over the Longford river and lake towards the South Downs. Although near to main routes, the hotel is 'off the beaten track' and guests enjoy total peace and tranquillity. The oldest part of the house dates from the 16th century and was an ironmaster's home, the extensive Victorian Dell Gardens behind the house being the site of his excavations. The gardens contain many shrubs and rhododendrons, together with giant gunnera and a rare collection of Royal Ferns. Snowdrops, bluebells and daffodils provide sheets of colour in the Spring. Reception rooms are exceptionally comfortable with the aura of a private house and no formal reception desk! Indeed the house can be hired for exclusive use and is a popular wedding venue. AA ❀ ❀ cuisine is served in the elegant dining room and caps the experience of staying in one of the most comfortable small hotels in the south east.

🛏 16 (inc 4 suites) ✔ ⛫ ♨ ♪ ✎ 🐴 ❀ 🐕 (£15 + £5 p.n) **P**
👥 100 🚗 **WiFi**

Rates Double/twin room including breakfast from £165. Dinner, b&b from £105 pppn.

Meals 3 course tdh dinner £42.50; tdh, lunch & special diets available; last orders 2100; breakfast from 0730.

Other facilities Golf, riding 5 miles. Tank driving and quad biking on estate.

💷 Amex, Mastercard, Visa & Switch accepted. Open all year.

Flackley Ash Hotel, Restaurant & Leisure Club
Peasmarsh, Nr. Rye, East Sussex TN31 6YH
T (01797) 230651 **F** (01797) 230510
E enquiries@flackleyashhotel.co.uk **W** www.flackleyashhotel.co.uk

This is one of Sussex' most charming country house hotels. It has an indoor swimming pool and leisure complex, with hydro pool, gym, steam room, saunas, aromatherapy, beauticians, sun terrace and games lawn. The Georgian house radiates a warm and friendly atmosphere, with individually decorated bedrooms. Dining by candlelight in the conservatory or overlooking the hotel's gardens, the restaurant boasts menus using the finest local produce. Staff are friendly, helpful and professional. Owners, the Betteridge family, ensure a quality stay for business and leisure guest alike. Rye is only a few miles away with its many historic buildings including the 15th century church, the Ypres Tower, the famous Landgate and Henry James' Georgian residence, Lamb House. There is plenty to do in the area, with antique shops, potteries, local crafts and boutiques and a Thursday market. The fellow *Cinque Port*, Winchelsea, is nearby, as is Camber Sands, with its beautiful beach and safe bathing. In addition there are famous castles, abbeys and gardens to visit.

Rates B&b from £67.50 per person sharing; dinner, b&b from £89.50.
Meals A la carte menu & Residents menu.

Getaway Breaks 4 nights, dinner, b&b from £79.50 pppn + free upgrade if available; 5 nights from £75.50 pppn; 6 nights from £66.50 pppn; 7 nights from £58.50 pppn.

Other facilities Beauty treatments.

All major credit cards accepted except American Express & Diners Club. Open all year.

East Sussex, Peasmarsh

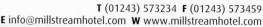

The Millstream Hotel & Restaurant

Bosham Lane, Bosham, Chichester, West Sussex PO18 8HL

T (01243) 573234 **F** (01243) 573459
E info@millstreamhotel.com **W** www.millstreamhotel.com

The Millstream is situated in the heart of old Bosham, an historic village with a fine Saxon church on the shores of Chichester Harbour. It combines the elegance of a small English country house with the character and charm of an 18th century malthouse cottage. Each bedroom is different and there are two suites across the bridge in the thatched Waterside Cottage. The AA ⑳ ⑳ Restaurant overlooks the gardens and is renowned for its excellent cuisine. It offers a selection of English and European dishes, prepared with the best available fresh produce and complemented by a list of fine wines from an established cellar. A more casual *Brasserie* was opened in Summer 2012. The charming sitting room, with its deep cushioned armchairs, grand piano, bowls of freshly cut flowers and tranquil atmosphere, is the ideal place to meet up with friends over afternoon tea or an aperitif, play cards or just relax with a good novel or magazine. At one point the garden is bisected by the eponymous Millstream which flows past the gazebo. Bosham is an ideal centre from which to explore this area of outstanding natural beauty and historical interest.

🛏 35 (inc 3 suites) 🕊 ♿ ❀ ⓠ 🚶 🎿 📶

Rates Single with breakfast from £99; double from £159.
Meals 3 course tdh dinner £34; special diets available; last orders 2115; breakfast from 0730.

Leisure Breaks Bosham Breaks – 2 nights dinner, b&b, from £92 per person per night; third night (Sun or Thurs) from £65.
Other facilities Golf, sailing, squash, riding and watersports nearby.

💷 All major credit cards accepted. Open all year.

West Sussex, Bosham

The Broads, Norfolk

East of England

Norfolk claims to have more sunshine than any other area of the country. Recently the North Norfolk Coast has become fashionable but the Norfolk Broads and Suffolk Coast have always been popular with yachtsmen. High-tech Cambridge is an expanding city with good communications while Hertfordshire and Essex have excellent transport links into the capital as well their own enclaves of beauty and seclusion.

NORFOLK

CAMBRIDGESHIRE

SUFFOLK

BEDFORDSHIRE

HERTFORDSHIRE

ESSEX

Hotels guide

Essex	page 63
Hertfordshire	page 65
Norfolk	page 66
Suffolk	page 69

Aldeburgh, Suffolk

Hadleigh, Essex

Further information:
East of England Tourism
Tel: 0333 3204202
www.visiteastofengland.com

BEDFORDSHIRE AND HERTFORDSHIRE

Principal attraction in **Bedfordshire** is Woburn Abbey, the still inhabited home of the Dukes of Bedford, which stands in a 3000-acre park and is now part of Europe's largest drive-through Game Reserve. The 18th century mansion's 14 state apartments are open to the public and the art collection includes works by Rembrandt, Holbein and Velasquez. Nearby is **Whipsnade Zoo**, where 2000 animals roam a 500-acre park.

Luton Hoo is a fine Robert Adam designed house in a 1200-acre Capability Brown designed park. South Bedfordshire's Chiltern landscape gives way to the fertile plains of East Anglia north of Bedford.

Woburn Safari Park

Hatfield House

Hertfordshire too has its fair share of stately homes, with **Hatfield House**, built from 1707 by Robert Cecil, first Earl of Salisbury, leading the way. Nearby **Knebworth House** is the venue for several summer concerts and events. Roman walls, mosaic floors and part of an amphitheatre are still visible at **Verulanium**, **St Albans**.

Much Hadham, where the Bishops of London used to have their country seat, is a showpiece village. Britain's first 20th century new towns were built in this northern commuter belt at **Welwyn Garden City**, **Letchworth** and later **Stevenage**. Welwyn in particular retains a certain art deco attraction.

Knebworth House

CAMBRIDGESHIRE AND ESSEX

Cambridge is a city of colleges, each founded for the personal glorification of the founder as an act of piety. The city's winding streets are lined with old houses, colleges and churches, while the gently flowing Cam provides a serene backdrop to the architectural wonders. **Kings College Chapel**, started by Henry VI in 1446 should not be missed. The **Fitzwilliam Museum** is one of Europe's treasure houses, with antiquities from Greece and Rome. Outside the city the Technology Park leads the world in computer science and research. **Peterborough** has a fine Norman cathedral with three soaring arches whilst **Ely** has had an abbey on its cathedral site since AD 670.

Western Essex borders London and has fast trains to Liverpool Street. Further east the **Blackwater** and **Crouch** estuaries provide havens for yachts and pleasure craft.

Peterborough Cathedral

St Botolph's Priory, Colchester

Cambridge

Some of the east's loveliest countryside is on the Suffolk Border around **Dedham Vale**, where Constable and Turner painted. County town **Colchester** was founded by the Romans and its massive castle keep, built in 1067 on the site of the Roman Temple of Claudius, houses a collection of Roman antiquities. At the western end of the county, Stansted Airport continues to expand and roads east are being upgraded accordingly.

Cley-next-the-Sea, Norfolk

NORFOLK

Norfolk is not as flat as Noel Coward would have it, as any cyclist will tell you. Nevertheless cycling or walking is a good way to see the county.

In the **west** the county is thickly afforested - **Thetford Forest** is said to be the oldest in England. In the east it is crisscrossed by waterways and lakes known as **The Broads** - apparently the remains of medieval man's peat diggings!

The county town of Norfolk and unofficial capital of East Anglia is **Norwich**, a finely planned city whose cathedral walls are decorated with biblical scenes dating from 1046. In addition there are 30 medieval churches in central Norwich alone and many interesting streets and shops to explore. Near **Kings Lynn** in the north west of the county is **Sandringham**, the royal palace bought by Queen Victoria for the then Prince of Wales.

The **North Norfolk** coast has become known as 'Chelsea-on-Sea' and good restaurants and hostelries abound from **Hunstanton** in the west to **Cromer** in the east. House prices in this area now rival those in the home counties.

SUFFOLK

Suffolk is famous for its winding lanes and pastel painted thatched cottages. This is a rich county, from the time when wool was the money crop of Middle England. See the great churches of **Lavenham**, **Sudbury** and **Long Melford**.

Aldburgh, Suffolk

Suffolk's coast, with its inlets and estuaries is popular with yachtsmen. **Framlingham Castle**, near **Aldeburgh**, stands intact since the 13th century. Aldeburgh itself is the home of the Benjamin Britten Music Festival at Snape, this year running from 13th - 29th June.

The hills and valleys on the Suffolk-Essex border open up to magnificent skies, captured in paintings by Constable, Turner and Gainsborough. The Heart of Constable Country is **Nayland** and **Dedham Vale**.

County Town **Ipswich** now has a buzzing waterfront and the ports of **Harwich** and **Felixstowe** are a great seafront day out.

Halesworth, Suffolk

60

Audley End

Audley End House & Gardens
(01799) 522842
www.english-heritage.org.uk/audleyend
One of England's finest country houses,
Audley End is also a mansion with a
difference. Enjoy a great day out.

Brentwood Cathedral
(01277) 232266
www.cathedral-brentwood.org
The new Roman Catholic classical Cathedral
Church of St Mary and St Helen incorporates
part of the original Victorian Church.

Woburn Abbey
(01525) 290333
www.woburnabbey.co.uk
Visit the home of Afternoon Tea to enjoy
priceless treasures, uncover fascinating
stories, and explore the beautiful gardens.

Hatfield House
(01707) 287010
www.hatfield-house.co.uk
Over 400 years of culture, history and
entertainment.

Holkham Hall
(01328) 710227
www.holkham.co.uk
A breathtaking Palladian house with an
outstanding art collection, panoramic
landscapes and the best beach in England.

Houghton Hall & Gardens
(01485) 528569
www.houghtonhall.com
Houghton Hall is one of the finest examples
of Palladian architecture in England. Built in
18th century by Sir Robert Walpole, Britain's
first Prime Minister.

Kentwell Hall & Gardens
(01787) 310207
www.kentwell.co.uk
A beautiful mellow redbrick Tudor Mansion,
surrounded by a broad moat, with rare
service building of c1500. Interior 'improved'
by Thomas Hopper in 1820's. Still a lived-in
family home.

Lavenham Guildhall of Corpus Christi
(01787) 247646
www.nationaltrust.org.uk
Once one of the wealthiest towns in Tudor
England, Lavenham oozes charm and
character. With timber-framed houses and
magnificent church, a visit to picturesque
Lavenham is a step back in time.

Oxburgh Hall
(01366) 328258
www.nationaltrust.org.uk
A romantic, moated manor house built by the
Bedingfeld family in the 15th century, they
have lived here ever since.

Peckover House & Gardens NT
(01945) 583463
www.nationaltrust.org.uk/peckover
Peckover House is an oasis hidden away in
an urban environment. A classic Georgian
merchant's townhouse, it was lived in by the
Peckover family for 150 years and reflects
the Quaker lifestyle.

Holkham Hall

HUDSON'S
HISTORIC HOUSES & GARDENS
MUSEUMS & HERITAGE SITES

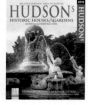

For more suggestions
of great historic days
out across Britain visit
www.hudsonsheritage.com

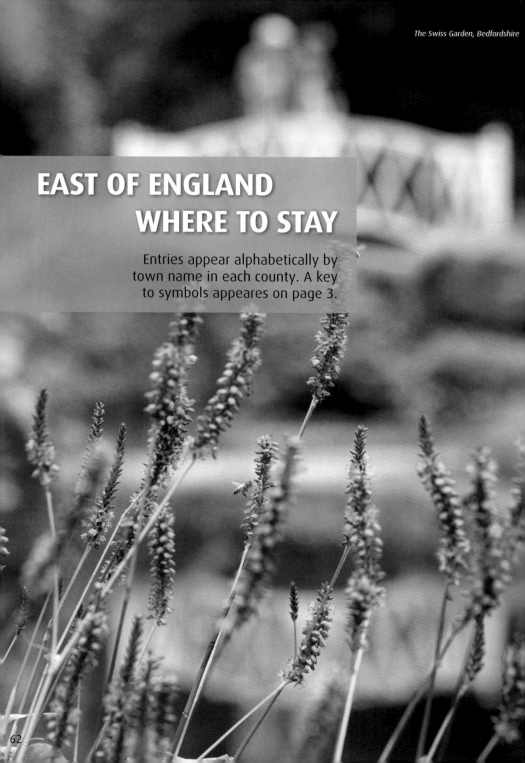

EAST OF ENGLAND
WHERE TO STAY

Entries appear alphabetically by
town name in each county. A key
to symbols appeares on page 3.

Maison Talbooth is a Victorian house which has been owned by the Milsom family for over 40 years and is one of the leading hotels in East Anglia. It lies on the Essex/Suffolk border, ½ mile from the picturesque village of Dedham and overlooking the beautiful Dedham Vale, famous Constable country. The 12 comfortable bedrooms are divided into four categories: principal suites with hot tubs, de luxe suites, superior suites and standard suites. All have marble bathrooms, bedrooms with flat screen TVs, minibars, goose feather duvets, Egyptian cotton sheets, upholstered headboards and large mirrors. The top floor has a spa with two double treatment rooms. As well as a tennis court, there is a swimming pool in the grounds, with changing rooms and showers, decking and a hot tub. Serious eating takes place at *Le Talbooth*, the AA ◉ ◉ restaurant nearby. This 16th century timber building was originally a toll booth. It overlooks the river Stour and private rooms can be hired. Outside one can sit under an architectural sail or wander in the large garden. Beyond, a marquee makes an idyllic setting for a wedding or function.

🛏12 (1 ≈) ✂ ➡ 🗄 🖥 🅿 ⊙ 🐎 ✄ ⁄ 🔟 ♨ ▦ 24 ❄ ⚕ ⅄ 🖨 ⚲ ⤳ 🜸 🐾 (Wi-Fi)

Rates Double including breakfast from £225.
Meals Le Talbooth fine dining restaurant 3 course £45; courtesy Range Rover from hotel; lunch & special diets available. Last orders 2100; breakfast from 0700.

Leisure Breaks Spa breaks and family breaks available. See website.
Other facilities Massage, DVD/Satellite TV. Golf, riding nearby.
£ All major credit cards accepted. Open all year.

Essex, Dedham

The Pier at Harwich

The Quay, Harwich, Essex CO12 3HH

T (01255) 241212 **F** (01255) 551922
E pier@milsomhotels.com **W** www.milsomhotels.com

The Pier was built in 1862 in the style of a Venetian palazzo to provide overnight accommodation for passengers travelling by train and ship to the Continent. Gerald Milsom bought The Pier in 1978 and opened a seafood restaurant. It is wonderfully situated overlooking the harbour at the confluence of the Stour and Orwell rivers. Across the water is Shotley Yacht Marina with Felixstowe in the distance. Yachts and boats can be chartered from the hotel by arrangement. The visitor enters a most attractive Brasserie. The ambience is rustic but comfortable with scrubbed floors, Farrow & Ball cream and taupe paintwork, framed posters and wooden mirrors. Diners jot down their orders on a notepad and hand them to one of the helpful staff. An elegant wooden staircase leads to the Harbourside AA ◉ ◉ on the first floor. The restaurant with fine views over the twin estuaries of the Stour and Orwell takes its influence from the sea. The Harbourside specialises in seafood, much of which is landed in the harbour opposite. Seven of the ensuite bedrooms are in this main building, seven in the adjacent Angel, all very attractive, with a nautical flavour and panoramic sea views. There is a comfortable sitting room, with bar and eating area and large screen TV, which can be hired for private functions.

🛏14 ✂ ☺ 🛏 🧖 🚶 🖥 🍴 🔍 ⬇ 🅿 🐕 🎿 📶

Rates Double room including breakfast from £120.
Meals Harbourside (closed Monday & Tuesday) & Ha'penny restaurants. Alc, lunch & diets available. Last orders 2130; breakfast from 0700. All day dining in Ha'penny from 12 noon.

Leisure Breaks Fishing Breaks, Sailing Breaks – 2 night packages available.
Other Facilities DVD/Satellite TV. Golf nearby.

£ All major credit cards accepted. Open all year.

Essex, Harwich

Redcoats Farmhouse Hotel
Redcoats Green, Nr. Hitchin, Hertfordshire SG4 7JR
T (01438) 729500 **F** (01438) 723322
E sales@redcoats.co.uk **W** www.redcoats.co.uk

Near the village of Little Wymondley, set amidst rolling Hertfordshire countryside, yet only a few minutes from the A1, lies the 15th century Redcoats Farmhouse. It has been in the Butterfield family for generations and in 1971 Peter and his sister Jackie Gainsford converted the building into an hotel. Today it retains its relaxed and easy going country atmosphere. Bedrooms are either in the main house, some with crooked floors and all with exposed beams, or in the converted stables. Recently Jackie's son Ben has joined the management team and two rooms in the old house were converted into a luxury suite, called *Bobbie's Room*, named after a favourite aunt whose room it used to be. The dining room and the conservatory serve outstanding cuisine that have won an AA ® for the past eight years. The à la carte menu changes every month or two, making best seasonal use of local products. The daily menu may include such dishes as fresh sardines and char grilled lamb rump on rosemary mash. Breakfast, winner of a special AA award, is equally memorable with devilled kidneys and kedgeree often on the menu. Two self-catering cottages are available to rent.

🛏 14 (+ 2 s/c cottages) ☺ 🐎 🐕 ♨ 20 🐾

Rates Single room with breakfast from £72; double from £105.
Meals Last dinner orders 2130. Restaurant closed Sunday night. Two intimate private dining rooms.

Leisure Breaks One night from £165 per couple, dinner, b&b.
Other Facilities Tennis 1 mile, golf 1☐ miles. Closed Dec 26–Jan 3.

£ Amex, Visa, Mastercard, Switch accepted.

Hertfordshire, Redcoats Green

The Norfolk Mead Hotel

Church Loke, Coltishall, Norfolk NR12 7DN
T (01603) 737531 **F** (01603) 737521
E info@norfolkmead.co.uk **W** www.norfolkmead.co.uk

Anna & James Holliday took over The Norfolk Mead in early 2013 and have transformed the hotel. The 13 bedrooms have been refurbished in contemporary style and are named after hedgerow plants and herbs which can be foraged for in Norfolk; *Samphire, Mulberry, Hawthorn, Sorrel* and so on. Three suites have free standing baths in the rooms and the other nine have large 'rain' showers. There is also *Crab Apple*, a converted garden pavilion, and *Sweet Chestnut Cottage* in the grounds, each sleeping up to four. James and Anna both come from catering backgrounds and Anna, who is the hard working chef, also runs Anna Duttson Events, catering for outside events and receptions. They plan to open the 'garden room' in the grounds to cater for up to 150 wedding or meeting guests. The menu, which changes monthly, uses local produce wherever possible. We had pan seared scallops with puy lentils, a duo of spring lamb, slow cooked shoulder and lamb cutlets, with a delicious baked lemon cheesecake to finish. Breakfast was equally delicious with home baked bread, jams and cereals. The hotel's front lawn leads to The Mead with wild flowers and birdlife. There are splendid walks nearby and the hotel has a rowing boat for rent.

🐾12 🅿 🐴 🐕 (£8 p.n) 🏨 ❄ 🧍 🎣 🦆 🛗 ♿ 🎿 🎾 📶

Rates Single room with breakfast £115–£165; double £125–£175; Dinner, b&b £160–£210 per double room; Sweet Chestnut Cottage from £230
Meals Alc & special diets available; last orders 2100; breakfast from 0730.

Other Facilities Riding and golf nearby.

💷 Major credit cards accepted. Open all year.

Norfolk, Coltishall

Beechwood Hotel

Cromer Road, North Walsham, Norfolk NR28 0HD
T (01692) 403231 **F** (01692) 407284
E info@beechwood-hotel.co.uk **W** www.beechwood-hotel.co.uk

67

A special welcome from hosts Don and Lindsay, a friendly and informal atmosphere, 17 comfortable bedrooms, fabulous food from a creative Head Chef, a Heritage coastline, a Royal country retreat and the Norfolk Broads close by, is the Beechwood recipe for a great Short Break! The AA ◉◉ restaurant is the hub of the hotel. Cuisine is modern British with a Mediterranean influence. Head chef Steven Norgate prepares a *ten mile dinner*, celebrating local ingredients, sourced, where possible, within ten miles of the hotel. Starter might be slow roasted pork belly with pineapple ice cream, followed by Sheringham lobster. Cromer crab, Morston mussels and Thornham oysters also feature in season. Do leave room for dessert – the sticky toffee pudding is to die for. After dinner you can sink into a leather sofa by the bar for coffee or a liqueur. Bedrooms are delightful with giant beds, Vi-spring mattresses, squashy pillows and fluffy bathrobes. Some have free standing baths and French windows opening onto the peaceful garden.

🛏 17 (inc 8🚭) ⚞ ⚒ ☺ ✿ 🔊 🐕 (£10 p.n)

Rates Single room wth breakfast from £88; double from £100.
Meals Tdh 3 course dinner £38; Sunday lunch & special diets available last orders 2100; breakfast from 0730.

Leisure Breaks Available all year: dinner, b&b from £65 pppn. Min 2 night stay. Complimentary Sundays – please enquire.
Other Facilities Golf, riding, fishing nearby.

💷 Major credit cards accepted. Open all year.

Norfolk, North Walsham

Broom Hall Country Hotel
Richmond Road, Saham Toney, Thetford, Norfolk IP25 7EX
T (01953) 882125 **F** (01953) 885325
E enquiries@broomhallhotel.co.uk **W** www.broomhallhotel.co.uk

Broom Hall is a family-run Victorian country house set in 15 acres of garden and parkland in the peaceful West Norfolk countryside. The traditional English gardens are laid out with mixed and herbaceous borders and mature trees. Bedrooms are spacious and airy with pretty bedspreads and most have views over the grounds. Newly refurbished reception rooms retain ornate moulded ceilings. Dining is either in the informal Ivy Room (also open for lunches) or in the Swallowtails fine dining restaurant. Both use fresh local produce where possible and both pride themselves also on their mouth-watering homemade desserts. Homemade cream teas are another treat. There is an indoor heated swimming pool. The whole house can be hired for a special occasion. Two of the five cheerful ground floor rooms in the converted stable block are suitable for disabled access. The air-conditioned conference room can double as a ballroom. Within easy driving distance are Sandringham, Blickling Hall, Thetford Forest Park and the trans-Norfolk Peddars Way.

🛏15 ♿ ☺ ⚲ ⚐ 🐕 (£5 p.n) 🅿 50 ♦♦♦ 40 📷 📶

Rates Single room with breakfast from £75; double from £95.
Meals 3-cse alc dinner £21–£32; lunch & bar snacks avail; last orders 2030.

Leisure Breaks Winter Breaks available Oct–mid-March, 2 days dinner, b&b £240 per room/3 days £360. Weekly rates available on request.
Other Facilities Massage & beauty treatments by arrangement. Fishing, golf, riding, cycling, walking, shooting nearby.

💷 Major credit cards accepted. Open all year exc. Dec 26–Jan 2.

Norfolk, Thetford

Wentworth Hotel
Wentworth Road, Aldeburgh, Suffolk IP15 5BD
T (01728) 452312 **F** (01728) 454343
E stay@wentworth-aldeburgh.co.uk **W** www.wentworth-aldeburgh.com

69

The Pritt family have been the owners of this charming Victorian hotel for over 90 years and they are continually upgrading and refurbishing it. The hotel is ideally situated on the seafront of this historic sailing town of Aldeburgh, also a centre for music lovers worldwide. The atmosphere is very much that of a country house. The lounge is attractively furnished with antiques and decorated in restful yellows and russets, picking out the colours of the elegant Crown Derby china. The walls are hung with a large collection of Russell Flint prints. The cuisine is excellent, offering local produce such as shellfish (the famous Aldeburgh sprats), fresh fish and asparagus. Bedrooms are individually decorated, many with sea views and all with a copy of *Orlando the Marmalade Cat*, the children's story set in *Owlbarrow* (Aldeburgh). Superior rooms have king size beds and there is a lovely pine panelled suite on the ground floor. A new wing has just opened across the road 'Darfield House' containing another ten contemporarily furnished bedrooms and the Gallery Room, a meeting room for up to ten delegates.

🛏 35 ♿ ▥ ☎ ⚓ ⛵ **P**

Rates Single room with breakfast from £73; double from £146.
Meals 3 course tdh dinner ca. from £24; lunch & special diets available; last orders 2100.

Leisure breaks See our website for current offers.
Other Facilities Golf, watersports nearby.

💷 Major credit cards accepted. Open all year.

Suffolk, Aldeburgh

70

milsoms Kesgrave Hall
Hall Road, Kesgrave, Ipswich, Suffolk IP5 2PU
T (01473) 333741 **F** (01473) 617614
E reception@kesgravehall.com **W** www.milsomhotels.com

Kesgrave Hall is the latest jewel in the Milsoms crown (– *see Maison Talbooth, and the Pier at Harwich in the Essex section of this guide*). It is a former Grade II Listed Georgian mansion which has been transformed into a contemporary dining experience backed up by 23 stylish bedrooms. When our inspector had lunch, the terrace and dining room were heaving with contented diners. The menu is imaginative and eclectic, ranging from a tasty sandwich to fresh fish from Harwich and beef from neighbouring Suffolk farms – all served with cheerful efficiency. Bedrooms are divided into five categories: standard, superior, deluxe and 'principal' or 'best rooms'. All are quiet and luxurious, with crisp linen and fluffy towels. They are competitively priced and beautifully designed, with the very latest TVs and MP3 players. Nestling in 38 acres of parkland, Kesgrave Hall is the perfect base for exploring the Suffolk Heritage Coast and the surrounding towns and villages as well as being a good business base – easily accessible from the A12. There are 3 private meeting/dining rooms – *The Mess & The Bunker*.

Rates Double from £130 including full breakfast.
Meals Restaurant, 3 course ca. £25; alc, lunch & special diets available; last orders 2130 (2200 Fri & Sat); breakfast from 0700. All day dining from 12 noon.

Special Breaks Golf, fishing & sailing breaks available.
Other Facilities Golf, sailing nearby.

£ Major credit cards accepted. Open all year.

Suffolk, Ipswich

HUDSON's HERITAGE Explorer

Hatfield House, Hertfordshire

An exciting touring pass

Opening the door to the country's heritage attractions

www.hudsons-explorer.com

3, 7, 14 or 28-day passes

Visit as many participating attractions as you wish during the fixed-day period

Prices start from just £49.00 per Adult

Complimentary full-colour guidebook

Available to buy online and in person at selected outlets

Amazing value! Visit heritage attractions for less than £6.40 per day* SAVE MORE WITH EVERY VISIT!

RHS Garden Wisley, Surrey   Bamburgh Castle, Northumberland   Roman Baths, Somerset   Portsmouth Historic Dockyard

STATELY HOMES • HISTORIC HOUSES • CASTLES • GARDENS • ABBEYS & CATHEDRALS • WORLD HERITAGE SITES

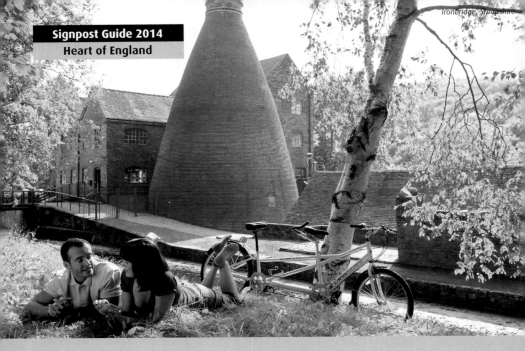
Ironbridge, Shropshire

Heart of England

The Heart of England: a name that defines this lovely part of the country so much better than its geographical name: The Midlands. Like a heart it has many arteries and compartments, from the March counties of Shropshire and Herefordshire through the West Midlands, birthplace of the Industrial revolution, via the light industrial East Midlands out to the Lincolnshire Wolds.

DERBYSHIRE LINCOLNSHIRE
NOTTINGHAM-SHIRE
STAFFORDSHIRE
SHROPSHIRE RUTLAND
LEICESTERSHIRE
WEST MIDLANDS NORTHAMPTONSHIRE
WORCESTERSHIRE WARWICKSHIRE
HEREFORDSHIRE

Hotels guide

Further information:
Peak District & Derbyshire
www.visitpeakdistrict.com

Visit Herefordshire
www.visitherefordshire.co.uk

Nottingham Park

Belton, Rutland

DERBYSHIRE

'There is no finer county in England than Derbyshire. To sit in the shade on a fine day and look upon verdure is the most perfect refreshment' - JANE AUSTEN.

'I assure you there are things in Derbyshire as noble as in Greece or Switzerland.' – LORD BYRON.

Derbyshire, home of the UK's first National Park, the **Peak District**, has been popular with home grown holidaymakers for more than 200 years. It is convenient for **Sheffield** and **Manchester** and right in the middle of the country, well served by road and rail connections

Matlock Bath, Derbyshire

It forms the beginning of the **Pennine Chain** and its reservoirs and hills are second to none in beauty. It is excellent walking, riding and cycling country and the **Buxton** Festival, increasingly a pan-arts occasion, has achieved international recognition. The 17th century Palladian **Chatsworth**, seat of the Duke of Devonshire, is one of the most visited houses and gardens in the country.

Buxton, Derbyshire

Chatsworth House, Derbyshire

Malvern Hills

Herefordshire's ruined castles in the border country and Iron Age and Roman hill-forts recall a turbulent battle-scarred past. **Offa's Dyke**, constructed by King Offa of Mercia in the 8th century marks to this day the border with Wales. Today the landscape is peaceful, with comfortable small towns and villages and Hereford cattle grazing in pastures beside apple orchards and hop gardens.

Hereford, co-venue of the Three Choirs Festival, has an 11th century cathedral and the Mappa Mundi. In the west, the **Wye** meanders through meadows and valleys, past **Hay-on-Wye**, now best known for its annual Book Festival and plethora of second hand bookshops, with over one million titles on sale.

The Broadway Tower

Wye Valley

Worcestershire borders the West Midlands complex and serves as a dormitory area for many Birmingham workers. **Worcester** too has a famous cathedral, cricket ground, and 15th century Commandery, now a Civil war museum. **Great Malvern**, still a Spa town, is famous as the birthplace of Sir Edward Elgar, who drew much of his inspiration from the countryside around. The annual Malvern Festival celebrates him and George Bernard Shaw, whose plays were first premiered there.

Evesham is the centre of the fruit growing area and **Droitwich** still has briny water in its spa baths, where visitors can float.

Birmingham

BIRMINGHAM, WARWICKSHIRE & WEST MIDLANDS

The Industrial revolution of the 19th century led to the growth of **Birmingham** into Britain's second city - *the city of a thousand trades*. Its prosperity was based on factories, hundreds of small workshops and a network of canals, all of which helped in the production of everything from needles and chocolate to steam engines and bridges. Grand public buildings expressed a sense of civic pride. Nowadays the city has one of the best concert halls in Europe, an International Airport & Exhibition Centre and is learning through its entrepreneurial spirit, to adjust after the gradual erosion of its car and components industries.

Warwickshire's most visited town is **Stratford-upon-Avon**, the bard's birthplace, with three theatres playing Shakespeare and other dramatists' work. It is also a well preserved Tudor town on the banks of the

Avon. The city of **Warwick** is dominated by its 14th century castle (alas the furniture has gone) and its museums. Many family activities are staged at the castle throughout the year. **Meriden**, near the city of Coventry, claims to be the centre of England.

The **West Midlands** is an urban area, criss-crossed by motorways, and still representing the powerhouse of Central Britain. **Coventry**, its main city, rose like a Phoenix from the Ashes after the last war and its 1962 cathedral stands next to the ruins of the former 14th century edifice. **Wolverhampton** has been called Capital of the Black Country, made famous through its ironwork. **Walsall**, birthplace of Jerome K Jerome, has three museums. **Sutton Coldfield** and **Solihull**, sometimes known as Birmingham's Hampstead and Wimbledon, have proud civic traditions.

Lincoln

LEICESTERSHIRE, NORTHAMPTONSHIRE, LINCOLNSHIRE & NOTTINGHAMSHIRE

Leicestershire's uplands are home to some of the country's best known hunts and her pastures also fuel one of the county's main exports: Stilton Cheese. **Leicester** itself is a cathedral city with a 2000-year history, now host to a modern university and light industry. **Belvoir Castle** in the east dominates its vale and **Rockingham** was built by William the Conqueror.

Northamptonshire too has its share of stately homes. County town **Northampton** is famous for its shoe making, celebrated in the Central Museum and Art Gallery. **Silverstone** in the south of the county is home to the British Grand Prix. **Althorp** was the birthplace and is now the resting place of the late Princess of Wales.

Nottingham's castle dates from 1674 and its university is reputedly the most sought after in England. Its Lace Centre illustrates the source of much of its wealth. Today diggers and builders are testament to the city's continued expansion. To the north the remains of **Sherwood Forest** provide a welcome breathing space.

Lincolnshire is said to produce one eighth of food placed on British tables and its wide open meadows are testament to this. Gothic triple-towered **Lincoln Cathedral** is visible from the Fens from miles around, whilst **Burghley** in the south hosts annual Horse Trials and is a top tourist attraction.

Salcey Forest

Sherwood Forest

SHROPSHIRE AND STAFFORDSHIRE

Shropshire is another March county that saw much conflict between English and Welsh, hostilities between warring tribes and invading Romans. The **Wrekin** and **Stretton Hills** were created by volcanoes and in the south the **Long Mynd** rises to 1700 ft and has panoramic views of much of the Severn plain. **Ironbridge**, near the present day Telford, is said to be where the Industrial Revolution started in Britain.

County town **Shrewsbury** was an historic fortress town built in a loop of the river **Severn**, whereas **Ludlow**, with its 11th century castle, is now one of the gastronomic high spots of Britain. A. E. Housman, an English classical scholar and poet, best known for his cycle of poems A Shropshire Lad, is buried in its churchyard.

Ironbridge

Bridgnorth

Staffordshire, squeezed between the **Black Country** to the south and **Manchester** to the north is home to the **Potteries**, a union of six towns made famous by Wedgwood, Spode and other ceramic designers.
Lichfield has a magnificent three-spired 13th century cathedral and was birthplace of Samuel Johnson.

Wedgwood Visitor Centre

Chatsworth House, Derbyshire

Burghley House
(01780) 752451
www.burghley.co.uk
Burghley House, home of Cecil family for over 400 years is one of England's greatest Elizabethan houses.

Chatsworth
(01246) 565300
www.chatsworth.org
The home of the Duke and Duchess of Devonshire, Chatsworth is one of the country's greatest Treasure Houses.

Burghley House, Lincolnshire

Cottesbrooke Hall & Gardens
(01604) 505808
www.cottesbrooke.co.uk
Dating from 1702 the Hall's beauty is matched by the magnificence of the gardens and the excellence of the picture, furniture and porcelain collections.

Deene Park
(01780) 450278
www.deenepark.com
Home of the Brudenell family since 1514, this 16th century house incorporates a medieval manor with important Georgian additions.

Grimsthorpe Castle, Park and Gardens
(01778) 591205
www.grimsthorpe.co.uk
Building styles from 13th century. North front is Vanburgh's last major work. State rooms and picture galleries including tapestries, furniture and paintings.

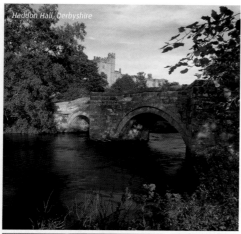
Haddon Hall, Derbyshire

Rockingham Castle, Northamptonshire

Deene Park, Northamptonshire

Haddon Hall
(01629) 812855
www.haddonhall.co.uk
Haddon Hall sits on a rocky outcrop above the river Wye near the market town of Bakewell, looking much as it would have done in Tudor Times.

Holdenby
(01604) 770074
www.holdenby.com
Once the largest private house in England and subsequently the palace of James I and prison of Charles I, Holdenby has recently been seen in the BBC's acclaimed adaptaion of 'Great Expectations'.

Lamport Hall & Gardens
(01604) 686272
www.lamporthall.co.uk
The home of the Isham family for 400 years, Lamport Hall contains an outstanding collection of furniture and paintings.

Rockingham Castle
(01536) 770240
www.rockinghamcastle.com
Rockingham Castle stands on the edge of an escarpment giving dramatic views over five counties and the Welland Valley below. Built by William the Conqueror, the Castle was a royal residence for 450 years.

Woolsthorpe Manor
(01476) 862823
www.nationaltrust.org.uk/woolsthorpe-manor
Issac Newton, scientist, Master of the Royal Mint and President of the Royal Society, was born in this modest 17th century manor house in 1642 and developed his ideas about light and gravity here.

HUDSON's
HISTORIC HOUSES & GARDENS
MUSEUMS & HERITAGE SITES

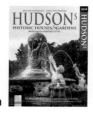

For more suggestions
of great historic days
out across Britain visit
www.hudsonsheritage.com

HEART OF ENGLAND
WHERE TO STAY

Entries appear alphabetically by
town name in each county. A key
to symbols appeares on page 3.

There has been an Inn here for so long that it is uncertain when it was built. Originally the Peacock Inn owned by the Duke of Rutland, it became the property of the Duke of Devonshire (and still is) in 1830. Becoming The Cavendish in the early 1970's it has been operated since 1975 by Eric March, latterly with Philip Joseph under contract on behalf of Chatsworth Estates. A closely knit team is dedicated to looking after guests as individuals, not merely room numbers. The hotel exudes a quiet elegance, with extensive artworks and antiques and regular refurbishment work. Stay in one of the generous 'Inn' rooms in the original Peacock Inn section of the hotel or the beautifully appointed 'standard' rooms, which are anything but standard. For the ultimate indulgence you can also stay in the Redesdale Suite. This self contained two storey suite can be accessed by its own private entrance. The AA ◉ ◉ awarded dining room is overseen by Chef Mike Thompson, using the freshest, locally sourced ingredients wherever possible. And perfect for that relaxing afternoon English afternoon tea with fresh baked scones and homemade fruitcake can be sampled daily. Add to this the glorious views over Chatsworth Estate from every bedroom window, snuggle down in soft, fluffy robes and the result is that elusive element – tranquillity.

🛏24 ⁙ ♪ ⌕ 🍴 ⌑ 🔲 ❖ 🅿 🚐 🚶 📶

Rates Single room from £139 +5% service Room only; Double room from £177+5% service Room only.

Meals Breakfast from 1000; dinner from £20.

Other Facilities Gallery restaurant and Garden room.

Awards & accreditations AA ◉◉ restaurant.

💷 Major credit cards accepted.

Derbyshire, Baslow

Biggin Hall Hotel
Biggin-by-Hartington, Buxton, Derbyshire w
T (01298) 84451
E enquiries@bigginhall.co.uk **W** www.bigginhall.co.uk

Biggin Hall is an historic old hall of 17th century origin, situated 1000 ft above sea level in the Peak District National Park. The Hall is Grade II* Listed and stands in its own grounds of some eight acres. There are eight bedrooms in the main house and a further 13 in converted buildings in the grounds: the lodge, the bothy and the courtyard. Dinner is a daily changing menu of traditional home cooking with the emphasis on local ingredients and free range wholefoods. Guests have a choice of two sitting rooms and will feel very much at home in this exceptionally welcoming, comfortable house. Hosts James Moffett and Steven Williams will be able to recommend walking itineraries and traffic-free cycle trails. There are several historic houses nearby: Haddon Hall, Chatsworth and Kedleston Hall. Also close by are important archeological sites including Arkwrights Mill, Cromford Canal, Ecton Hill lead and copper mines and Magpie lead mine – Britain's deepest. Packed lunches can be arranged and there is even stabling if you wish to bring your horse or pony.

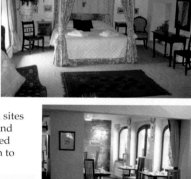

🛏21 🔌 🕱 ♻ 🐕 (in bothy/annex) ⫶⫶⫶ 20 🅿

Rates Double/twin room from £90 (apartments)/£106 main house & bothy. Double as single from £80.
Meals Dinner b&b from £122 per night for two (midweek low season) to £174 (weekend high season). Packed lunches available.

Leisure Breaks Seasonal specials – midweek from £122 per night, dinner, b&b including packed lunch and glühwein. Sorry – no children under 12.
Other activities Cycling, fishing nearby.

💷 Major credit cards accepted. Open all year.

Derbyshire, Biggin-by-Hartington

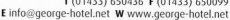

The George Hotel

Main Road, Hathersage, Derbyshire S32 1BB

T (01433) 650436 **F** (01433) 650099
E info@george-hotel.net **W** www.george-hotel.net

The George has been welcoming travellers for over 500 years, first as an alehouse, and, since 1770, as an inn. It is ideally placed in the centre of the Peak District, near to Chatsworth and the Ladybower Reservoir, yet only 12 miles from Sheffield. The George offers a superb choice of great value standard and luxury accommodation that will ensure that you're well rested and looked after for the duration of your stay – but of course, there's nothing standard about George's standard, it has beautifully appointed rooms which cater to all creature comforts. If you're planning a climbing or walking holiday in the Peak District, you can wash away the day's efforts in gorgeous en suite bathrooms, wrap yourself up in soft, fluffy towels and enjoy a warming brew. The Public rooms are comfortable and always have fresh flowers and the award-winning restaurant, under the supervision of Chef Helen Heywood, has an ever changing menu. A dedication to homemade excellence means that guests can enjoy a wide selection of freshly produced tasty treats; from bread to preserves, petit fours to pasta – if it can be made in the kitchen, it will be. There is also boardroom for meetings or private dining and a Banquet Suite for functions and wedding receptions.

Rates Single room with breakfast from £68 + 5% service, Room only; Double from £146 + 5% service, Room only.

Meals 2 course dinner from £29.25, 3 coures from £36.95.

Awards & accreditations AA ◎ ◎ restaurant.

£ Major credit cards accepted.

Derbyshire, Hathersage

84

Losehill House Hotel & Spa
Edale Road, Hope, Derbyshire S33 6RF
T (01433) 621219 **F** (01433) 622501
E info@losehillhouse.co.uk **W** www.losehillhouse.co.uk

Losehill House is a unique country retreat in the Hope Valley in Derbyshire, where service and style are of the utmost importance. The hotel is furnished in modern style with common areas and passageways finished in solid oak. The beautifully furnished bedrooms, including family suites and deluxe Kings, all have modern facilities, including flat screen TVs and DVD players. Most overlook the stunning surrounding countryside. When we stayed, we were recommended a walk up Lose Hill which affords excellent views and is well signed. This worked up a good appetite for our delicious table d'hôte dinner, taken in the Orangery overlooking the valley. Hope Station, with its single track line, provides rail links to Sheffield and the north west. The hotel is available for exclusive wedding or function use. This is the very heart of the Peak District and the Pennine Way starts near the hotel. After a day's walking or sightseeing, why not curl up with a good book or take a dip in the indoor heated pool or the outdoor tub? The Spa treatment rooms offer a totally relaxing experience. Children are welcomed. AA ★★★★ ◎ ◎

21 (inc 4 ⚌) 🐾 🗺 🐕 🏊 📺 💆 🍷 🍴 ☺ 📻 🛋 👤 ⚏ 🅿 🛏 🐾 📶

Rates Single room with breakfast from £135; double from £165.
Meals Alc dinner ca £35; lunch & special diets available; last orders 2130; breakfast from 0730.

Leisure Breaks Spa Breaks from £300 lunch, dinner, b&b, two x 1 hour spa treatments. Easter & Xmas Breaks also available.

Other activities Riding, fishing, golf, sailing, caving/abseiling nearby.

£ Major credit cards accepted. Open all year.

Derbyshire, Hope

The Peacock, owned by the Haddon Estate of nearby Haddon Hall, has recently been refurbished to a very high standard. Its 15 bedrooms are decorated in contemporary style, with thick curtains, pinpoint reading lights and lots of little extras. Power showers are at just the right temperature. There are three dining rooms and a comfortable lounge, strewn with magazines and scrapbooks about the hotel. Dan Smith supervises cuisine in the AA ❀❀❀ restaurant, serving international dishes, making best use of local fish and game. There is an intimate bar for that after dinner liqueur. Chatsworth and the many beauties of Derbyshire are nearby and for walkers, the Pennine Way starts close at hand. The hotel provides an excellent selection of maps for shorter walks starting from the hotel. The Peacock has long been known as a fishing hotel and guests can experience some ten miles of the best trout fishing in the UK on the Wye and Derwent rivers. The Haddon estate's river keeper is always on hand to give advice. There is golf, shooting, riding and a fitness centre nearby.

🛏 14 (inc 2 🛏 & 1 suite) ❀ 🐕 (£10 p.n) 🎣 🚶 🅿 📶

Rates Single room with cont'l breakfast from £90; double from £155; Suite from £275
Meals Alc 3 course dinner ca. £57; 3 course lunch £16.50; special diets available; last orders 2100; breakfast from 0730. No fine dining lunch times & Sunday evening.

Leisure Breaks Sunday Special, dinner, b&b – see our website for details.

Other activities Riding, shooting, golf, fitness centre nearby.

💷 Major credit cards accepted. Open all year exc. 2 weeks early January.

Derbyshire, Rowsley

86

Aylestone Court
2 Aylestone Hill, Hereford, Herefordshire HR1 1HS
T (01432) 359342
E enquiries@aylestonecourt.com **W** www.aylestonecourt.com

Aylestone Court, near to Hereford town centre and the railway station is a quiet nine bedroom townhouse, personally run by the Kay mother and son team. Décor is smart and contemporary throughout. Each bedroom is individually styled with rich materials, fluffy towels, restful colour schemes and up-to-date TV/DVD players and Wifi throughout. Two rooms are licensed for civil weddings. The dining room overlooks the pretty walled garden. A menu might start with baked stilton and walnut avocado, followed by Paradise green pork (free range) and herb sausage , with a dark chocolate and amaretto *torte* to finish. A lighter bar menu is available in the Club Room. A meeting room with all modern amenities is available for up to 30 people. In summer months the hotel hosts exhibitions and serves afternoon tea in the Orangery Café. Garden holidays and Heritage Breaks have been introduced this year. Treasures in the superb 11th century Hereford cathedral include brasses, the chained library, a copy of the Magna Carta and the famous 14th century Mappa Mundi.

Rates Single with breakfast from £79; double from £98. Dinner, b&b from £98 single/£138 double.
Meals 3 course tdh dinner from £29; bar lunches; last orders 2200; breakfast from 0700, Afternoon teas.

Leisure Breaks Hill House 2 night package £180 (not available Xmas).

£ All major credit cards (exc. Diners) accepted. Open all year.

Herefordshire, Hereford

Castle Street, Hereford, Herefordshire HR1 2NW
T (01432) 356321 **F** (01432) 365909
E info@castlehse.co.uk **W** www.castlehse.co.uk

Castle House is an elegant Grade II Listed Georgian town-house situated near the cathedral in this historic city. All 24 rooms and suites are exceptionally comfortable, fresh and original without being minimalist or English Country House. Decor is bold, with tapestries, paintings and plenty of fresh flowers. Each bedroom has flat screen TV, CD player, WIFI, fridge and welcoming sherry decanter. Bathrooms are of marble and wood. There are two ground floor suites (one adapted for disabled guests) leading out into the gardens, which overlook the tranquil castle moat. This year eight further bedrooms have been opened in the nearby 'No 25'. Award winning chef Claire Nicholls creates memorable lunch and dinner menus, including a seven-course *Taste of the Marches* menu, in the AA ⍟⍟ Restaurant and in the Castle Bistro, offering the best of contemporary British cuisine using local ingredients, some from the hotel owner's farm. Hereford is steeped in history, having been the old capital of Mercia. The cathedral's famous Mappa Mundi and Chained Library are within walking distance, as are the main shopping areas.

🛏 24 (inc 2 🛏) ❊ ⊙ ⌨ ♿ ⚐ ☲ **P** 🏃 🐎 🐾 **WiFi**

Rates Single/double/twin including breakfast from £130.
Meals 3 course dinner in Bar/Bistro from £22; Taste of Marches 7 course tdh £50; lunch & special diets available; last orders 2130; breakfast from 0700.

Leisure Breaks 2-night weekend breaks available. See website for current offers.

💷 All major credit cards accepted. Open all year.

Herefordshire, Hereford

The Chase Hotel
Gloucester Road, Ross-on-Wye, Herefordshire HR9 5LH
T (01989) 763161 **F** (01989) 768330
E res@chasehotel.co.uk **W** www.chasehotel.co.uk

The Chase Hotel is a stately mansion set in 11 acres of parkland on the outskirts of Ross-on-Wye. It has recently been modernised to provide a smart 36-room country hotel. Bedrooms have voicemail telephones & modem points, WIFI Internet access as well as the usual amenities. Executive and four-poster rooms enjoy the extra comfort of a feature or jacuzzi bathroom. Harry's AA ® Restaurant is contemporarily furnished. Chef Richard Barchill combines traditional British classic dishes with European/ Mediterranean influences. A typical starter might be sautéed king scallops with king prawn ravioli, soy and ginger butter sauce followed maybe by roast beef fillet with sautéed calves liver with wild mushrooms, spinach and white truffle jus.

Traditional Sunday lunch and an excellent selection of bar snacks are also available. Weddings, conferences and special events can be organised; also balloon flights, canoe trips down the river Wye and other team building activities. Good walks start from the hotel, through picturesque Ross and along the river towpaths. The stunning March country is all around.

🛏 38 (inc 2 🛏) 🎧 ✿ 🏧 ☉ 🗐 🍴 ⚷ ✂ 🅿 🚶 📶

Rates Single inc. breakfast from £105; double/twin inc bfst from £125.
Meals 3 course alc from £27.50; lunch, special diets available; last orders 2200; breakfast from 0700.

Leisure Breaks Please see our website for current special offers.
Other facilities Satellite/SKY TV. Birdwatching, fishing, golf, indoor pool, tennis, watersports nearby.

Awards & Accreditations Winners of the 'Hotel & Pub Grounds' category in the *Heart of England in Bloom* Awards 2012.

£ All major credit cards accepted. Open all year exc. 24–28 Dec.

Herefordshire, Ross-on-Wye

The Manners Arms

Croxton Rd, Knipton, Nr. Grantham, Lincolnshire NG32 1RH

T (01476) 879222 **F** (01476) 879228
E info@mannersarms.com **W** www.mannersarms.com

The Manners Arms, formerly *The Red House* and originally a Hunting Lodge built for the 6th duke, has been thoughtfully restored and decorated to make a superior Restaurant with Rooms in the shadow of Belvoir Castle. The ten bedrooms are all individually and comfortably furnished. The largest ones are on the top floor and there are two good singles. The AA ⊚ restaurant is a destination in its own right and attracts diners from a wide radius. Emphasis is on locally sourced modern free range British food. Starters include fresh crab and homemade terrines. Main course might be heart of rump or a fresh fish special. There is a good wine list or four kinds of real ale to choose from in the bar, including one brewed in the Vale of Belvoir. Lighter bar menus are also available Monday to Saturday at lunch or supper time. These and breakfast can be enjoyed in the conservatory or in fine weather on the terrace. This area is also licensed for civil wedding ceremonies and civil partnerships and can seat up to 50 guests.

🛏 10 (5 🚭 only) ❄ 🎠 ⵊ 🐾 (£10) 🅿 🏍 📶

Rates Single room inc. breakfast from £70/with dinner from £100; double from £90/with dinner from £140.

Meals Sunday lunch two courses £14.50 or three courses £19.50; last orders 2100; breakfast from 0700.

Leisure breaks Please see our website for current special offers.

💷 All major credit cards accepted. Open all year.

Lincolnshire, Nr. Grantham

The Talbot Hotel
New Street, Oundle, Northamptonshire PE8 4EA
T (01832) 273621
E talbot@bulldogmail.co.uk **W** www.thetalbot-oundle.com

The Talbot Hotel, in the centre of the fine market town of Oundle, dates from Elizabethan times. The oak staircase was brought from nearby Fotheringay Castle, down which it is said that Mary, Queen of Scots descended on the way to her execution in 1587. The Bulldog Hotel Group completed a major restoration and refurbishment project in 2012 and one of the highlights is the new open plan *Sun Room* which extends into the old courtyard and is a great place to enjoy lunch or afternoon tea. Cuisine is traditional British, all freshly prepared and making use of local produce where possible, and has recently been awarded AA ⊕. After dinner, relax in the main bar with open fireplaces. The 34 bedrooms are made up of standard, feature rooms and suites, some with four-posters and separate sitting areas. All are super comfortable with

Beltrami linen, *White Company* toiletries and free internet access. The company's *Greensleep* initiative means that, for every hotel room sold, a tree is planted, so you can sleep soundly in the knowledge that you are helping the environment! The hotel is fully licensed for weddings and is equipped with the latest in conference facilities.

🛏34 ☺ ⤵ 🐕 ♿ 🐎 ♨ 100 🅿 🐕 📶

Rates Single room with breakfast from £95; double from £125.
Meals 'The Eatery' Restaurant, 3 course tdh dinner ca. £30, alc menu starters from £5, mains from £10. Lunch & special diets available; last orders 2130; breakfast from 0700.

Other facilities Fishing & walking nearby.

💷 All major credit cards accepted. Open all year.

Northamptonshire, Oundle

Whittlebury Hall, Conference, Training Centre, Hotel & Spa
Whittlebury, Nr. Towcester, Northamptonshire NN12 8QH

91

T (01327) 857857 **F** (01327) 857867
E reservations@whittleburyhall.co.uk **W** www.whittleburyhall.co.uk

Whittlebury Hall is a modern Georgian-style building surrounded by parkland and golf courses. Inside rich furnishings and fabrics combine to create an impressive hotel. All bedrooms are spacious doubles with many modern touches and thoughtful extras. Suites come with whirlpool spa bath and double shower. An apéritif can be taken in the Silverstone Bar before heading to either the informal Astons Restaurant or the fine dining AA ◉ ◉ Murrays. Bentleys, a third outlet, provides a pizza and pasta option. The award winning Day Spa has the very latest in health, fitness and beauty facilities. For the energetic there is an extensive Gymnasium. Or there is the whirlpool spa set amongst Roman ruins, together with a steam room and sauna. A range of beauty treatments is on offer, from facials to massage, Heat and Ice Experiences and body wraps. Day Spa Packages and Spa Breaks are available to both residents and outside members. Adjacent to the hotel the independent Whittlebury Golf Course offers a choice of four 9-hole courses to challenge every level of handicap.

🛏213 ✂ ♿ 🎦 ♨ ⛽ ☉ ▣ 🐎 ♂ 🦢 🏃₁₈ 🚶 ✓ ∪ ♪ ⌕ ✒ 🎣
🏃 ♨ ⚓ ⌂ 🍴 🏋 🎿 🏠 ⛏ ⚞ 52x ♨♨♨ 500 **P** 200 🚴 (WiFi)

Rates Single room inc. breakfast from £200; doubles from £250, Sunday – Thursday. Friday and Saturday dinner, b&b from £260 single/£370 double.
Meals Astons, Bentleys, Murrays Restaurants; meals from £17.50; Sunday lunch, special diets available; last orders 2130; breakfast from 0700.
Leisure Breaks Spa Breaks, Silverstone Circuit & Hotel Breaks. See website.
Other activities Sailing 15 miles; squash 5 miles.
Awards & accreditations England for Excellence Silver Award 2011.
£ Mastercard, Visa & Diners cards accepted. Open all year.

Northamptonshire, Nr. Towcester

Langar Hall
Langar, Nr. Nottingham, Nottinghamshire NG13 9HG
T (01949) 860559 **F** (01949) 861045
E info@langarhall.co.uk **W** www.langarhall.com

I always love my visits to Langar Hall. Although close to Nottingham, it is beautifully situated overlooking the Vale of Belvoir – a lovely country house, built in 1837, standing beside an early English church, with glorious views over the gardens and parkland. The Hall is the family home of Imogen Skirving, whose father used to entertain famous cricketers of the 1930's. Langar still attracts cricket lovers and famous old cricketers. The public rooms are delightful. The charming proprietor and her excellent team make every effort for their guests' happiness. Chef Gary Booth & his team work hard to produce excellent, reasonably priced menus of French and English food, using local produce, garden vegetables and herbs, Langar lamb, local stilton, game from the Belvoir estate, fish direct from Brixham. This year we had delicious seared scallops, followed by guinea fowl, then gooseberry pudding. All the bedrooms are charming and uniquely furnished. A truly lovely spot, with a peaceful and relaxing atmosphere.

🛏 10 🐕 🐾 🎵 🐴 (by arr't - £10 fee) ♦♦♦ 20 P 20

Rates Single room inc. breakfast from £95; double from £130; suite from £195.
Meals 2 course AA ⊛ ⊛ tdh dinner weekdays £25; alc menus from £35; lunch from £18.50; special diets available; last orders 2130; breakfast from 0700.

Leisure Breaks Sunday & Monday nights, dinner b&b from £150 per room per nt.
Other activities Newark antique fair. Trent Bridge cricket, Belvoir Castle, Belton House and Burghley House near by.
Awards & accreditations 2013 winner of Food & Travel magazine for Britain's best rural hotel.

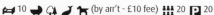

£ Mastercard & Visa cards accepted. Open all year.

Nottinghamshire, Langar

Barnsdale Lodge Hotel

The Avenue, Rutland Water, Nr. Oakham, Rutland LE15 8AH

93

T (01572) 724678 **F** (01572) 724961
E enquiries@barnsdalelodge.co.uk **W** www.barnsdalelodge.co.uk

Overlooking Rutland Water and the undulating hills of England's smallest county, this former 17th century farm-house, adjacent to the estate of the Earl of Gainsborough, is an idyllic retreat for anyone wishing to escape. Lovingly restored, Barnsdale is located to the north east of Oakham, with its market square and specialist boutiques and shops. Bedrooms offer complete relaxation. Two are specially designed for disabled guests, some are inter-connecting or four-poster and many offer views towards Rutland Water. Dining is in one of three dining rooms, the conservatory or, weather permitting, in the courtyard garden. All are usually full of local, contented diners. Eggs, herbs and vegetables come form the hotel's own hens and vegetable garden. There is a Meadow Walk (for dogs) and Highland cattle to observe. Conferences, wedding receptions, product launches and private parties take place in the separate Banqueting Suite. *Vicienté at Barnsdale,* the hotel's beauty therapy room, offers the ultimate in relaxation and pampering. New this year is the adjoining William Wheelwright hair salon. On and around Rutland Water, there is sailing, wind-surfing or cycling.

🛏️ 44 ♿ ☺ 🐕 🔟 🐎 (£10 p.n) 🏃 ♦♦♦ 200 🅿️ 🐾 📶

Rates Single room including breakfast from £80; double from £95; Retreats 3 nights from £300, 7 from £495.
Meals AA ◉ dinner tdh 3 course from £28.50; alc, lunch & special diets available; last orders 2130; breakfast from 0700.

Leisure Breaks Stay three nights and receive free entrance into Geoff Hamilton's famous Barnsdale Gardens. Rates from £325.50. Please ask for details.
Other facilities In-house beauty treatments, relaxation massage. Riding, birdwatching, sailing, fishing, cycling, Rock Bloc climbing, watersports nearby.
£ All major credit cards accepted. Open all year.

Rutland, Oakham

Soulton Hall
Wem, Nr. Shrewsbury, Shropshire SY4 5RS
T (01939) 232786 **F** (01939) 234097
E enquiries@soultonhall.co.uk **W** www.soultonhall.co.uk

16 generations of the Ashton family have cherished this ancient Shropshire manor house set in 500 acres of private country estate and woodland, as John and Ann Ashton, and son Tim do today. Guests here are treated like members of the family. Drinks are taken in the cosy drawing room, whilst making a choice from the four-course menu. This is served in the elegant candle-lit dining room, using local ingredients including game from the estate and fruit from the garden. Rooms in Soulton Hall boast wood panelling and mullion windows whilst further ground floor accommodation is available in the Carriage House and Cedar House. The 18th century Soulton Court (across the lawn) provides a unique setting for weddings and conferences. Soulton, with its walled gardens and extensive grounds, is a peaceful spot in which to just relax. It is a working 'sustainable' farm and also an excellent base from which to explore the beauties of the Shires and the Welsh Marches, as well as the Ironbridge Gorge and the cities of Shrewsbury and Chester. The Welsh Hills and border castles are also within easy reach. Soulton is one of the best kept secrets of Shropshire.

8 (inc 2) (£10 p.n) P 50 150+

Rates Single with breakfast from £55; double from £110.
Meals 4 course tdh dinner £38.50–42; spec. diets available; last orders 2030.

Conference Tariff Room hire from £96; 24-hr residential rate – on application
Leisure Breaks Winter breaks – 10% discount; complimentary dinner on some bookings.

Other Facilities Fishing, shooting, golf, riding nearby.

All major credit cards accepted. Open all year.

Shropshire, Nr. Shrewsbury

The Mytton & Mermaid Hotel
Atcham, Shrewsbury, Shropshire SY5 6QG

T (01743) 761220
E reception@myttonandmermaid.co.uk **W** www.myttonandmermaid.co.uk

A fine, family owned country house hotel on the banks of the river Severn, three miles from Shrewsbury town centre. It has the charm of an old coaching inn, having stood on the old A5 London-Holyhead route. In the 1930s, it was bought by Sir Clough Williams Ellis of Portmeirion and Romney Bay House fame (*see Kent section of guide*). It was extended and converted into a hotel, assuming the name Mytton & Mermaid, the mermaid being the crest of Portmeirion. Today it enjoys lovely views and sweeping river lawns. The 16 bedrooms range from the Mytton four-poster through to the Courtyard rooms. Nice touches within the bedrooms include homemade flapjacks and a wide range of coffee and teas. The heart of the hotel is the AA ⊛ ⊛ Restaurant, which uses Shropshire local produce where possible, with seasonally changing menus. Afternoon tea with homemade cakes has become very popular. Food is available 7am until 10pm and includes childrens' and vegetarian or vegan menus. Picnic hampers can be supplied. The hotel offers mini breaks, and the Mytton Sunday break is a delight. The hotel also owns the quaint oak-beamed Bramble Cottage opposite the nearby National Trust Attingham Park. This provides a self-contained or self-catering alternative for up to six people.

🛏 16 📠 🅿 🎠 🛁 🐓 🐕 £10 per dog 🎷 ❀ 🚶 👪 100 🚲 170 📶

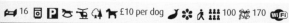

Rates Single room with breakfast from £75; double from £110.

Meals 3 course tdh dinner £25 per person; Seasonal alc menu; Last orders 2200; breakfast from 0715 Monday - Friday & from 0800 Saturday - Sunday.

Leisure Breaks Please see website for current special offers.

Other Facilities Golf 2 miles; Riding 5 miles.

💷 All major credit & debit cards accepted. Open all year except Christmas Day.

Shropshire, Shrewsbury

North West

The North West, with the Lake District, is one of the most visited areas of Britain, yet it was only opened up by the railway some 150 years ago. Wordsworth and Tennyson's poetry helped to spread the word then about this remarkable, natural corner of Britain and it has remained popular ever since.

CUMBRIA

LANCASHIRE

MERSEYSIDE   GREATER MANCHESTER

CHESHIRE

Hotels guide
Cumbria page 103

Forest of Bowland

Blackpool

Arnside Knot

Further information:
Cumbria Tourist Board
Tel: 015398 22222
www.golakes.co.uk

Lancashire & Blackpool Tourist Bd.
Tel: 01257 226600
www.visitlancashire.com

CHESHIRE AND LANCASHIRE

The stark industrial towns of **Runcorn** and **Warrington** contrast sharply with the charms of the old walled city of **Chester** and the picturesque villages that dot **Cheshire**'s countryside. Iron age forts, Roman ruins, medieval churches, Tudor cottages and elegant Georgian and Victorian stately homes are among the many attractive sights of the county. **South Cheshire**, like Cumbria to the north, has long been where the magnates of the cities of Liverpool and Manchester have made their abode. It has good communications, pretty countryside with the wilder terrain of the Peak District and North Wales within easy reach.

Norton Priory Museum, Runcorn

Chester

Lancashire's **Forest of Bowland** is an area of outstanding natural beauty with wild crags, superb walks, streams, valleys and fells. **Blackpool** on the coast has been the playground of the North West for many years and still draws millions of holiday makers every year, attracted to its seven miles of beach, illuminations, Pleasure Beach Amusement Park and golf. **Morecambe, Southport, Lytham St Annes** and **Fleetwood** also offer wide beaches, golf and bracing walks. **Lancaster**, a city since Roman times, has fine museums, castle and university and an imitation of the Taj Mahal, the Ashton Memorial.

Morecambe Bay

Lake District

CUMBRIA

In this lovely corner of England, **The Lake District**, there is beauty in breathtaking variety. It is loved by many who come back time and again to its inspirational magic, brilliant blue lakes and craggy mountain tops.

The central Lake District with its mountains, lakes and woods is so well known and loved that there is a tendency to forget that the rest of Cumbria contains some of the most varied and attractive landscape in Britain. In the east of the county, the lovely peaceful **Eden Valley** is sheltered by the towering hills of the Pennines, and everywhere are dotted charming little red sandstone villages. **Alston**, with its cobbled streets is the highest town in England, and has been used for numerous TV location sets.

Cumbria's long coastline is itself full of variety. There are rocky cliffs with myriad sea birds, sandy estuaries, miles of sun-trapping sand dunes and friendly harbours, and everywhere something interesting to see, from reminders of the Roman occupation to the **Flookburgh** shrimp fishermen who go fishing not in boats, but on tractors!

Lake District

Cumbria

Lake Windermere

Wherever you choose to stay in Cumbria, you will not be far away from beautiful scenery and there is a wide choice of accommodation from gracious country house hotels to country inns and bed & breakfasts. Don't think that Summer is the only time when Cumbria is beautiful. In Autumn the deciduous woodlands and bracken coloured hillsides glow with colour. In Winter, the snow covered mountain tops stand out in dazzling magnificence against blue skies. In Spring, you can discover the delights of the magical, constantly changing light and the joy of finding carpets of wild flowers. This is really the best time of the year to go walking or climbing - spending each day in the fresh air, to return in the evening with a healthy appetite to enjoy a delicious Cumbrian meal by the fireside in a cosy pub or friendly hotel.

There are many holidays in **Lakeland** which offer both activity and instruction in a range of sports - walking, climbing, orienteering, potholing, cycling, riding, golf, sailing, sailboarding, canoeing, fishing and water-skiing. Although beware - **Lake Windermere** has banned any boat faster than 30 knots.

A good way to take in the beauty of this unique area is to plan your own personal route on foot or cycle. The **Cumbria Cycle Way**, designed to avoid all the cyclist's problems like main roads and precipitate inclines, takes a circular route 250 miles long

around this beautiful county. There are also good cheap public transport services, and where the big coaches cannot go, Mountain Goat minibuses run, even over the steepest mountain passes.

For a change from the great outdoors, there is a wealth of historic houses to visit, including a uniquely constructed thatched farmhouse, stately homes that have seen centuries of gracious living and the small cottages where famous writers have lived without having their style cramped. Other houses are important because of their architecture, like the round house in **Belle Isle** or majestic **Hutton-in-the-Forest**, which has a central tower dating from the 14th century, surrounded by later additions.

The Cumbrian climate is ideal for gardens and the area is famous for the rhododendrons and azaleas which grow in abundance.

You will find out more about the secrets of this ancient kingdom by watching, or even joining in with some of its old customs, many of which are unique to Cumbria. There are traditional agricultural shows displaying the essence of the English countryside - spiced in Cumbria with local specialities like hound trailing, which is like hunting but without the fox and fell races: crazy lung-bursting ascents of the nearest hill, followed by bone bruising descent.

Martindale

Liverpool

LIVERPOOL AND MANCHESTER

Liverpool was an important city long before The Beatles emerged from their Cavern in the Swinging Sixties. It grew from a village into a prosperous port, an entrepot where emigrants sailed for the New World and immigrants arrived from Ireland.

Today the ocean going liners are fewer, but the new dock complex ensures that the city is as vibrant as ever. Liverpool's waterfront regeneration is led by the **Albert Dock Village**, which includes the **Maritime Museum** and **Tate Gallery Liverpool**. The city has two modern cathedrals, a symphony orchestra, eight museums and Britain's oldest repertory theatre The Playhouse. It has two commercial radio stations and the popular TV programmes The Liver Birds, On the Waterfront and Brookside were made here. Liverpool has seen the opening of several contemporary hotels and it has over 100 cafés and restaurants with many gastronomes making the short trip to **Chinatown** to sample oriental culinary delights.

Manchester's prosperity can be traced back to the 14th century when Flemish weavers arrived to transform a market town into a thriving boom city at the forefront of the Industrial Revolution. It is now known as *The Capital of the North* and is a great centre of learning and culture as well as of economic success. The city that spawned 20 Nobel Prize Winners and where Rutherford worked on splitting the atom has not been resting on its laurels. It is rich in galleries, museums, libraries and theatres. The **City Art Gallery** displays its famous pre-Raphaelite collection while the **Halle Orchestra** regularly fills the **Bridgewater Hall**. At **Granada Studios** Coronation Street's Rovers Return Pub can be seen. The city boasts a booming 24/7 economy, has high quality shopping and sporting (particularly football) traditions and is within an hour's drive of the Peak District and Lake District National Parks. It too has spawned a family of boutique hotels.

The Long Gallery, Manchester

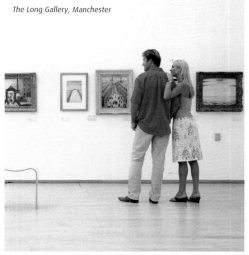

HUDSON'S HISTORIC HOUSES & GARDENS HIGHLIGHTS

Cholmondeley Castle Gardens
(01829) 720383
www.cholmondeleycastle.com
Cholmondeley Castle Garden is said by many to be among the most romantically beautiful gardens they have seen. Visitors can enjoy the tranquil Temple Water Garden, Ruin Water Garden, memorial mosaic, Rose garden & many mixed borders.

Holker Hall & Gardens
(015395) 58328
www.holker.co.uk
Holker is the family home of Lord & Lady Cavendish. Steeped in history, this magnificent Victorian Mansion of neo-Elizabethan Gothic style was largely re-built in the 1870's following a fire, but origins date back to the 1600's.

Kirklinton Hall

Kirklinton Hall
01697) 748292
www.kirklintonhall.co.uk
Adjacent to the 12th century de Boyville stronghold, Kirklinton Hall is said to have been built from it's stone. The Hall has been a Restoration Great House, an RAF base, a school, a gangsters' gambling den and worse.

Leighton Hall
01524) 734474
www.leightonhall.co.uk
Nestled in 1,550 acres of lush grounds, this romantic, Gothic house is the lived-in home of the famous Gillow furniture family.

Levens Hall & Gardens
(015395) 60321
www.levenshall.co.uk
Levens Hall is an Elizabethan mansion built around a 13th century pele tower. The much loved home of the Bagot family.

Muncaster Castle
(01229) 717614
www.muncaster.co.uk
A treasure trove of paintings, silver, embroideries and more. With acres of Grade 2 woodland gardens, famous for rhododendrons and breathtaking views of the Lake District.

Peover Hall & Gardens
(01565) 724220
www.peoverhall.com
A Grade 2 listed Elizabethan family house dating from 1585. Situated within some 500 acres of landscaped 18th century parkland with formal gardens.

Rode Hall & Gardens
(01270) 873237
www.rodehall.co.uk
The Wilbraham family have lived at Rode since 1669. The house stands in a Repton landscape and extensive gardens include a woodland garden which has many species of plants & flowers.

Tabley House
(01565) 750151
www.tableyhouse.co.uk
Tabley, a Grade I listed building, was designed by John Carr of York for the Leicester family. It contains one of the first collections of English paintings, including works of art by Turner, Reynolds, Lawrence, Lely and Dobson.

HUDSON'S
HISTORIC HOUSES & GARDENS
MUSEUMS & HERITAGE SITES

For more suggestions of great historic days out across Britain visit
www.hudsonsheritage.com

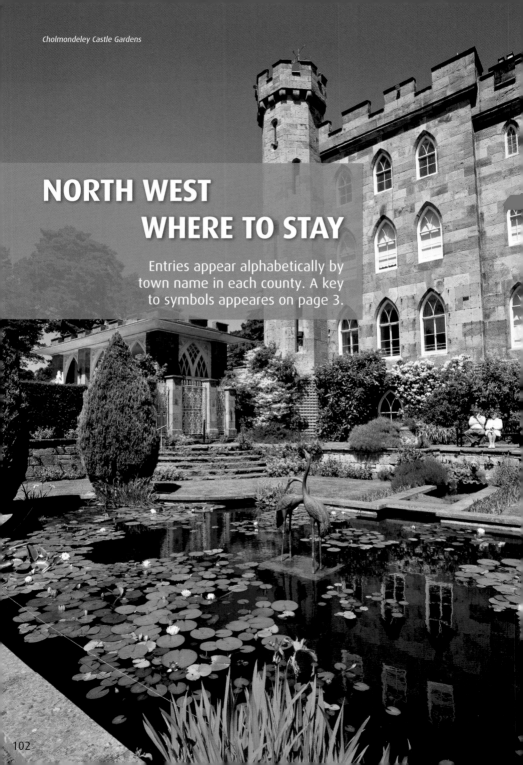

Cholmondeley Castle Gardens

NORTH WEST
WHERE TO STAY

Entries appear alphabetically by town name in each county. A key to symbols appeares on page 3.

Lovelady Shield Country House Hotel
Nenthead Road, Nr. Alston, Cumbria CA9 3LF

T (01434) 381203 **F** (01434) 381515
E enquiries@lovelady.co.uk **W** www.lovelady.co.uk

Lovelady Shield. The name conjures up an image of the peace and tranquillity that you will certainly find in this gracious country house hotel. Set beside a river in a wooded valley high in the Pennines, just 2¼ miles from Alston (England's highest market town), this quiet retreat is an ideal situation for exploring the border country, the Lake District, Hadrian's Wall and the Yorkshire Dales. Only 35 minutes from the Penrith exit of the M6, via the dramatic A686 – one of the world's top drives – it is a very pleasant stopover. The owners, Mr & Mrs Haynes, together with their friendly staff, are maintaining the hotel's tradition of warm hospitality and service. The rooms in the extension have every comfort and amenity: DVD/CD players, power showers in the bathrooms and squishy duvets. Chef Barrie Garton produces imaginative and beautifully presented meals and has been awarded AA ֎ ֎ for his cooking. Service in the pretty dining room is discreet and attentive. The hotel is well furnished and welcoming, with log fires. There are two self-catering cottages in the grounds. A very peaceful spot.

Rates Single room with breakfast from £85; double from £170.
Meals Tdh ֎ ֎ dinner £44.50; bar lunches & special diets available; last orders 2030.

Leisure Breaks November–March, midweek, dinner, b&b from £140 per night for two people; weekend from £160 per person.

Other Activities Shooting, golf, riding nearby.

£ All major cards accepted. Open all year.

Cumbria, Alston

Borrowdale Gates Country House Hotel
Grange-in-Borrowdale, Keswick, Cumbria CA12 5UQ

T (01768) 777204 **F** (01768) 777195
E hotel@borrowdale-gates.com **W** www.borrowdale-gates.com

Originally a private residence situated on the edge of the historic hamlet of Grange, Borrowdale Gates maintains the lovely homely atmosphere of a genuine country house, where the cares of the world just ebb away. Location is sublime. Set in two acres of wooded gardens, with a backdrop of high, rising fells, close to the shores of Derwentwater, the hotel offers seclusion without remoteness. Its aspect is perfect, providing panoramic views of the dramatic lakeland scenery. Wonderful lakeland cooking, an outstanding wine list and personal service all combine to create a memorable guest experience. The lounges have picture length windows and log fires and make an ideal place to read, chat or enjoy afternoon tea. Bedrooms, ten of which are on the ground floor, have every amenity and are wonderful to return to after a day's invigorating walking or sightseeing. All have views of the surrounding valley, fells or farmland. Guests can also relax in the gardens with unspoiled views of Castle Crag, the famous Jaws of Borrowdale and the distant Scafell Pike.

Rates Single room with breakfast from £67; double from £134.
Meals 3 course tdh dinner £39. Alc, lunch & special diets available; Last orders 2030; breakfast from 0800.

Leisure Breaks Specialised weekend and other breaks available – see website.
Awards & accreditations AA ★★★ & AA ◉ cuisine.

Other Activities Golf, fishing, riding, sailing nearby.

All major credit cards accepted. Open all year except January.

Cumbria, Nr. Keswick

RELAIS &
CHATEAUX.

Gilpin Hotel & Lake House
Crook Road, Nr. Windermere, Cumbria LA23 3NE
T (015394) 88818 **F** (015394) 88660
E hotel@thegilpin.co.uk **W** www.thegilpin.co.uk

105

Meticulously run by the Cunliffe family, Gilpin Hotel is set in 20 tranquil acres of woodland, moor and country gardens. The family is assisted by a team of dedicated and long serving staff whose experience shows at every corner. Just 12 miles from the M6 and almost opposite Windermere Golf Course ('*the miniature Gleneagles*'), this AA ★★★★ Relais & Châteaux hotel is at the heart of the Lake District's wealth of sightseeing, heritage and activities. Seven rooms lead directly onto the gardens and six Garden Suites have decked gardens with hot tubs. 2010 saw the opening of Gilpin Lake House (a mile away) which sits on its own four-acre lake with private spa, boat-house, boat, cedarwood hot tub, indoor pool, salt snug and 100 acres of private gardens and grounds. Accommodation consists of six stunning suites which exclusively share these facilities (the house can also be booked for exclusive use). A chauffeur will take guests to the main hotel, where they can enjoy AA ❀❀❀ cuisine. As in the main house, décor by Christine Cunliffe uses exquisite fabrics, wonderful upholstery, with delicious art on the walls and luxurious bathrooms.

🛏26 ❀ �’ 🕏 🏃 🎧 ▶18 🅿 40 🐾 (WiFi)

Rates Single room with breakfast & 5 course dinner from £225; double from £335.
Meals 5 course tdh dinner £58; 3 course Sunday lunch £35; alc 3 course lunch from £30.

Leisure Breaks Special 3–5 night breaks from £235 per night, dinner, b&b; 10 nights from £195 pn, dinner,b&b. Golf breaks also available.
Other Facilities In-room spa treatment. Leisure Club & gym, riding, fishing, sailing, food safaris, spa, sauna nearby. Dedicated spa for Lake House guests.

Awards & accreditations Catey's Independent Hotel of the Year 2012. AA England Hotel of the year 2012. Condé Nast Johansens Country House Hotel of the Year 2013.

💷 All major credit & debit cards accepted. Open all year.

Cumbria, Windermere

Oak Bank Hotel

Broadgate, Grasmere Village, Cumbria LA22 9TA
T (015394) 35217 **F** (015394) 35685
E info@lakedistricthotel.co.uk **W** www.lakedistricthotel.co.uk

Like many hotels in the Lake District, Oak Bank was originally a private merchant's house built in 1872. It became a hotel in 1920 and its central location in the heart of Grasmere puts all the Lake District attractions within easy reach. It is a short walk from St Oswald's Church, final resting place of William Wordsworth, whose Daffodil Garden and Dove Cottage are nearby. Glynis and Simon Wood own and personally manage Oak Bank, ably assisted by a small band of loyal staff, including head chef Darren Comish, who presides over the AA ® ® Restaurant. This has become a destination in its own right, using top quality fresh ingredients, locally sourced where possible. They make their own bread, pasta, sauces, jus and sorbets. A selection of fine wines from around the world is available to complement the dining experience. The dining room overlooks the hotel garden, a short walk down to the river Rothay. There are a selection of rooms to suit all tastes and budgets, from standard double to superior four poster and the superb Acorn Suite, a large ground floor room with its own entrance, a super king size bed and spa bathroom. All bedrooms are individually and stylishly decorated, with flat screen TV, luxury toiletries and hospitality tray. Hotel guests can use the nearby Langdale Spa if they want an indoor swim or spa experience.

🛏 14 🔟 🅿 ⚡ 🐾 ❄ ⚡ 🛜

Rates Single room with breakfast from £73.50; double from £87.00; plus dinner from £20.00 per person.

Meals 3 course tdh dinner £35; Alc available; Lunch available; vegetarian & special diets available; Last orders 2000; Breakfast from 0815.

Other Facilities Spa nearby; Golf 8 miles; Bicycle hire 4 miles.

Awards & accreditations AA ® ®, Michelin recommended restaurant.

£ All major credit & debit cards accepted, except American Express.
Closed 2 - 16 January, 3 - 14 August & 24 - 26 December.

Cumbria, Windermere

Located in the beautiful Forest of Bowland, just a mile outside the village of Chipping, the Gibbon Bridge is one of Lancashire's finest, privately owned, four star hotels. For over thirty years it was the family farm, until its conversion into a sumptuous country hotel by owner Janet Simpson and her late mother, Margaret. The hotel has continued to evolve over the years and the most recent development is a Victorian-style Orangery. Gibbon Bridge has to be experienced to fully appreciate the unique ambience and special charm which captivates those who stay there. A roaring log fire and welcoming atmosphere lead guests to enjoy superior accommodation and surroundings; 23 acres of award winning gardens, and a wonderful restaurant with a deserved reputation for delicious food. Additional facilities include: executive meeting rooms, private and al fresco dining, civil wedding ceremonies and receptions, tennis court and helicopter pad. For business or pleasure, the Gibbon Bridge offers a superb location and comes highly recommended. Winner of the Lancashire Life Food & Drink Awards 2010-2011 Lancashire Hotel of the Year.

🛏30 ♨ ⚓ ⚒ 🖥 ❄ 🅿 ⚲ ⚓ 🐾 📶

Rates Single room with breakfast from £90; double with breakfast from £140.
Meals 2 course tdh dinner £16.45 3 courses £20.45; 3 course Sunday lunch £24.45.

Leisure Breaks Please see our website for current special offers.

Awards & accreditations Winner of the Lancashire Life Food & Drink Awards 2010-2011 – Lancashire Hotel of the Year. Visit England Four Star Silver Award.

💷 All major credit & debit cards accepted. Open all year.

Cumbria, Windermere

Signpost Guide 2014
Yorkshire & North East

Yorkshire & North East

Yorkshire, Durham and Northumberland – fiercely independent counties which make up the North East. Yorkshire includes two national parks, the Dales and the North Yorks Moors, James Herriot and Last of the Summer Wine country. Northumberland's border lands have high moors, ragged cliffs, sandy beaches and offshore islands. The dynamic city of Newcastle divides it from County Durham, with its fine cathedral and castle.

NORTHUMBERLAND
TYNE & WEAR
DURHAM   TEESSIDE
NORTH YORKSHIRE
EAST RIDING
WEST YORKSHIRE
SOUTH YORKSHIRE

Hotels guide

Northumberland page 115
North Yorkshire   page 116

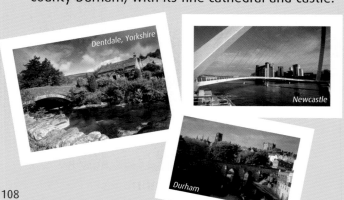

Dentdale, Yorkshire

Newcastle

Durham

Further information:
Yorkshire Tourist Board
Tel: 0844 888 5123
www.yorkshire.com

North East England
www.visitnortheastengland.co.uk

108

NORTHUMBERLAND

Bamburgh Castle, Bamburgh

Northumbria is an undiscovered holiday paradise, where the scenery is wild and beautiful, the beaches golden and unspoiled and the natives friendly. The region is edged by the **North Sea**, four national parks and the vast **Border Forest Park**.

Its **eastern** sea boundary makes a stunning coastline, stretching 100 miles from Staithes on the Cleveland boundary, to **Berwick-on-Tweed**, England's most northerly town, frequently fought over and with the finest preserved example of Elizabethan town walls in the country. In between you'll find as many holiday opportunities as changes of scenery.

Inland there's **Hadrian's Wall**, the **National Park**, hills, forests, waterfalls, castles, splendid churches and quaint towns. Visitors can trace man's occupation of the region from prehistoric times: rock carvings, ancient hill forts, Saxon churches, Norman priories, medieval castles, through a wealth of industrial archaeology.

Berwick-upon-Tweed

The region has a rich maritime heritage too. Ruins like **Dunstanburgh** or fairy-tale **Lindisfarne** are relics of a turbulent era. You can take a trip from **Seahouses** to the **Farne Islands** - a marvellous bird sanctuary and breeding ground of the Atlantic Grey Seal.

Agriculture is one of the region's most important industries. **Heatherslaw Mill** near Ford, (a delightful model village) has a restored waterdriven corn mill and agricultural museum. Fans of One Man and His Dog can see the skills of shepherd and dog at numerous sheepdog trails and county shows in the summer.

Holy Island

Newcastle-upon-Tyne, once a shipbuilding centre, is a rejuvenated city of proud civic tradition, fine restaurants and theatres, with one of the liveliest arts scenes outside London. The **Theatre Royal** is the third home of the Royal Shakespeare Company and a venue for major touring companies. The **Metro Centre** in neighbouring **Gateshead** attracts shoppers form all over the North East with more than 300 outlets and 11 cinema screens.

Durham's Norman cathedral, once a prison, soars above the plain and was the Bishops Palace from 1072 to 1837. Find the small **University and Oriental Museum**, housing a unique collection of Chinese, Indian & Egyptian Art.

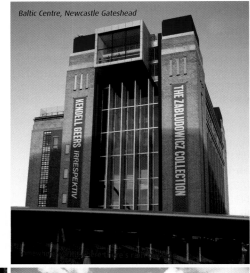

Baltic Centre, Newcastle Gateshead

Durham Cathedral

York

YORK

No visit to the North East would be complete without savouring the delights of **York**. Wherever you turn within the city's medieval walls, you will find fascinating glimpses of the past. These can be seen in the splendours of the 600-year old **Minster**, the grim stronghold of **Clifford's Tower**, the **National Railway Museum**, the medieval timbers of the **Merchant Adventurers' Hall** and the **Jorvik Viking Centre** which illustrates life in a 10th century Viking village. Throughout the city, statues and monuments remind the visitor that this was where Constantine was proclaimed Holy Roman Emperor, Guy Fawkes was born and Dick Turpin met his end.

North York Moors National Park

NORTH YORKSHIRE

So rich in history, **North Yorkshire** boasts some of the country's most splendid scenery. The **North York Moors National Park** has 500 square miles of hills, dales, forests and open moorland, neatly edged by a spectacular coastline. Walking, cycling and pony trekking are ideal ways to savour the scenery; alternatively take the steam train from Pickering to Grosmont on the famous **North Yorkshire Moors Railway**.

Numerous greystone towns and villages dotted throughout the **Moors** are ideal bases from which to explore the countryside. From **Helmsley**, visit the ruins of **Rievaulx Abbey**, founded by Cistercian monks in the 12th century. In **Hutton-le-Hole**, moorland life is depicted in the **Ryedale Folk Museum**. Likewise the **Beck Isle Museum** in **Pickering** provides an insight into the life of a country market town. A few miles down the road, you'll find **Malton**, once a Roman fortress,

and nearby **Castle Howard**, the setting for *Brideshead Revisited*.

From the Moors, cross the A1 for a total change of scene. Wherever you go in **The Dales**, you'll come across visible reminders of the rich and changing past. In medieval days, solid fortresses like **Richmond** and **Middleham** were built to protect the area from marauding Scots. **Knaresborough**, the home of the prophetess Mother Shipton, **Ripley** and **Skipton** all had their massive strongholds while **Bolton Castle** in **Wensleydale** once imprisoned Mary, Queen of Scots. The pattern of history is also enshrined in the great abbeys, like **Jervaulx Abbey**, near **Masham**, where the monks first made Wensleydale cheese, **Eastby Abbey** on the banks of the river **Swale**, and the majestic ruins of **Fountains Abbey** in the grounds of **Studley Royal**.

Bridlington

WEST, EAST & SOUTH YORKSHIRE

For centuries cloth has been spun from the wool of the sheep grazing in the **Pennine uplands**. The fascinating story of England's industrial heritage can now be seen in the numerous craft centres and folk museums throughout **West Yorkshire**. To enjoy the countryside, take a trip on the steam hauled **Keighley and Worth Valley Railway**.

Stop off at **Haworth**, home of the Bronte sisters, and experience the rugged atmosphere of Wuthering Heights. Not far from Haworth is **Bingley**, where the Leeds & Liverpool canal makes its famous uphill journey. In the past, coal barges came this way; nowadays holiday makers in gaily painted boats have taken their place.

Whitby

Leeds itself is now a vibrant city with its Victorian shopping arcades, Royal Armories Museum, Corn Exchange and lively arts scene.

Moving into the **East Riding**, the scenery changes again. From the dramatic 400 ft high cliffs at **Flamborough Head**, there sweeps south a 40-mile stretch of perfect sandy beach. Along this coastline you will find the boisterous entertainment centres of **Cleethorpes** and **Bridlington** or the quieter attractions of **Hornsea** and **Withernsea**. The Wolds are near all these seaside resorts and **Beverley**, with its magnificent 13th century minster and lattice of medieval streets, is a jewel of architectural heritage. **Hull** is a modern city rebuilt since the war, linked to **Lincolnshire** via the 1452 yd **Humber Bridge**.

The area around **Sheffield** - the steel city - in **South Yorkshire** is dominated by the iron and steel industries. Cooling towers and power stations still nudge the M1 motorway as it cuts through this industrial heartland. Sheffield was the first city in England to pioneer free public transport. The Industrial Museum and City Museum display a wide range of Sheffield cutlery and oplate. Meadowhall shopping centre, with 270 stores under one roof, is a must visit for shopaholics.

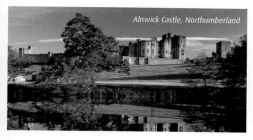
Alnwick Castle, Northumberland

Alnwick Castle
(01665) 511100
www.alnwickcastle.com
Home to the Duke of Northumberland's family, the Percys, for over 700 years; Alnwick Castle offers history on a grand scale.

Bamburgh Castle
(01668) 214208
www.bamburghcastle.com
These formidable stone walls have witnessed dark tales of royal rebellion, bloody battles, spellbinding legends and millionaire benefactors. With fourteen public rooms and 3000 artefacts, including arms and armour, porcelain, furniture and artwork.

Beamish Museum
(0191) 3704000
www.beamish.org.uk
Beamish Museum is an award-winning museum vividly recreating life in North East England in Georgian, Victorian and Edwardian times.

Burton Agnes Hall & Gardens
(01262) 490324
www.burtonagnes.com
A magnificent Elizabethan Hall containing treasures collected over four centuries, from the original carving and plasterwork to modern and impressionist paintings.

Castle Howard
(01653) 648333
www.castlehoward.co.uk
Designed by Sir John Vanbrugh in 1699 Castle Howard is undoubtedly one of Britain's finest private residences.

Chillingham Castle
(01668) 215359
www.chillingham-castle.com
20 Minutes from seaside or mountains. 4 stars in Simon Jenkins' 'Thousand Best Houses' and the very first of The Independent's '50 Best Castles in Britain & Ireland'.

Harewood House and Gardens
(0113) 2181010
www.harewood.org
Harewood is one of the finest Treasure Houses of England, in the setting of Yorkshire's most beautiful landscape.

Newby Hall & Gardens
01423 322583
www.newbyhall.com
Its beautifully restored interior presents Robert Adam at his best. It houses rare Gobelins tapestries and one of the UK's largest private collections of classical statuary.

Raby Castle
(01833) 660202
www.rabycastle.com
Surrounded by a large deer park, with two lakes and a beautiful walled garden with formal lawns, yew hedges and an ornamental pond, Raby Castle was built by the mighty Nevill family in the 14th century, and has been home to Lord Barnard's family since 1626.

Skipton Castle
(01756) 792442
www.skiptoncastle.co.uk
Skipton Castle, over 900 years old, one of the best preserved, most complete medieval castles in England.

For more suggestions of great historic days out across Britain visit
www.hudsonsheritage.com

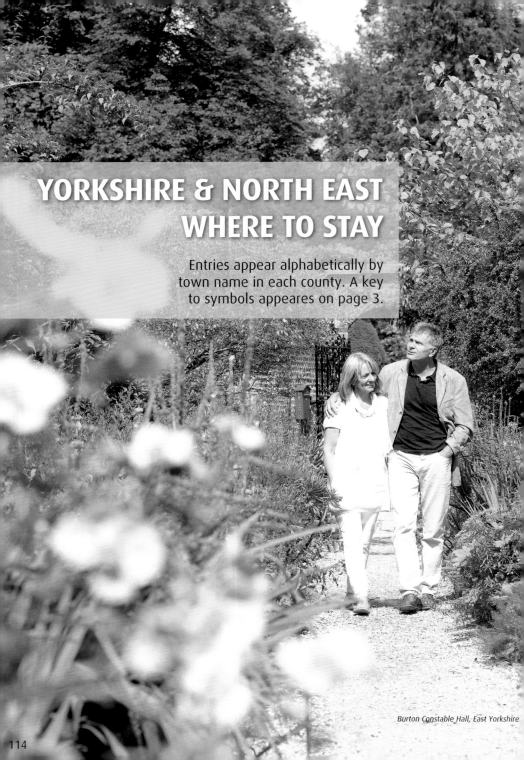

YORKSHIRE & NORTH EAST
WHERE TO STAY

Entries appear alphabetically by
town name in each county. A key
to symbols appeares on page 3.

Burton Constable Hall, East Yorkshire

Waren House Hotel
Waren Mill, Belford, Northumberland NE70 7EE
T (01668) 214581 **F** (01668) 214484
E enquiries@warenhousehotel.co.uk **W** www.warenhousehotel.co.uk

115

Set in six acres of gardens and woodland, Waren House is a peaceful and tranquil centre from which to visit one of this country's most naturally beautiful and historic areas, largely unspoiled by tourism and the commercial world. The castles of Bamburgh, Dunstanburgh, Alnwick and Warkworth are all easily accessible. The Holy Island of Lindisfarne is nearby. There is a wealth of birdlife along miles of magnificent coastline, particularly at Budle Bay and the Farne Islands. After a day's sightseeing, you can return to the quiet luxury of Waren House where owners Peter and Anita Laverack and their staff will pamper you. Set in landscaped grounds, the hotel offers three suites and 12 individually styled bedrooms, including some ground floor. In the evening guests can enjoy a gastronomic treat in Grays Restaurant, a favourite with local and resident alike. Specialising in locally sourced ingredients, it has been awarded an AA ⍟. As you enjoy the hospitality, reflect on your good fortune at having stopped here, rather than speeding by on the A1 without discovering the splendours of this historic region and of Waren House in particular.

🛏 15 (inc 3 suites & 2 🛏) 🍴 ♿ ✂ 🐕 🧍 🚭 ℚ **P** 📶

Rates Single/double room with breakfast from £65.
Meals Tdh dinner £42; special diets available; last orders 2030.

Leisure Breaks Two nights, 5 course dinner, b&b from £190 per room per night.

Other Activities Golf 2 miles, riding 5 miles.

💷 Major credit cards accepted. Open all year.

Northumberland, Bamburgh

The Sportsman's Arms Hotel & Restaurant

Wath in Nidderdale, Pateley Bridge, Harrogate HG3 5PP

T (01423) 711306 **F** (01423) 712524
E sportsmansarms@btconnect.com **W** www.sportsmans-arms.co.uk

The Sportsman's Arms Hotel and Restaurant nestles close to the river Nidd (on which it has fishing rights) at Wath in Nidderdale – a conservation village, and one of the most picturesque and unspoiled villages in a beautiful part of the Yorkshire Dales. Reached by a pack horse bridge and set in its own gardens, this attractive 17th century mellow sandstone building attracts you like a magnet. Once inside, the cosy lounges, log fires, bar and charming, softly lit restaurant exude warmth and this and the welcome and hospitality of owners Jane and Ray Carter will remain with you throughout your stay. The local reputation for the Sportsman's Arms is that it is a first class restaurant with bedrooms. However this is not fair to the bedrooms which are comfortable and tastefully decorated, retaining many original features. At the heart of the Sportsmans Arms, however, is the restaurant and the first class food and wine on offer. Working with the best fresh local game, fish and vegetables, the Sportsman's Arms provides a feast for its guests.

🛏 12 (inc 1 suite) 🍴 ♿ 🐕 ✎ 🎣 🅿 30 📶

Rates Single room with breakfast from £80; double room from £120.
Meals Alc dinner; lunch & special diets available; last orders 2100.

Leisure Breaks End October–mid March Nidderdale Midweekers – 2 persons sharing, min stay two nights, dinner, b&b from £140 per person Sun–Thurs inc.

💳 Visa, Mastercard & Switch cards accepted. Open all year (exc. Xmas Day).

North Yorkshire, Nr. Harrogate

Lastingham Grange
Lastingham, Nr. Kirkbymoorside, York YO62 6TH
T (01751) 417345 **F** (01751) 417358
E reservations@lastinghamgrange.com **W** www.lastinghamgrange.com

117

It is easy to see why guests return time and again to this charming hotel situated on the edge of the Moors in the historic village of Lastingham, a peaceful backwater in the heart of the North York Moors National Park. The old, stone-walled country house, built around a courtyard and set within 10 acres of attractive gardens, is owned and personally run by the Wood family. Their charming friendliness and hospitality sets the mood for all guests to feel at ease in this elegant and tasteful country home. The atmosphere is unhurried and peaceful, the south facing terrace providing a tranquil setting in which to relax and enjoy the beautiful rose garden. The welcoming hall, the spacious lounge with its open fire, the comfortable bedrooms with their impressive views, the excellent food, the attention to detail and the location make the Grange a perfect spot for a restful break. In the village is the 7th century Church of St Mary with its ancient crypt, mentioned by the Venerable Bede in AD 731 and where Holy Communion is still celebrated every Wednesday morning.

Rates Single room with breakfast from £130; double room from £199.
Meals Tdh dinner £39.50; lunch from £20; Sunday lunch from £29.50; special diets available; last orders 2030.

Leisure Breaks 2 nights, dinner, b&b, two sharing, £265 per room per night. See also website.
Other Facilities Riding 4 mile and golf 5 miles nearby.

£ Major credit cards accepted. Open March–beginning of December.

North Yorkshire, Lastingham

The Traddock
Austwick, Settle, North Yorkshire LA2 8BY

T (015242) 51224 **F** (015242) 51796
E info@austwicktraddock.co.uk **W** www.the traddock.co.uk

The Traddock is a country house hotel surrounded by the breathtaking scenery of the Yorkshire Dales National Park, located just off the A65 between Skipton and Kendal. The Reynolds family owners take pride in the informal, relaxed style of their hotel, which is lovingly furnished to create a relaxed atmosphere as soon as you step over the threshold. Each en suite bedroom is individually decorated with all the comforts you would need, from Sheridan cotton sheets and duck down duvets (or sheets & blankets if preferred) to LCD TVs and free WiFi throughout. Most have impressive views of the surrounding countryside. The award winning AA ⊛ ⊛ Restaurant, a member of the *Slow Food UK* movement, uses only the finest local and organic seasonal products including Dales' bred beef. There are over 70 wines to choose from, and three comfortable lounge bars in which to relax before and after dinner, in front of an open fire on a winter's night. Austwick and the Yorkshire Dales National Park offer dramatic scenery and walks. Nearby is Ingleborough Cave and the famous Ribblehead Viaduct, bearing the Settle to Carlisle Railway.

🛏 12 (4 📶 only) ♨ 🅿 ❀ 🚲 🐑 🔊 🎱 🐾 (£5 fee) 🏃 🎠 📶

Rates Single room with breakfast from £85; double room from £95.
Meals 3 course tdh dinner £30; lunch from £20; Sunday lunch from £28.50; special diets available; last orders 2100; breakfast from 0800.

Other Facilities Golf, riding, sailing nearby.

💷 Visa & Mastercard accepted. Open all year.

North Yorkshire, Settle

The Devonshire Arms Hotel & Spa

Bolton Abbey, Skipton, North Yorkshire BD23 6AJ
T (01756) 710441 **F** (01756) 710564
E res@devonshirehotels.co.uk **W** www.thedevonshirearms.co.uk

119

Owned by the Duke and Duchess, the Devonshire Arms has been welcoming travelers since the early 17th century. The hotel's rich heritage, combined with the most modern facilities, make it a gem worth discovering, and once discovered, returning to. Enjoy a warm Yorkshire welcome and settle into your room to ponder whether to explore the 30,000 acres of the Bolton Abbey Estate or enjoy the stunning Dales with picturesque riverside walks and pretty tea shops serving hearty Yorkshire afternoon teas. After these exertions, unwind in the secluded Devonshire Health Barn with pool, steam room, spa pool, gym, tennis and bicycles. The less energetic can enjoy a luxurious massage and beauty treatment or just sink into one of the deep squishy sofas in front of a roaring log fire. Best of all is the food. Whether dining in the elegant Burlington Restaurant or in the vibrant Devonshire Brasserie & Bar, you will enjoy freshly prepared top quality produce, much of it from the hotel's own gardens or from local producers. The award winning wine list boasts over 2500 bins – a treat for even the most discerning wine lover. Nearby Harrogate is famous for its antique shops and rich history.

🛏 40 🐾 🍴 ♟ 🅿 🍽 🏃 ♿ 🍸 📺 🎿 📶

Rates Single room with breakfast from £110; double with breakfast from £160.
Meals The Burlington - 3 course alc dinner £65, 8 course tasting menu £75; alc, special diets available; last orders 2130; breakfast from 0730. The Devonshire Brasserie and Bar - dinner, lunch and special diets available; last orders 2100.

Leisure Breaks Please see website for current special offers.

£ Major credit cards accepted. Open all year.

North Yorkshire, Skipton

120

The Devonshire Fell
Burnsall Village, Skipton, North Yorkshire BD23 6BT
T (01756) 729000 **F** (01756) 729009
E res@devonshirehotels.co.uk **W** www.devonshirefell.co.uk

The Devonshire Fell is in the heart of Wharfedale overlooking the river and the picturesque village of Burnsall, across to the hills of the Yorkshire Dales. Décor, chosen by the Duchess, is chic and modern, with the use of rich fabrics and bold, bright colours. Public rooms have soft squishy sofas, comfy armchairs, a huge wood burning stove and original contemporary art, creating a warm and inviting atmosphere, somewhat in contrast to the building's traditional Edwardian exterior. Dining choices are the relaxing conservatory or the attractive Bistro. Cuisine has been awarded AA ◎ ◎ and is enhanced by excellent wines chosen from the nearby Devonshire Cellars at Bolton Abbey, together with cask and guest ales from local breweries. Menus take advantage of fresh, local produce available daily. Guests receive complimentary access of our Devonshire Health Spa, just 5 minutes' drive away. They may also explore the Bolton Abbey Estate with 80 miles of footpaths and nature trails, riverside café and pretty village with 12th century Augustinian priory church. The Dales Way follows the meandering river Wharfe past the hotel and all around is the spectacular Dales countryside with caverns, waterfalls and fells to explore.

🛏 12 🐕 🅿 🏃 📶

Rates Single room with breakfast from £85; double room with breakfast from £110.

Meals Dinner, lunch and special diets available; last orders 2100; breakfast from 0800.

Leisure Breaks Please see website for current special offers.

 Visa & Mastercard accepted. Open all year.

The Coniston Hotel & Country Estate

Coniston Cold, Skipton, North Yorkshire BD23 4EA

T (01756) 748080 **F** (01756) 749487
E reservations@theconistonhotel.com **W** www.theconistonhotel.com

Nestled in the heart of the Yorkshire Dales, this property is part of the 1400-acre Coniston Estate. It is home to a shooting ground (CPSA Premier Plus standard), falconry centre, Land Rover 4x4 experience and fly fishing on the 24-acre lake or river Aire. Archery, target golf and mountain bike hire is also available. Maps are given to guests setting out on trails across the estate. Hotel facilities include free WiFi, making it an ideal place to meet for a business get-together or for a friends and family party. The Bannister suite caters for up to 150 banqueting guests or 200 conference delegates. The Huntsmans Lodge and Terrace is the perfect place to unwind, with stunning panoramic views of the Yorkshire Dales. Items such as morning coffee, lunch, Yorkshire Tapas and afternoon tea are on the all-day menu. Alternatively guests can enjoy a meal in the popular Macleod's Restaurant. This serves a traditional array of home cooked foods sourced locally or indeed from the estate itself. AA ★★★★ Hotel.

71 ✠ ⅃ ⚇ ☒ ⚘ ⚒ (£10 fee) ⚹ 6x ⚏ 200 **P** ⚘ ⚒ ♪ ☺ ⚹
⚒ ♿ ⚲ ◎ ⚞ (WiFi)

Rates Single room with breakfast from £90; double from £99, superior supplement £25. Luxury room supplement £50.

Meals 3 course tdh dinner £32; alc, lunch & special diets available; last orders 2130; breakfast from 0730.

Leisure Breaks A variety of breaks are available at different times of year.

Other Facilities Falconry centre, hovercraft, Dragon Boat racing, Honda Pilots.

£ Major credit cards accepted. Open all year.

North Yorkshire, Skipton

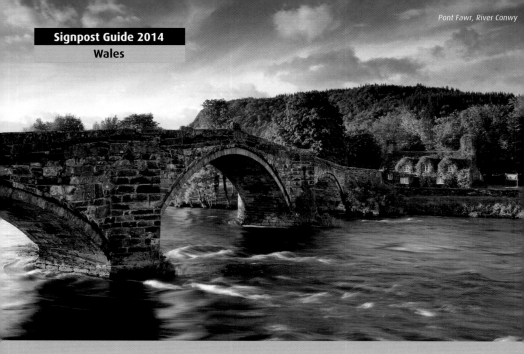
Pont Fawr, River Conwy

Wales

Wales is a land of untouched green countryside, beautiful coastline, lakes and forests, hidden valleys and high mountains. It has three National Parks, five official Areas of Outstanding Natural Beauty and long stretches of protected Heritage Coast, not to mention its own language, traditions and culture. It is also very accessible from London and the Midlands, making it an ideal short break or holiday destination.

Hotels guide

Cardiff
Raglan Castle, Monmouthshire
Barafundle Bay

Further information:
VisitWales
Tel: 08708 300 306
www.visitwales.com

Beaumaris Castle

North Wales has been attracting holiday visitors for over two hundred years - Wordsworth, Samuel Johnson, Turner, Nelson, George Burrows, Bismarck and Wellington to name a few. Nowadays the area still attracts artists, poets, politicians and sailors but the range of accommodation and attractions make North Wales a perfect venue, whatever choice of holiday.

Hotels, restaurants and inns are continually improving their standards and now compare with the best in Britain. Added to this North Wales has the unfair advantage of some of the best scenery in the world, the road from **Dolgellau** to **Taly-Lynn** having heart-stopping views. **Snowdonia** is justly famous for its magnificent mountains, lakes and forests but the **Hiraethog Mountains** in the north east, **The Berwyns** south of Llangollen and the beautiful river valleys of the **Conwy**, **Clwyd**, **Dee** and **Glaslyn** have a magic all of their own. The variety of the scenery is what impresses first time visitors. Within six miles of the resort of **Llandudno** you can find the peace of the **Carneddau**, one hundred square miles of beautiful mountain moorland, dotted with Neolithic tracks, standing stones, Bronze Age sites and beautiful lakes, without a single main road crossing it.

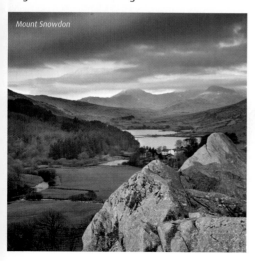
Mount Snowdon

The past surrounds the visitor to North Wales. The history of man can be traced from the Neolithic tombs of 6000 years ago to the Iron Age hill forts that were inhabited when the Roman legions arrived, then through the cells and abbeys of the early Celtic church to the nonconformist chapels of the 19th century so admired by Sir John Betjeman.

The 12th century Welsh castles and 13th century castles of Edward 1st reflect a more turbulent time, but what masterpieces of military architecture they left us - **Conwy**, **Caernarfon**, **Rhuddlan** and **Beaumaris** are breathtaking in their size and splendour, while the Welsh keeps of **Dolwyddelan**, **Dinas Bran** and **Dolbadarn** will appeal to more romantic souls. Medieval towns such as **Conwy** and **Ruthin**, the splendid Elizabethan and Jacobean farmhouses and the tiny cottages show the ordinary side of life in the 16th-18th centuries.

The Industrial Revolution brought changes to North Wales. Slate was the major industry and the slate caverns of **Blaenau Ffestiniog** or **Glyn Ceiriog** and **The National Slate Museum** at **Llanberis** can be explored today. Most of **The Great Little Trains of Wales** were first used to carry slate from the mines to the harbours, the one notable exception being the **Snowdon Mountain Railway**.

As soon as you cross the border into Wales, the scenery changes, the road signs seem unpronounceable and warm hospitable people greet you. The language, music and heritage of Wales add a special dimension. Croeso means Welcome and you will hear it often.

Bala Lake

MID WALES

Mid-Wales is a land of dramatic contrasts in which the pleasures of coast and countryside can be equally enjoyed. It is an area of immense natural beauty. Much of the **Snowdonia National Park** lies in this area.

A relaxing way to see these natural wonders is on horseback. Both the novice and the experienced rider will find fabulous pony trekking country. Alternatively, a ride on one of the **Great Little Trains of Wales** is a must for all steam enthusiasts. The **Cambrian Mountains** are Wales' backbone, an upland region where hamlets and farms nestle in the folds of seemingly endless hills. In this area farming life is centred around a series of strategic small towns, linked by splendid mountain roads or old drovers' ways, such as **Llanidoes**, with its 16th century market hall, standing almost at the centre of Wales at the confluence of the **Severn** and **Clywedog** rivers.

In **Mid Wales** life revolves around the historic market towns and former spa centres, while the coastline is dotted with small fishing villages and popular seaside resorts.

The **western** districts are strongholds of Welsh culture, where the language is in everyday use. Expansive sandy beaches, spectacular estuaries and rugged cliffs lead down to secluded coves. Mid Wales has always had a seafaring tradition. Schooners used to set out from the little ports of

Aberaeron, **Aberdovey**, **Aberystwyth**, **Barmouth** and **New Quay**. Today the harbours are still bustling but with a different type of craft. Some of the most spectacular roads in the British Isles are in this area. Try **Dolgellau** to **Taly-Llyn** or **Trawsfynydd** via **Llyn Celyn Lake** to **Bala**. But beware! New car launches and motorcycle rallies have also discovered their beauty!

To the **east** of Mid Wales are the **Welsh Marches** with their traditional half-timbered black and white buildings. Many centuries ago this area was governed by the Marcher Lords on behalf of the King.

Further back in time, Offa, an 8th century Saxon king, built a massive dyke to keep marauding Welsh forces out of his kingdom. Significant traces of these earthworks remain along the border, forming the basis of **Offa's Dyke Trail**, a long distance walkway of 168 miles north to south. At Knighton a special **Heritage Centre** illustrates the significance of the Dyke.

Dolwyddelan Castle, Snowdonia National Park

The whole of **mid-Wales** has a colourful and exciting history. Apart from the many castles, other popular attractions are the museums reflecting Welsh rural life: woollen weaving, pottery and craft work and these are to be found in displays at **Llandrindod Wells**, **Llanidloes**, **Machynlleth**, **Aberystwth**, **Tre'r Ddol**, **Newtown** and **Welshpool**. At Llandrindod Wells, a display of the Spas of Wales has been opened. There is also the opportunity to take the water here in the original pump room. The annual **Royal Welsh Show** is held nearby.

Pembrokeshire

SOUTH WALES

Starting in the south east, Wales' boundary with England is marked by the **Black Mountains**, north of **Abergavenny**, rising to 2660 feet at **Waun Fach**. **Hay Bluff**, near **Llanthony Priory** affords amazing views westwards. Great castles are the legacy of Llywelyn the Great's resistance to the English, whereas ancient monastic settlements embody the solitude sought by the Augustinian and Cistercian orders. The **Brecon Beacons National Park** includes breathtaking reservoirs, waterfalls and caves.

Further **south**, near **Newport**, is **Caerleon**, which was the site of the Roman fortress of Isca, built AD75. **Tintern Abbey**, in the **Wye** valley, is one of the finest relics of Britain's monastic age. It was founded in the 12th century by Cistercian monks, rebuilt in the 13th and sacked by Henry VIII during the Dissolution of the Monasteries. **Offa's Dyke**, part of an 168-mile rampart built by King Offa of Mercia to keep the Welsh out, and now a noted walk, runs past Tintern's ghostly empty portals.

North west of **Cardiff** is the late 19th century **Castell Coch** (Red Castle), a mixture of Victorian Gothic and fairytale styles. Well preserved is 13th century **Caerphilly Castle**, with its famous leaning tower. Further **west**, outside **Port Talbot**, the visitor comes to

Margam Country Park, 850 acres including an Iron Age hill fort, a restored abbey church with windows by William Morris, **Margam Stones Museum** with stones and crosses dating form the 5th-11th centuries and the main house with its 327ft orangery.

The **Gower Peninsula**, west of **Swansea**, is a secluded world of its own, with limestone cliffs, remote bays and miles of golden sands. It is the Riviera of South Wales. Sites not to miss include 13th century **Weobley Castle**, the ruins of **Threecliff Bay** and **Gower Farm Museum** with its 100-yr old farm memorabilia. Near **Carmarthen** is Dylan Thomas' village of **Laugharne**, in whose churchyard he is buried. Up country are the **Dolaucothi** gold mines, started by the Romans and re-opened from 1870 to 1938, now a museum.

The rugged Pembroke coast is guarded on its western rim by Britain's smallest city - **St David's**, whose cathedral was founded by the eponymous saint in the 8th century and is still used today. Around St David's and indeed all around the county runs the spectacular and excellently maintained **Pembrokeshire Coastal Path. The Pembrokeshire Coast National Park** has moorlands rising gently to the Preseli Hills. Here again Stone Age forts and Norman castles reflect the area's ancient history.

CARDIFF

Cardiff, Wales' capital, is essentially a young city, even though its history dates back many centuries. The development of its docks during the Industrial Revolution for the export of Welsh iron and coal was the basis of its prosperity. **Cardiff Castle** is part Roman fort, part medieval castle and part 19th century mansion. Its Chaucer Room has stained glass windows depicting the Canterbury Tales. Its Summer Smoking Room has a copper, brass and silver inlaid floor. The **National Museum of Wales** houses a wealth of exhibits, from impressionist paintings to examples of Swansea porcelain.

Cardiff Castle

The Cardiff Bay development area is very impressive, with dual carriageway access from the M4 (west). The **Cardiff Millennium Stadium**, one of the finest in Europe, plays host regularly to capacity audiences of 70,000. Cardiff is now firmly established as the decision making capital of Wales, following the opening of the National Assembly in July 1999.

The city has facilities one would normally associate with a city of three times the population. On the cultural side the BBC Welsh Symphony Orchestra has its home there with major conference and concert venues in the **St Davids Hall** and **Motorpoint Arena Cardiff**. It is an important shopping and entertainment centre, the facilities combining the elegance of the old Edwardian arcades with St Davids Shopping Centre and the pedestrianisation of much of the central shopping and commercial area. The city's links with the rest of the UK are enhanced by the M4 and the now double Severn bridge. The A470 goes north via **Merthyr Tydfil** and the beautiful **Taf Fawr Valley** to **Brecon** and beyond and there is an international airport just west of the city.

Millenium Stadium

Aberglasney Gardens

(01558) 668998
www.aberglasney.org
Aberglasney is one of Wales' finest gardens - a renowed plantsman's paradise of more than 10 acres with a unique Elizabethan cloister garden at its heart.

Bodnant Garden

(01492) 650460
www.nationaltrust.org.uk/bodnant-garden
Bodnant Garden is one of the finest gardens in the country not only for its magnificent collections of rhododendrons, camellias and magnolias but also for its idyllic setting above the River Conwy with extensive views of the Snowdonia range.

Caernarvon Castle

Caernarvon Castle

(01286) 677617
www.cadw.wales.gov.uk
The most famous and perhaps the most impressive castle in Wales, built by Edward I.

Cardiff Castle

(029) 2087 8100
www.cardiffcastle.com
2000 years of history has shaped Cardiff Castle into a spectacular and fascinating site at the heart of one of the UK's most vibrant cities.

Dyffryn Gardens

(02920) 593328
www.nationaltrust.org.uk/dyffryngardens
These Grade I listed gardens feature a collection of formal lawns, intimate garden rooms and extensive arboretum and reinstated glasshouse.

Fonmon Castle

(01446) 710206
www.fonmoncastle.com
Fonmon is one of few medieval castles still lived in as a home, since being built c1200. Take the guided tour through the fascinating history of the Castle, its families, architecture and interiors.

Gwydir Castle

(01492) 641687
www.gwydircastle.co.uk
Situated in the beautiful Conwy Valley and is set within a Grade I listed, 10 acre garden. Gwydir is a fine example of a Tudor courtyard house, incorporating re-used medieval material from the dissolved Abbey of Maenan.

The Hall at Abbey Cwm Hir

(01597) 851727
www.abbeycwmhir.com
It is one of Wales' finest examples of Victorian Gothic Revival archiecture, and is surrounded by beautiful and noteable 12 acre gardens.

Tintern Abbey

(01291) 689251
www.cadw.wales.gov.uk
Tintern is the best-preserved abbey in Wales and ranks among Britain's most beautiful historic sites. The great Gothic abbey church stands almost complete to roof level.

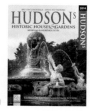

For more suggestions of great historic days out across Britain visit **www.hudsonsheritage.com**

127

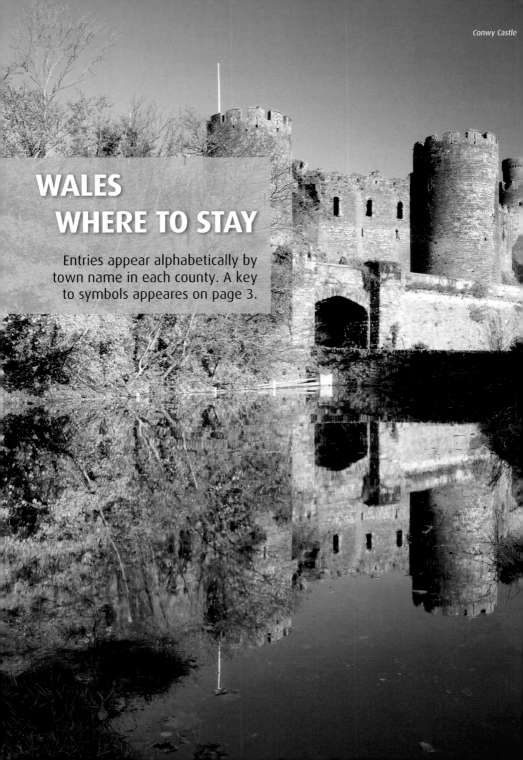

WALES
WHERE TO STAY

Entries appear alphabetically by
town name in each county. A key
to symbols appeares on page 3.

Tre-Ysgawen Hall Country House Hotel & Spa

Capel Coch, Llangefni, Anglesey LL77 7UR

T (01248) 750750 **F** (01248) 750035
E enquiries@treysgawen-hall.co.uk **W** www.treysgawen-hall.co.uk

Reached along a private wooded drive, Tre-Ysgawen is set in 11 acres of landscaped gardens and woodland a short drive inland from the breathtaking east coast of Anglesey. The house has been sympathetically and luxuriously refurbished and extended to become one of the leading country house hotels in North Wales. Bedrooms in the main house are large and high-ceilinged, individually designed and decorated in traditional period style while the rooms in the Courtyard Wing are more modern in design. Tre-Ysgawen Spa, built and equipped to the highest standards, was converted from the Victorian stable block and retains many of the original features including the Clock Tower. Facilities include a 16m level deck pool, steam room, sauna, whirlpool, beauty/therapy suite and air-conditioned gymnasium. New this year is the thermal suite. Tre-Ysgawen is in the middle of the bewitching Isle of Anglesey with its safe, clean beaches, spectacular scenery and challenging golf courses. Tre-Ysgawen Hall provides the perfect environment for a luxury break for both mind and body.

29 (inc 2 suites) 🛏 200 **P** 100

Rates Single room with breakfast from £104; double/twin from £134; 4-poster from £284.
Meals 5 course tdh dinner £35.95; alc, lunch & special diets available; last orders 2130.

Leisure Breaks See our website for latest offers.

Other activities Golf, watersports, sailing, Anglesey Coastal Path nearby.
Awards & accreditations Visit Wales Gold Award.

£ & all major credit cards accepted. Open all year.

Anglesey, Llangefni

Miskin Manor Hotel & Health Club
Miskin, Llantrisant, Nr. Cardiff CF72 8ND
T (01443) 224204 **F** (01443) 237606
E reservations@miskin-manor.co.uk **W** www.miskin-manor.co.uk

Miskin Manor has a long history dating back to the 10th century. It was rebuilt in the 19th century along its present lines. In the war it was a hospital and after that was converted into flats. It became an hotel in 1986 and was bought by the Rosenberg family in 1997. The family and loyal staff have transformed it into one of the leading venues of South Wales, popular equally with business travellers not wishing to be in the city centre, leisure guests touring South Wales, wedding guests and conference planners. It sits in its own 25-acre parkland situated a short distance from Cardiff amongst spectacular gardens. The interior is baronial with moulded ceilings, oak panelling and chandeliers yet the attitude is friendly and inviting. Bedrooms are spacious, many overlooking the gardens, which are triple winners of Wales in Bloom 2011, 2012 and 2013. There are three dining rooms serving award winning cuisine, locally sourced if possible, including Brecon venison and Welsh black beef. The recently expanded Health Club has indoor pool and gymnasium and offers many treatments, therapy and exercise classes.

43 (inc 5)

Rates Single room with breakfast from £110; double from £155. Self-catering lodge, 2 x doubles available, please contact for rates.

Meals AA ◎ ◎ Meisgyn Restaurant alc dinner 3 course ca £35; lunch & special diets available; last orders 2130; breakfast from 0700.

Leisure Breaks See website for latest special offers.
Other Facilities 24 hour reception, massage, WiFi, Golf nearby, App.

Major credit cards accepted. Open all year.

Cardiff, Llantrisant

Holyhead Road, Betws-y-Coed, Conwy County LL24 0AY
T (01690) 710219 **F** (01690) 710603
E royaloakmail@btinternet.com **W** www.royaloakhotel.net

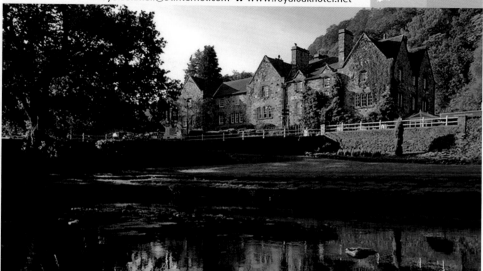

Privately owned and personally run, the Royal Oak Hotel is a picturesque former Victorian coaching inn overlooking the river Llugwy centrally located in the delightful village of Betws-y-Coed. All 27 three-star graded ensuite rooms have modern facilities with free WiFi and LCD televisions with Freeview. Deluxe 4-posters, feature bathrooms and family rooms are also available. Guests have a choice of three dining venues: the stylish AA ® Llugwy River Restaurant, highlighting the best of local Welsh produce, the contemporary vibe of the Grill Bar or the Stables which hosts regular music events and has *alfresco* dining. The Royal Oak is the perfect setting for sophisticated socialising or casual get togethers. Adjoining the hotel is the Stables Lodge, great for walkers, climbers and cyclists. All rooms are on the same floor with lift access. Guests also have use of a drying room and bike storage facilities as well as complimentary use of the Stations Leisure Complex nearby. The Royal Oak is the ultimate base for exploring all of Snowdonia's wonders or enjoying multi activity adventures, or just soaking up the panoramic scenery – its all here!

🛏27 ✂ ☺ ♟ ✈ ⛏ 85 **P** 85 🐾 📶

Rates Single room with breakfast from £80; double from £115.
Meals 4 course tdh dinner from £25; alc, lunch & special diets available; last orders 2045 (2100 weekends); breakfast from 0745.

Leisure Breaks Lazy Weekend Special – 3 nights, including Sunday lunch, from £145 per person.
Other Activities Golf, fishing, indoor pool, gym, riding, watersports nearby.

💷 Major credit cards accepted. Open all year.

Conwy, Betws-y-Coed

The Groes Inn
Tyn-y-Groes, Nr Conwy LL32 8TN
T (01492) 650545 **F** (01492) 650855
E enquiries@groesinn.com **W** www.groesinn.com

There has been an inn in this spot since 1573 when The Groes was on the main coach route between London and Holyhead. The Groes Inn is a true family-run hostelry, whose decor reflects the personality of the hosts: from stone cats lounging in the fireplace to the inn's collection of Victorian hats and shields. There is even a display of saucy Victorian postcards, but no jukeboxes or gaming machines! AA ® cuisine specialises in local delights: local game, Welsh black beef, Conwy crab, mussels and plaice from the sea around Anglesey. Puddings are another delight with a selection of homemade ice creams. There is an extensive wine list and you should try Groes Ale. Bedrooms are smartly and individually decorated; some with balconies. All have magnificent views, either of Snowdonia's foothills or of the Conwy valley. There is a private suite - The Gallery - for meetings. The Groes Inn is the perfect spot for a short break, ideally placed for visiting Conwy Castle, Bodnant Gardens & Snowdonia. Nearby is the self-catering High Cabin – complete hillside seclusion with an outdoor hot tub – and also a luxury cottage, also with a hot tub, '14' in the heart of Conwy town.

🛏 14 (inc 4 suites) ✂ ♿ ⚬🐾 (£20 per stay) 👥 20 🅿 150 🛏

Rates Single room with breakfast from £91; double from £125. High Cabin from £195 per nt. min stay 2 nts.
Meals Alc dinner (ca. £30 3 course), lunch, bar snacks & special diets available; last orders 2100; breakfast from 0730.

Leisure Breaks 2 nights, dinner b&b, two sharing, from £70 pppn.

Awards & accreditations AA ★★★★★ ® Inn, 2008 Good Pub Guide Inn of the Year. Wales Dining Pub of the Year. The Independent 2011 Top 50 Hotels UK Cask Mark.
Other Activities Golf, fishing, water-sports, sailing, shooting, indoor pool, tennis, riding, mountain walking nearby.

💷 Major credit cards accepted. Open all year.

Conwy, Nr. Conwy

St Tudno Hotel
The Promenade, Llandudno, Conwy LL30 2LP
T (01492) 874411 **F** (01492) 860407
E sttudnohotel@btinternet.com **W** www.st-tudno.co.uk

Situated at the far end of Llandudno's fine promenade, opposite the pier, St Tudno is one of Wales' leading hotels and has won many prestigious awards. Owner Martin Bland and his charming and efficient staff make guests feel instantly at home. The Terrace Restaurant has outstanding murals of Lake Como and Italian-style décor. Chef Andrew Foster has built the restaurant's reputation up to being one of the best in Wales, with plaudits from Clarissa Dickson-Wright and Bill Bryson, among others. Excellent bar meals are also available at lunchtime and the number of locals who rendezvous for this is evidence of their popularity. The lounges have a Victorian theme with comfortable chairs and restful colours. Bedrooms are individually decorated, the 'suites' on the front being the most comfortable. Special touches include Villeroy & Boch china, bathrobes and Molton Brown toiletries. Alice Liddell, better known as Lewis Carroll's *Alice in Wonderland,* stayed here in 1861 at the age of eight. St Tudno is ideally situated for visits to Snowdonia, Conwy & Caernarfon Castles, and Bodnant Gardens.

18 (inc 🛏 & 🚪) 🍴 🐱 🥂 ⬆ 🐴 💻 🐕 ♿ 🚲 **WiFi**

Rates Single with breakfast from £80; double from £100. Meals Alc dinner Terrace Restaurant; lunch & spec. diets available; last orders 2130 (Sunday 2100); breakfast from 0730.

Leisure Breaks Winter Special Offers per pers dinner, b&b 2 nights (exc Xmas / Bank Hols) from £140. Weekend Specials and Romantic Getaways – see website.
Other Facilities Sailing, squash, tennis, dry ski-ing ½ mile. Riding 5 miles.

Awards '*A Wine Lover's Paradise*' – Wine Magazine 2009. British Tea Council Award of Excellence. AA ⍟ ⍟ cuisine. Visit Wales Gold Award 2013.

£ All major credit cards accepted. Open all year.

Conwy, Llandudno

Trefeddian Hotel
Aberdovey (Aberdyfi), Gwynedd LL35 0SB
T (01654) 767213 **F** (01654) 767777
E info@trefwales.com **W** www.trefwales.com

The Trefeddian Hotel stands in a commanding position overlooking Cardigan Bay, one mile west of Aberdovey, a village with many attractions and fast becoming a centre for many outdoor activities. The Cave-Browne-Cave family own and run this first class family hotel, celebrating 110 years in 2014. They are constantly making improvements, with a major refurbishment of the swimming pool planned for completion in early 2014, to include a new spa bath. The lounges are spacious, light and peaceful and have also been refurbished. The bedrooms, most with views of Cardigan Bay, are comfortable and elegantly decorated. The five-course dinner menu changes daily and offers a good choice of well presented traditional English-French cuisine, using an abundance of local produce and complemented by a well chosen wine list, with a good range of half bottles. The Trefeddian faces a four-mile stretch of sandy beach and is ideally located for beach strolls, playing golf, walking in the hills or rambling by lakes, rivers and waterfalls. The courtesy and efficiency of the staff create a happy, welcoming atmosphere that sees many guests returning year after year.

🛏 59 (+3 s/c appts) 🦽 ⊞ △ ⏏₁₈ 🔍 ✒ 🔍 ⚋ ⚘ ⚰ 🏔 🍴 🅿 📶

Rates Dinner, bed & breakfast from £73 per person.
Meals 5 course dinner £29.50; childrens' supper; lunch & special diets available; last orders 2100.

Special Breaks Spring, Autumn & Winter Breaks available. Special 5 night rates Sun–Fri. See website for further details.

Other Facilities Riding, cycling, fishing, boat trips nearby.

💷 Mastercard, Visa & debit cards accepted. Open all year except Christmas.

Gwynedd, Aberdovey

Palé Hall

Palé Estate, Llanderfel, Bala, Gwynedd LL23 7PS
T (01678) 530285 **F** (01678) 530220
E enquiries@palehall.co.uk **W** www.palehall.co.uk

135

Palé Hall is a delightful discovery for the discerning visitor – a lovingly restored Victorian country manor set in refreshingly tranquil and beautiful surroundings. Queen Victoria herself warmed to Palé's welcome during her visit in 1889 and her bath and bed are still in use today. The present family owners are proud to maintain the Hall's great tradition of hospitality. The elegance and grandeur of Palé remain unchanged while the amenities have been discreetly enhanced to the highest standards. We are sure Her Majesty would have approved. Each individually appointed bedroom overlooks the grounds and bathrooms have been refurbished. *Palé Jewellers*, based at the hotel, is a small but personal business devoted exclusively to Welsh gold jewellery from Cymru y Metal and Clogau Gold. The

Hall lies in an unspoiled area of lush valleys and gentle hills, making it a paradise for many outdoor activities: fishing, shooting, riding and mountaineering. Lake Bala is the largest natural lake in Wales (4½ miles long) and it is the only habitat of the trout-like *gwyniaid*. A steam railway runs alongside it.

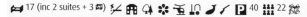

🛏 17 (inc 2 suites + 3 🛏) 🍴 🏨 ⚙ ❀ 🥂 🔟 ♪ ✓ **P** 40 ♨ 22 🐾

Rates Single room with breakfast from £90; double from £125.

Meals Tdh Restaurant; lunch & special diets available; breakfast from 0800.

Other Facilities Golf, fitness centre/gym, riding, watersports, sailing, 4x4 driving nearby.

Accreditations Visit Wales ★★★★ Gold Award Hotel.

£ Most major credit/debit cards accepted. Open all year.

Gwynedd, Bala

Glen-yr-Afon House Hotel
Pontypool Road, Usk, Monmouthshire NP15 1SY
T (01291) 672302 **F** (01291) 672597
E enquiries@glen-yr-afon.co.uk **W** www.glen-yr-afon.co.uk

The award-winning Glen-Yr-Afon House Hotel offers relaxation and a high level of personal service and attention, all in a rural location in the lovely county of Monmouthshire overlooking the banks of the River Usk. Only five minutes' walk from the pleasant market town of Usk, this is a great base from which to explore South Wales, being only 15 minutes from the M50 and 10 minutes from the M4. Glen-Yr-Afon is an imposing and elegant Victorian house retaining many original features, yet sympathetically updated. Many of the guest bathrooms have benefited from recent refurbishment. Privately owned, the business opened its doors in March 1974 and is home to Clarkes restaurant which offers a range of locally sourced menu choices and an extensive wine list. Business people and wedding parties are well catered for with a function suite seating 140 whilst the charming Library is an intimate room suitable for anniversaries, dinner parties and smaller functions for up to 20 people. Glen-Yr-Afon's sister Hotel, The Three Salmons Hotel, a traditional coaching inn is just a 5 minute stroll into the town.

🛏 27 (+ 🏠) ⚒ ♿ 🐴 (£10 per stay) 👥 140 🐾 📶

Rates Single room with breakfast from £99; double from £136.
Meals Alc restaurant; special diets available; last orders 2145.

Leisure Breaks Any two-night break, dinner, b&b for two sharing from £150 per person.
Other Facilities Complimentary broadband hotspot. Croquet, golf, fishing, tennis, gliding, country walks nearby.

💷 All major cards accepted. Open all year.

Monmouthshire, Usk

Wolfscastle Country Hotel

Wolfscastle, Haverfordwest, Pembrokeshire SA62 5LZ

T (01437) 741225 **F** (01437) 741383
E info@wolfscastle.com **W** www.wolfscastle.com

137

Wolfscastle is a friendly country house hotel and restaurant, formerly a vicarage, situated between Haverfordwest and Fishguard, just off the A40. It is still known locally by its original name *Allt Yr Afon* ('Wooded Hill by the River'). It is excellently located for exploring the Pembrokeshire Coast and National Park, the Preseli Hills and St David's – Britain's smallest cathedral city. Tregwynt Woollen Mill and a number of craft and pottery workshops are also nearby. The 20 bedrooms, which have all been newly refurbished and fitted with 32" flat screen TVs, are either in the old vicarage part of the house or in the more modern rear part of the building. New for 2013 was a stylish extension to the front of the building with a cosy residents' lounge and brasserie style dining area. Wolfscastle's location and hospitality make it popular for conferences and weddings. It has been under the same ownership for over 35 years, and has gained a well deserved reputation for good food and friendly relaxed service, which will guarantee a memorable stay here.

🛏 12 ✗ 🐾 (£5 fee) ❀ 🚶 **P** ♨ 150 🎫 📶

Rates Single room with breakfast from £82; double from £118.
Meals Alc ⊚ restaurant; lunch & special diets available; last orders 2100; breakfast from 0700.

Leisure Breaks Two days, dinner, b&b from £154 per person.
Other Facilities Digital freeview TV.

💳 Major credit cards (exc Diners) accepted. Closed 24–26 December.

Pembrokeshire, Haverfordwest

Warpool Court Hotel
St David's, Pembrokeshire SA62 6BN
T (01437) 720300
E info@warpoolcourthotel.com **W** www.warpoolcourthotel.com

The Warpool Court is in a wonderful position overlooking the wild Atlantic and within a few minutes' walk of the famous St. David's Cathedral. It is owned by Peter Trier, whose charming daughter Marianne helps the very professional and 'hands-on' manager Rupert Duffin. You can be assured of good food, gracious living and a warm welcome. Bedrooms are divided into Grades A to F, the best *Premier* rooms having recently opened on the second floor. The walls of the Ramsey Room are decorated with nursery tiles and, lying in the bath of the Skomer Room, you can look out onto Skomer Island. Mark Napper's Garden Room Restaurant has a high reputation for good food, backed by a fine selection of well chosen wines. He has many years' experience of tempting hotel guests and local diners, who come from a wide radius, to celebrate 'that special occasion' here. The lounge bar, with its array of antique tiles, provides a relaxed atmosphere for that pre-dinner drink. There are numerous outdoor activities nearby and you can access the Pembrokeshire Coastal Path at one of its most dramatic stretches directly from the hotel's gardens.

🛏22 ✂ 🐕 🐈 (£10 p.n) ⊙ 🍳 🎣 ⚲ 🏃

Rates Single room with breakfast single from £110; twin/double from £130.
Meals tdh dinner 2 course £28 or 3 course £35.00 Sun – Sat; lunch & special diets available; last orders 2115.

Special Breaks Please visit our website.
Other Facilities 9-hole golf course, watersports, boat trips, riding nearby.

💳 All major cards accepted. Open 1 April – 1 November.

Pembrokeshire, St David's

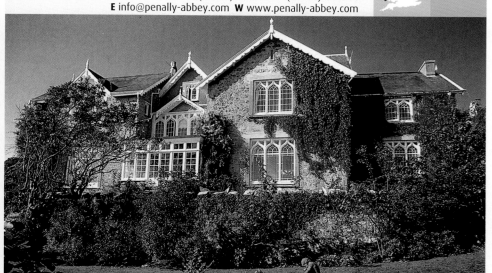

Penally Abbey is a fine country house rich in character and old world charm, a favourite with many celebrities. Standing in five acres of gardens and woodlands with magnificent views over Caldey Island and Carmarthen Bay, it exudes an air of peace and tranquillity that belies its monastic past. The hotel stands on the site of a 6th century abbey and there is a ruined medieval chapel and a wishing well in the garden. Larger and more individual bedrooms in the main Abbey House are individually and originally furnished with antiques, many having four posters. The Coach House is an adjoining converted stable block resembling four stone cottages. Each has its own front door and is furnished in a cottage style. Dining is a romantic candle-lit affair, making use of the best seasonal local produce. There is a lot to see and do in this corner of Wales. Tenby has a sheltered harbour, Georgian and Regency houses, medieval castle ruins, town walls and a 13th century church. Tenby golf course is almost opposite the hotel and the Pembrokeshire Coastal Path passes nearby.

🛏12 🎿 🍴 🎯 ✿

Rates Single room with breakfast from £110; dinner b&b from £135. Double/twin b&b from £148; dinner, b&b from £198.
Meals 3 course tdh dinner for non-residents £36/2 course £29.50. Special diets available; last orders 2045.

Leisure Breaks See website for Welsh Winter Welcome Breaks with roaring log fires.
Other Facilities Golf, sea bathing, riding, shooting, fishing nearby. Exploring the National Park.
£ All major cards accepted. Open all year.

Pembrokeshire, Tenby

Scotland

Scotland is a proud nation that has much to be proud about....famous inventors, writers, politicians, beautiful countryside that is a playground for the sportsman. Golf, sailing, fishing, shooting, stalking are all available in abundance. Golf was invented at St Andrews four centuries ago. With a range of flights now available from the south, all this is easily within range for a weekend or short break.

Hotels guide

Further information:
VisitScotland
Tel: 0845 2255 121
www.visitscotland.com

Castle Stalker

Glasgow

Kintyre, Strathclyde

GLASGOW

Glasgow, Scotland's 'Second Capital' and largest city is one of the liveliest and most cosmopolitan destinations in Europe. It has been reborn as a centre of style and vitality, set against a backdrop of outstanding Victorian architecture. It was European City of Culture 1990 and UK City of Architecture and Design in 1999.

Glasgow boasts world famous art collections, some of the best shopping in the UK and the most vibrant nightlife in Scotland. A 'must see' is the Art Nouveau splendour of Scotland's best known architect **Charles Rennie Mackintosh**, whose inimitable style adorns attractions such as **The Lighthouse**, **Glasgow School of Art**, **House for an Art Lover** and the **Hunterian Museum & Art Gallery**. **Kelvingrave Art Gallery and Museum** displays a unique collection of European art and a famous array of European arms and armour.

Gallery of Modern Art

Art and Culture are important in Glasgow life with its many galleries and museums - most with free admission. The choice of over 20 includes the world's first **Saint Mungo Museum of Religious Life and Art**, the renowned **Burrell Collection** and the contemporary **Gallery of Modern Art**. **Glasgow Cathedral** is built near the church site said to have been constructed in the 6th century by the city's founder, St Mungo. The **The Riverside Museum** has a showroom of Scottish-built cars and the Clyde Room of ship models. **The Peoples' Palace**, in Glasgow's East End, is a social history museum covering the city's history since 1175. It has a purse and ring which once belonged to Mary, Queen of Scots.

Glasgow's revitalised riverside offers numerous options for leisure and entertainment, including the city's newest attraction, the £75m **Glasgow Science Centre**. This exciting development is an attractive titanium-clad complex which includes an IMAX cinema and a science mall.

The Burrell Collection

River Clyde

EDINBURGH

Edinburgh is the jewel in Scotland's crown. The jewel has many facets: fortified hilltop architecture, sweeping Georgian crescents, tree-filled valleys, medieval cobbled crescents, graceful bridges soaring across chasms and green parks.

Its centrepiece is **The Castle** which dominates the city from its volcanic rock. It was the traditional home of Scottish kings and queens and now the Scottish Crown Jewels are kept in the **Old Royal Palace** where Mary, Queen of Scots gave birth to the future James VI of Scotland, James I of England. At the other end of **Royal Mile** is **Holyroodhouse**, Her Majesty the Queen's official residence when in Edinburgh. Mary, Queen of Scots, lived here from 1561-1567 and today the picture gallery has portraits of 89 Scottish kings. Also in the **Old Town** is **John Knox House**, former home of Scotland's religious reformer and **St Giles Cathedral**, the high kirk of Edinburgh, with its famous Crown Spire, dating from the 15th century.

Holyrood Palace

Edinburgh Festival

Edinburgh Castle

The 18th century **New Town**, north of Princes Street, is the largest single area of Georgian architecture in Europe, officially recognised by the EU. Numerous architects in the 18th & 19th century endowed the city with a wealth of meritorious buildings, both private and public. **Georgian House**, in Charlotte Square, has rooms furnished as they might have been in the city's Golden Age, 1796. Nearby the **West Register House** has a fascinating collection of documents from Scotland's past.

Today the highlight of Edinburgh's cultural year is the **Festival** in August, which is the largest pan-arts festival in the world. As well as the official festival, there are over 500 'fringe events' where many of today's leading actors, comedians and writers have cut their teeth, and also a film and literary festival. The **Scottish Parliament**, opened in the new **Holyrood House** in 2004 after years of delay.

Girvan, South Ayrshire

THE LOWLANDS

Rich, rolling farmland, rugged sea coasts and Clyde coast islands characterise the **south of Scotland**. It is a land of ancient abbeys, castles and historic houses and also boasts strong literary connections, with both **Robert Burns** and **Sir Walter Scott** having lived here. Robert Burns lived around Dumfries where his house and favourite drinking haunt, **The Globe Inn**, still stand and Scott in the **Lammermuirs** of **East Lothian**, where sheep now graze and skylarks soar where bitter battles once raged.

The **Tweed** meanders from the coast along the border to rise in the **Pentland Hills**, whereas the coast of **East Lothian** is dotted with castle remains, golf courses and looks out to the bird sanctuary of the **Bass Rock**. **Stranraer** is the gateway to Northern Ireland and the A75 streaks through Dumfries & Galloway bearing freight to its port.

The real Scotland starts right at the border. Different accents in the shops, different beer names in the pubs and different money notes are just three of the ways in which Scotland stamps its personality straight away. Even the scenery changes and the hazy blue peaks of the **Cheviot** and **Elidon Hills** have lifted the hearts of many a traveller crossing Carter Bar on the A68. Crossing from Carlisle towards Edinburgh the traveller passes Bruce's Cave and there are numerous castle remains where he fought the English. The A7 scenic route passes through the gentle hills of **Eskdale** and the **Moorfoots**.

Then there are the forests and wild moors of upland **Galloway** and the vivid greens of **Ayrshire**'s rich pastures, with the steep mountainous profile of **Arran** as a backdrop. Wherever you travel here, you can be sure of a real Scottish welcome.

143

CENTRAL SCOTLAND

Argyll, the **Isles**, **Loch Lomond**, **Stirling** & the **Trossachs** form the birthplace of Scotland and are the cradle of its Christianity and nationhood as well as the focal point of much of its dramatic history. Here you can savour the atmosphere of the **Hebridean Islands**, the charm of rural villages, and trace the footsteps of heroes like St Columba, Sir William Wallace, Robert the Bruce, Mary, Queen of Scots and Rob Roy.

These are lands where you can glimpse an eagle, an osprey, a wildcat, a fine antlered stag, or even whales and dolphins. And if the fancy takes you, you can enjoy the spectacle of **Highland Games**, the warmth of a traditional Celtic folk night or the flavour of a local food festival.

Skye, in the **west** is a magical island of mountains (**The Cuillins**), deep lochs and Iron Age forts. It is now linked to the mainland by a (free-of-charge) road bridge. The islands have a harsh history, with Norse invasions, fierce clan feuds and the Highland Clearances that followed Culloden. **Argyll and Bute**, warmed by the Gulf Stream, have many spectacular gardens whereas **Stirling** and the **Trossachs** are Scotland's first **National Park**, encompassing 720 square miles of superb walking country. **Rob Roy's** grave can be seen at **Balquhidder** on **Loch Voil** and **Inchmahone Priory**, **Port of Menteith** was once the childhood home of Mary, Queen of Scots. Stirling was the site of Wallace's famous victory over the English in 1297.

From the heather moorland around **Loch Rannoch** in **West Perthshire** and the **Pitlochry Drama festival** to the well manicured golf courses of **St Andrews** in Fife, where golf was invented 400 years ago, there is always plenty to do and see in this Central Scottish belt.

Highland Games

Trossachs National Park

Buachaille Etive Mor

The **north east** of Scotland likewise is blessed with outstanding scenery. The majestic **Grampian** mountains dominate the skyline to the **west** whilst **Aberdeen**, Scotland's third largest city, has a vibrant, prosperous air.

The Malt Whisky Trail from, **Aviemore**, through **Speyside** to **Huntly**, takes in seven major distilleries and cooperage, all open to the public. There is also the **Castle Trail** on **Royal Deeside** which takes in 11 of the finest gems the region has to offer, including **Balmoral**. On the **coast** are empty beaches, interspersed with picturesque fishing villages and dramatic clifftop scenery waiting to be explored. The ski slopes of **Glenshee** and **Aviemore** are readily accessible, championship golf courses are there to be played.

THE HIGHLANDS

Sutherland and the far **north** of Scotland have some of the most unspoiled terrain in Europe. They have much to offer - spectacular mountains, majestic glens and mirror-like lochs form the backdrop to picturesque towns, isolated crofts, towering castles and pagoda-topped distilleries. A startling variety of wildlife also makes its home in the sea lochs and glens where an unbroken thread of human history reaches back into the mists of time. There are ruined brochs of the Iron Age people and carved stones left by Dark Age picts. Nowhere else in the British Isles are you able to drive for 30 miles without seeing a habitation or another car, but beware, the single track (with passing places) roads of the north west are unsuitable for trailers or caravans.

This is some of Britain's best walking and climbing country; also the land of the **Helmsdale**, arguably Britain's best salmon river. History, legend and romance and the great outdoors combine seamlessly here to guarantee visitors a warm Highland welcome and a truly memorable holiday.

Balmoral Castle

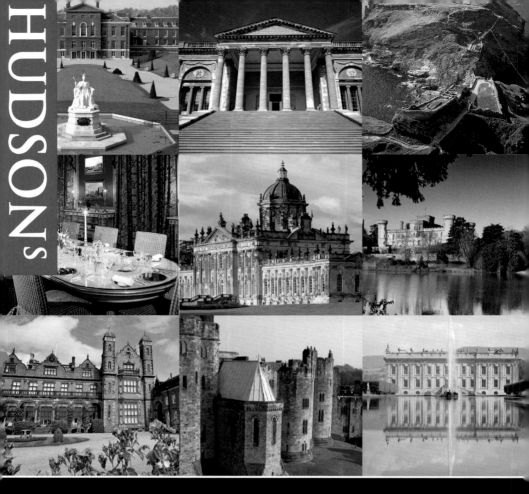
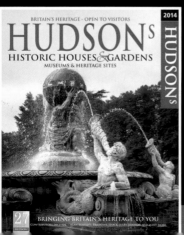

HUDSON'S HISTORIC HOUSES & GARDENS HIGHLIGHTS

Cawdor Castle
(01667) 404401
www.cawdorcastle.com
A must see romantic fairy-tale Castle of historical beauty and one of the most outstanding Stately Homes in Scotland.

Dalmeny House
(0131 331) 1888
www.dalmeny.co.uk
A family home which contains Scotland's finest French treasurers. Dine in splendor, and enjoy sea-views over superb parkland.

Dumfries House

Dumfries House
(01290) 425959
www.dumfries-house.org.uk
A Georgian Gem, nesting within 2,000 acres of scenic Ayrshire countryside in south west Scotland.

Dunvegan Castle & Gardens
(01470) 521206
www.dunvegancastle.com
Experience living history at Dunvegan Castle, the ancestral home of the Chiefs of Clan MacLeod for 800 years.

Hopetoun House
(0131) 331 2451
www.hopetoun.co.uk
Hopetoun House is a unique gem of Europe's architectural heritage and undoubtedly 'Scotland's Finest Stately Home'.

Inveraray Castle & Garden
(01499) 302203
www.inveraray-castle.com
Inveraray Castle & Garden - Home to the Duke & Duchess of Argyll and ancestral home of the Clan Campbell.

Manderston
(01361) 883450
www.manderston.co.uk
Manderston, together with its magnificent stables, stunning marble dairy and 56 acres of immaculate gardens, forms quite a unique emsemble.

Mount Stuart
(01700) 503877
www.mountstuart.com
One of the World's finest houses - Mount Stuart, ancestral home of the Marquess of Bute, is a stupendous example of Victorian Gothic architecture set amidst 300 acres of gloriously landscaped gardens.

Scone Palace & Grounds
(01738) 552300
www.scone-palace.co.uk
Scone Palace is home to the Earls of Mansfield and is built on the site of an ancient abbey.

Stirling Castle
(01786) 450000
www.stirlingcastle.gov.uk
Experience the newly refurbished Royal palace where you can explore the richly decorated King's and Queen's apartments. Take the guided tour where you can hear tales of the castle's history.

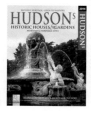

HUDSON's
HISTORIC HOUSES & GARDENS
MUSEUMS & HERITAGE SITES

For more suggestions of great historic days out across Britain visit
www.hudsonsheritage.com

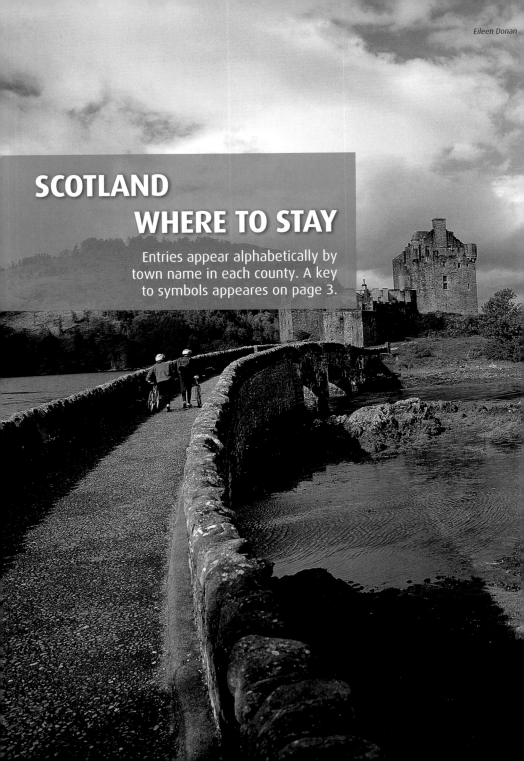

Eileen Donan

SCOTLAND
WHERE TO STAY

Entries appear alphabetically by
town name in each county. A key
to symbols appeares on page 3.

Loch Melfort Hotel
Arduaine, by Oban, Argyll PA34 4XG
T (01852) 200233 **F** (01852) 2002145
E reception@lochmelfort.co.uk **W** www.lochmelfort.co.uk

149

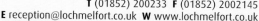

Loch Melfort Hotel is a unique retreat set in 17 acres of the romantic Gulf Stream-warmed coast of Argyll. Recently bought by Calum and Rachel Ross who have already made quite an impression! Public rooms have been upgraded and are ideal venues for tea with homemade shortbread, a wee dram or just a relax gazing out to sea. Five of the bedrooms in the Canadian Lodge style annexe have been designated Superior with extra touches of luxury to make your stay special. Ten of the annexe bedrooms are on the ground floor. The five bedrooms in the former Campbell family home, which is the main building, have King-size beds, two being designated Junior Suite and Master Bedroom. All 25 bedrooms have stunning views out over Asknish Bay towards the islands of Jura, Shuna and Scarba. There is much to do in this coastal area of exceptional natural beauty. The NTS Arduaine Garden is next door, boat trips can be arranged to the Corryvreckan whirlpools, horse riding is available and walks and further. Argyll garden visits recommended. Dining in the AA ◉ ◉ Asknish Bay Restaurant is another experience to savour. Choose from freshly caught langoustine, lobster and crab, Islay scallops, select meat and game from nearby Barbreck Farm and fresh vegetables and herbs, all sourced locally. A less formal option is available in the Chartroom II Bistro, with has high chairs and a childrens' menu available. Staying here is an unforgettable experience.

🏇 25 🅿 📻 🎠 🛶 🏌 ⚓ £8.50 p.n 🐓 🍴 ❀ ⚔ / 🚶 ⛺ 14 🐾 (WiFi)

Rates Single room with breakfast from £104; double with breakfast from £144.
Meals 3 course tdh dinner £38; alc available; lunch available; special diets available; last orders 2100; breakfast from 0745.

Leisure Breaks 2 nights dinner b&b from £90 pppn; 3 nights dinner b&b from £83 pppn; 4 gourmet nights per year.

Other Facilities Riding, sailing & watersports nearby - 3 miles.

💷 All major credit & debit cards accepted except American Express.
Hotel open 1 February - 30 November & Christmas bookings.

Argyll & Bute, Oban

Craigadam House
Crocketford, Kirkpatrick Durham, Castle Douglas DG7 3HU
T (01556) 650233 **F** (01556) 650100
E inquiry@craigadam.com **W** www.craigadam.com

Craigadam is a small country house in the midst of a 25,000 acre sporting estate. It is an imaginative conversion of 18th century farm buildings which open onto a delightful courtyard. Each bedroom suite has its own front door and theme. Whether it be Victorian, Indian, Chinese or Traditional Scottish, each is charming with sitting area and large bathroom. Craigadam is also the family home of Celia and Richard and is filled with antiques, family pictures and fresh flowers from the pretty garden. Guests are treated like old friends, with communal dining around a large oak table. There is a snooker room and open fires burn throughout. The hosts provide a country house atmosphere with many guests taking advantage of the fishing, shooting and stalking available. Outdoor enthusiasts can also go hiking, rambling, birdwatching or can play golf locally. Celia is known for her delicious cooking and generous portions. Meat and fish come from the estate – game in season and lamb and beef from the hill. There is even a shop to stock up with goodies to take home as a souvenir of a memorable stay. Craigadam also has a self catering cottage for six available to rent.

Rates Single room with breakfast from £62; double from £94.
Meals 3 course tdh dinner £28.50; special diets available; last orders 1900.

Other Facilities Sailing, golf, riding, tennis, watersports nearby.

Major credit cards exc. Amex accepted. Open all year exc. Christmas.

Dumfries & Galloway, Castle Douglas

Blackaddie Country House Hotel

Blackaddie Rd, Sanquhar, Dumfriesshire DG4 6JJ

T (01659) 50270; **F** (01659) 495935
E ian@blackaddiehotel.co.uk **W** www.blackaddiehotel.co.uk

A superb small hotel set in its own gardens on the banks of the river Nith, one of Scotland's great yet little known salmon rivers and with extensive views across Scotland's Southern Upland Way. Blackaddie has recently been awarded 3 GOLD Stars from VisitScotland. Seven beautiful bedrooms and suites, many of which overlook the gardens or the river some with stunning bathrooms. There are also two self-contained cottages in the grounds, each with fully fitted kitchen, for those who wish to be independent. But who would when the hotel boasts food to rival the best anywhere? It is far and away above what one would expect in a small tucked away country house hotel. Chef/Proprietor Ian McAndrew has held a Michelin star for many years in previous restaurants and his menus use fresh local produce with all dishes prepared on the premises. There's a lot to see and do in this unspoiled corner of south west Scotland with extensive biking, walking, fishing and riding in the area. There are also historic houses such as Dumfries House and Drumlanrig Castle within a short drive with Caerlaverock and Threave castles nearby. Glasgow 45 miles and Edinburgh 70 miles.

🛏 7 (1 🐾 only) ✂ ❄ 🐕 🦃 🦆 🎣 🏇 🅿 ▦ 25 📶

Rates Single room with breakfast from £80; double from £110; suite from £180.
Meals Alc dinner, gourmet menu; lunch & spec. diets avail. Last orders 2100. Bfst from 0730.
Leisure Breaks 2 nights dinner, b&b from £85.00 ppers per nt; 3 nights from £78.00 pppn; 4+ nights from £70.00 pppn. Gourmet menu & breaks available.
Other Facilities Flat screen TVs + Freeview+DVD players. Golf, swimming, fishing nearby.
Awards and accreditations VisitScotland Silver Award for Food from Eat Scotland. Gold Plate – Hotel Review Scotland, ★★★★★ Exceptional Food Review, Winner – Scottish Hotels Award 2009/11/12.
£ Visa, Mastercard, Switch, Amex, Maestro accepted. Open all year.

Dumfries & Galloway, Sanquhar

Flodigarry Country House Hotel
Flodigarry, Staffin, Isle of Skye IV51 9HZ
T (01470) 552203 **F** (01470) 552301
E info@flodigarry.co.uk **W** www.flodigarry.co.uk

The Dutch have always loved The Highlands and Paul and Bette Hemming fulfilled their dream by acquiring Flodigarry in 2013. Flodigarry is a sheltered haven amidst the dramatic scenery of northern Skye, magnificently situated with panoramic views across the sea to the Torridon mountains. The surrounding cliff and mountain scenery is amongst the finest in the British Isles, with the famous towering pinnacles of the Quiraing providing a remarkable skyline inland. Lying immediately to the south is the broad sweep of Staffin Bay, one of the most beautiful on the island. Capture the breathtaking views, Jurassic scenery and fresh air. Walk the coast and see sharks, whales, seals, otters and puffins. There are 11 bedrooms in the main house and a further seven in Flora Macdonald's Cottage in the grounds. These are cosy with low ceilings, ground floor rooms having direct garden access. Flora lived here after she assisted Bonnie Prince Charlie 'over the sea to Skye' and ultimately to France. Sample in both restaurants some of Skye's finest seafood and locally caught fish, not forgetting Highland Lamb and famous Scottish Beef. Capture the magic of Flodigarry.

🦴 18 ✂ 🐕 £20 🚶 ⛳ 🔍 ♨ 30 🅿 40 📶

Rates Single room with breakfast from £80; double from £110.
Meals Broad alc menu; bar, bistro, lunch & special diets available.

Leisure Breaks Special Breaks available: Autumn Gold, Winter Magic, Great Winter Escapes, Spring Breaks etc. See website.
Other Facilities Boat trips, sea fishing, loch fishing.

💷 Visa & Mastercard accepted. Open all year.

Highland, Isle of Skye

Viewfield House
Portree, Isle of Skye, Highland IV51 9EU
T (01478) 612217 **F** (01478) 613517
E info@viewfieldhouse.com **W** www.viewfieldhouse.com

153

Viewfield House offers a unique opportunity to stay in style and comfort in what has been the home of the Macdonald family for over 200 years. The house stands in extensive wooded grounds on the outskirts of Portree, overlooking Portree Bay and within easy walking distance of the centre. Guests eat in Victorian splendour beneath family portraits or mementoes from India. The ten bedrooms, each with individual temperature control, are tastefully decorated, each in their own style, with several overlooking the bay. There is plenty to do on Skye: boat trips to Rona, Raasay or round the harbour, fishing, sailing, walking in the Cuillin Hills, pony trekking and golf. Or you could visit the otter haven at Kylerhea or take a scenic drive around the coast admiring the striking scenery and visiting Dunvegan Castle, home to the MacLeod Clan. When you return exhausted after your excursion, sit down in peace and quiet in the spacious drawing room with a cup of tea or a wee dram by the open fire. Three course dinners are available along with rates for Dinner, Bed & Breakfast. Hugh may also recommend other local seafood restaurants.

🛏 10 ✂ ♿ ❄ 🐦 🔊 🏃 ✒ 🐕 **P** 📶

Rates Single room with breakfast from £65; double from £120.
Meals Dinner, 3 course ca. £25 available at 1930.

Other Facilities Fishing 2 miles, golf 9 miles, riding 3 miles. Sailing, squash, shooting, indoor pool within 1 mile.

Leisure Breaks 3 days b&b gets 5% discount; 5 days b&b gets 10% disc + free bottle of house wine.

💳 Visa & Mastercard accepted. Open April–October.

Highland, Isle of Skye

Eddrachilles Hotel
Badcall Bay, Scourie, Sutherland IV27 4TH
T (01971) 502080 **F** (01971) 502477
E enq@eddrachilles.com **W** www.eddrachilles.com

Presbyterian ministers had a knack of choosing perfect sites for their Manses and Eddrachilles is no exception. Sheltered by gentle hills and with stunning views, this is a place to escape to. The owners are enthusiastic about their home and enjoy sharing it with their guests. Everything is home produced with a selection of home smoked produce and homemade charcuterie. The menu changes daily with a wine list of over 70 bins and over 140 malt whiskies. The seafood is outstanding and the beef, venison and lamb from Highland farms unsurpassed. The Restaurant is now located in the conservatory with outstanding views over the islands. The north of Scotland is unique. Its remote and untouched beauty can be best explored on quiet single-track roads, or by one of numerous scenic walks and climbs over beach, cliff and hill, many starting directly from the hotel. Handa Island, the famous bird sanctuary, can easily be visited by boat from nearby Tarbet. There is no restriction on the number of brown trout which may be caught on nearby hill lochs.

Rates Single with breakfast from £80; single dinner, b&b from £99. Double b&b from £110; dinner, b&b from £148 per room.
Meals Last orders for dinner 2000; bar lunches & special diets available.

Leisure Breaks Reduced rates for stays of 3, 6 or 10 days.
Other Facilities Children welcome.

Amex, Switch, Visa & Mastercard accepted. Open April 1 – October 1.

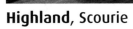

Highland, Scourie

Channings is a four-star townhouse hotel, about one mile from Princes Street and the city's main shopping area but in a quiet residential area. It has the feel of a Scottish country home. The polar explorer Sir Ernest Shackleton lived at No 14, now part of the hotel, from 1904 to 1910, and the top floor de luxe rooms are called the Shackleton Suites, named after the explorer and his doughty fellow adventurers. Elsewhere are many prints from the expeditions, together with a copy of a journey planner. Accommodation is a mix of 41 antique and contemporarily furnished rooms, each one different and with every modern convenience. The AA ® Channings Restaurant is a delightful neighbourhood bistro with a relaxed atmosphere. Reasonably priced seasonal menus are available Tuesday-Saturday, remember to leave room for a caramelised British plum crème brulee or a dark chocolate financier with Madagascan ice cream. Channings makes an excellent base for Edinburgh visitors who are happy to be away from the centre. Friendly staff will help with parking and with local information. Channings is a sister hotel of The Howard, at the northern end of the New Town.

Rates Single room from £62; double from £94.
Meals Available 6pm until 9.45pm 2 courses £18.50, 3 courses £25.50, lunch available at the Bar from 1200 till 2145.

Leisure Breaks Please see website for special offers.
Other Facilities Golf, the botanic gardens, modern galleries.

Major credit cards accepted. Open all year.

Midlothian, Edinburgh

156

The Howard
34-36 Great King Street, Edinburgh, Midlothian EH3 6QH
T (0131) 557 3500
E reception@thehoward.com **W** www.thehoward.com

The Howard is an intimate and discreet luxury 5-star hotel occupying three Georgian townhouses in the heart of Edinburgh city centre. A key feature of the service at the Howard is the team of butlers, who take care of everything from car parking to serving you one of their famous afternoon teas. Each of the 18 luxuriously individually furnished bedrooms bears the name of an Edinburgh street. Style is traditional elegance with rich fabrics, plush carpets and fine reproduction furniture. Bathrooms come with fluffy towels, luxurious bathrobes and roll top baths. The Atholl Restaurant started life as a private dining room for The Howard residents and quickly evolved into a much sought-after restaurant in Edinburgh. Award winning chef William Poncelet's dinner might start with Mallaig scallops or braised pork belly, followed by slow cooked Pentland lamb shank with spiced couscous as a main course, and rounded off with a raspberry crème brulee with walnut shortbread. The Howard is the ideal base for visiting the city, being tucked away in a quiet Georgian terrace in the New Town, yet only a 10-minute walk from Princes Street.

🛏 18 🛌 2 🅿 ✂ 🖥 📶 ⬆ ↕ ⚑ 🛋 🐾 📶

Rates Single room from £135; double from £185.
Meals 3 course dinner from £35, special diets and lunch available, last orders 2200, breakfast from 0700.

Other Facilities Golf, drawing school

💷 Major credit cards accepted. Open all year.

Midlothian, Edinburgh

Roman Camp Country House Hotel & Restaurant

Callander, Perthshire FK17 9BG

T (01877) 330003 **F** (01877) 331533
E mail@romancamphotel.co.uk **W** www.romancamphotel.co.uk

The Roman Camp Hotel stands in 20 acres of gardens on the bank of the river Teith. The house dates from 1625 and was originally a hunting lodge for the Dukes of Perth. It was converted to an hotel in 1939 by the Brown family, who are still the hosts today. Public rooms are exceptionally comfortable, with deep sofas and armchairs, roaring fires in winter and fresh flowers in summer. The heart of the house is the library with its rich oak panelling and adjoining secret chapel. The AA ⊛ ⊛ ⊛ Restaurant is an inspiring oval room of elegant proportions, with soft modern classical décor. Cuisine is modern Scottish, making best use of freshest local produce. A number of smaller private dining rooms are suitable for special occasions or private parties. Each bedroom, several on the ground floor, is individually furnished with rich fabrics and antiques. Sumptuous marble jacuzzi bathrooms have underfloor heating. Weddings and small conferences can also be catered for. Callander is in the Loch Lomond and Trossachs National Park, Rob Roy country, yet convenient for Stirling and just over one hour from both Glasgow and Edinburgh.

🛏 15 (inc 1 ♿) ⊙ 🖾 🅿 ➡ 🐾 ⊞ 120 🕴 🕼 🐴 🌸 🎵 🐾 📶

Rates Single room with breakfast from £100; double from £155.

Meals 4 course tdh dinner £50. Alc, lunch & special diets available. Last orders 2100; breakfast from 0745.

Leisure Breaks Low season midweek breaks – 2 nights dinner, b&b from £396 per room.

Other Facilities Golf, sailing, watersports nearby.

💷 Amex, Visa, Diners & Mastercard accepted. Open all year.

Perth & Kinross, Callander

The Four Seasons Hotel
St Fillans, Perthshire PH6 2NF
T (01764) 685333 **F** (01764) 685444
E info@thefourseasonshotel.co.uk **W** www.thefourseasonshotel.co.uk

The Four Seasons sits in glorious countryside on the banks of Loch Earn. The hotel faces south west, down to the loch; the view changing with the seasons: fresh, new colours in Spring; long, light summer evenings with spectacular sunsets, morning mists in Autumn and snow covered Monros in Winter. Originally built in the early 19th century for the manager of the lime kilns, the main house then became the schoolmaster's house. Converted in the 1990s, it has been extended over the years into the comfortable hotel it now is, with recently refurbished sitting rooms, 12 bedrooms and, in the grounds, six chalets, ideal for families, and a holiday apartment. Upstairs there is a small, comfy library, with books for every taste, and a collection of CDs. The hotel has its own jetty and there is a 9-hole golf course in the village. The cuisine has been awarded AA ❀ ❀, dining being either in the *Meall Reamhar* (High Hills) Restaurant, or in the less formal *Tarken* room. The Four Seasons provides a wonderful base from which to explore Perthshire and the Heart of Scotland.

🛏 18 ⚘ 🍴 🎣 ⚡ ⛵ 🚣 👤 🏊 🐕 ⛤ **P** 50 🎿

Rates Single room with breakfast from £54; double from £108.
Meals 3 course tdh dinner; alc, lunch & special diets available; last orders 2100; breakfast from 0830.

Leisure Breaks Four for three, three for two, romantic, wine tasting, walking, art, Christmas and Hogmanay breaks available.
Other Facilities Golf & riding nearby.

Open March–December; weekends only March, November & December.

💷 Major credit cards + Switch accepted.

Perth & Kinross, St Fillans

Atholl Palace Hotel
Pitlochry, Perthshire PH16 5LY
T (01796) 472400 **F** (01796) 473036
E info@athollpalace.com **W** www.athollpalace.com

159

The Atholl Palace, a stunning Victorian hotel, towers above Pitlochry, the tourist capital of the Highlands, with beautiful views on all sides. It started life as a Hydropathic Establishment whose history is chronicled in its own museum. Refurbished bedrooms range from singles through family suites and four posters to Turret rooms (ideal for honeymooners) and Highland Lodges in the grounds, cottages, self-catering apartments and the Manor House. Recently an 8-bedroom manor house has also become available. Close by there are endless things to do and see. Sports include golf, tennis, fishing, walking, mountain biking, pony trekking, kayaking and pitch'n putt. Other local attractions include the amazing 'salmon ladder', historic Blair Castle (with the only private army in the British Isles), the House of Bruar – the 'Harrods of the North' – the shops of Pitlochry and the renowned Festival Theatre. In the evening, return to the hotel to enjoy a drink in the bar, and dine in the Verandah Restaurant with its growing reputation for quality food making best use of local produce.

🛏90 ⚒ ♿ 🧍 ♨ 🦯 🖥 🔌 ❋ 🛋 🍷 ⛪ ♞ 🎠 ⋮⋮⋮ 200 🅿 ⛳ 🎣 🐟 🏌 🏇

Rates Single room with breakfast from £59; double from £99.
Meals 3 course tdh dinner; alc, lunch & special diets available; last orders 2100; breakfast from 0730.

Leisure Breaks Please see our website.
Other Facilities Fishing, golf, riding, sailing, watersports nearby.
£ Major credit & debit cards accepted. Open all year.

Perth & Kinross, Pitlochry

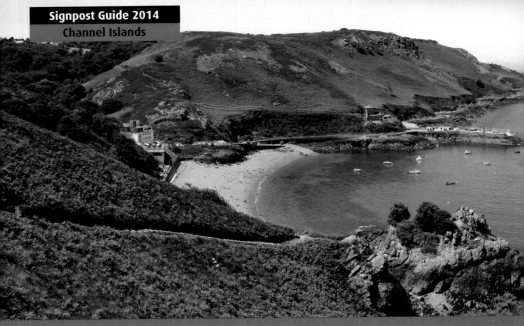

Bouley Bay, Jersey

Channel Islands

Britains' southernmost islands lie some 14 miles off the French coast, yet despite many French place names, they have not been owned by France since William the Conqueror. Each has its own appeal: Alderney's St Annes has the character of a Normandy village, Guernsey has strong links with fishing and the sea; Jersey is a cosmopolitan offshore financial centre; Herm and Sark are car-free zones.

ALDERNEY

GUERNSEY
HERM
SARK
JERSEY

Hotels guide

Jersey	page 165

Pea Stacks, Jerbourg Point

Vazon Bay, Guernsey

Jersey

Further information:
Jersey Tourism
Tel: 01534 448 800
www.jersey.com

160

GUERNSEY

Guernsey is a veritable haven for the holiday maker with a modern airport, excellent harbour and a wide range of available accommodation. Street names are displayed in both English and French. Now and again you catch a snatch of conversation between islanders in *patois* - a halfway dialect.

Moulin Huet Bay

The island was once under the domination of the Norman dukes, then vassals of the French king. William II of Normandy, crowned William I of England in 1066, established the connection with England and ever since the Islands have been part of the dominion of the Kings of England, but never part of their kingdom. **St Peter Port**, the capital, is a flourishing commercial centre with a busy harbour. From the castle ramparts throughout the summer, there booms the noonday gun - shades of the old Hong Kong.

Guernsey has many unique attractions for the visitor. The **Little Chapel** is the smallest in the world, lavishly decorated with pottery and shells and with room for only five worshippers at a time. **Victor Hugo** lived in exile in the town for 15 years and his former home, Hauteville House, is now a museum. There are a host of museums, a butterfly centre and a variety of archeological sites; also spectacular cliff walks and beautiful countryside to explore.

The island is famous for its delicacies, not least Guernsey Gache, a sort of fruit loaf. A good place to buy some would be the Thursday **Old Guernsey Market**. Traditionally dressed stall holders sell all manner of island produced wares from freesia corms to the famous eponymous sweaters. There is much to fascinate the holiday maker on Guernsey.

The islanders, proud of their heritage, will afford the warmest of welcomes.

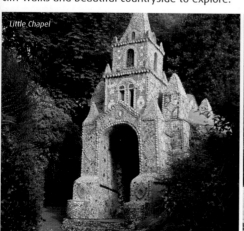
Little Chapel

St Martin

JERSEY

Jersey is the largest and most southerly of the Channel Islands, 100 miles south of England, yet only 14 miles from the French coast. Measuring just 45 square miles, it's an island big enough to lose yourself in, yet small enough to feel at home.

Leave the car behind and make tracks on foot or pedal along green country lanes for a breathtaking discovery of the island. The 96-mile cycle network has been designed to give precedence to pedestrians and cyclists, allowing you to discover new sights and experiences.

Jersey fits an encyclopaedic amount of history into its pocket book size and it comes to life everywhere. In just a short distance, it is possible to travel from prehistoric to postwar times. In the east is **Mont Orgueil Castle**, overlooking Grouville Bay. Originally built in the 13th century as a first line of defence against the French.

Mont Orgueil Castle

Ouaisne Bay and St Brelades Bay

St Helier

The Maritime Museum uses state-of-the-art interactive displays to celebrate Jersey's long association with the sea. **The Jersey War Tunnels** record the occupation of Jersey during the second world war.

The Durrell Wildlife Conservation Trust is a 'must see' for any visitor to the island. First established in 1963 by Gerald Durrell, it is set in 40 acres of parkland and aims to save as many threatened species as possible from extinction.

Jersey may measure just nine miles by five, but it is packed with interesting things to see and do. Whatever your age and whatever time of year you visit, you will be assured of a warm welcome.

St Peter Port, Guernsey

ALDERNEY, HERM AND SARK

Alderney is the third largest Channel Island, just 1.5 miles wide and 3.5 miles long, yet with 3000 friendly and welcoming inhabitants. It is only eight miles from France yet is known as 'the most English' of the islands, with a fledgling off-shore finance and E-commerce sector. It has an abundance of flora, fauna and wildlife, including black rabbits and white hedgehogs, beautiful beaches and a relaxed friendly lifestyle.

Sights include **St Anne's Church**, often referred to as The Cathedral of the Channel Islands, the **Alderney Society Museum**, covering the island's history and development, the cinema, library and **Alderney Railway**, the only one in the Islands, dubbed The Orient Express, running at weekends and Bank Holidays in the summer and a favourite for railway enthusiasts and children alike. The **Alderney Lighthouse**, which was automated in 1997, is open to the public.

Herm is three miles from the Guernsey coast and is reached by a daily 20-minute catamaran service. There is a regular boat connection (20 minutes) to the nearby island of Sark. 200 years ago 400 people lived on Herm, largely employed in quarrying stone which was subsequently used to build

St Peter Port Harbour, Guernsey. The island was purchased by the State of Guernsey after the war and leased out to the late Major Peter Wood until 1980. Herm measures just half a mile square, and the island can be covered on foot within a couple of hours. It has unspoilt beaches and a clean, unpolluted environment, with no cars allowed.

Sark is the smallest of the main Channel islands, located some 80 miles off the south coast of England. Although only three miles long and half a mile wide, it boasts 40 miles of picturesque coastline. There are no cars; travel is by bicycle or horsedrawn cart. Sark used to have the last feudal constitution in the western world, being governed by a seigneur, who held the island in perpetuity from the monarch. From 2007 the island's parliament, The Chief Pleas, has been made up for the first time of elected representatives drawn from the island's 600 residents. **The Seigneurie** is open to the public and its beautiful walled gardens are one of Sark's most popular attractions. In 2011 the International Dark-Sky Association designated Sark as a 'Dark-Sky Community' and the first Dark-Sky island in the world as Sark is sufficiently clear of light pollution to allow naked-eye astronomy.

Bouley Bay, Jersey

CHANNEL ISLANDS
WHERE TO STAY

Entries appear alphabetically by
town name in each county. A key
to symbols appeares on page 3.

The Moorings Hotel

Gorey Pier, St Martin, Jersey JE3 6EW

T (01534) 853633 **F** (01534) 857618
E reservations@themooringshotel.com **W** www.themooringshotel.com

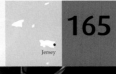

Jersey

The Moorings Hotel & Restaurant enjoys a true Jersey picture postcard location. It is situated below the historic ramparts of Mont Orgeuil Castle on the waterfront of Gorey Harbour. The Hotel & Restaurant has a husband and wife team at the helm – Joanne is front of house with the kitchen in the hands of husband/chef Simon Walker. You could not wish for a better team to run this hotel where such warm, friendly hospitality is extended. Rooms are well presented and have all facilities expected by today's travellers. Many enjoy stunning sea views across the harbour towards Grouville Bay. The AA ❀ ❀ Restaurant is one of the island's finest with Simon excelling in the kitchen. Both the table d'hôte and à la carte menus offer a wonderful selection of Island produce with the accent on local seafood. Presentation, menu choices and service are all exemplary. The Pier Bar & Bistro offers a more casual dining experience. The *al fresco* terrace is the place to absorb the warmth of this delightful hotel while watching the sun set. This is a great location and Gorey and The Moorings should be on every Jersey visitor's list. Highly recommended.

 15 🏇 🎠 🦢 🜋 🔍 △ **WiFi**

Rates Single, bed & breakfast from £57.50 per night; double/twin from £115.
Meals Walkers Restaurant alc. Lunch & special diets available.

Leisure Breaks Stay seven nights half-board for the price of six. Four nights b&b for the price of three.

£ All major credit cards accepted. Open all year.

Jersey, Gorey

SIGNPOST
SELECTED PREMIER HOTELS 2014

For more fantastic hotels, special offers, reviews and news visit
www.signpost.co.uk

Sign up to our monthly Newsletter for exclusive hotel offers.

Recommending the UK's Finest Hotels since 1935

www.signpost.co.uk

LOCATION MAPS

Numbers in the magenta ovals on the following maps denote page numbers of Signpost approved hotels. Turn to these pages for full details of accommodation in the area where you are looking.

PAGES 174- 175

PAGES 172 - 173

PAGES 170 - 171

PAGES 168 - 169

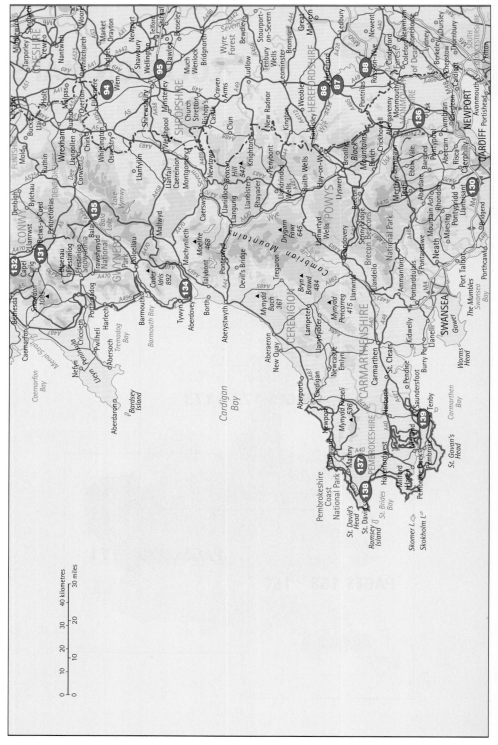

168

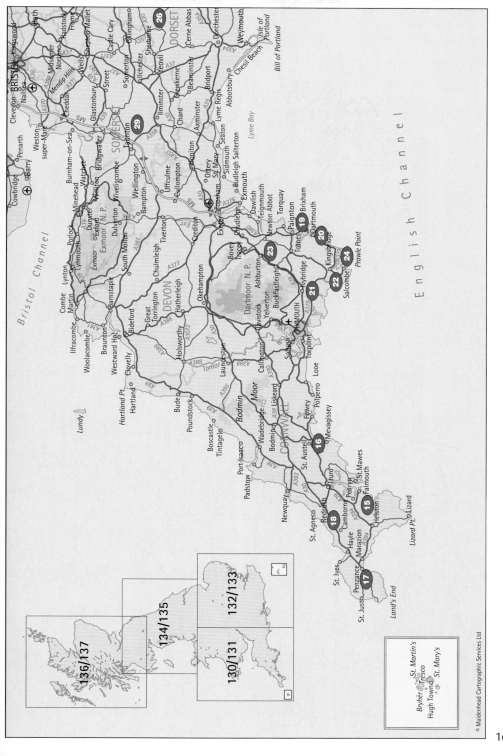

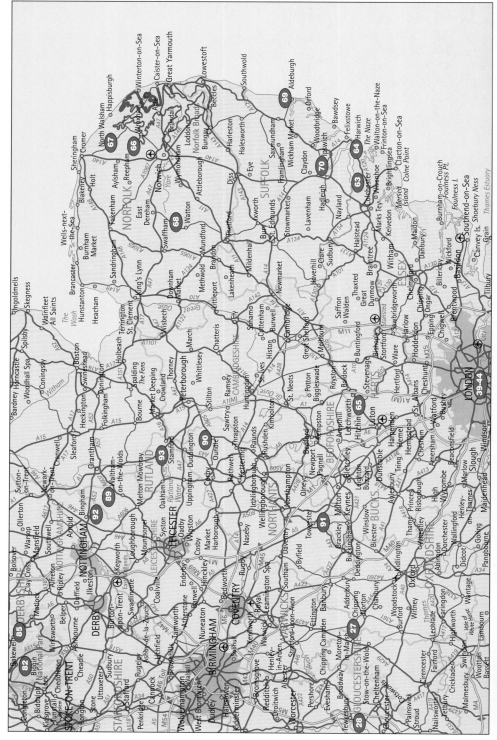

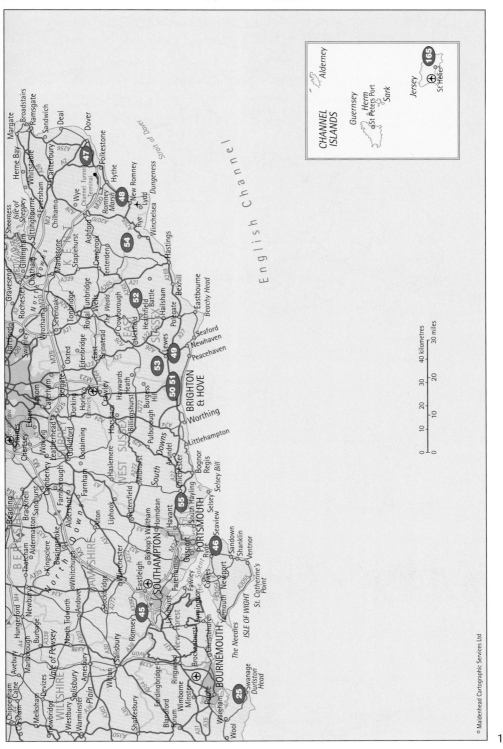

CHANNEL ISLANDS

Alderney

Guernesey
St Peters Port Herm
Sark

Jersey
St Hélier 165

English Channel

Margate
Broadstairs
Ramsgate
Sandwich
Deal
Dover
Folkestone 47
Hythe
New Romney 48
Romney Marsh
Dungeness
Strait of Dover
Winchelsea
Rye
Hastings 54
Bexhill
Battle
Hailsham 52
Polegate
Eastbourne
Beachy Head
Seaford
Newhaven 49
Peacehaven
Lewes 51 50 53
BRIGHTON & HOVE
Worthing
Littlehampton
Bognor Regis
Selsey
Selsey Bill
Chichester 55
Havant
South Hayling
PORTSMOUTH
Seaview 46
Sandown
Shanklin
Ventnor
St. Catherine's Point
ISLE OF WIGHT
Newport
Cowes
SOUTHAMPTON 45
Eastleigh
Winchester

BOURNEMOUTH 25
Poole
Swanage
Durlston Head

WILTSHIRE
HAMPSHIRE
BERKSHIRE
SURREY
KENT
EAST SUSSEX
WEST SUSSEX

0 10 20 30 40 kilometres
0 10 20 30 miles

© Maidenhead Cartographic Services Ltd

171

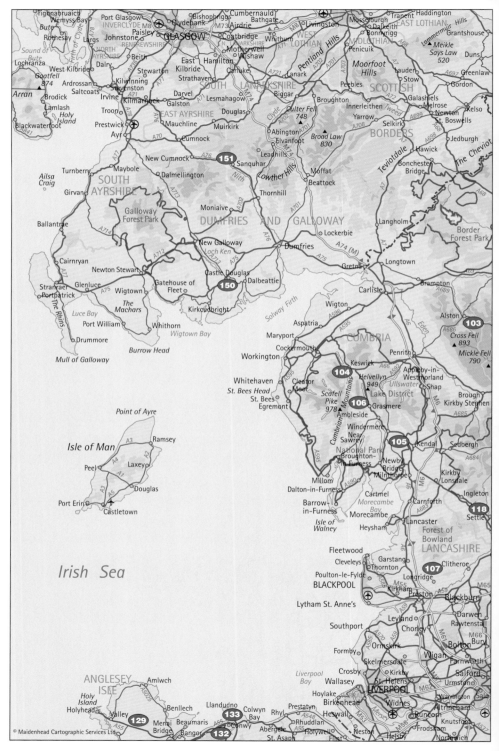

© Maidenhead Cartographic Services Ltd

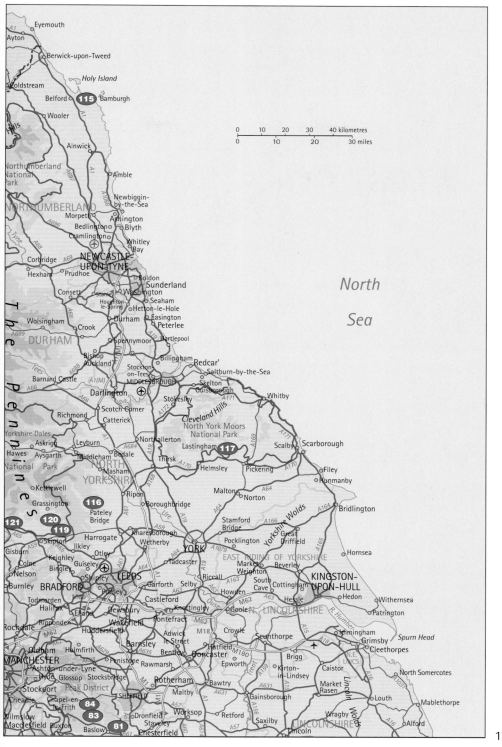

173

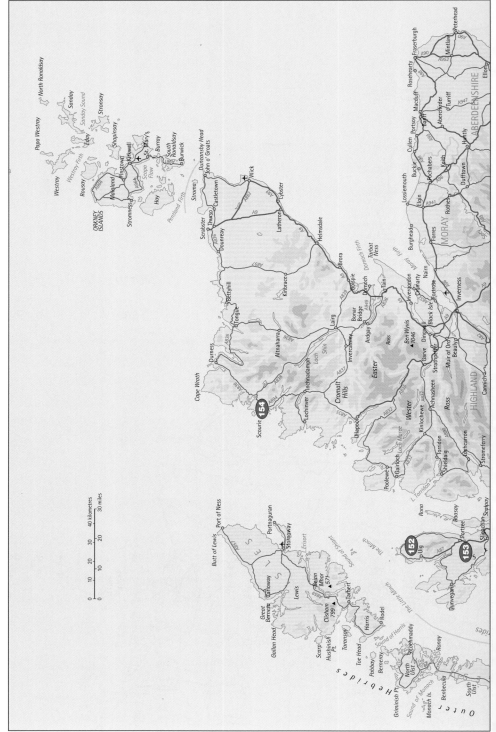

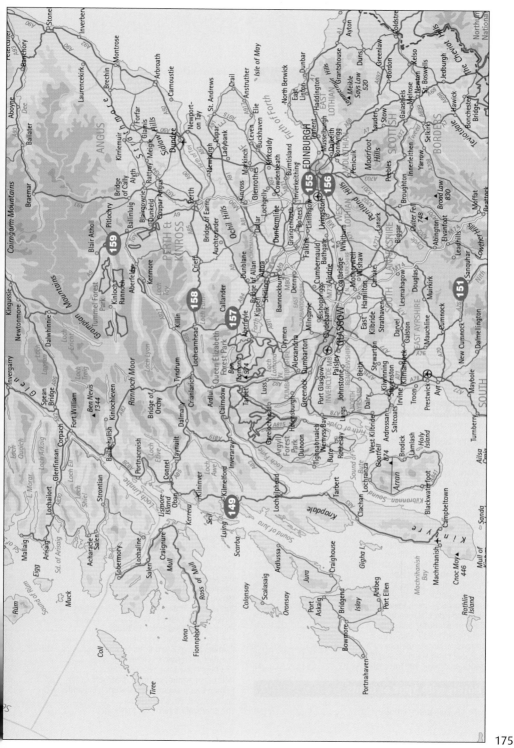

Hotels by Facilities

Hotels with Golf ▶9 ▶18

(own course or special arrangements with adjacent course)

Budock Vean Hotel, Falmouth 15
Channings, Edinburgh 155
Gilpin Hotel & Lake House, Windermere 105
Knoll House Hotel, Studland Bay 25
Trefeddian Hotel, Aberdovey 134
Whittlebury Hall, Nr. Towcester 91

Hotels with Conference Facilities ⁙

(for 60 or more delegates)

Atholl Palace Hotel, Pitlochry 159
Barnsdale Lodge Hotel, Oakham 93
The Berry Head Hotel, Brixham 19
The Coniston Hotel, Skipton 121
Deans Place Hotel, Alfriston 49
Flackley Ash Hotel, Peasmarsh 54
Glen-yr-Afon House Hotel, Usk 136
Ilsington Country House Hotel, Ilsington 23
The Mytton & Mermaid Hotel, Shrewsbury 95
Newick Park Hotel, Lewes 53
Penventon Park Hotel, Redruth 18
Roman Camp Country House Hotel, Callander 157
Royal Oak Hotel, Betws-y-Coed 131
Searcys Roof Garden Rooms, SW1 39
The Talbot Hotel, Oundle 90
Tre-Ysgawen Hall, Llangefni 129
Whittlebury Hall, Nr. Towcester 91
Wolfscastle Country Hotel, Haverfordwest 137

Hotels with Swimming Pools ⸚

(⸚ = indoor pool)

Atholl Palace Hotel, Pitlochry ⸚ 159
The Berry Head Hotel, Brixham ⸚ 19
Broom Hall Country Hotel, Thetford ⸚ 68
Budock Vean Hotel, Falmouth ⸚ 15
Dart Marina Hotel & Spa, Dartmouth ⸚ 20
The Devonshire Arms Hotel, Skipton ⸚ 119
Flackley Ash Hotel, Peasmarsh ⸚ 54
Gilpin Hotel & Lake House, Windermere ⸚ 105
Ilsington Country House Hotel, Ilsington ⸚ 23
Knoll House Hotel, Studland Bay ⸚ 25
Losehill House Hotel, Hope ⸚ 84
Maison Talbooth, Dedham ⸚ 63
Miskin Manor Hotel, Llantrisant ⸚ 130
Newick Park Hotel, Lewes 53
Penally Abbey, Tenby ⸚ 139
Penventon Park Hotel, Redruth ⸚ 18
The Priory Bay Hotel, Seaview IOW 46
St Tudno Hotel, Llandudno ⸚ 133
Tides Reach Hotel, Salcombe ⸚ 24
Tre-Ysgawen Hall, Llangefni ⸚ 129
Trefeddian Hotel, Aberdovey ⸚ 134
Warpool Court Hotel, St David's ⸚ 138
Whittlebury Hall, Nr. Towcester ⸚ 91

Hotels with Spas or Gyms ⵣ

Atholl Palace Hotel, Pitlochry 159

Budock Vean Hotel, Falmouth 15
Craigadam House, Castle Douglas 150
Dart Marina Hotel & Spa, Dartmouth 20
The Devonshire Arms Hotel, Skipton 119
Flackley Ash Hotel, Peasmarsh 54
Ilsington Country House Hotel, Ilsington 23
Knoll House Hotel, Studland Bay 25
Losehill House Hotel, Hope 84
Maison Talbooth, Dedham 63
Miskin Manor Hotel, Llantrisant 130
Penventon Park Hotel, Redruth 18
Tides Reach Hotel, Salcombe 24
Tre-Ysgawen Hall, Llangefni 129
Whittlebury Hall, Nr. Towcester 91

Hotels who Accept Pets 🐕

(can be charged)

Abbey Hotel (The), Penzance 17
Aylestone Court, Hereford 86
Barnsdale Lodge Hotel, Oakham 93
Beechwood Hotel, North Walsham 67
Berry Head Hotel (The), Brixham 19
Biggin Hall Hotel, Biggin-by-Hartington 82
Blackaddie Country House Hotel, Sanquhar 151
Borrowdale Gates Country House, Nr. Keswick 104
Broom Hall Country Hotel, Thetford 68
Budock Vean Hotel, Falmouth 15
The Coniston Hotel, Skipton 121
Corse Lawn House Hotel, Nr. Tewkesbury 28
The Cottage Hotel, Hope Cove 22
Craigadam House, Castle Douglas 150
Dart Marina Hotel & Spa, Dartmouth 20
Deans Place Hotel, Alfriston 49
The Devonshire Arms Hotel, Skipton 119
The Devonshire Fell, Skipton 120
Farthings Country House Hotel, Taunton 29
Flackley Ash Hotel, Peasmarsh 54
Flodigarry Country House, Isle of Skye 152
The Four Seasons Hotel, St Fillans 158
Glen-yr-Afon House Hotel, Usk 136
The Groes Inn, Nr. Conwy 132
Ilsington Country House Hotel, Ilsington 23
Knoll House Hotel, Studland Bay 25
Langar Hall, Langar 92
Lastingham Grange, Lastingham 117
Loch Melfort Hotel, Oban 149
Lovelady Shield Country House, Alston 103
Maison Talbooth, Dedham 63
The Manners Arms, Nr. Grantham 89
milsoms Kesgrave Hall, Ipswich 70
Miskin Manor Hotel, Llantrisant 130
The Mytton & Mermaid Hotel, Shrewsbury 95
Newick Park Hotel, Lewes 53
The Norfolk Mead Hotel, Coltishall 66
The Peacock Hotel, Rowsley 85
Plumber Manor, Sturminster Newton 26
The Pier at Harwich, Harwich 64
The Priory Bay Hotel, Seaview IOW 46
Redcoats Farmhouse Hotel, Redcoats Green 65
Roman Camp Country House Hotel, Callander 157
Soulton Hall, Nr. Shrewsbury 94
The Sportsman's Arms, Nr. Harrogate 116

Hotels with Fishing 🎣

(✓ = + game shooting)

Hotels with Disabled-Friendly Rooms ♿

These are hotels who have indicated to us that they can cater for guests of restricted mobility. This may mean ground floor rooms and a lift or a wide-entrance room with a fully adapted bathroom with wet room shower, rails, red pulls etc.

We recommend that guests with limited mobility check with hotels before booking.

Hotels Licensed for Civil Weddings 💍

Hotels by Location

Flackley Ash, East Sussex

HUDSON'S MEDIA LIMITED

Published by: Hudson's Media Ltd
35 Thorpe Road, Peterborough, PE3 6AG
Tel: 01733 296910 Fax: 01733 568099

Publisher: Malcolm Orr-Ewing.
Production team: Lisa Barreno, Sarah Phillips, Gemma Wall,
Rhiannon McCluskey, Rebecca Owen-Fisher.
Design: Jamieson Eley.
Hotel Inspectors: Malcolm Orr-Ewing, Paul Riley, Suzie Wessley.

Retail Sales: Compass – Tel: 020 8996 5764

Photography credits: © VisitEngland: Visit Peak District, Visit Northumberland,
Jameskerr.co.uk, New Forest District CouncilVisit England, Visit Dorset, North
Somerset Council, English Riviera, Iain Lewis, English Heritage, Cotswolds.com,
Nick Turner, Hudson's Media Ltd, Alex Hare, Sudeley Castle, Clive Burling, Visit
Kent, Arundel, 1066 Country Marketing, Andrew Marshall, Diana Jarvis, Visit
Brighton, Luke Rogers, Hampshire, Broads Authority, Julia Claxton, Visit Essex,
Woburn Safari Park, Suffolk Coastal, Experience Nottingham, Linda Bussey,
Chatsworth House Trust, Ironbridge, Stewart Writtle, Visit Blackpool, Marketing
Cheshire, Blacks, Marketing Cheshire, Newcastle Gateshead, NYMNPA, Colin
Carter, Visit Hull & East Yorkshire, Visit County Durham.

© VisitBritain Images: Pawel Libera, Visit Britain, Adam Burton, Stephen
Spraggon, David Crap, Joanna Henderson, Daniel Bosworth, Britain on View,
Tower of London, Historic Royal Palaces, David Sellman, Rod Edwards, Tony
Pleavin, Peter Seaward, Adrian Houston, Martin Brent, Jason Knott, Visit
Northumberland, Andy Tryner, Lee Beel, David Angel, Simon Kreitem, Joe
Cornish, James McCormick, Simon Winnall, Dennis Hardley, Grant Pritchard,
Jersey, Visit Guernsey.

Front cover: Maison Talbooth, Essex.
Back cover: Top, Atholl Palace, Perthshire. Bottom, Langar Hall,
Nottinghamshire.
Maps: Maidenhead Cartographic Services